SUBALTERN SILENCE

NEW DIRECTIONS IN CRITICAL THEORY

NEW DIRECTIONS IN CRITICAL THEORY

Amy Allen, General Editor

New Directions in Critical Theory presents outstanding classic and contemporary texts in the tradition of critical social theory, broadly construed. The series aims to renew and advance the program of critical social theory, with a particular focus on theorizing contemporary struggles around gender, race, sexuality, class, and globalization and their complex interconnections.

Contesting the Far Right: A Psychoanalytic Critical Theory Approach, Claudia Leeb

Another Universalism: Seyla Benhabib and the Future of Critical Theory, edited by Stefan Eich, Anna Jurkevics, Nishin Nathwani, and Nica Siegel

Fascist Mythologies: The History and Politics of Unreason in Borges, Freud, and Schmitt, Federico Finchelstein

Selected Writings on Media, Propaganda, and Political Communication, Siegfried Kracauer, edited by Jaeho Kang, Graeme Gilloch, and John Abromeit

Crisis Under Critique: How People Assess, Transform, and Respond to Critical Situations, edited by Didier Fassin and Axel Honneth

Praxis and Revolution: A Theory of Social Transformation, Eva von Redecker

Recognition and Ambivalence, edited by Heikki Ikäheimo, Kristina Lepold, and Titus Stahl

Hermeneutics as Critique: Science, Politics, Race and Culture, Lorenzo C. Simpson

Critique on the Couch: Why Critical Theory Needs Psychoanalysis, Amy Allen

Capitalism on Edge: How Fighting Precarity Can Achieve Radical Change Without Crisis or Utopia, Albena Azmanova

A Time for Critique, edited by Didier Fassin and Berbard E. Harcourt

Transitional Subjects: Critical Theory and Object Relations, edited by Amy Allen and Brian O'Connor

For a complete list of books in the series, please see the Columbia University Press website.

SUBALTERN SILENCE

A Postcolonial Genealogy

KEVIN OLSON

Columbia University Press
New York

Columbia University Press
Publishers Since 1893
New York   Chichester, West Sussex
cup.columbia.edu
Copyright © 2024 Columbia University Press
All rights reserved

Library of Congress Cataloging-in-Publication Data
Names: Olson, Kevin, author.
Title: Subaltern silence : a postcolonial genealogy / Kevin Olson.
Description: New York : Columbia University Press, [2023] | Series: New directions in critical theory | Includes bibliographical references and index.
Identifiers: LCCN 2023032159 (print) | LCCN 2023032160 (ebook) | ISBN 9780231214469 (hardback) | ISBN 9780231214476 (trade paperback) | ISBN 9780231560351 (ebook)
Subjects: LCSH: Haiti—Colonization—Case studies. | Silence—Political aspects—Haiti—Case studies. | France—Colonies—America—Administration—Case studies. | France—Colonies—America—Race relations—Case studies. | Haiti—History. | Spivak, Gayatri Chakravorty. Can the subaltern speak. | Foucault, Michel, 1926-1984.
Classification: LCC F1923 .O45 2023 (print) | LCC F1923 (ebook) | DDC 325/.37294—dc23/eng/20231019
LC record available at https://lccn.loc.gov/2023032159
LC ebook record available at https://lccn.loc.gov/2023032160

Cover design: Milenda Nan Ok Lee
Cover art: nidpor / Stockimo / Alamy

For Ulrike

Contents

Acknowledgments ix

PART I. INNOVATIONS IN SUBORDINATION: COLONIAL PUBLIC SPHERES

1. The Sounds of Silence 3
2. Silence as an Achievement: Marronage 30
3. Unsettling Silences: The Perils of Poison 79
4. Phantasmatic Public Spheres: The Paranoid Style in French Colonialism 100
5. Disruptive Object: The Tricolor Cockade and the Fear of Black Jacobins 136

INTERLUDE

The Shifting Horizon of Modernity: Placide Camus, Apprentice Printer 163

PART II. POSTCOLONIAL TRANSFORMATIONS

6. Times of Exception: Subaltern Silence in the Revolutionary Caribbean 173
7. Revolution Within a Revolution: Postcolonial Liberalism and the Army of Sufferers 201

8 The Force of Farce: Emperor Soulouque and the Art of
Racial Caricature   238

9 Silent in Plain Sight: We Are All Postcolonial Now   288

Notes   317

Bibliography   341

Index   353

Acknowledgments

The best thing about writing this book has been the conversations I have been privileged to have along the way. The project began as a small, somewhat quirky essay for the Poor Theory project, a collaboration with Ackbar Abbas, David Theo Goldberg, and Gabriele Schwab in the Critical Theory Institute of the University of California, Irvine. I am very grateful for their camaraderie and creative spark during our many conversations around the project. Rocío Zambrana organized the stimulating conference *Immanent Critique: New Directions* at the University of Oregon that gave me an incentive to write that essay and set it on a path to becoming much larger.

Verena Erlenbusch-Anderson has made many insightful contributions to this book with her thoughtful comments on the manuscript and lively conversations while I was writing it. I am similarly grateful to Neil Roberts for his rich reflections on the manuscript. Colin Koopman is a genealogical fellow traveler who has been a sustained source of inspiration in this project. Stacey Liou has been a wonderful dialogue partner throughout and has talked me through many of these ideas as I was formulating them. Sarah Farmer is my generous archives coach and ambassador to the world of French history. I am very grateful to Amy Allen for including this book in her excellent series and for everything she does to open spaces for creative thought. Wendy Lochner at Columbia University Press has been a joy to work with, and I deeply appreciate her enthusiasm for this project. My UC Irvine political theory colleagues Daniel Brunstetter, Simone Chambers, Mary McThomas, and Keith Topper continue to create a rich environment for our shared undertakings.

I am equally grateful to all those who commented on parts of the manuscript or provided pointers and ideas along the way: Libby Anker, Lawrie Balfour,

Banu Bargu, Jane Bennett, Nahum Chandler, Natalie Cisneros, Ian Coller, Maeve Cooke, Yasmeen Daifallah, Don Deere, Andrew Dilts, Kevin Duong, Alessandro Ferrara, Carlos Forment, Jason Frank, Lyat Friedman, Vince Golden, Jane Gordon, Yiwen Huang, Katelyn Kelly, Margaret Kohn, Sina Kramer, Chung-jae Lee, Horacio Legras, Ainsley LeSure, Mary Beth Mader, Patchen Markell, Bill Maurer, Ladelle McWhorter, Jaeyoon Park, Kaushik Sunder Rajan, Kamal Sadiq, Bonnie Sheehey, George Shulman, Brad Stone, Massimiliano Tomba, Alejandro Vallega, Antonio Vázquez-Arroyo, and Christopher Zurn. Patchen and Lawrie have my additional warm thanks for our wonderful discussions about the art of crafting a book.

This book first took shape in the oak-paneled chambers and deep woodlands of the Château de la Bretesche, France. It was the perfect environment to commune with the disappeared world of parchment, wood, and stone from which this genealogy is drawn. I am deeply grateful to the Albert and Elaine Borchard Foundation for an extraordinary sabbatical. My special thanks to Janna and Kristen Beling for their wonderful support and Odile Juhel for her warm welcome during my stay.

I would like to extend my gratitude to all of the institutions that made their collections available for this work, particularly the American Antiquarian Society; the Archives Nationales and the Bibliothèque Nationale de France in Paris; the Archives Nationales d'Outre-Mer in Aix-en-Provence; the Château de Versailles; Google Labs; the John Carter Brown Library of Brown University; the Library Company of Philadelphia; the Musée de la Révolution Française in Vizille, France; the National Museum of American History in the Smithsonian Institution; the Newberry Library in Chicago; and the U.S. National Archives and Records Administration.

An earlier version of chapter 5 was published as "Epistemologies of Rebellion: The Tricolor Cockade and the Problem of Subaltern Speech," *Political Theory* 43, no. 6 (2015): 730–52.

I owe a whole different kind of gratitude to the dear friends, fellow denizens, community members, and daily people who make up the substance of life and brighten my days. I will not name you all, but you have my warmest thanks. My sisters Shannon and Mikaela have been wonderful companions and co-conspirators for many decades. I'm very grateful to them and our extended family for our rich life together. Ulrike is, as always, the first audience for these ideas and my very best accomplice in many adventures.

PART I

Innovations in Subordination

Colonial Public Spheres

CHAPTER 1

The Sounds of Silence

There is a story we like to tell about the waves of self-liberation that ended colonialism. Once upon a time, subordination was the product of brutality, violence, and intimidation. In this colonial past, subaltern populations were held down by force and terror. Their ability to rise up depended upon equal and opposite exertions of force and terror. But, the story goes, we are past all of that now. Democracy, civil rights, and globalized capitalism have pushed aside naked violence in the postcolonial present. We now live in a world well regulated by discourse and democracy, equality and civil rights, public accountability and free speech. Subordination has been uprooted by modernity.

Or so the story goes. Of course, things have never been that simple. The old colonial project of subordination has never gone away but has instead taken new and more subtle forms. Where people were once held in check by force, they are now devalued, discounted, and rendered invisible. Subordination has become light and diaphanous at the same time that it has become more widespread. Contemporary forms of subordination subsist among the great modern innovations of law and politics. They are, to be precise, an integral *part* of those forms of modernity. Such techniques of subordination are broadly diffused throughout our society. Their subtle, diffuse, and largely invisible character is what makes them so effective. For exactly these reasons, that which does *not* attract our attention should cause us the gravest concern.

This book aims to excavate the layers of silence that surround subaltern subordination. It has a simple thesis: that modernity was accompanied by the development of ingenious new forms of subordination. They operate through shifting articulations of participation, agency, invisibility, and absence. In their newest, most contemporary forms, they can subjugate entire societies and groups of people with minimal effort. These forms of subordination are alive and well, proliferating among us. The people subjected to them are in certain ways invisible and absent from our society, perceived in ways they did not create and would not choose.

Consider these traces from the early years of European modernity:

> Eh! eh! Bomba, hen! hen!
> Canga bafio té
> Canga moune dé lé
> Canga do ki la
> Canga li.

This cryptic text was copied down in a time when our present constellation of cultures, institutions, and technologies was first falling into place. It was probably transcribed in the 1770s, appearing in a footnote to a celebrated, encyclopedic account of the French slave colony of Saint-Domingue, what is now Haiti.[1] The author tells us that it is the transcription of "an African song." He adds that "the first sounds of the first line are pronounced very openly, and the last two of the same line are only muffled inflections." Beyond that he does not speculate about the song's meaning, identify in what language it is spoken, or recount any other details of its transcription. The voices of enslaved Africans are included in a narrative of colonial life, but as ciphers, consigned to a footnote without further explanation.

The author is a bit more forthcoming about the context in which the song appears, however. He describes it as part of "the vaudou dance." This is a kind of initiation ceremony in which the Vaudou King draws a circle on the ground, placing an initiate within it while handing him a packet of herbs, horse hair, pieces of horn, "and other similarly disgusting objects." He strikes the initiate on the head lightly with a small wooden paddle while intoning the "African song," which is repeated in chorus by others around the circle. The initiate then begins to shake and dance. The singing and dancing continue until the Vaudou King orders it to cease. At that point he strikes the initiate lightly on the head again, and he becomes part of the sect.

The author understood vaudou as more than just a dance, and even more than just a religion. He characterizes it as a political structure and a way of euphemizing black religious practices so they could pass unnoticed in plain view. In this sense, he parses subtle meanings out of the "vaudou dance" and other rituals. He even ascribes to them a kind of cryptifying intent, a way of being hidden in plain sight. He carefully transcribes the "African song" as the primary utterance of this practice but passes it along to his readers without further comment. It becomes a cipher, untranslated but carefully recorded. It is held up as something meaningful, yet without an attempt to interpret what that meaning might be.

Because of the indifference of this treatment, the Africans' voices, thoughts, and intentions are abandoned to silence. Anything they might have been trying to say—to one another or the transcriber—is lost within the casual indifference of the transcription itself. Their voices are heard in a certain way yet silenced in a much more cosmic sense. This indifference may have been a slight on the transcriber's part, a judgment that what was being said was not worthy of attention. Or it may simply have registered the cryptified nature of the practice itself, the extent to which the Africans sought to obscure the meanings of their own actions. The silence reproduced in this passage is itself ambiguous, possibly a result of casual indifference and possibly an intentional achievement of those who are silenced. In sum, the "African song" presents a kind of enigma: it is both present and absent, both fully articulated and uninterpreted, both carefully preserved and ignored.

In contrast, consider a rather different text. This one directly imposed silence rather than merely transcribing it. It is a caricature that appeared in a Parisian satirical newspaper in 1850 (figure 1.1). There was a span of some eighty years between the transcription of the "African song" and the publication of this drawing, *Soulouque après sa mort*. Translated, the title reads "Soulouque after his death. Emperor Soulouque, carefully stuffed, becomes the prize decoration in a cabinet of great curiosity."[2] The Emperor Soulouque in question was the much maligned, much ridiculed head of the Haitian government from 1847 to 1859. He was also very much alive and ruling Haiti—the former Saint-Domingue—at the time of the drawing. This makes the image a rather broad parody of what his death might look like.

Soulouque looks quite simian in this vision, similar to some of the great apes one might find in a nineteenth-century zoo. We are told that this specimen was not alive, however, but "carefully stuffed." He is shown preserved in a bell jar, a device that became popular in the nineteenth century for transporting

SOULOUQUE APRÈS SA MORT.
L'empereur Soulouque, soigneusement empaillé, devient le principal ornement d'un cabinet de haute curiosité.

Figure 1.1 Cham, *Soulouque après sa mort*, Le Charivari, April 12, 1850, 3.

botanical specimens back to Europe. The reference to "a cabinet of great curiosity" is a multilayered joke. It plays on the idea of a cabinet of curiosities, another upper-class diversion. It was typically a room used to display wonders of natural history, archaeology, and anthropology.[3] In this case, the wonder is Soulouque, who seems quite curious about his audience and is also implied to be "curious" in the sense of rather odd.

All of this collecting and exoticism reduces Soulouque to a bizarre spectacle. A frock-coated bourgeois gapes in amazement at the curiosity before him.

Soulouque is dressed like a Napoleonic general, yet he seems more monkey than man. In spite of his careful preservation, he does not look at all dead. Rather, he seems to be returning the bourgeois's gaze with a lively, artless curiosity. Soulouque is a spectacle of manlike monkeyness, both curious and curiosity, artless and art. He is not a living, speaking political ruler but an object of ridicule. Although Soulouque is quite animated, he is also silenced—by parody, devaluation, and laughter.

The "African song" and *Soulouque après sa mort* inhabited very different worlds. The "African song" was recorded during the zenith of Saint-Domingue's prosperity as a sugar-producing slave colony. The people chanting the song were enslaved workers; the conditions of their captivity were notoriously brutal. In contrast, *Soulouque après sa mort* appeared several decades after the enslaved people of Saint-Domingue had liberated themselves in a striking, world-historical revolution. They had formed the free, independent nation of Haiti. Faustin Soulouque, the subject of this caricature, was their constitutionally chosen ruler.

In theory, these two vignettes should reflect such differences, one mirroring the oppression of colonialism, the other the freedom of the postcolonial order. Things were not so simple, however. Instead, they are characterized by continuously developing forms of subaltern subordination. We see this in germinal form in the "African song." It displays an ethnographic attention to something unknown and uncomprehended that is worth recording. It is observed with meticulous attention and carefully transcribed. However, we also see a casual disregard for the semantic import of these utterances. The "African song" is consigned to the archives as an untranslated, coded mystery with no further investigation. The author displays a rather striking lack of curiosity about what is being said or intended. No attempt is made to inquire into the meaning or significance of these words. This combination of ethnographic thoroughness and consignment to the footnotes of history says volumes about the attitude taken toward the Africans and their song. It is interesting, curious, but not terribly meaningful or important.

Soulouque après sa mort intensifies and further develops tendencies that were germinating in the "African song." It is a highly racialized form of representation. Rather than disregard and incomprehension, it trades in racial stereotyping and grotesquery. It is euphemized as humor in a way that mimics the innocence of the "African song," yet it scarcely succeeds in disguising its sharply biting political edge. This particular image works its effects through a multilayered set of references. It is representation about representation: a caricature of a man put on display because of his highly exotic character, and, on the other hand, the amazed scrutiny of the European upper classes at this artless specimen. Humor is used to mask the sting of the representation, allowing a highly stigmatizing portrayal to pass as innocent fun.

The development of modern subordination, I will argue, lies in the arc between the "African song" and *Soulouque après sa mort*. The first image was catalogued during the fullest flowering of French colonialism and the early days of a modern, transatlantic public sphere. The other was drawn after the French had long since been sent packing and Haiti had governed itself for four decades. In the space of these eighty years we move from casual disregard and incomprehension to a shrewd, pictorial skewering. Each text marks a characteristic point in the development of specifically modern forms of subordination. Those techniques were embryonic in the eighteenth century and reaching maturity by the mid-nineteenth. Each, in its own way, constitutes forms of visibility and presence that simultaneously silence and devalue.

In these vignettes we see the origins of new, more subtle, uniquely modern forms of subordination. They use *silence* as a mode of subordination, and they achieve that silence in insidious new ways. They are all the more powerful for their seemingly subtle and inconsequential character. These techniques operate in plain view, through shifting articulations of discourse and publicity, within the modern public sphere, rendering some people socially and politically invisible, others worthless or irrelevant. Where people were once held in check by brutality, force, and violence, they are now devalued, discounted, and stripped of importance and coherence. We see subordination becoming ever lighter and more diaphanous as it matures in the colonial world and blossoms in the postcolonial.

Together, the "African song" and *Soulouque après sa mort* mark two points in a much broader history of subaltern subordination. The former lies in the early years of this phenomenon and the latter in its fully mature form some eighty years later. This trajectory has continued into the present. Today such forms of subordination are broadly diffused throughout our society. The subtle, abstract, and largely invisible character of such techniques is what makes them so effective. In their most contemporary forms they can subjugate entire societies and groups of people with minimal effort. The people subjected to them are visible in our society, yet perceived in ways they did not create and would not choose.

SUBALTERN SILENCE

This book is a critical history of these new forms of subordination. As the violence, force, and brutality of colonialism were gradually overthrown in the eighteenth and nineteenth centuries, other techniques were quietly adopted to take their place. These are much more abstract, diffuse—and ultimately, pervasive. They became increasingly widespread and sophisticated as colonialism was pushed aside and the world took on its contemporary form. These ingenious new techniques subordinate people through silence.

Silence is quite often a metaphor in this history, standing in for a wide array of different phenomena. Some of them involve literal silence, such as de jure prohibitions on speaking or appearing in public, bans proscribing a person's ability to testify in court, or lack of protections for speech. Others are quite different: having one's identity, actions, or existence devalued through misunderstanding, misrepresentation, invisibility, incomprehension, dismissal, or delegitimation. As a result, one could not exhaustively catalog the shifting forms of subaltern silence. However, one can characterize trends in the practices of silencing themselves. Here we trace out broader changes in the subtle, endlessly permuting character of these practices—how they are put in place and simultaneously resisted, how they fail to be absolute and somehow leave openings for speech and agency. We see that modes of subordination can at times constitute the conditions of possibility for reaction against them. New forms of silence can create bases for improvised agency. There is nothing automatic or dialectical about this relationship. Rather, it is a fragile and contingent achievement, one in which people capitalize on ephemeral opportunities or simply arrive at a new and better set of circumstances through unintended consequences.

My point of entry for theorizing subaltern silence is Gayatri Spivak's pathbreaking question "Can the subaltern speak?" Spivak poses this question to open up the puzzles of understanding others across time and through the effects of subordination. These paradoxes go quite deep. If a subject is truly silent, then trying to liberate that subject from subordination carries the implicit risk of misunderstanding the nature of the problem and further perpetuating it. More radically, it poses the danger of speaking on behalf of the subaltern in a way that masks what the subaltern might be trying to say, drowning out subaltern speech and replacing it with one's own. Even further, it is possible to mistakenly constitute a subaltern subject out of whole cloth, imagining a silent subject and attributing subordination and interests to her in a way that cannot be verified and thus becomes inherently problematic. These effects can occur as a result of casual disregard, the daily business of colonial and postcolonial life. However, they also confront well-intentioned efforts to free the subaltern from such systems of subordination. Spivak shows us that there are dangers all around, and the project of confronting them is ambiguous, difficult, and inherently problematic.

I arrive at the idea of subaltern silence by inverting Spivak's question. Rather than asking "Can the subaltern speak?" my investigation tries to discover the conditions and practices that produce subaltern silence. That is to say, it asks what the shifting forms and qualities of silence are, what the practices of silencing that create subaltern subordination in a given place and time are. The difference is a subtle but important one. Spivak's question is one of epistemic possibility. It asks whether it is possible for us to understand what may or may not have been intended by some subaltern subject trying to speak. This is a rather narrow question, probing whether or not we truly understand the subaltern. In contrast, "In what ways is the subaltern made silent?" is a question of degrees, conditions, practices, and limits. Silence functions as a limit condition in this analysis. Arrayed around it, we observe various departures from silence. This allows us to ask what the conditions of silence are, what its gradations are, what the methods, technologies, and practices of silencing are, how complete this silence is, what its character is, and what forms of voice, presence, and agency sneak through the cracks. From this perspective, subaltern silence describes a constantly permuting play of silences and subordinations. They are driven by mobile and diverse strategies of subordination and desubordination, a cat-and-mouse game of endless improvisation.

That back-and-forth dynamic, the constant play of opposing tendencies, historicizes the problem of subaltern subordination. It allows us to ask how subaltern silence changes over time. It prompts us to note that our contemporary condition has a history, and that history has many vital things to say about how we wound up here and how we might change it.

I will trace these changes in a genealogy of subaltern silence. This history shows that contemporary forms of subordination have their roots in specific colonial and postcolonial practices. I will try to show how forms and tactics of subordination that originated under colonialism were retooled in new, more subtle forms under postcolonial conditions. These ineffable forms of subordination are exercised through our collective knowledge, belief, and understanding. The past several centuries have been marked by a continual development and diffusion of such techniques. Revealing these dynamics allows us to better combat their effects.

To frame this genealogy, we need to be clear what "silence" is. I do not mean this in a necessarily literal sense. Rather, it is a term of art that encompasses many phenomena. We can see this by analogy to Spivak's question, "Can the subaltern speak?" When Spivak posed this question, she was actually gesturing toward a much broader epistemological problem. "Speech" in her exploration is shorthand for a broad set of questions about representation, comprehension, and presence. Problems of subaltern speech concern aporias of incomprehension across cultural and historical distance. They are about the legibility of certain kinds of people as subjects, about the extent to which they can be comprehended in their own terms within dominant cultures.

Similarly, we can say that people are silenced when they are made imperceptible or incomprehensible. They are thought to have nothing to say, or if speaking, are thought to be saying nothing. Similar to Spivak's question about speech, this becomes a broad investigation of social presence and absence. It is both a matter of whether one appears to others and more specifically *how* one appears—through what schemata of perception, in what value-saturated field of visibility.

These phenomena are much too complicated to be characterized only as a matter of "speech." We need to supplement this metaphorical language with additional idioms and vocabularies: a broadly sensory vocabulary that includes the visible and the material in addition to the audible. This would valuably capture how people can be "invisible" in Ralph Ellison's sense, for example: seen yet unseen; seen yet ignored so profoundly that they fall outside of one's notice.[4] In a more epistemic vein, we might consider similar problems of comprehensibility and legibility. People can be understood as saying something and as having something to say or not. Even more radically, we must be aware of epistemologies that foreclose the existence of certain kinds of people. They drop out of perception, knowledge, and therefore social reality. Each of these idioms captures a different aspect of subaltern silence. I will use them to reflect changing manifestations of the problem, construed in a suitably broad, nuanced, and often metaphorical way.

Some might be troubled by this profusion of terms and how it constantly changes metaphors for subordination. This is actually a carefully calibrated feature of my analysis. It is important that the precision of the terminology not exceed that of the subject matter. The fact that no single set of terms or metaphors can capture this phenomenon indicates how complex and ineffable it is. Given this complexity, it would be dangerously limiting to talk only about "subaltern speech." It tends to channel our thought in subtle ways toward a conception of politics consisting principally of discourse. In fact, subaltern subordination takes many forms. Discourse is one of them, but not the only or the most important one. Given the broad range of phenomena that create subaltern silence we need a similarly broad and flexible language for characterizing it. With its changing metaphors and shifting accents, this language is richly evocative and descriptively powerful. It prevents the kind of reductivism that would come from focusing on speech only in a literal sense.

There is one core feature that unites all of the phenomena I will be examining. As subordination enters its modern age, it migrates from specific sites of violence and intimidation to a more general and abstract plane. It is enacted increasingly by means of *publicity*, the developing public spheres of the eighteenth and nineteenth centuries. These developments were uniquely modern, tied to some of the most prized cultural and technical innovations of the modern age. They operated through cherished institutions such as the public sphere, freedom of the press, free discourse, print technologies that made possible increasing mass circulation of words and images, and the culture of discourse and information that arose around them. This enterprise had an important point of inflection and acceleration in 1764, when the first newspaper went into print in colonial Saint-Domingue. The existence of a periodical press added new technologies and new means to the project of subaltern subordination. It now increasingly became a matter of whether and how one could appear in the public domain. The issues of the visibility, audibility, legibility, and epistemic presence of subordinated people changed character. All increasingly became issues of the more abstract, mediated public domain.

These developments were particularly prominent in some of the hotspots of modernity, the places where subordination was most profitable. That is to say, they were vital elements of colonialism. These technologies became so useful for subordination, however, that they were retained and transformed in the postcolonial era. Tendrils of colonial practice survived after colonialism, insidiously shaping how life is lived by many of the globe's current inhabitants. These innovations have become central to contemporary life. They have new technical forms: the internet, social media, the explosion of information and the proliferation of technologies to create and propagate it. However, the broader set of institutions, technologies, and cultures they represent have been at the cutting edge of subordination since at least the 1760s.

SHIFTING MODES OF SUBORDINATION

The genealogy of subaltern silence observes an arc of shifting forms, from the naked violence of colonialism to the euphemized epistemic violence of the postcolonial present. In its later phases, the genealogy reveals a symbolic politics of erasure, occlusion, invisibility, disruption, containment, and delegitimation. It shows how silence can be produced amid a proliferation of discourse. It reveals different ways of being placed into silence: injunctions against speech, decoupling of discursive spheres, creation of invisibility and nonpresence, and techniques for delegitimating entire categories of people. Above all, it brings to the fore constant struggles over silence, showing how it is occasionally pushed back and occasionally unwinds of its own accord. This is a complex politics that involves a wide variety of material and performative responses, one that is also traversed by powerful affective currents.

In sum, this genealogy focuses on how a politics of meaning comes to occupy an increasingly central role in subaltern subordination. This occurs partly through unexpected means: rumor, affect, ignorance, supposition, and disjointed communication. It occurs across a wide variety of discursive, symbolic, and material practices. I will try to render these typically unnoticed relations vivid as a way of better understanding the changing landscape of subordination. I am particularly interested in moments of disruption, when the project goes awry as a result of its own incoherence and the destabilization of those it means to subordinate.

To follow the course of these developments, I will trace out the connections, disjunctions, conditions of possibility, lines of descent, and shifting imaginaries that render some things intelligible and others not. I am interested specifically how subaltern silence functions as a mechanism of devaluation and delegitimation and how it is resisted and contested. Such a history shows how forms of subordination are threaded throughout our other practices and how they arise, change, permute, and disappear. It aims to reveal the ubiquity and subtlety of subordination in everyday life.

This genealogy provides some surprising insights. I will argue that silence is not always a form of subordination. Rather, it can sometimes be a *response* to subordination, an achievement chosen when other choices seem unpalatable or foreclosed. Subordination itself sometimes comes from surprising sources, including newspapers and magazines. Equally surprising are some of the ways in which colonial subordination was destabilized. Rumor, supposition, hearsay, fear, anxiety, and paranoia undercut what seemed like an ironclad system of oppression, problematizing it from within. Ultimately, I will argue, subordination took on an increasingly abstract character under these pressures, becoming more efficient and less noticeable. Ironically, the most widely dispersed forms of subaltern subordination arrived in what was portrayed as an era of postcolonial freedom.

This analysis theorizes subaltern silence in the domains in which our social, political, and cultural lives are shared. It is a story of our shared forms of perception and how they are mediated in the modern world. It is thus a story of the material forms such perception takes: its means of production and distribution, and how new technologies influence thought and practice. Important transformations emerged in the mid-eighteenth century in both Europe and the colonial Caribbean, particularly in the dense web of connections between them. These are the origins of now familiar technologies of modern publicity: newspapers, books, journals, broadsheets, pamphlets, brochures, prints, engravings, learned societies, salons, the "republic of letters," the public square, legislative assemblies, and public spectacles.

Jürgen Habermas draws a careful genealogy of modern publicity in *The Structural Transformation of the Public Sphere*.[5] Whereas he celebrates the democratizing potential of public spheres, however, I will show that their history has a substantial dark side. The tools and practices of publicity also operated as tools of domination in their early history. They functioned as adjuncts to much more forceful, violent, de jure forms of subordination. These technologies underwent important transformations in the postcolonial context. They moved to center stage as new, efficient, and insidious technologies of subaltern subordination. In this postcolonial context they emerged as the basis for subtle mechanisms of delegitimation, exclusion, invisibility, opacity, and silence. This history exactly parallels

Habermas's. It reveals other dimensions of publicity, ones that were not liberating but subordinating. In that sense, my book stands as a counterhistory to that other genealogy of the public sphere.

The "African song" is emblematic of this counterhistory. It represents striking aspects of the public sphere that Habermas does not discuss. The author transcribing the African song was Louis-Élie-Médéric Moreau de Saint-Méry, a prolific chronicler of life in Saint-Domingue. He was a white creole, born in the neighboring colony of Martinique. Moreau de Saint-Méry was educated in law in France and returned to practice in Saint-Domingue.[6] He was a founder of the Cercle des Philadelphes, a scientific society in the Caribbean colonies modeled on ones in Europe. The book containing the "African song" is his encyclopedic compendium of geography and life in the French colony, *Description topographique, physique, civile, politique et historique de la partie française de l'isle Saint-Domingue* (A Topographical, Physical, Civil, Political, and Historical Description of the French Part of the Island of Saint-Domingue). The vast span of this work was a product of many decades of observation, collection, and document-hoarding. It chronicles the zenith of the colonial era in Saint-Domingue, viewed from a perspective after that zenith had passed and the colony was riven by revolutionary conflict. Moreau de Saint-Méry's book was published in Philadelphia in 1796, where he had settled in exile from the French and Haitian Revolutions. He operated a publishing and bookselling operation there and was of fixture of the city's expatriate intellectual life. The documents he hoarded still exist. They are now housed in the French colonial archives in Aix-en-Provence, and they form one of the archival bases for this book.[7] There is thus a complex sense in which some of my own observations on subaltern silence are filtered through Moreau de Saint-Méry's proclivities, perspective, and taste as a consumer of information.

The *Description* represents a certain kind of Enlightenment publicity. It reflects an impulse to collect, organize, and disseminate knowledge that is very characteristic of the era. Written in the colonies, published in the United States during the French and Haitian Revolutions, the *Description* exemplifies another aspect of the colonial public sphere: its extension around the Caribbean basin and across the Atlantic. It was part of a multilocal, transatlantic domain of discourse and print that was rapidly developing at this time. It extended across the Caribbean colonies to cities on the American mainland such as Cayenne, Charleston, and Philadelphia, and to Europe itself. In this sense, Moreau de Saint-Méry was at the cutting edge of enlightened discourse and technical innovation of his time, particularly as it mapped onto the hottest economic frontier of the era: colonial capitalism.

Moreau de Saint-Méry's *Description* also exemplifies the ways that the public sphere became an innovative tool of modern subordination. The public sphere arose hand in hand with European colonialism, articulating powerful forms of subaltern silence. Seen from this perspective, the history of the modern public sphere is also a history of constituent exclusions, blockages, elisions, and silences. It is a story of openness and closure, the attempt to create a colonial normality and the countervailing efforts by colonial subjects to disrupt that common sense. This broadened and subversive counterhistory allows us to trace some of the ways that such phenomena were structured into the development of the public sphere and have persisted ever since.

Although this book is a genealogy of subaltern silence, it is just as much a history of moments in which subordination failed to work, in which the subaltern "spoke" in one way or another. It is not, however, simply an account of the ways that subordinated subjects spoke covertly to one another or mobilized forms of subaltern agency. Excellent studies of that kind have already been written. Julius Scott's *The Common Wind* pieces together a wonderful history of subterranean currents of discourse in colonial Saint-Domingue. James Scott's *Weapons of the Weak* is a landmark account of cryptified forms of subaltern agency.[8] My book heads in a rather different direction. It aims to problematize such projects, showing how fraught and difficult subaltern agency can be and how misleading it is to romanticize or rely upon the agency of the subordinated in any straightforward way. This will very much be a discussion of the weapons of the weak and the agency of the dispossessed, but I will argue that those issues are anything but straightforward.

In contrast, Michel-Rolph Trouillot's *Silencing the Past* provides a promising example of how to proceed.[9] Trouillot probes moments in which an unreflective Eurocentrism causes interpreters to see European agency and ideas in non-European places, ignoring the rich texture of subaltern politics. His analysis of the "three faces of Sans Souci," for instance, is a powerful demonstration of how to read silences from well-known archival materials. Trouillot poses the question of why the Haitian King Henri I named his palace Sans Souci. The answer is *not*, Trouillot argues, because he wanted to pay homage to the Prussian King Frederick II, whose famed palace was also called Sans Souci. Instead, Trouillot makes a persuasive argument that the palace celebrates a victory by Henri over Jean-Baptiste Sans Souci, a vanquished rival who had defied Henri's authority. By digging deeply into this question, Trouillot is able to reveal a whole set of silences about African culture in Haiti, tensions between creole and African revolutionaries, and the silencing of those who are not legible in European terms.

Trouillot provides a wonderful example of how to pursue silences in the archives and why pursing them matters. I will follow lines of inquiry very similar to his, with three notable departures. First, Trouillot framed his project with some valuable reflections on the nature of historical interpretation and its relation to power in colonial contexts. Our understanding of such topics has considerably deepened in subsequent decades, however. In coming chapters I will show that there is much more left to say on these themes. In that sense, my project can be seen as a considerable expansion, updating, and methodological refinement of the kinds of insights framed by him. Second, like Spivak, Trouillot burrows deeply into specific examples and opens their complexities up to view. I will do so as well, but I will attempt to situate those instances in a much broader historical tableau that reveals additional complexities over time. A genealogy of subaltern silence allows us to develop a coordinated set of investigations that is more complex, diachronic, and far-reaching. Third, in the examples he provides us Trouillot seems concerned to push his analyses to a determinate conclusion. By the end of his treatment of Sans Souci, for instance, he is quite clear that silencing has occurred and that it takes the forms I have described. Because of the cautions I adopt from Spivak, I will rarely be able to proceed in this way. Often my analyses will remain suspended in ambiguity. They operate in vague, difficult, ineffable situations, and the interpreter's treatment must preserve this ambiguity rather than seeking to erase it.

Although my aim is to go well beyond Spivak's original question about subaltern speech, this book does implicitly respond to it. Yes, I will claim, the subaltern can occasionally speak, through a wide variety of means that evolve along with correspondent forms of silencing. I will devote a great deal of energy to highlighting the subtle texture of that silence and its opposites. Much of this is odd and unexpected, not what we usually think of as subaltern "voice." In this history, the subaltern finds new opportunities to speak through rumor, symbolic representation, disruption, fear, and even by means of the very apparatus of subordination itself. In short, this phenomenon operates in a wide variety of ways. Contingency, change, and improvisation are very much the point of this study. Subaltern silence takes richly varied forms, ones that reflect the complex character of subordination in the contemporary world.

Ultimately, this genealogy is the prehistory of characteristic tendencies that we still live with today. My real focus in these pages is a media-obsessed culture fixated on exciting new communication technologies that make possible new forms of wealth, social relation, knowledge, and radical new epistemologies. It is a sharply divided, hierarchical society with substantial racial tensions. There are pronounced differences of wealth and poverty both within and between nations, and its elites are acquiring dazzling fortunes from globalized trade and overseas investments. It is a society that can be strikingly indifferent or cruel to those it exploits. New epistemologies, new media, and tools of the increasingly networked culture are drawn into this project of domination in subtle and polymorphous ways. Ironically, they are also widely celebrated as vectors of a new wave of democracy and political equality.

I am referring, of course, to the explosion of print in eighteenth-century Europe, the rapid efflorescence of public spheres during that time, the unbounded optimism of technical innovation that characterized that age, and the colonial projects of conquest and enslavement that accompanied them. This could easily be mistaken as a description of the present day, however. Contemporary societies are plagued by forms of subordination that grow ever more subtle and diffuse. They are forms of invisibility, erasure, racialization, delegitimation, and disregard. Such silences play across many axes of labor and social status: racialized minorities, refugees, migrants, the undocumented, global reserve armies of labor, and those classed as members of the Global South. These silences trace lines of privilege and disadvantage on a global and transnational scale. To understand them, we would do well to examine such problems in previous eras of globalization and technical innovation. The particular era I will focus on is one of wooden ships, paper publications, and plantation slavery. Yet it is also a past that is in many ways strikingly contemporary, one that established the scripts and conditions of possibility for much of what happens in our present moment.

INSURRECTIONS OF SUBJUGATED KNOWLEDGES

It is clear that I am greatly indebted to the insights of Gayatri Spivak and Michel Foucault in this study. Such ancestry leaves me in the difficult position of a child of bickering parents, however. Their forced cohabitation often requires one to adjudicate conflicts and differences of opinion.

Readers of "Can the Subaltern Speak?" will remember that Spivak framed her cosmic question as a rebuke to Foucault. Her most far-reaching criticism focused on Foucault's idea that genealogy could help to create a space for "insurrections of subjugated knowledges."[10] She takes issue with the assumption that "the oppressed, if given the chance... *can speak and know their conditions.*"[11] She thereby accuses Foucault of tacitly reintroducing an essentialist notion of the subject—a charge she also levels against the Subaltern Studies group and others.[12] In this case, it is something like the illusion of a subaltern whose knowledge is subjugated and can be liberated.

Spivak also charges Foucault with trying to speak in place of a silenced subaltern. She says, "The banality of leftist intellectuals' lists of self-knowing, politically canny subalterns stands revealed; representing them, the intellectuals represent themselves as transparent."[13] Her inquiry shows that systematic misconstrual, miscomprehension, and misunderstanding are endemic to subalternity. They are created and ramified across gaps of power, precarity, culture, and time. Attempts to help the subaltern speak are equally embroiled in these problems. Speaking on behalf of the subaltern threatens simply to reproduce subaltern silence. When the subjectivity of the subaltern cannot be known, any attempt to speak on the subaltern's behalf risks a kind of ventriloquism in which the illusion of liberated speech is actually an artifact of the interpreter's own agenda. Claiming to speak on behalf of a silent subaltern merely entangles one in problems of power and subordination rather than resolving them. When one postulates a silenced or lost voice that can be recovered by the intellectual, the act of recovery itself becomes a form of epistemic erasure.

In Spivak's diagnosis, even efforts at comprehension can be problematic. Attempts to understand a silenced subaltern can lead to a systematic misconstrual. It can mistake the interpreter's biases and misconstruals for a genuine understanding of the subaltern. The result is another form of ventriloquism, one that substitutes itself for anything the actual person may be trying to say. The seeming interpretive ambiguity of understanding the subaltern is not an artifact of academic inquiry but a symptom of subordination itself. Attempting to remove that ambiguity merely substitutes one form of subordination for another.

Spivak uses these criticisms to highlight the great complexity of subaltern silence and the ways that well intentioned advocates can perpetuate it. She makes an effective case for deromanticizing the oppressed and thinking in much more complex ways about desubjugation.

Whether these charges actually hold for Foucault is a complicated question that I will not tackle directly. Just briefly, though, it is worth noting that Spivak's criticisms often rely on Foucault's own statements about the theoretical and methodological import of his work. This is not a terribly good interpretive strategy, especially in Foucault's case. His understanding of what he was doing often lagged behind the sheer intuitive brilliance of his investigations. Foucault often struggled to understand the implications of his own work, and his interviews, lectures, and published statements do not do an adequate job of plumbing their significance.

Rather than decide Foucault's guilt or innocence, it is much more useful to offer a Foucauldian retort to Spivak's charges. That is the aim of this book: to take Spivak's cautions on board while capitalizing on the advantages of Foucault's techniques. Over the course of these chapters, I will try to show that the arc connecting the "African song" and *Soulouque après sa mort* is in many ways a Spivakian story of subordination-as-silence. This genealogy traces constantly shifting technologies of subordination that produce subaltern silence in novel ways during several centuries of colonial and postcolonial history. In short, this book is a syncretic fusion of Spivak and Foucault that tries to tap the insights of both.

To think about this project, it is useful to consider how a genealogy of subaltern silence might relate to Foucault's other work. Most obviously, it takes genealogy in a direction that Foucault did not pursue. His detailed, insightful analyses of the "Classical Age" in Europe ignore the centrality of colonialism to that era. He was a compelling and insightful analyst of the forms of power that characterized European societies of the seventeenth and eighteenth centuries and the ways that they were deployed as forms of knowledge and practice. However, those forms of knowledge and practice were not restricted to the European continent, precisely because so much of their intellectual, political, and economic energy was directed elsewhere. This is the period of European domination of much of the rest of the planet. Colonialism provided the basis for a vast expansion of European wealth during this time and was a central preoccupation of its intellectual energies. It is baffling that these phenomena are not interwoven with Foucault's genealogies of this period.

Spivak is blunt on this point. She writes, "It is well known that Foucault locates one case of epistemic violence, a complete overhaul of the episteme, in the redefinition of madness at the end of the European eighteenth century. But what if that particular redefinition was only a part of the narrative of history in Europe as well as in the colonies? What if the two projects of epistemic overhaul worked as dislocated and unacknowledged parts of a vast two-handed engine?"[14] Here Spivak advances the thesis that colonialism was part and parcel of the history of epistemic violence that Foucault does reveal, an unacknowledged half of a "vast two-handed engine." The implication, which is entirely correct, is that colonial histories were not simply parallel to histories of epistemic violence in Europe, but inherently a part of them. As Spivak has noted, Foucault's brilliant work on European intellectual culture fails to look beyond Europe, even though European intellectual culture, politics, and business were quite busy with the rest of the world. In his analyses, "the clinic, the asylum, the prison, the university—all seem like screen-allegories that foreclose a reading of the broader narratives of imperialism."[15]

I will pick up this thread of Spivak's criticism and amplify it considerably. The project I have outlined should have been on Foucault's agenda, but it was not. There are obvious parallels between this genealogy and the ones he did write, however. Colonialism was a fertile site for the development of discipline, confinement, penality, marginalization, exclusion, and normalization of many kinds—the themes that are so vivid in *Discipline and Punish*. Its formative period was exactly during the Classical Age on which Foucault lavished so much attention, especially in *The Order of Things* but equally in his other works of the 1960s and 1970s. Reciprocally, colonialism was deeply intertwined with the development of the modern institutions that he catalogued, developing at the same time and in contact with those institutions. I will tack back and forth between colony and metropole to demonstrate the depth of this intertwinement. My aim is to show how subaltern silence increasingly becomes an effect of European instruments of communication and speech. Ironically, the very same institutions and technologies that claim to undo tyranny and democratize speech turn out to be particularly subtle and effective tools of subaltern subordination. The ties between European modernity and colonial subordination are dense and unavoidable. The technologies of European liberation were also technologies of subaltern silence.

Although Foucault never addressed the centrality of colonialism to European modernity, he did reflect in important ways about race. His most sustained treatment is in *"Society Must Be Defended,"* the Collège de France lectures of 1976.[16]

There his discussion is provocative and unusual. It is not a history of practices that led up to our current understanding of race, with its differentiation of humans into groups through a complicated logic of phenotype, ancestry, and culture. Rather, it is a more elemental history of conflict between groups, reminiscent of Carl Schmitt's friend/enemy distinction as played out in actual history.[17] It is one that Foucault characterizes as a history of dominations and subjugations.[18]

For Foucault the development of racial thinking is the prehistory of biopolitics. In its biopolitical form, he sees race as intimately connected with sexuality, an aspect of his work that Ann Laura Stoler makes lucid in *Race and the Education of Desire*.[19] Sexuality becomes a crucial point of control in the effort to govern the fecundity and health of a population. Racism is the ultimate biopolitical expression of this transformation. Races are populations pitted against one another; state racism is the project of governing a race as a population. This project finds its ultimate expression in twentieth-century genocide, particularly in Nazism as its most extreme and rigorous form. Foucault had made this clear in *The History of Sexuality, Volume 1*, a text peppered with references to race and racial thinking as themes deeply intertwined with concerns about sexuality.[20] Foucault's readers seldom notice this aspect of the book, however, even in the wake of Stoler's influential treatment.

As attentive as Foucault was to issues of race, the elision of colonialism from his work is striking. Foucault's analyses of race are always bounded within continental Europe. As such, they are curiously divorced from European projects of colonial domination, globalized capitalism, and enslavement. Of course, these overseas adventures were the epitome of biopolitics: the marshaling of colonized bodies and forces for production, concerns about the fecundity of enslaved populations, the control of sexuality to separate the races and ensure the coherence of "race" as a criterion of domination, and so on. In fact, the site of biopolitical racialization was much more often the colonies than Europe proper. All of this is curiously missing in Foucault's analysis, when arguably it should be at its heart.

Spivak points us in a helpful direction for the critique of colonialism and its aftermath. She works immanently within a number of specific examples, opening them up delicately to reveal paradoxes, conundrums, and aporias associated with subalternity. We might refer to this interpretive strategy as *problematization*.

Spivak focuses on largely forgotten figures to ask questions about historical interpretation, archival loss, the representation of others, and the problematic position of the intellectual. She first explored these puzzles within the story of a suicide in the family, a distant relative whose complex personal and political life was misunderstood by her descendants. In *A Critique of Postcolonial Reason*, those themes are expanded to a much broader tableau. Here she shifts nimbly between the local and the global, showing how forms of silencing can have an utterly banal and quotidian character but derive from global financial capital and international aid. Her examples range widely: a royal figure in India under British colonial administration during the nineteenth century; a contemporary Japanese fashion designer; immigrants in the contemporary geopolitical-economic landscape; efforts by highly resourced NGOs to solicit local participants in processes of "improvement" and "development." Each moment in this eclectic analysis captures the broad sweep of gigantic social, political, and economic forces that invest individual subjects and lives and produce subordination on a global scale.

Problematization is a powerful tool in Spivak's hands. It allows her to note the changing character of British colonialism, for instance, in an implicitly genealogical way. In this her work is not unlike Foucault's. However, she does not pursue the larger project that these examples imply. Missing is a more general, synthetic characterization of what subaltern silence is, how it arises, and how it permutes over time. She does not trace the shifting forms of exclusion, marginalization, mediation, and contestation of colonial processes. The result is a lack of attention to how subaltern silence is constituted and contested.

In this sense, Spivak's interpretive strategy is also a form of *exemplification*. It allows her to dive deeply into the complexities of a given instance, showing how meanings are lost over time through the incomprehension and forgetting of later generations. However, this analysis remains synchronic rather than diachronic. Although the complexities she details frequently stretch across time and are problematic because of their temporal character, we can draw no broader conclusions about the flow of history from them. As a result, the weight of such an analysis rests on the exemplarity of its individual examples.

In sum, Spivak's approach suffers from a kind of pointillism. It maintains a somewhat narrow focus on the specificities of particular cases, often particular people. She shows how these instances are ramified through history or across cultural contexts, but these instances remain... instances, not effectively drawn together into a broader analysis of subaltern speech. Her brilliant analyses tend to focus on individual subject positions and the ambivalent and paradoxical situations in which they exist.

My project weaves together these various strands, combining Spivak's attention to the aporias of postcoloniality with Foucault's fertile approach to historiography. At the same time, it tries to address Foucault's neglect of colonialism while correcting Spivak's methodological pointillism. The question of subaltern silence taps issues that have long histories, ones that have permuted over the years and recur in potent new forms in the present. They are issues with particular resonance in European modernity and its colonial past. To take full advantage of Spivak's insights about problematization and exemplification while avoiding their limitations, I will trace them across a broader canvas and longer time frame, employing genealogical techniques that can tap some of the riches hidden there. This approach is oriented toward sifting through the record of silence, speech, presence, and agency, observing gaps and holes in the archive, what is saved and what is lost, and developing interpretive and epistemic insights for thinking about these issues over an extended span of time.

As a genealogy, the book aims to provide an indirect response to Spivak's charges against Foucault. Rather than rebut her critique with theoretical arguments, I try to demonstrate the richness of insight that can be generated through a careful genealogy. If the proof is in the pudding, then this book is intended as pudding.

That is not to say that it aims to refute Spivak's criticisms, however. Instead, she considerably raises the bar for a successful analysis and poses questions that require departures from Foucault's usual techniques. Subaltern silence is not a totalizing status or a foreclosed destiny, but an interpretive caution to be navigated for both those who would be silenced and those who try to interpret them. The task is to trace the conditions under which subaltern speech might emerge, to create interpretive bridges across time and culture that might discover what the subaltern was or is trying to say.

HOW DO WE WRITE A GENEALOGY OF SUBALTERN SILENCE?

How, then, do we write a genealogy of subaltern silence? This project poses unique challenges. It aims to chart the production of silence, which is to some extent a process of erasure, blockage, and occlusion. At the limit, subaltern silence seems to imply total inaudibility or invisibility—a complete lack of social presence. By definition, there could be no evidence of someone silenced in this way: no perception, no record, no trace, no contact. As a result, to write the history of subaltern silence would be to write the history of a nonobject, an absence, a lack, a negativity, of something that is invisible or epistemically nonexistent, of something that cannot be brought into view in any determinate way.

Because of this unique dilemma, a genealogy of subaltern silence is a perplexing task that requires some methodological soul-searching. Genealogy typically traces the history of a specific institution or practice: prisons, sexuality, the human sciences. A genealogy of subaltern silence is a considerably different enterprise. It is a critical history of people and practices that are by definition obscured from view or only suspected to exist. It is a history of absences, opacities, nonevents, nonobjects, suspected objects, or inferred objects. We enter tricky epistemological terrain if we try to use traditional Foucauldian categories to theorize such phenomena. Foucault famously characterized knowledge as having a productive power to create new subjectivities and new kinds of subject. It is not immediately clear what this would mean in the case of silence, however. It seems paradoxical to talk about the production of a new form of subjectivity as invisible, undetectable, and unknowable. "Production" implies a positivity that seems inconsistent with subaltern silence as absence and erasure.

Of course, subaltern silence in its pure form is a limit case. At the limit, there may well be forms of silence and subordination that remain forever invisible. A truly silent subaltern would be one so thoroughly occluded from social participation that he or she would be unknowable. Moving beyond that theoretical limit case, however, there are penumbras of effects surrounding the silences we are seeking. We can characterize shifting qualities and forms of silence. Some of these are side effects of the production of silences, or reactions to it on the part of those still present, or partial and incomplete forms of silence that provide insights into the broader phenomenon. To work on this basis, one must seek out anomalies within the archive and observe what can be seen around their peripheries. One can then project back to the center, inferring what must be there to produce such effects. We may not be able to observe subaltern silence itself, but we can seek out the practices of silencing that produce it, the shadows it casts on bordering phenomena, and the times when its production is incomplete, contested, or changing.

I will operate on the assumption that subaltern silence has often been wrapped into broader and more abstract processes of colonialism and modernization. Sometimes these are ambiguous, ineffable, or trail off to a vanishing point in the production of subordination. The next chapter, for instance, asks about the significance of the first newspaper in the French Caribbean. It will turn out to have a lot to do with an odd transmogrification of subaltern agency. This practice was an attempt to resignify subaltern agency in a way that was only partly successful. While aiming to use the print media as a tool of subordination, colonial elites partly missed their mark and created an unsettling vision of subaltern agency. Both the intended subordination and its misfired alternative resulted in subaltern silence, but the distance between them provides us with a kind of parallax: a way to read colonial modernization as the production of subaltern silence.

Here we can make a useful distinction between subaltern silence, which can pass unnoticed, and the *practices* of silencing that produce it. In what follows I will be careful to draw out these practices as specific *dispositifs*, specific apparatuses and technologies, that produce silence in characteristic ways. Much of my genealogy will trace particular changes and permutations in these practices, attempting to reveal the forms of silence and subordination that they leave behind. We will see that such practices multiply and diversify considerably over time, giving rise to a sometimes dizzying array of ways to produce silence. At the same time, important overall tendencies will emerge that I will be careful to draw out.

Another angle of parallax comes by focusing on sources that have *not* been silenced. Many archival documents were left by people of power and privilege. Such people are more likely to be *creators* of silence than its victims. Nonetheless, the archives often register traces of silence that resulted from their actions. The powerful were typically quite happy to record their own actions and opinions, and they had privileged means to do so. This record is always suspect, subject to substantial distortions and misunderstandings. Reading it carefully can provide useful information, however. Sometimes it records action that can be interpreted as reaction. This might be the observed results of unseen actions, the gravitational force of subaltern silence causing disruptions in the orbits of those around it. Characterizing such phenomena requires a careful mapping of the disruptions surrounding an apparently nonexistent object. Sometimes it traces reactions of pride, cruelty, or distain; at other times, fear, panic, or paranoia. These affective responses can provide a valuable index of elite reactions to subordination or its failure. Such considerations require a genealogy to explore new registers of interpretation. They go beyond writing a history of knowledges to consider epistemologies of fear, ambiguity, ignorance, and uncertainty.

Of course, most genres of silence are partial and incomplete rather than absolute. They involve the relative muting, invisibility, and obscurity of some people relative to others. In some cases, this is the result of successful resistance. We will see moments in nineteenth-century Haiti, for instance, in which subordinated subjects push back against their own silence. They had been out of view as silenced subjects, but sudden bursts of revolutionary energy, repeated several times in the early nineteenth century, reveal what was hidden during the interim. These attempts to contest silence were brief and ultimately unsuccessful, but they display the underlying dynamics at work in producing that silence. They force us to notice silenced subjects who might otherwise have remained out of view.

In this sense, genealogy can reveal slippages over time, moments when the subaltern manages some sort of presence only to be resubmerged in silence. This will be a particular preoccupation of chapters 6 and 7, where I will explore how subaltern subjects are pushed out of visibility and reemerge into view repeatedly during a fifty-year span of Haitian history. Here the historical dimensions of genealogy are a particular advantage.

All of these strategies acknowledge the inherent problems of writing the genealogy of a nonobject. They are not simply pragmatic workarounds but careful attempts to assess who *does* speak when the subaltern does not, and how what *is* present relates to what is absent. There is never a simple relation between the two; instead it is a constant interpretive challenge. As Arlette Farge put it, "You develop your reading of the archives through ruptures and dispersion, and must mold questions out of stutters and silences."[21] In this case, I am interested in molding not just questions but entire genealogies out of stutters and silences. The challenges are correspondingly greater, but also hold out the promise of teaching us many important things.

Of necessity, this project has complicated relations with the archive. The sources I have been describing are different from those we are used to dealing with in genealogy. Foucault focuses almost exclusively on learned treatises and other academic texts. This seems quite appropriate if one is writing a history of the human sciences. However, this approach would be a substantial distortion in the study I am outlining. The forms of absence and subordination I have described are produced not only by academic works like Moreau de Saint-Méry's *Description*. Pamphlets, broadsheets, newspapers, journals, engravings, maps, letters, speeches, memoirs, and manuscripts all become important resources in puzzling out the sources of silence. This project requires a considerable *expansion* of the archive compared with those of Foucault.

Ultimately, though, none of these sources stands as an authoritative account of what was said and done. The problem of subaltern silence necessitates a self-reflexive engagement with our sources of information and the forms of opacity that shadow them. Our attitude must be correspondingly more complex, one of vigilance and suspicion to identify ambiguities and explore their significance. Sometimes the question is "What events are reported in this document?" but just as often, "What is the constitutive force of what this document says and the way it circulated?" I am equally interested in what *does not* appear in the print media as what does. This will be a history of things not-said and not-done to a large extent.

As a result, the archive itself is considerably problematized in this enterprise. We must pay close attention to its construction, what is there, what is not, who is represented, who is not, and try to triangulate and approximate the sources of silence that result. This will involve reading around the edges of that which is not there, showing where it is absent, speculating about what might have been or what might still be in its empty place. Thus, my relationship with the archive and with documentary history becomes much more complicated.

I will be arguing that subaltern silence was both an implicit goal and an ambiguous achievement during colonial times. To trace this phenomenon, we must operate simultaneously on two separate levels, taking account of (1) the silences produced by and/or eluding colonial elites in their attempts to rule and (2) the silences produced by and/or eluding our current understanding of this archival past. These two levels are isomorphic. Unknowability across lines of social difference *within their time* is in many ways similar to unknowability across lines of social and temporal difference *from their time to the present*. I will therefore execute a careful double move throughout this genealogy, trying to characterize specific forms of subaltern silence within specific eras while also being attentive to the forms of silence that result from the construction of the archive across time—what was preserved and what was lost—and our attempts to interpret it. Subaltern silence produced in earlier years comes down to us as silence within the archives now, but silence in the archives now does not necessarily indicate subaltern subordination then. Telling the difference will be a constant interpretive preoccupation as we proceed.

The production of subaltern silence is never constituted by a unified set of practices, nor is it opposed by a unified set of practices. Rather, it is a vast web of interrelated phenomena. As a result, a comprehensive genealogy is neither possible nor desirable in these circumstances. Instead I will try to trace out some important strands of this web, focusing on practices that seem particularly salient for their era.

This genealogy traces a discontinuous history that reflects the heterogeneous, topsy-turvy world it tries to understand. It reveals shifting modes of subordination that change in characteristic ways over time, a mosaic of closures, exclusions, and forms of resistance. New openings for subaltern voice are met with innovative new strategies of silencing. This will be a story of fits and starts, complex mixtures of practice and counterpractice, conditions of possibility or impossibility, and endlessly permuting forms of action, speech, and silence. It will observe instances in which opportunities for action were seized against impossible odds, and others where difficult situations were navigated with great difficulty and ambivalent results. The eclecticism of this account is very much a reflection of the underlying phenomenon.

From this perspective, it will be possible to see more durable patterns of subaltern silence: its sources in colonialism, in the institutional and cultural practices of European modernity, in technical innovations, and even in well-intentioned projects of political progress and social improvement. These currents become visible from the perspective of an always permuting production of silences and always innovating practices of contestation.

CHAPTER 2

Silence as an Achievement

Marronage

1685-1790

We clamor for the right to opacity for everyone.

—Édouard Glissant

The first half of this book examines the complex, subtle, and odd traces of subaltern silence under colonialism. Some of them can be discerned only with careful interpretive triangulation. Others are stories of contest and struggle in which the subaltern achieves some form of publicity while fighting the undertow of silence. They are not strictly speaking about "speech," but about a complex set of relations between discourse, materiality, performativity, and affect. I will try to show that when the subaltern cannot speak in the colonial slave colony, discourse is displaced into other domains. These material practices carry performative effects. The performativity of the silenced subaltern is often a destabilizing one. The result is problematization and epistemic rupture. It disrupts attempts to normalize colonialism and slavery, exposing the hypocrisy of these projects. Chief among these are the tensions between subaltern subordination in the colonies and democratic revolution at home. As a result of problematization, those hypocrisies are now experienced as unease, unsettlement, fear, anxiety, and paranoia. Although colonial subalterns could not speak, they gained other forms of publicity and provoked strong affective reactions in the process. These other forms of publicity, I will argue, formed a continual subversion of subaltern silence in French colonialism.

This chapter focuses on the fugitivity of enslaved people. Known as "marronage" in the French colonies of the Caribbean, such forms of escape were a paradigmatic pursuit of freedom by the enslaved. A maroon was a person fleeing the brutal confines of slavery to reclaim her or his self-determination. This flight could be temporary, as when a slave vanished from a plantation but returned later. Or it could be a more permanent seizure of freedom, an attempt to constitute a life completely outside the system of enslavement. In the Caribbean colonies, this often took the form of maroon settlements in the hinterlands where slaves could constitute a new life according to their own plans and designs.

As such, marronage is above all a story of freedom, resistance, and the corresponding efforts of repression on the part of slaveowners and the colonial administration. In this chapter, however, I will focus on other less obvious aspects of this phenomenon. I will treat marronage as both an effect of and an attempt to resist subaltern silence. This perspective highlights the epistemic force of the act of escape and its complex double character as a form of silence.

Such treatment may seem counterintuitive. Marronage *was* above all a practice of flight rather than thought. The counterintuitive character of this claim, however, is precisely my point. It reminds us that the question whether the subaltern can speak is only obliquely about speech. It is more profoundly a question of how subordinated peoples can become epistemically present. Marronage reveals unexpected modalities that subaltern people can use to make themselves present when that presence is blocked, silenced, or forcibly excluded. It is, in this sense, an example of epistemology pressed into the service of rebellion. It is an attempt to regain subaltern agency when speech is not an option. Marronage thus provides a particularly good illustration of the dynamics of publicity and performativity, showing us how material acts can have a public, imaginary, and subversive effect.

RACIALIZATION, SUBORDINATION, AND SILENCE

Subaltern silence was a sustaining condition of slavery. The captive population was forced into submission through various coercive measures. In French colonialism, this was a long-term, systematic project with many strands: the establishment of colonial governments, the enunciation of laws regulating conduct in the colonies, and the informal disregard for those laws when they limited brutality and violence towards the enslaved. Silence, an inability to complain, lodge claims, or react, was a core feature of this oppression.

As I noted in chapter 1, it is often easiest to characterize such silences by the practices creating them. In the early years of French colonialism two such forms of practice were especially common. *Silencing through law* functioned in a straightforward way to formally strip people of voice, presence, and personhood. It operated through legal definitions of who could speak, who could testify, who could hold positions of authority and responsibility, who could function as a normal adult member of society. People who were legally excluded from these capacities were thereby silenced in corresponding ways. At the same time, *silencing through violence* relied on the intimidating force of painful and harmful treatment to keep people quiet. It was sometimes official, coded into the laws of slavery, but it was also quite often extralegal or illegal, operating alongside, in supplement to, or in defiance of the law. This treatment was frequently improvised, random, capricious, vicious, gratuitous, and excessive. The violent behavior of slaveholders and their auxiliaries created a regime of terror that further extended the silence of people who were already silenced through law. It caused enslaved people to minimize their presence and voice as a way of escaping notice, since being singled out for attention could often carry such high costs.

These domains of colonial practice are well known, so I will not dwell on them here. What interests me more are the subtle, less obvious practices of silencing that began to take root in this environment. They would continue to grow and develop from the seventeenth to the nineteenth centuries, and they will be the ultimate focus of our interest.

Processes of racialization and dehumanization worked to rationalize enslavement. They promoted imaginaries that framed enslaved Africans and their descendants as inferior and invisible. They thereby constituted a population of people who were not really people, people who did not figure in the developing institutions of European democracy, legality, or publicity. These people were not allowed to "speak" in any meaningful sense: either by challenging stigmatizing norms, making claims about the injustice of their treatment, resisting it, or demonstrating their humanity and thereby undermining the idea that enslavement was improper. Here the erasure of voices, plans, ideas, and presence combined with physical enslavement and violence to constitute the social death that Orlando Patterson so eloquently describes.[1] Such silences fulfilled a vital epistemic function for the maintenance of enslavement and colonial domination. They permitted the normalization of such practices by silencing those who would oppose them.

In French colonialism, a key feature of this project was the interpellation of enslaved Africans and their descendants as *nègres*. This was a complex and variable concept that signified both black and slave in certain ways. As Laurent Dubois has noted, "it is a particularly capacious and shifting term in French, layered with uses and counteruses, shot through in a sense with centuries of struggle over its very meaning."[2] It is Franz Fanon's primary focus when he describes the injuries of racial interpellation. Readers of *Black Skin, White Masks* will remember Fanon's famous anecdote of being pointed at by a child, who cries out: "Mother, look at the *nègre*, I'm scared!" ("*Maman, regarde le nègre, j'ai peur!*").[3] Fanon insightfully describes the existential impact of this label, which he characterizes as woven by whites "out of a thousand details, anecdotes, and stories." Léopold Senghor and Aimé Césaire seized control of the term and revalorized it as an affirmative theory of *négritude*.[4] More recently, Achille Mbembe has detailed some of the idea's complexity and significance in his *Critique de la raison nègre*. His concise assessment is that "From a strictly historical point of view, the word '*Nègre*' refers above all to a phantasmagoria."[5]

I do not want to perpetuate the injuries that Fanon describes. However, it is important to trace parts of the construction of French racial thinking as they bear on the history I am discussing. Following the gradual evolution of this racialized language will provide us with genealogical insight into what Spivak might refer to as "the track of ideology."[6]

The word *nègre* occurs constantly in the archives of French colonialism, and the corresponding figure becomes a central part of fabricating subaltern silence. Its meaning shifts in subtle and complex ways, intertwining ideas of racial identity and enslavement. As Dubois noted, there are no good translations of *nègre* into English, and it must be carefully distinguished from Anglo-American racial language that might seem similar. To avoid misleading translations and false anachronisms, I will leave *nègre* and its cognates untranslated when working with original sources. This is not to perpetuate the language of racial thinking but to detail its formation and effects.

Fanon had finely tuned genealogical instincts when he described the figure of the *nègre* as a creation of whites, formed out of a thousand details, anecdotes, and stories. Indeed, this figure consolidated slowly over decades and centuries of quotidian use. The history of those changing meanings tells us much about French colonial racialization, denigration, and ultimately, subaltern silence.

In its early years during the seventeenth and eighteenth centuries, *nègre* traveled a path similar to *esclave*. Both were terms for slave, and they were often used interchangeably in variable and changing ways. During this time, *esclave* meant slave in a strict and narrow sense. *Nègre*, in contrast, had a richer and more complex range of meanings. It also signified slave, but with variable layers of identity and valuation. *Nègres* were not simply slaves, but African or African-descended slaves with unique associations of raciality, submission, inferiority, and eligibility for violent and sexualized treatment.

The Code Noir is an early document in that history. It was a comprehensive set of legal regulations proclaimed by Louis XIV in 1685 that governed slavery in all of the French colonies. *Le Code Noir* was the common name for this act, but its original title was *Edit du roy, touchant la police des isles de l'Amerique françoise* (Edict of the King on the Policing of the Islands of French America).[7] Here policing is used in the historically specific sense that Michel Foucault has done so much to explain: a set of governmental techniques designed to enhance the splendor and forces of the state.[8] In this context, it describes the effective management of the colonies to ensure profitability and maximize state benefit, which includes above all managing their enslaved labor force.

The edict legally codifies the status of slave, using the language of both *nègre* and *esclave* interchangeably. Both are contrasted with "les maîtres," their masters. The act regulates the *"marché des Nègres,"* the market in *nègres* (art. 7), and refers to at one point to "planters who buy newly arrived *nègres*" (art. 2). On the other hand, it declares that *esclaves* are *meubles*—moveable property (art. 44). It forbids them from bearing arms and specifies a carefully calibrated series of corporal punishments for repeated attempts at fugitivity (art. 38). If there is a difference in usage here, it seems that *nègre* refers to those newly arrived, who then become *esclaves* as they are more formally incorporated into the practices of slavery.

We see a similar phenomenon in an alternative version of the Code Noir promulgated by Louis XV in 1724: *"Édit du roi, touchant l'état et la discipline des esclaves nègres de la Louisiane"* (Edict of the King on the State and Discipline of *Esclaves Nègres* of Louisiana).[9] Here *esclave* and *nègre* are brought together: not the same, but each representing part of a compound idea. A reprint of the original Code Noir by the royal presses in 1735 follows similar lines. Here the reference to policing the colonies was retained. However, that task was made more specific with a reference to *"la discipline et le commerce des nègres et esclaves"* in a revised subtitle.[10] The parallelism of and oscillation between *nègre* and *esclave* reveals the terms to be on more of an equal footing, but again, not identical. A different tack occurs in a pair of legal briefs of 1742 that address the question whether slaves are property [*meubles*]. In one case, the question is "whether *nègres* should be considered property," in the other, "whether *esclaves* are property." The answer is carefully read out of various articles of the Code Noir, primarily using the abstract legal term *esclave*.[11]

This tendency to prefer *esclave* in the adjudication of legal questions, particularly ones referring to the Code Noir, continued on in subsequent decades.[12] By the mid-eighteenth century, however, references to "*esclave*" in daily discourse would almost entirely disappear as its meaning was absorbed into "*nègre*" as both black and slave. In this sense, *nègre* supplanted *esclave* as a word that amply covered both meanings. It thus spanned the abstract legal sense of esclave as a person who could be owned, but also incorporated overtones of racialized inferiority. Those ideas were quietly merged and became naturalized as part of the unseen infrastructure of the colonial state. At this point the figure of the *nègre* had more or less consolidated.

There were, however, moments of problematization when something that seemed natural was suddenly called into question. This happened chiefly when some technical distinction had to be made between racialized subjects and enslaved subjects. As manumissions became more common, prompting growing anxiety from the state, the phrase *nègre libre* came into use. It indicated someone who was *nègre* but free. The idea of a *nègre libre* was clearly counterintuitive to some extent and had to be carefully specified. In contrast, the term "*esclave nègre*" had long disappeared. It was not necessary to stipulate enslaved status if one had already said *nègre*. Those two ideas coincided by this point, and only required commentary when one wanted to separate them.

This is all part of what Charles Mills calls the period of de jure white supremacy, the formation of legally coded racial relations.[13] It is part of the long, slow consolidation of the concept of race. We can see Mills's point clearly here, that the legal apparatus of slavery does not simply regulate the commodification and ill treatment of persons, but also accretes a great deal of cultural and imaginary meaning. That is not simply a matter of abstract racial categories, but of the ability of a term such as *nègre* to instantiate those racial ideas at the level of specific identities and individuals.

My point is not to document the construction of racial thinking in French colonialism. That is a vast and complex project that would encompass the entire legal, institutional, and cultural apparatus of racism, colonialism, and enslavement in the colonies. Rather, my point is to trace much more narrowly the ways in which *nègre* was intertwined not only with the idea of an enslaved person, but also with silence. In short, this history of racialization takes on more specific form by constituting subaltern silence.

Esclave remained a dry and abstract legal category. Its use in the Code Noir is telling, because it seems to assume that a person with normal human tendencies and characteristics is being interpellated into the status of *esclave*. As I noted earlier, the Code describes *nègres* arriving into the colonies from Africa and establishes progressively more narrow specifications of them as *esclaves*. This includes a number of things one might ordinarily expect people to do, which are now prohibited: bearing arms (art. XV), meeting with one another (art. XVI), selling fruits, vegetables, firewood, herbs, or animals (art. XIX), and holding public office (art. XXX). Some kind of background personhood is assumed, which is hereby legally dismantled point by point. This process is almost literary in character. It culminates with the declaration that esclaves are property, are thereby subject to the law of property and inheritance. By the end of this narrative arc in which they are carefully stripped of human characteristics, *esclaves* have become legally silent.

The figure of the *nègre* had a much wider daily circulation and was correspondingly more complicated. There was an entire art of government dedicated to achieving docile and useful *nègres*. It aimed, effectively, at a state of silence, one in which the *nègre* would become a useful instrument with no other human presence. The means of achieving this through brutality and violence are well known, so we need not explore them here. It is worth noting that these practices had a governmental character, however. There is a vast archive about the best means of achieving docile enslaved bodies that should have had an important place in Foucault's *Discipline and Punish*. That literature discussed various forms of physical punishment and torture, described the use of various techniques and implements, and gave advice about the most effective and efficient means for achieving compliance. Unlike forms of punishment from the same era in Foucault's narrative, however, these extrajudicial forms of violence did not aim at the avowal of truth, the confirmation of guilt, or the production of the criminal.[14] Rather, this was a project of erasure: of rendering people inhuman and silent.

As Foucault might have noted, however, the very attention devoted to this project indicates its problematic status. Whereas *esclave* was simply constituted as silent under the law, *nègre* had richer connotations and was therefore much more unstable. The project of dehumanization, racialization, and silencing seems to have carried the risk of the re-emergence of personhood. At times *nègres* seemed to be up to something. They seemed to be animated by projects and designs. This provoked anxiety, because it problematized both the silence of the *nègres* and the assumption that they lacked agency and intention.

I am referring to silence in the broad sense I have already discussed: *nègres* should be seen but not be legible as people. Their depersonalization and constitution as productive property hinged on losing their comprehensibility as humans. In this scheme, they could not speak because they were not the kind of thing that spoke. This is a most radical example of what Spivak meant by a subaltern unable to speak.

Here we see the development of practices that create silence by redescribing and normalizing people's identities. We could call them *silencing through resignification*. They symbolically reposition such identities, degrading them and displacing any other identity, words, thoughts, or ideas that the subaltern may have tried to express. These practices follow a more general model of *silencing through displacement*—of identities, voices, and actions—that becomes a common thread through many new practices of silencing that develop at this time. We will see it in many other guises as the decades go on, and its forms will continue to permute and multiply in coming centuries.

The specific practices of resignification I have been describing are rooted in law, but they would quickly extend to many other domains of colonial culture. Such practices emerge slowly as adjuncts to the silencing effects of law and violence, rationalizing codes and measures that produce silence. However, their effects are distinct from, and ultimately much more powerful than, the silencing force of law and violence.

In this era, the silence of *nègres* was an active pursuit of their enslavers, but it was always a delicate achievement. *Esclave* and *nègre* functioned in tandem as means of pursing subaltern silence, both under law and in carefully calibrated practice. *Nègre* eventually became the dominant term of discourse, where its instabilities became all the more apparent. Through that lens we can see various moments when the project of subaltern silence was problematized and destabilized. They reveal tensions and contradictions plaguing the creation of a silent but laboring subaltern.

SPACES OF EXCEPTION

Marronage emerges as a specific problematization of subaltern silence. *Marron* was a neologism developed by French colonists to describe escaped slaves. They adapted it from their Spanish counterparts, who had borrowed it from the Arawak and Taíno people who originally inhabited the Caribbean islands. In Spanish, *cimarrón* originally referred to feral cattle, then to enslaved native people who had escaped, then to enslaved Africans. Since the French had no word for this, they converted the Spanish to *marron*.[15] This word is typically coupled with *nègre* in many documents of the time: *nègre marron*. "Fugitive slave" would be a rudimentary translation of this term, but that misses all of the resonances I just discussed. As a modification of *nègre*, *nègre marron* is a subtle reinflection of that complex state of subalternity. One might read between the lines of common usage at this time to flesh out some of its implicit connotations. It indicates, from the perspective of colonial elites, that something has gone wrong with the process of racialized subordination. The suppressed surplus of personhood that elites feared in the *nègre* had reasserted itself. In that sense, *nègre marron* is an African or African-descended, inferior, captive, owned, laboring being who has destabilized the status of subordination that *nègre* is supposed to represent.

Not surprisingly, marronage was co-originary with Caribbean slavery itself. It was one of the most elemental responses to enslavement, and one of the most avidly policed, legislated, and punished. One account dates the beginning of slavery in French Saint-Domingue to 1505, and the first recorded fugitive slaves to 1520.[16] Such forms of fugitivity were a central part of slavery in the Spanish, Portuguese, English, Danish, and Dutch colonies as well. In this sense, marronage and the measures levelled against it were a widely shared set of practices in the New World slave colonies.

The spirit underlying marronage was similarly elemental. It was a desire for freedom from cruelty and subordination, enacted through flight.[17] Such departure could take the form of a temporary, episodic absence followed by return, or it could take more permanent form. Sometimes slaves would disappear to go to town, perhaps to sell produce from their garden plots on markets days. Visiting friends and relatives also necessitated absence. One overseer in Saint-Domingue reported capturing twenty-seven maroon slaves in his area, "as many in the slave huts as in the hills."[18] Slaves would also vanish temporarily to attend religious ceremonies jointly organized by people from multiple plantations. Vaudou, for instance, was a creole religious tradition that provided a counterweight to plantation life and gathered slaves in remote locations for joint celebrations.[19] Such gatherings are thought to have been crucial to the planning of the slave revolt in 1791 that launched the Haitian Revolution.[20]

At other times, marronage was not simply an episode of temporary freedom, but a more permanent escape. Some maroon slaves fled to cities and port towns, where they could pass themselves off as free. Others fled to nearby colonies or took jobs as sailors. Makandal, Boukman, and Henri Christophe, principal revolutionary leaders in Saint-Domingue, were maroons from Jamaica and Saint Kitts. Still others formed alternative communities in remote hinterlands, not only in Saint-Domingue, but famously in Jamaica, Cuba, and the South American coast as well. These communities were often carefully concealed and fortified. They chose leaders and established a village life completely separate from the slave economy of the plantation.[21] These communities formed one of the chief points of resistance to slavery, and by extension, one of the chief threats to plantation owners' control.[22]

The significance of marronage as a material practice of freedom cannot be underestimated. It was an improvised, everyday form of resistance that helped enslaved people mitigate a terrible situation. In this sense, it takes a place alongside other such forms of coping, well characterized by Saidiya Hartman: "work slowdowns, feigned illness, unlicensed travel, the destruction of property, theft, self-mutilation, dissimulation, physical confrontation with owners and overseers."[23] Among this list, however, marronage had properties not shared by these other strategies. It allowed people to regain control of their lives in a relatively more complete form.

Marronage reveals additional complexities when viewed from the perspective of subaltern silence. It not only gave people certain forms of freedom but also made possible forms of sociality and communication. It seems to have produced extensive networks of covert communication across the slave colonies. Julius Scott has done a wonderful job of puzzling out the traces of these networks, which were typically well hidden from elite eyes and thus obscured from the archive as well. For instance, he recounts a number of examples in which slave owners were stunned at the speed with which news could propagate through slave communities, often over large distances, when slaves seemed to be well accounted for and under firm control.[24]

Marronage also produced a rearticulation of space. Maroons moved from a space of constraint and violence to one of freedom. They were able to improvise new spaces that could be occupied with relative freedom. The necessity to remain hidden and uncaptured still imposed significant limitations, so such spaces of exception were typically limited to the mountain hinterlands in Saint-Domingue. Nonetheless, these spaces were freely chosen and stood outside of the plantation system.

By creating such heterotopic zones of freedom, these spaces made it possible for slaves to flee the forced silence under which they had been placed. In doing so they exchanged one silence for another. The new silence of marronage consisted of not needing to speak, being left alone by removing oneself from the geographical location of control and violence. It was freely adopted as an alternative to the subaltern silence of the plantation and the society that surrounded it. In this sense, marronage renegotiated the silence of being *nègre*. It substituted a different kind of silence: out of sight, out of commodification, out of biopolitical exploitation, out of brutalization, out of control.

We can think of this by analogy to what Édouard Glissant calls opacity: the value of being obscure, not being understandable, not being legible.[25] Glissant frames opacity as a form of freedom. In his account, it is a kind of epistemic freedom, a freedom from the need to be understood or understandable in the terms of the dominant culture. Similarly, when maroons fled the plantation, they ceased needing to account for themselves. They avoided authority and hid from scrutiny, becoming cryptic and unpredictable. Maroon communities had a kind of shadowy existence in the peripheries of the colony and much about them remained speculative. The passage of maroons from plantation to plantation, or from the hinterlands into the plantations, happened in this penumbra of obscurity.

In this sense, marronage was truly another form of subaltern silence. It was, however, one quite different from that instituted by colonial elites. It was silence as an achievement. This silence was voluntarily chosen, struggled for, carefully guarded and preserved. Such achieved silence replaced the forced silence of the slave society. It was a simple and direct expression of what we could call, paraphrasing Justice Louis Brandeis, a desire to be left alone.[26] The creation of spaces of exception from the plantation system made this new form of silence possible. It was a basis for enslaved people to exchange a forced silence that was part of the apparatus of subordination for a silence that created freedom. Both were forms of subaltern silence, but one was freely chosen and generated further forms of freedom. In homage to Glissant, we might call these practices *self-silencing through opacity*.

PUBLICITY AND PSYCHIC EXCESS

As we have already noted, enslaved people were silenced in the colonies through de facto and de jure exclusion from public life, demotion to a subordinate status in domains that they were permitted in, and a sharp focus on repression. The repressive apparatus was particularly brought into play to combat marronage. A large part of the administrative correspondence and petitions to the colonial government surrounding marronage focused on organizing expeditions to round up maroon slaves and hunt out maroon communities. There are pages and pages of such correspondence spanning most of the eighteenth century. It testifies to the great attention devoted to such tasks and the evident idea that the colonial government should take this on as a project that required funds and military resources beyond the means of individual plantation owners.[27]

Paramilitary groups known as *maréchaussée* were assembled to conduct such manhunts. They were composed primarily of former slaves and mixed-race colonists and served as intermediaries to conduct the colonial state's tasks of repression. Specially trained "Spanish dogs" were brought in from Cuba to assist in this task. They were particularly prized for their abilities to track, seize, and sometimes kill escapees. These practices underlined the quite literal and graphic senses in which enslavement was a form of predatory capitalism.[28]

The Code Noir established a brutal and carefully graduated set of punishments for marronage. They became more and more severe with repeated offenses: first disfigurement, then incapacitation, and finally death. However, the Code also set limits on the treatment of slaves, freeing them from work on Sundays and religious holidays, forbidding inhumane treatment, and outlawing their murder. It thereby established drastic punishments for marronage, but it also outlawed even more draconian ones regularly meted out by slave owners. In spite of this, recaptured maroons often experienced informal and illegal treatment that was much more severe than the Code allowed.[29]

With such tensions between law and actual practice in the background, discourse about marronage often turned around the idea of reforming the Code Noir. We see reform proposals across the Caribbean colonies throughout the early 1700s. In 1705, a former governor of Saint-Domingue made a proposal, rejected by the king, to make castration the penalty for a third offense of marronage.[30] This, ironically, was designed as a progressive reform measure. It would have been less severe than the prescribed death penalty. A more severe proposal from Martinique in 1742 was particularly concerned with the prospect of maroons arming themselves. It proposed the death penalty for any maroon caught with a weapon, including a knife.[31] Another proposal in 1758 complains of growing disorder in the colonies and says that the penalties prescribed by the Code Noir are not severe enough to discourage marronage and revolt. It proposed accelerating the schedule of penalties so that the longer a slave remained maroon, the more severe the penalty. Maroons who have been fugitive for a month would be branded on the shoulder with a *fleur de lys*, the emblem of the French monarchy, and have their ears cut off. Those maroon for six months would be branded on the other shoulder with a *fleur de lys* and be hamstrung. A year of fugitivity would be punished with death. These penalties were already part of the Code for repeat offences, but under this proposal they would be brought to bear on first-time offenders as well.[32]

Such responses to marronage display two important characteristics: publicity and excess. The Code Noir was a written, public law. It seems to have been well known among colonial elites, given their continual efforts to reform it. A particular rationality was built into this legal apparatus. Its carefully graduated schedule of punishments clearly aimed at deterrence. It operated on the presumption that a properly graduated system of penalties could shape behavior in the desired manner. The deterrent effect of that system would in turn depend upon the force of representation, however. Graphic punishments, an escalating scale of pain and disfigurement, and restraints on owners' mistreatment of slaves all had symbolic and public functions. They relied on public exposure and notoriety for their force. Such measures had a very specific ideational content and aimed at a general, undefined audience: a "public." It imagined a rather different public from the one we are used to thinking about, however: it was the public of enslaved colonial subjects, the public of those who were to be put in terror by the potential violence that the law required to be enacted upon them. The punishments meted out on the basis of the Code had a kind of public semiotics: they were publicly visible forms of mutilation, and at the limit, public execution. The law was thus designed to function as public spectacle.[33] It prescribed graphic forms of punishment that were inherently public, thus relying on the public imagination of such punishments for its deterrent effect. Ideally, knowledge of the measures stipulated in the law would shape behavior in themselves, making its actual use unnecessary. If marronage was prevented by public knowledge of the law, then there would be no need for its complex regime of ever-more-severe torture.

However, the Code Noir was issued from a distant metropole and was frequently ignored in favor of more capricious, unregulated, and vicious treatment. Such treatment often displayed a great degree of vengeance, bizarre cathexes, and excess psychic energy. Louis de Jaucourt captured the spirit of this phenomenon well in his *Encyclopédie* article on torture, saying that it "is an inexplicable phenomenon that the extension of man's imagination creates out of the barbarous and the cruel."[34] Punishments were often sadistic in ways that went beyond the carefully graduated schedule of tortures. Jean Fouchard enumerates a truly horrifying list of practices that were banned by the Code Noir yet were practiced with some frequency in the colonies.[35] These punishments carried an excessive psychic charge that well surpassed the goal of preventing marronage.

Saidiya Hartman has argued that we should not aestheticize the violence exercised on slaves by relishing its description, a point that is well taken here.[36] However, the aestheticization of violence is very much the issue in this case, so we must recount at least some of the details. Consider, for instance, the interrogation transcript of an enslaved man identified as *le nègre* Thomas about the reasons for his fugitivity. He explains that he fled out of fear of the depraved punishments his overseer meted out on fellow slaves. The transcript follows the conventions for court documents of the time, recording questions and answers in a terse and businesslike manner:

Questioned what the Sieur Chapuihet did to kill the slaves.
Responded that said Sieur Chapuihet put said slaves, the ones who died, in a prison cell on the plantation of which he is the overseer, and buried alive others on said plantation, saying that they had caused an animal to die through their mistreatment.

The accused goes on to tell of his father, whom the overseer sent to the prison of another plantation where he died after a month, and two others who were put in a cell for two or three weeks, then removed and buried alive.

> It was this example that terrified the accused and caused him to go maroon out of fear of meeting the same fate....
>
> Questioned whether he didn't know that it is prohibited for slaves to go maroon, under penalty of having their ears cut off and being marked with a *fleur de lys* on the right shoulder for the first infraction, of having their hamstrings cut and being marked again on the left shoulder with a *fleur de lys* for the second infraction, and being hung for the third infraction.
>
> Responded that he didn't know that, but was maroon because he was afraid of being killed like his father.[37]

The interrogator accurately recounts the details of the Code Noir's regime of punishment, with its carefully escalating schedule of mutilation, accompanied by the question "did he know about it?" Slaves' knowledge of such punishment is clearly important to the legal establishment. However, it is not the Code Noir that the slave is aware of, but the informal and gratuitously violent treatment in actual operation. He was unfamiliar with the details of the Code Noir but well acquainted with the master's flair for cruelty. In this case, the spectacular punishment that occupied people's consciousness was not that of the Code Noir, but the excessive and illegal practices being improvised on the plantation.

This exchange illustrates some important features of marronage. The Code Noir established legal guidelines that both prescribed and limited punishments. As such, it also aimed to establish an official symbology of state power over both slaves and masters. However, this law was routinely ignored in the colonies. In its place was an even more excessive regime of torture that seems to have had a more powerful symbolic effect. Such punishments were often an over-the-top spectacle, one that symbolized with surplus vividness the power of the planter and colonial state to enact retribution, intimidation, and vengeance. Like the Code Noir, they also relied on publicity for their effect. This merely emphasizes the importance and character of publicity in this case. The official publicity of the law seems to have been largely unknown by those who were intended as its audience, its public. Competing with it was much more direct observation of punishments meted out to specific people on local plantations, as well as the rumor that surrounded them. The symbolics of state power competed in public spheres with the symbolics of gratuitous cruelty exercised by slave owners and overseers. The carefully calibrated schedule of physical punishments coded into the law was largely a subject for administrative correspondence. The potential victims of these punishments had other public spheres and their attention was focused on more immediate, local, and unregulated threats. In short, the official, printed law of the French crown competed with other strands of publicity in the colonies that also aimed at a spectacular effect through vividness and excess.

INNOVATIONS IN PUBLICITY, 1764

A notable innovation in colonial publicity came to Saint-Domingue in 1764. The first newspaper published on the island appeared on Wednesday, February 1st. The *Gazette de Saint-Domingue* was to be published weekly in the northern port town of Cap Français (figure 2.1). On the first day of publication, there was much to get caught up on. Much of the news concerned the aftermath of the Seven Years' War, which had ended the previous year and caused major realignments in the possession of Caribbean colonies. The paper opened with an article on the difficulties faced by German businesses in recovering from the war. This was followed by an update on ministerial politics in Britain, including a note on the large number of British military casualties in Cuba.

Then came what must have been welcome news. The king had commissioned nine ships to carry royal decrees and administrative correspondence between France and the Caribbean colonies on a monthly basis. These ships would also accept mail from ordinary citizens to establish a regular post across the Atlantic and Caribbean. The newspaper celebrates "all the utility" that will result from this innovation.

And finally, on to local news. There were several obituaries for plantation owners who had died. Fifty-two ships were in port from various locations. Five of these were slave traders, listed with the origin and number of slaves they carried. A new public market would be opening in Cap Français. The king was levying new taxes for the defense of the colony. There was a long article about Jesuits in the colonies. A list of ships about to depart to various destinations. A small

Figure 2.1 *Gazette de Saint-Domingue*, Prospectus, January 10, 1764. Bibliothèque Nationale de France, Paris.

section of commodity prices, headed by four different grades of sugar, as well as indigo, coffee, and cotton. And to close, a brief section of advertisements: a pottery manufacture for sale; the ship *Saint Marie*, equipped with eighteen cannons and fifty sailors, would be leaving on March 15, taking freight and passengers to Nantes, Bordeaux, and Marseille.

Such was print journalism in the mid-eighteenth century. All of this adds up to a snapshot of colonial life, seen from the perspective of planters and the colonial administration. For them it would have marked a significant leap forward in the development of a colonial public sphere, similar in form and intent to the one then taking shape in Europe. It extended European conventions of public discourse to the colonies, providing a patina of European civilization. Similarly, the opening of regular mail service made possible the exchange of news and ideas and was also a vital part of this expanding public sphere.

Benedict Anderson describes the profound epistemic effects of newspapers, creating an impression of simultaneity and shared experience among their readers.[38] The new colonial public sphere had a similar effect. It created a kind of colonial normality, a feeling of accounting for everything important that was happening in the colony. As a result, the press had enormous powers of reification and normalization, but ones that were largely benign and unnoticed. It constituted a kind of synchronicity and shared reality among a community of readers.

This transplanted sense of European normality was constituted with some notable omissions, however. Slavery, the economic base of the Caribbean colonies, was mentioned only briefly in the paper, and only in the context of commerce. It was featured obliquely in a list of ships in port conducting business, which in several cases was the slave trade.

The oddity of this vision of the normal becomes clearer in the second issue of the *Gazette*, published one week later. The format was largely the same. First was international news from Russia, Poland, Amsterdam, and France. Then came local news, including a report on a ministerial decree forbidding colonial *nègres* and mixed-race people (*mulâtres*) from traveling to France, out of concern for the "disorder" resulting from the number of them accumulating there. After that was news of ships coming and going from port, followed by commodity prices and classified advertisements.

Something new appears, however, in a small, quiet editorial note at the beginning of the classified section. It says,

> N. B. Since the establishment of the *Gazette de Saint-Domingue*, there seems to be great enthusiasm for us to include, as one of the articles with the most general utility, an account of *Négres marons* [sic.] who have entered the various jails of the colony. Monsieur the Intendant has been happy to agree to this for the satisfaction of the public, and has given the necessary orders as a result. We will be careful to report the name, apparent age, nation, and branding of each *Négre* as exactly as possible.[39]

The eager-to-please, happy-to-be-of-service character of the announcement stands in sharp contrast to its equally matter-of-fact brutality. Escaped *nègres* who have been recaptured will be described so that they can be retrieved by their owners. Those descriptions will include identifying brands and other useful information. This, after only a week of circulation, has apparently been an enthusiastic request of readers. Both the editor and the chief administrator of the colony agree to provide the information as something of "the most general utility" to the public.

Fugitive slave notices were not a new idea. They had already existed in the British colonies for some decades. The *Virginia Gazette*, for instance, began publishing them a month after it was established in 1736, along with notices for stray horses and runaway servants and convict laborers.[40] Many other papers in the British-American colonies printed similar advertisements. The *Gazette de Saint-Domingue* thus imported a practice that was already established in the well-developed Anglophone public spheres to its north.

With no further commentary, the issue concludes with a miscellany of classified advertisements: the ship *Jenny*, commanded by Jacques Villeneau, is accepting freight bound for Bordeaux; an apothecary named Menot is selling a successful remedy for children's stomach worms as well as "ophthalmic water" and medicine for toothaches; a coffee plantation is for sale; a surgeon named Loubeau is selling a remedy for venereal disease; and so on.

In subsequent weeks the first notices for *nègres marrons* appeared, in a format that quickly became routine (figure 2.2):

> Thelemaque, from Nago, belonging to Sieur Couturier of Fort-Dauphin, branded on the right chest P. CHARRIER and below that AU CAP, arrested at Cap Français the 10th, with a clog on the left foot.

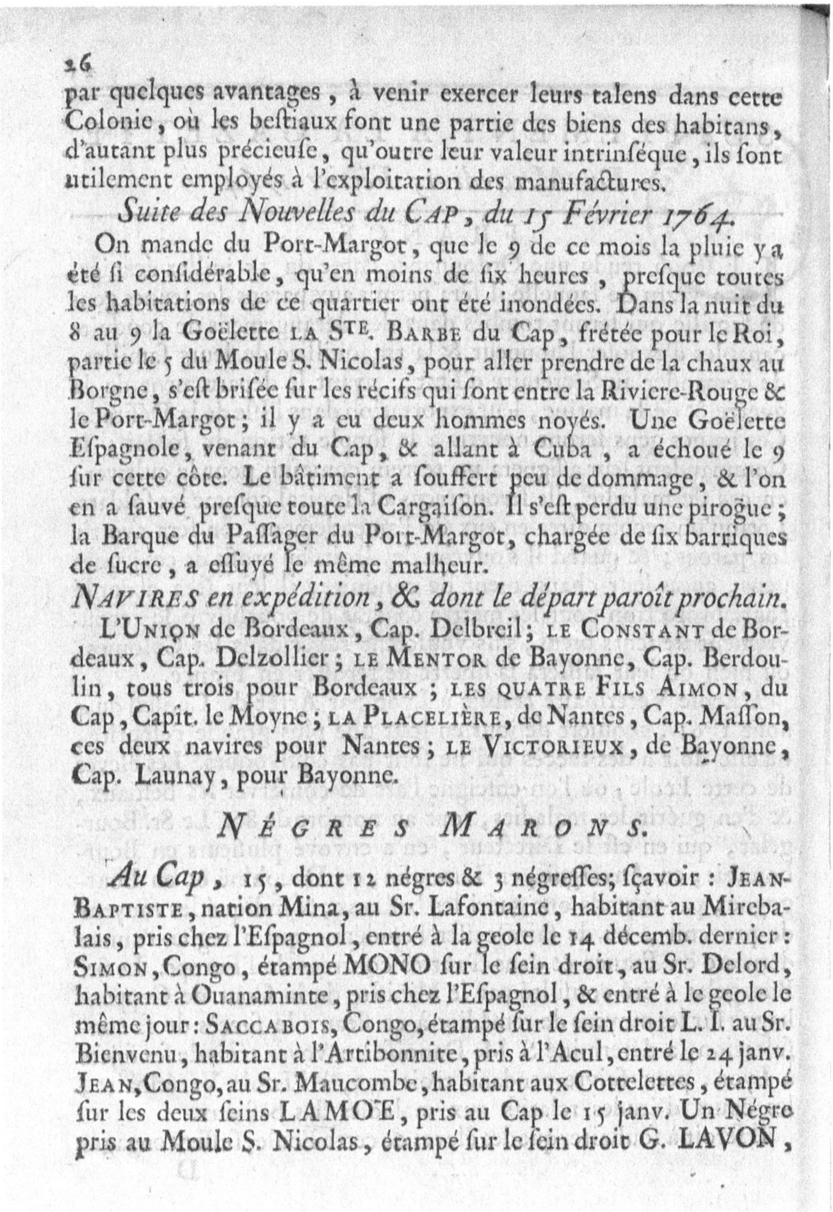

par quelques avantages, à venir exercer leurs talens dans cette Colonie, où les bestiaux font une partie des biens des habitans, d'autant plus précieuse, qu'outre leur valeur intrinséque, ils sont utilement employés à l'exploitation des manufactures.

Suite des Nouvelles du CAP, du 15 Février 1764.

On mande du Port-Margot, que le 9 de ce mois la pluie y a été si considérable, qu'en moins de six heures, presque toutes les habitations de ce quartier ont été inondées. Dans la nuit du 8 au 9 la Goëlette LA S^{TE}. BARBE du Cap, frétée pour le Roi, partie le 5 du Moule S. Nicolas, pour aller prendre de la chaux au Borgne, s'est brisée sur les récifs qui sont entre la Riviere-Rouge & le Port-Margot; il y a eu deux hommes noyés. Une Goëlette Espagnole, venant du Cap, & allant à Cuba, a échoué le 9 sur cette côte. Le bâtiment a souffert peu de dommage, & l'on en a sauvé presque toute la Cargaison. Il s'est perdu une pirogue; la Barque du Passager du Port-Margot, chargée de six barriques de sucre, a essuyé le même malheur.

NAVIRES en expédition, & dont le départ paroît prochain.

L'UNION de Bordeaux, Cap. Delbreil; LE CONSTANT de Bordeaux, Cap. Delzollier; LE MENTOR de Bayonne, Cap. Berdoulin, tous trois pour Bordeaux; LES QUATRE FILS AIMON, du Cap, Capit. le Moyne; LA PLACELIÈRE, de Nantes, Cap. Masson, ces deux navires pour Nantes; LE VICTORIEUX, de Bayonne, Cap. Launay, pour Bayonne.

NÉGRES MARONS.

Au Cap, 15, dont 12 négres & 3 négresses; sçavoir : JEAN-BAPTISTE, nation Mina, au Sr. Lafontaine, habitant au Mirebalais, pris chez l'Espagnol, entré à la geole le 14 décemb. dernier : SIMON, Congo, étampé MONO sur le sein droit, au Sr. Delord, habitant à Ouanaminte, pris chez l'Espagnol, & entré à le geole le même jour : SACCABOIS, Congo, étampé sur le sein droit L. I. au Sr. Bienvenu, habitant à l'Artibonnite, pris à l'Acul, entré le 24 janv. JEAN, Congo, au Sr. Maucombe, habitant aux Cotrelettes, étampé sur les deux seins LAMOE, pris au Cap le 15 janv. Un Négre pris au Moule S. Nicolas, étampé sur le sein droit G. LAVON,

Figure 2.2 *Gazette de Saint-Domingue*, February 15, 1764. Bibliothèque Nationale de France, Paris.

Rose, Congolese *Négresse*, about 60 years old, belonging to Sieur Cuvert, planter in Dondon.

Lise, Tiamban *Négresse*, belonging to Sieur Baconnais of Limbé, entered jail on the 3rd of this month.

In Port-au-Prince, three *Négres*: Phaéton, Congo, branded C. MICHEL, 20 to 25 years old; Adrien and Bossal, also Congo, no brand, all three arrested the same day at the Spanish border, and put in jail February 12th.[41]

In the beginning, maroon notices were used only to list those who had been captured and were awaiting retrieval. They soon expanded to other functions, however, also describing slaves who had gone missing and were being sought. By August, this section easily surpassed the amount of print devoted to shipping news, commodity prices, or obituaries, often filling a fifth of the newspaper. Clearly the public was not only satisfied but enthusiastic about the new feature.

A set of conventions quickly developed around the new genre. The idea was to give as rich a description of the slave as possible so that he or she could be identified. Slaves would be described by national origin, distinguishing marks and brands, physical characteristics, age, things they brought with them into fugitivity (often a horse or clothing), and occupational skills that they might use to establish themselves somewhere else. Sometimes the remark is made that they may be trying to pass as a free person. Often smallpox scars are described as a distinguishing feature.

We can understand these features of publicity with the categories Foucault has bequeathed us. The published descriptions are individualizing. They aim at a form of surveillance made possible by the new technologies of publicity. Individualized subjects become visible and identifiable, thus more easily brought back under control (for those still at large) or repossessed (for those already in captivity). The careful effort at description is a vital aspect of this *dispositif*. It differentiates individuals out of subaltern obscurity, makes them visible, and thereby renders them subject to surveillance, arrest, and repatriation.

The target of this effort was precisely subaltern silence itself. Maroons had managed to achieve a new form of subaltern silence, one that was chosen rather than imposed, one that provided autonomy by removing them from authority and possession. Maroon notices aimed at piercing this obscurity, bringing maroons back under control through the harsh light of publicity. They aimed at a kind of *excessive visibility*, one that used rich description to make black bodies and black subjectivities surveyable and identifiable.[42] This visibility was intended to have a normalizing force, reinscribing maroons in the apparatus of colonial control and making it possible to re-silence them. Such a *silencing through excessive visibility* was not a distinct form of silencing; it would not yet be sufficient to silence someone by itself. Rather, these practices were designed to function in tandem with law and violence. They were, at this point in their development, adjunct means of silencing. In this sense, maroon notices were the third move in a sequence. Slaves had been silenced through law and violence; some managed to reject such silence in favor of a different silence that gave them freedom; and now publicity was being used as a counterstrategy of control. Silencing through law and violence, self-silencing through opacity, and silencing through excessive visibility constituted move, countermove, and counter-countermove in an escalating dynamic of subaltern subordination.

There is another aspect of this practice, however. The individuation of maroons brought them into publicity in another sense. The individualizing descriptions of specific *nègres* constituted a new form of publicity that echoed the normalization of other colonial activities. Just like the prices of commodities and the presence of ships in port, *nègres marrons* now became part of the shared, everyday experience of the colonial public.

This individualizing publicity was literally denigrating in the sense of constituting enslaved people as *nègres*. On the other hand, it simultaneously problematized that status. They were ones who had broken free from the apparatus of control, at least temporarily, and reasserted some of the will and agency of which their designation as *nègre* tried to strip them. In short, this was an ambivalent form of publicity. It singled maroons out as criminal and *nègre*, but it also portrayed them as individuals with traits, features, skills, national and personal histories, and specific identities. As a result, the effects of such publicity are ambivalent as well. The figure of the *nègre marron* becomes more and more reified and normalized as part of colonial life. This, however, amounts to a problematization of the subordinate status of enslaved people. *Nègre marron* describes a dangerous subordinate, one whose suppressed personhood is recognizable through the agency of escape, but equally by having a carefully publicized name, nationality, and individual characteristics. This is no longer a silent and unknown subaltern, but one who has achieved some public presence, however ambivalent that might be.

The ambivalence of this practice is even clearer when some of the psychic baggage of individuation becomes visible. Consider the odd undercurrents in four advertisements placed in the *Affiches américaines* in 1783-1784 (figure 2.3).[43] Appearing over the course of several months, they advertise the desire of the lawyer M. Larchevêque-Thibaut for the return of a mixed-race slave named

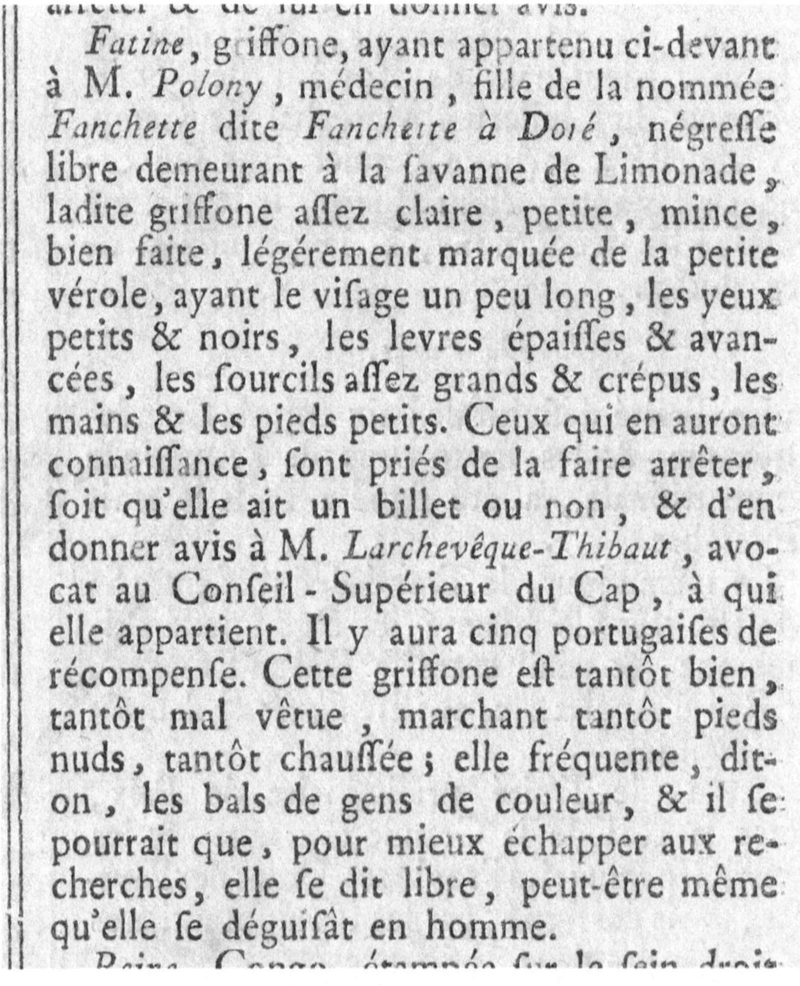

> *Fatine*, griffone, ayant appartenu ci-devant à M. *Polony*, médecin, fille de la nommée *Fanchette* dite *Fanchette à Doré*, négreffe libre demeurant à la favanne de Limonade, ladite griffone affez claire, petite, mince, bien faite, légérement marquée de la petite vérole, ayant le vifage un peu long, les yeux petits & noirs, les levres épaiffes & avancées, les fourcils affez grands & crépus, les mains & les pieds petits. Ceux qui en auront connaiffance, font priés de la faire arrêter, foit qu'elle ait un billet ou non, & d'en donner avis à M. *Larchevêque-Thibaut*, avocat au Confeil-Supérieur du Cap, à qui elle appartient. Il y aura cinq portugaifes de récompenfe. Cette griffone eft tantôt bien, tantôt mal vêtue, marchant tantôt pieds nuds, tantôt chauffée; elle fréquente, dit-on, les bals de gens de couleur, & il fe pourrait que, pour mieux échapper aux recherches, elle fe dit libre, peut-être même qu'elle fe déguifât en homme.

Figure 2.3 "Fatine." Detail of *Affiches américaines*, November 19, 1783, no. 47, 4. Bibliothèque Nationale de France, Paris.

Fatine. The nature of that desire is suggested by the richness of her description. Larchevêque-Thibaut delineates Fatine's features with finely observed attention, which grows richer in detail with each successive advertisement. She is described as small, thin, and well formed; fairly light in complexion, with some faint smallpox scars; her face is a bit long; she has small, bright, and lively eyes; her nose a bit aquiline; a handsome forehead; heavy, pronounced lips; bushy eyebrows; small, narrow hands and feet. She loves to attend dances and walks with her head held high, affecting the airs of a free woman. M. Larchevêque-Thibaut clearly had a fine appreciation for Fatine's qualities. Her failure to return during the months in which the advertisement was posted suggests that his affections were not reciprocated.

Larchevêque-Thibaut's finely detailed descriptions of Fatine evoke the deeply problematic ways in which enslavers had nonconsensual access to enslaved bodies. He may have understood himself as having a more mutual relationship with Fantine, but of course true reciprocity and consent were impossible under such circumstances. Sexual predation upon the enslaved was controversial in this era, but unfortunately not on behalf of the victims. Rather, it provoked worries about miscegenation, "concubinage," and white moral degeneracy.[44] The victims themselves were often blamed for such hypocrisies. A letter from the minister of the navy in 1727 is somewhat typical. Expressing dismay at the sexual "disorder" created by free *négresses* and mixed-race women (*mulâtresses*), he instructs his subordinates to control "the libertinage of these creatures."[45] That framing of subjects for discipline was a displacement for other realities, of course. It points toward the compulsive interest and anxiety generated by the sexual activities of white men toward nonwhite women. The discourse of female "libertinage" merely twisted this around and visited it upon the enslaved themselves.

Beyond these important issues of sexualization and sexual predation, the descriptions of Fatine reveal a broader tendency in the maroon slave notices. Fatine is advertised as a fugitive. She is at the same time given a rich public presence. Her descriptions are sexualizing, but as an extreme, highly cathected expression of the individualizing tendencies of the maroon notices. Again, this is an ambivalent form of publicity. In place of a silenced subaltern with absolutely no presence, we now have a name, a personality, a physical description, some idea of what her treatment might have been like, and the knowledge that she has escaped. This is individualizing publicity that gives Fatine presence where previously she had none.

Does the subaltern speak in such cases? No, at least not in the rich sense that one would like. People like Fatine were not allowed to speak in that sense. Thus we do not know what she thought, where she went, what she aspired to, or whether she achieved it. We do know certain things about her that we would not otherwise have known, however. She was written into the public record, given some presence and personality, interpellated into the public sphere. That description was filtered through the perspective of someone who had designs on and desires for her, yet it still stands as a partial, biased, ambivalent record of Fatine's agency, purpose, and personhood. She was enslaved, she was desired, she left. The traces of her pursuit in the public sphere allow us to understand certain things: about the degree of fine-detailed individuation that these notices were capable of; about the ways in which those descriptions spoke in place of the actual person being described; about the extremes of excess that excessive publicity was capable of. Fatine does not exactly speak, but she nonetheless achieves some traces of publicity, some ambivalent presence, that previously had been denied her.

RUPTURES IN THE FABRIC OF THE NORMAL

The public sphere is often seen as an idealized domain of free and open communication, vital to the propagation of ideas, rational argument, and universal human dignity. Less obvious is the sense in which it is thereby a political, social, and epistemic technology. It has the ability to circulate ideas and expose them to criticism, but it can also render them banal and naturalize the visions they create. Seen from this angle, the public sphere is a technology for creating common sense, a taken-for-granted state of affairs, an order of things. It serves as the technical means for achieving a unified picture of the world, what Oskar Negt and Alexander Kluge have called "an illusory synthesis of the totality of society."[46] It thereby normalizes and depoliticizes.

We can see such dynamics at work in the nascent public spheres of the colonial Caribbean. The *Gazette de Saint-Domingue* was established after a successful lobbying effort by commercial interests on the island. There had been a print shop in the 1720s, but the printer was jailed twice, and the shop shut down within two years. He incurred problems, among other reasons, for printing copies of the Code Noir. Because the laws regulating slavery were regularly flouted on the island, printing them seems to have been viewed as a hostile act.

In 1742, a request was made to establish two new print shops. They were supported on grounds of legal and business efficiency: publicizing laws, printing invoices and other forms needed for the conduct of business. Versailles resisted the proposal and never approved it. Again in 1761, the Chamber of Agriculture of Cap Français began lobbying vigorously for a printer, and after approval by the Ministry of Colonies, a printer from Nantes was recruited and given the letters patent needed to open his shop. He would have a monopoly on printing in Saint-Domingue, but also be subject to censorship and surveillance by the colonial administration. Thus was born the *Gazette de Saint-Domingue*.[47]

The *Gazette*'s format was characteristic of an emergent news genre taking shape in Europe at the time. It mimicked business papers like the *Journal économique*, which first appeared in Paris in 1751, the *Journal du commerce*, founded in Brussels in 1759, and the *Gazette du commerce*, published in Paris starting in 1763.[48] Like their colonial counterpart, these papers aimed at being "generally useful," which the *Gazette du commerce* described as a broadly educational mission "allowing people to understand general ideas about economics, to be familiar with the principles of commercial interests, to be instructed in useful and provocative news that stimulates the industry of artisans of all nations."[49] Among the useful news were listings of ships in port, commodity prices, and exchange rates. In comparison with the Saint-Domingue paper, the reporting in Europe reflects the much richer and more diverse economy concentrated at the colonial center. In addition to prices for sugar, indigo, and coffee, the *Gazette du commerce* also reported the going rate for elephant tusks, Dutch spirits, and truffles. Some of the ships it reported on were headed for Caribbean ports like Martinique and Saint-Domingue, but others were going to India, Angola, Galipoli, and Syria.[50] Not surprisingly, the design of the Paris paper was more sophisticated and the printing more elaborate. The colonial and metropolitan papers were largely the same in format and appearance, though, and followed similar genre conventions.

It is important to note that papers like the *Gazette* were not the organs of opinion and public expression that we might expect later in the century, such as the broadsheets, pamphlets, and political opinion journals of the revolutionary period.[51] This was a time of war across Europe and the Caribbean, and there was an assassination attempt on Louis XV in 1757. Under these conditions, the royal regime allowed the press to function only under censorship and surveillance. As a result, this press was not a politicizing one. The *Gazette* did not call the status quo into question, as would the highly political journalism of the French Revolution. By claiming to provide useful information and report on quotidian features of colonial life, it instead had a normalizing effect. Commodity prices, exchange rates, news from Europe, and ships in port were rendered as familiar and quotidian facts. Among these aspects of daily life was the slave trade, since slave ships and their cargoes were routinely reported as commercial traffic. From this perspective, what was not said was just as important as what was said. Missing were the quotidian aspects of slavery themselves: brutal subordination, extreme mortality rates, the disruption of families, sexual coercion, and so on. In these senses, the construction of colonial normality also constituted blindness to important parts of colonial life and silence for the subaltern subjects most victimized by it.

By August 1764, the *Gazette* had changed its name to *Avis divers et petites affiches américaines*. It also adopted a new title banner, promising that "Nothing would be left undone to make the paper interesting." The name was shortened to *Affiches américaines* in 1766 and the presses were moved to Port-au-Prince to better enable surveillance by the colonial state. Under this title, it remained the sole newspaper in Saint-Domingue until 1790.

The popularity of maroon notices only continued to grow during this time. During the next decade, the number would reach nearly four hundred per year. Starting in 1780 there was another rapid increase in such notices, peaking at more than nine hundred in 1789 (figure 2.4).[52]

The rapid increase in maroon notices is not surprising. Saint-Domingue went through a notable economic expansion in the 1770s that included significant increases in the numbers of enslaved people being imported into the colony. The annual average was just under eight thousand new slaves per year from 1739 to 1778. That number skyrocketed to more than twenty-six thousand per year from 1779 to 1790.[53] The increase in maroon notices from 1779 to 1789 exactly mirrors this trend. Thus it was not that slaves were running away at a greater rate, nor that slave owners were suddenly attaching greater interest to retrieving them, but simply that the size of the slave population was increasing at a dramatic rate. The ideational impact remains the same, however: maroon notices took up a greater and greater part of the newspaper, and their presence in the public sphere increased accordingly, stopping only when the *Affiches américaines* went out of print in 1790.

The practice eventually caught on in other publications across the Caribbean. *L'observateur américain* was published in Guadeloupe from 1776 to 1777, but it did not

Figure 2.4 Maroon slave notices in the *Gazette de Saint-Domingue* and *Affiches américaines*, 1765-1789. Data from the French Atlantic History Group, McGill University.

cover marronage. By the 1780s, however, the innovation had come to that island as well. The February 1785 issue of the Guadeloupe paper *Follicules caraïbes* carried a single, tentative maroon listing, sandwiched between a notice for a loose cow and subscription information for the paper. More prominently, it also featured an article entitled "Instructive Guide for the Management of a Plantation" which included a section on the punishment and prevention of marronage.[54] This included the observation that the whip has been shown to be ineffective at correction. "The best policy in that regard," the paper counsels, "will be to punish a first absence by three months in chains; the second by three years; and the third by death." By 1788 another paper, the *Gazette de la Guadeloupe*, was featuring a full-blown but small section of marronage listings.[55] Still later, the first newspaper of colonial Louisiana, the *Moniteur de la Louisiane*, was founded in 1794 by a refugee from Saint-Dominque who brought the innovation of maroon notices along with him.[56]

Meanwhile, back in Saint-Domingue the *Affiches américaines* was reporting on the arrival of the ship *Les Amis*, just in after a stormy crossing from Martinique. The crew related that both Martinique and Guadeloupe had suffered considerably under the "depredations" of maroon groups during the fall of 1786. These were maroon colonies established in inaccessible mountains, the sailors said, and there was some hope of a government venture to pursue and destroy them. The problematization, anxiety, and conflict around these events—real or imagined—may explain some of the newfound urgency attached to marronage in the press of the Lesser Antilles.[57]

The appearance of newspapers in the Caribbean colonies was just one element of a growing public sphere. Creole lawyers like Médéric-Louis-Élie Moreau de Saint-Méry—the chronicler of the "African song"—and Michel-René Hilliard d'Auberteuil found new opportunities in the colonial administration and used their newfound status to become commentators on the colony itself. Hilliard d'Auberteuil published *Considérations sur l'état présent de la colonie française de Saint-Domingue* in 1776.[58] As we have already seen in chapter 1, Moreau de Saint-Méry was a wide-ranging collector of information, documents, and letters from around the colony, with important correspondents across the Caribbean and Europe.[59] His massive multivolume *Description topographique, physique, civile, politique et historique de la partie française de l'isle Saint-Domingue* was sold in the United States, Germany, and France.[60]

These commentators contributed to the normalization of colonial life through the public sphere in ways similar to the newspapers. Newspapers create a sense of the simultaneity of events, as Anderson tells us, of conveying "everything that is happening today." Encyclopedic compendia like those of Hilliard d'Auberteuil and Moreau de Saint-Méry gave an impression of the totality of colonial life, of conveying "everything to be known about the colony." This was primarily its economy, its commerce, its relations with France, its plant life, and its settlement patterns, but not in any prominent way the extent to which its considerable prosperity was created by an enslaved labor force. Again the organs of publicity have a hypostasizing function, one that normalizes the status quo. That status quo submerged the majority of the population in silence.

Moreau de Saint-Méry's account is mostly devoted to quotidian details of geography and economy. There is, however, a brief frisson of unrest in its pages. He notes that a settlement of *nègres marons* had been living in the Bahoruco Mountains near Jacmel for several decades. Moreau de Saint-Méry recounts the military expeditions sent to kill or capture these people and root out their settlement, starting in 1702 and recurring with some frequency ever since. He focuses largely on the details of armed conflict: the number of troops deployed, the number of fatalities, and the "ravages" and "disorders" caused by the *nègres* on surrounding communities. Finally, a joint Spanish and French expedition was organized, which succeeded in dispersing the settlement and extracting a promise to pursue other *nègres marrons* in exchange for pardon, liberty, and bounties for those they captured. Moreau de Saint-Méry concludes, "These are the true details of the individuals who sometimes desolated vast tracts of countryside.... Their character is one of disquiet, and it is painted on their appearance. Fear agitates them all. One could write an entire volume on everything we can detail about their numbers and ways of being."[61]

Moreau de Saint-Méry never did write that volume, so these maroons remained a silent presence. To the extent that they did achieve notice in his work, it is chiefly as vectors of disorder who must be dealt with.

There is one figure who comes into sharper focus, however. It is a brief vignette, only one paragraph long, that starts suddenly in the midst of an account of the "ravages" of maroons and the military expeditions mounted against them. The vignette begins suddenly with no prelude: "This *nègresse* called Anne, having refused to follow the *nègres marrons*, was tied up, collared, and dragged along by force." It is the story of a black woman captured by a maroon band. The chief, "a creole of the woods named *Kébinda*," tries to give her to his valet as a concubine. She refuses, so he takes her for himself, which she also refuses. She tries to flee and is recaptured. The band wants to kill her; the chief intervenes. Anne eventually agrees to become his wife if he will marry her "*in a church*." They cross over the Spanish border to fulfill this agreement. While crossing she begins to scream; he is arrested. She is brought to the governor, who frees her under the name Faithful Anne. Kébinda dies a short time later, "of regrets from a love betrayed."[62]

Women make so few appearances in the colonial archive that it is worth noticing when they do. The story of "Faithful Anne" is one of those oddities of (male) enlightenment discourse that says volumes for what it does not say as well as what it does. Any real Anne who may have been its source is suffocated under so many layers of signification that it is difficult for her to speak. The story functions as a tiny morality play in which "Faithful Anne" resists the depredations of the maroon band and is rewarded for her loyalty to the world of colony and plantation. Her faithfulness is located specifically in siding, at her own great peril, with the colonial order. In other words, she is made to define the moralized borders of a binary opposition between colonial order and maroon band. The function of this story is clear enough in Moreau de Saint-Méry's narrative:

the maroons know no bounds of decency, but the colonial order rewards its faithful.

In light of this message, the ending of the story is rather unexpected and bizarre. Kébinda, the story's nominal villain, becomes a kind of gallant lover, spurned and betrayed, who dies of unrequited love. Perhaps Moreau de Saint-Méry thought it best to veer in this direction to take the sting out of the highly problematic sexual politics that he had otherwise implied. What begins as a story of kidnap and rape ends as a gallant tragedy. Or so it seems. The only thing that is clear is that Anne's appearance is sudden, brief, and highly stylized. She appears as a cipher of female virtue under duress. Moreau de Saint-Méry is so busy attributing other meanings to Anne that we have no idea who she really was, what she thought about the difficult act of navigation she was forced into, or the loyalty and piety attributed to her. In Spivak's sense, Anne could not speak.

In addition to the sorts of books published by Hilliard d'Auberteuil and Moreau de Saint-Méry, there was also a "republic of letters" in the colony modeled very consciously on metropolitan practice. Like its continental counterpart, this was an Enlightenment practice of intellectual exchange.[63] Its principal product was a broadly humanist, enlightened society of arts and letters called the Cercle des Philadelphes. The Cercle was established in 1784 with members across the Caribbean and France, and in cooperation and correspondence with similar societies in Europe. Among the list of honorary members were royal officials, governors of other Caribbean colonies, and "his excellency" Dr. Benjamin Franklin. The list of regular members included doctors, lawyers, nobles, a number of highly placed people in Europe and the United States, and the editor of the *Affiches américaines*. Not surprisingly, the Cercle received quite favorable coverage there.[64]

A prospectus published by the Cercle in a Guadeloupe newspaper notes that there is now a different "order of things" in the colonies, and our knowledge of their physical, natural, and moral history has not kept pace. The language could have come from the eighteenth-century French intellectuals in Foucault's *The Order of Things*—not only the "order of things" itself, but also the conjunction of different fields of study that will be "set in the order and natural relations" that can be represented in a "vast Tableau."[65] The prospectus characterizes this as the unified project of a "Society of Observers" that can serve the colony "with work that may be useful to it."

The Cercle was modeled on the learned societies in Europe at the time. It organized public meetings, publications, and essay competitions. Among these were a doctor reporting on experiments about disease-causing smells in hospitals; research on the customs of ancient Danes; a prospectus for a book about the "physico-economics" of tropical plants; another doctor talking about the necessity of public instruction for women about childbirth; a captain of artillery reading a piece of poetry; and a third medical doctor, discussing "the true sense of the expression 'philosophy.'"[66]

In all of these ways, the growing public spheres of the colonial Caribbean were explicitly modeled on European examples. They attempted to forge discursive connections with Europe to become part of an extended European public sphere. In these senses, they were oriented toward creating a kind of European normality in the colonies. They functioned in much the same way as their European models, using stylistic conventions that were also developing rapidly in Europe at this time. Within these evolving conventions, reportage functioned to thematize problem areas, open them to discourse, and weigh potential solutions. To this extent, public spheres served not only to construct problematics but also to capture and domesticate them.

At the same time, the colonial public spheres also aimed at refashioning the very idea of European normality. The Caribbean colonies, with their wealth, plantations, and slaves, were portrayed as part of an extended European order that participated in the quotidian affairs of Europe. To the extent that there were problems within this order, they became subjects for the normal problem-solving functions of the public sphere. Maroon listings were an outgrowth of this attitude. They were a local innovation very much in the spirit of the genre conventions of European public spheres. Marronage was constructed as a problem to be solved; maroon listings had "public utility" as a result. By extension, marronage became part of the normal fabric of Euro-colonial life.

Against this background we can see what is striking about marronage. The small, seemingly insignificant press innovations of 1764 mark a fundamental transformation in the problematics of slavery. The sudden popularity of maroon notices signals a fundamental shift in the form and role of publicity in expressing this problematic. Rather than private discourse oriented toward ever more spectacular punishment, marronage could now be problematized in public discourse. This shift testifies to the perceived failure of spectacular punishment as a form of deterrence. It marks an attempt to harness discourse and publicity as tools for reasserting domination, control, and the property relations peculiar to slavery. In this sense, 1764 is a point of inflection in the way marronage circulated within the colonial imaginary of Saint-Domingue.

These events are a point of inflection in another way as well. The Code Noir was a very public document, but one whose punishments were largely carried out in private. Their spectacular effect was limited to those within view of the spectacle. Similarly, attempts to deal with marronage by the colonial government treated maroons as an undifferentiated menace requiring an apparatus of manhunt and torture—either scattered individuals to be captured or maroon communities to be hunted out. With the innovation of publicity, maroons could be individually named, described, known, and publicized. As a result, individual subaltern subjects were now made present in the public sphere.

Therein lies the ambivalence of the publicity surrounding marronage. When enslaved people escaped, they actively subverted the property relations and domination that constituted them as fungible commodities. When this subversion was publicly advertised, it additionally brought slavery and its refusal squarely to the center of the developing public sphere. Marronage became part of the vision of the normal being created there, yet in the form of menacing, deviant behavior. The result was a tension within this new public definition of normality. Marronage problematized attempts to normalize slavery as a non-problematic fact of commerce. Instead, it revealed slavery to be problematically unstable, a potentially ungovernable aspect of the colonial order.

Starting in 1764, the production of a colonial order took a huge leap forward through the use of relatively new technologies, especially the mechanical printing of newspapers and a subscription model of distribution. In a narrow sense, the control of this discursive production lay with the publisher, but he was in turn licensed, inspected, and censored by the colonial government. In a broader and more diffuse sense, then, control was passively maintained by a particular class of white planters and their allies, most of whom had large capital stakes in the colonial plantation economy. Their control was manifest as a kind of colonial common sense which, *inter alia*, included maintaining the epistemic invisibility of slaves. In this sense, the ruling ideas of the colonial public sphere were the ideas of the ruling class, as Marx and Engels would have noted.[67]

Marronage disrupted this control. It did not literally put control of the production of discourse in the hands of the enslaved, but it disrupted the causal efficacy of the control enjoyed by the planter class. They could no longer produce an unproblematized, normal vision of the colonial order. In this sense, marronage produced discourse that was out of control. It was discourse about the colonial regime's failures to fully contain and subordinate slaves. It thereby not only disrupted the control of discourse, but also the *dispositif* of power and knowledge constituted by the colonial public sphere. Here marronage opened up an epistemic rupture in the colonial order of things by disrupting the colonial ruling class's own understanding of the world around it.

Marronage undermined the silence and invisibility of slaves by inserting subaltern agents into the public sphere. Rather than invisible subalterns, they became problematic agents of disruption. Rather than smoothly operating elements of the machinery of commodity production, they were perceived as unruly and disorderly. After 1764, maroons were able to unsettle the construction of a counterfactual normality for the slave colony by inserting themselves into the very apparatus of that construction. Marronage ruptured normality by reasserting the presence of subalterns who otherwise only appeared in this vision as voiceless and without volition.

We see that marronage had spillover effects that went beyond the direct pursuit of freedom. It ruptured attempts to establish a smoothly functioning mechanism for the extraction of profit from slave labor, provoking a response that was often viciously out of proportion to the acts it was designed to punish. When the colonial press became available as a new tool for normalizing this situation in 1764, marronage again inverted the situation. The wild popularity of maroon slave notices migrated the rupture to a whole new register, propagated it to a much wider audience, and thereby increased the sense of unease it provoked in colonial common sense.

INCITEMENT TO DISCOURSE

Maroon notices were only part of a wider proliferation of discourse around fugitivity. Shortly after their debut there was a marked increase in use of the term "marronage" itself. This was part of a generalized expansion of the problematic that marronage represented.

Before the 1760s the idea of marronage was largely unknown on the continent, at least among those not directly involved in the slave economy. A gallant love poem of 1729 by Antoine de Labarre de Beaumarchais reveals much of this.

Beaumarchais uses marronage as an extended metaphor for love in flight that cannot be seized or captured. The poem describes a jesting, flitting, audacious, cruel love that burns the heart. Maroon love knows neither respect nor shame; it comes and goes; it flutters like a butterfly. In a somewhat surprising reversal, it can even transform itself into a tyrannical master. It is useless to hide and lock up this love; it will always escape and find its freedom. After announcing this conceit, Beaumarchais envisions an imaginary critic: "But (someone will say) this is not a proper word. I've never seen the term maroon employed in any learned work." The poet responds with irony, "Great thanks, Monsieur the Critic... maybe with time it will find its way out of the tropics and become established in Europe."[68]

Using marronage as a metaphor for love conveys an air of romantic whimsy. It celebrates the freedom and caprice of the fugitive heart, but of course it also ignores the harsh realities of maroon life. In this sense, it reflects an incomplete and distant understanding of marronage. It is a romanticized projection of colonial realities as seen from an elite metropolitan perspective. As Beaumarchais indicates, the idea is not well known on the continent. To a metropolitan reader this conceit might have seemed somewhat naughty and risqué. It has an air of exoticism, reinforced by its placement in Beaumarchais's book next to an equally fictional "Excerpt from a Chinese tragedy" and "The Story of Topal-Osman Pacha, Grand Visir."

Starting with the innovations of the *Gazette de Saint-Domingue*, however, marronage became a more general topic of discussion. It began to show up with increasing regularity in the French press, not only in the colonies but the metropole as well. There was a notable increase of discussion just after 1764 and a rapid increase again in the 1790s (figure 2.5).[69]

This eruption of discourse occurred during a time in which the press on Saint-Domingue was blossoming into something like a full-blown public sphere. Starting in 1790 and running to approximately 1794, there was an enormous expansion of the colony's press. There were now a number of *Gazettes*, several *Journals*, several *Courriers*, and at least two more papers whose title included *Affiches américaines*. There was a significant new daily, the *Moniteur général*. There were several papers whose names revealed a clear Jacobin orientation: *L'ami de l'egalité ou annales révolutionnaires* and *Le patriote des Antilles*. This efflorescence mirrored that in metropolitan France at the time.

The increasing discourse about marronage has an interesting relationship with the dynamics we observed in the *Affiches américaines* in figure 2.4. In the *Affiches*, the number of maroon notices reached a peak of 911 just before the

Figure 2.5 Published frequency of *"marronage,"* 1765–1820. Google French dataset of 2012, courtesy of Google Labs.

paper went out of print in 1790. One might wonder why an innovation as popular as the maroon notices was not immediately adopted by other newspapers. To a student of Haitian history the reason is clear enough. The year 1791 marks the beginnings of widespread, well-organized revolts that threw the colony into full-blown insurrection. By 1804 Saint-Domingue had been taken over by formerly enslaved people, seceded from France, and declared itself the Republic of Haiti. During that time of revolutionary upheaval, maroon slave notices must have seemed quite beside the point. In many cases, planters were fleeing the colony for refuge in Charleston or Philadelphia.

During the same decades, however, the published use of "marronage" in the French-language press increased fourteen-fold.[70] Notices for maroon slaves vanished as talk of marronage increased dramatically. Why should two so similar phenomena, both pressed forward by marronage, show such stark and opposite tendencies? The answer is clear enough. The maroon slave notices graphed in figure 2.4 appear only in the *Affiches américaines*, published in Saint-Domingue, and thus reflect the specific circumstances of the Haitian Revolution. The discussion of marronage graphed in figure 2.5, on the other hand, registers across all French language publications of the era. It reveals a broader problematization of marronage and related phenomena that was provoked by the Saint-Domingue revolution. Marronage was seen as a precursor to revolution in other slave colonies. As such, this dynamic traces a more general problematization of slavery, fugitivity, and revolution that spurred a great deal of discourse.

We do not know exactly who conceived of implementing maroon notices in the French colonies or the exact character of the *ardeur* behind the idea. Was it the pull of losing one's "property," the destabilization of plantation life, the threat to the colonial order of things, or some other anxiety? Regardless of the exact motive, marronage seems to have exercised a propulsive force on the developing public sphere of Saint-Domingue. It pushed the topic of fugitive slaves onto the agenda with a zeal evident to both readers and publishers.

Michel Foucault describes a similar phenomenon in his genealogy of sexuality. Rather than find repression in modern sexuality, he found a great urge to speak about it, "a veritable discursive explosion."[71] This discourse increased in specificity and detail over time, contributing to "a constant optimization and an increasing valorization of the discourse on sex ... meant to yield multiple effects of displacement, intensification, reorientation, and modification of desire itself."[72] Ultimately, the steady impulse to anatomize sex in discourse created forms of knowledge and truth around sexuality.

Foucault describes this proliferation of talk as an incitement to discourse. It spurred people to single out sexuality as a focus of attention, to study it in minute detail, to reflect upon and modify their own sexual practices. This discourse constituted a new set of productive power relations. It produced new varieties of sexuality and new forms of sexual identity, connecting sexuality with many other currents of thought and practice in the eighteenth century—population, political economy, national prosperity. This incitement fed on itself, discourse producing more discourse. It thereby proliferated discursive power relations and the objects that are created through them.

Marronage also incited discourse, but in a form rather different from Foucault's. His genealogical studies focus on highly codified, well-developed areas of study. In these domains, knowledge has been carefully elaborated as a *disposif* of power. Foucault's genealogies of the human sciences reveal this in the development of specific domains of knowledge: philology, biology, political economy, psychiatry, medicine, criminology, sexuality. These are all stories of the constitution of bodies of knowledge that exert power as an essential mode of their operation. Such knowledge produces specific subjectivities: the insane, self-reflective criminals, sexual deviants. These new types are produced through discourse, and they are thereby invested in power relations from the very start. The same dynamic is at work in Foucault's extensive study of "truth-telling" as a practice of self-examination.[73] Here introspection and articulating the truth of one's self becomes a way of making the private public, constituting a self within discourse.

Marronage did not follow these patterns. It was not elaborated as an object of knowledge, even among the scientifically minded Cercle des Philadelphes. It did not become a systematic study of "colonial criminality" or a science of "slave deviance," which would then function as a regime of power. Nor was it a topic of self-examination on the part of colonial administrators or planters, a truth about themselves that they felt compelled to reveal through discourse. Instead, marronage followed a much rawer and untrod path, indicating important differences between colonial and metropolitan epistemologies.

Marronage incited discourse as a reaction to the perceived instability, danger, and uncertainty that it represented. Rather than investing subjects in a field of knowledge that produced and constituted their subjectivity (the mad, the criminal, the pervert), the discourse surrounding marronage operated in a more complicated way. It disrupted the formation of a colonial common sense that excluded slavery from view, constituting a *problematization* of truth rather than a new regime of truth. Marronage spurred discourse in the form of an open-ended disruption of knowledge, rather than a new science that constituted subjects and established facts. To be sure, this discourse did constitute the new identity category of the *nègre marron*, one novel enough that it could be named only by borrowing a neologism from Spanish. It did not aim to generate knowledge about maroons, however, but only identified and enumerated them. In so doing, it constituted a disruption of received opinion. This discourse thus served two functions that pulled in opposite directions and operated at cross-purposes to one another. On one hand it formed a productive, constitutive regime of power over its subjects, but on the other, it functioned as a disruptive *counterpower* that operated on their behalf.

As a result of the spontaneous, unreflective nature of the maroon notices, the proliferation of discourse around them was rather different as well. It constituted a relatively wide-open discursive field that encompassed many different themes in an unsystematic way. That discourse waxed and waned over time, responding to conditions of the moment. This included particular events, but equally, anxieties about things that could potentially happen (slave revolts, for instance); or things that might have already happened but were as yet unknown (such as maroon plots and conspiracies), as well as self-congratulatory narratives and even romantic poetry. This was not simply discourse *about* marronage but equally marronage intruding upon and provoking discourse.

This colonial scene requires a conception of the incitement to discourse quite different from Foucault's. Rather than focus on new forms of discourse that create new domains of knowledge, one's attention is drawn to the banal truths created by everyday discourse, especially the ones sanctified as facts because they are given legitimacy by the print media. Instead of an incitement to discourse that creates more power, new kinds of power, and greater investments of subjects in power, we see here an incitement to discourse that both promotes and disrupts power. In this case, the proliferation of discourse sowed the seeds of doubt and paranoia. It denaturalized the power created by that other discourse, the normalizing one of the everyday. It thereby constituted its own form of counterpower.

In all of these senses, marronage had a constituent effect on the colonial public sphere. It provoked substantial discussion of punishment and deterrence in the late seventeenth and early eighteenth centuries. It later became a wildly successful theme of Saint-Domingue's first newspaper. This was part and parcel of an incitement to discourse. Through this incitement, marronage promoted the growth and expansion of the public sphere itself. This is what I mean by its constituent effect: the technical capacities of print publication were lobbied for by the Chamber of Agriculture on Saint-Domingue because of their perceived usefulness. Such innovations, which made possible the institutionalization and expansion of the public sphere in the colony, were driven forward by perceived need. This is the sense in which marronage had a crucial role in *constituting* the colonial public sphere.

Here we can see the political complexity of marronage. It had a double effect in the colonial public sphere. On one hand it drove forward the development of the apparatus of publicity. On the other hand it created anxiety, incited discourse, and disrupted normality. This was a double movement of production and disruption. It promoted the development of technologies of publicity while at the same time using them to destabilize the colonial sense of normality.

THE DISRUPTIVE FORCE OF ABSENCE

It is worth emphasizing the extent to which discourse about marronage was driven by anxiety. We can see this clearly in the surplus affect surrounding marronage—in both its discussion and treatment.

Accounts at the time claimed that marronage was rare and there were only a few scattered maroons in the mountains.[74] David Geggus shares this opinion. He estimates that the number of maroons was a relatively small percentage of the number of slaves on the island. He also argues that the maroon communities in the Saint Domingan hinterlands were isolated and contained relatively few people. These communities had some influence on what would eventually become the Haitian Revolution, but Geggus concludes that that influence was small.[75]

In contrast to these estimates, the amount of psychic energy devoted to escaped slaves is striking. Many of the measures taken against marronage seem to go quite far beyond what might have been necessary to prevent fugitivity and protect planters' interests. This begins even with the Code Noir in 1685, with its progressively escalating schedule of physical mutilation. That was only a legal code, of course, and as the years went on, actual punishments became even more excessive and imaginative. The gruesome, Damiens-like character of these punishments seems to go well beyond what was needed for deterrence.[76]

Not only that, but we know that the measures taken against marronage were often unsuccessful. Colonial administrators complained that the Code Noir was not severe enough to discourage marronage and other "disorders."[77] Interrogation transcripts show that more extreme, improvised punishments were also frequently counterproductive. Thomas, the enslaved victim of Sieur Chapuihet, says that he fled to avoid such sadistic treatment. He was not aware of the elaborate semiotics of mutilation specified by the Code Noir, but he was terrified of his overseer's gratuitous violence. Rather than incline him toward obedience, this fear made him take flight.

In short, the attention devoted to marronage seems quite disproportional to its material importance. Something more seems to have been at work. This attention had a strong psychic charge. One frequently sees signs of underlying anxieties and fears in this archive, ones that were vague, threatening, and of unclear provenance. Marronage was symbolically linked to a number of other threats: raids on plantations, general slave insurrection, and the chafing, gnawing worry of small acts of sabotage and rebellion thought to be inspired by maroons. The prospect of such threats riveted the attention, but it was unclear how or whether they might arise. It was thus also unclear how much of a response might be sufficient to avoid them. The result was sometimes a disproportionate and excessive response, one that seemed to have no limits because its target was largely unknown.

We see, then, that there was an *incitement to practice* that stood alongside the incitement to discourse.[78] The chafing anxieties surrounding marronage had a broader inciting effect, motivating actions as well as words. Much of the aggressive response to marronage is traceable to the outsized importance that was placed upon it. This spur to action goes beyond a mere incitement of discourse. Otherwise put, there is a continuum between discourse and practice in these instances. Discursive practices are central to the working out of anxiety, but they are accompanied by other forms of working out as well.

It is important to be precise: marronage itself did not incite such activity. Rather, incitement came from the perception and imagination of marronage by colonial elites. It was not the actual practice of marronage that constituted such a pervasive problematization but the way it percolated through the colonial imagination. This imaginary of enslaved people on the loose disrupted the feeling of normality and problematized colonial common sense. Anxieties were generated as part and parcel of this imaginary, not directly out of the experience of marronage itself.

Problematization is an apt term for discussing the working out of colonial anxieties.[79] Unsettling phenomena provoked disquiet and thus became objects of consideration. The imaginary of marronage, for instance, focused the attention of colonial elites on its roots, effects, and character. This was frequently not the problematization one might have hoped for. In place of a sober reflection on the problematic character of enslavement, problematization frequently took unfortunate paths: proposals to enhance the severity of the Code Noir, for instance, or the sadistic violence of overseers like Sieur Chapuihet. In other words, problematization was a chafing itch that needed to be scratched. It brought particular themes to the fore for attention in a persistent manner. What paths that attention followed was, however, an entirely different question.

It is worth noting the extent to which anxiety animated a great deal of thought and activity in the colonies. Marronage was just one part of this dynamic. It was a member of a small family of material acts that had potent epistemic significance. We will see in coming chapters that subaltern silence had a more broadly disruptive effect on French colonialism. It characterized a web of interconnected anxieties: not only of fugitivity but also of fears about poisoning, abolitionist infiltrators, and the spread of revolutionary doctrines. All of these fears percolated through the elite classes of the colony as vague and unverifiable threats.

Subaltern silence was a principal source of such anxieties. Silencing was a goal for colonial elites. It was a form of subordination that was required for colonial domination and slavery. The achievement of this silence created a whole host of worries, however. The silent subaltern was an unknowable and thus unnerving figure. One never quite knew what might be happening behind the façade of silence. This unknowability made the potential dangers of colonialism surface vividly in the elite imagination. Where silence seemed to be observed, much greater dangers could be imagined: a subaltern who was not *actually* silent but instead plotting, conspiring, and committing secret harms. In short, this amounted to an imaginary *unsilencing* of the subaltern. Ironically, this imaginary unsilencing is itself a further form of silencing. The silent subaltern, imagined as secretly *non*-silent, takes on a shadowy presence that is purely phantasmatic. It creates a new, imaginary identity and attributes characteristics to it. This is another variation on the *silencing through displacement* that we have already observed: substituting an imagined identity for whatever the subaltern might actually have had to say. This one is distinctive, however, for its highly affect-driven, phantasmatic character and the way it postulates an invisible possession of agency by those who seem to be silent. In recognition of this convoluted configuration, we might call it *silencing through imaginary unsilencing*.

All of these silences, densely connected with one another, certainly had an unnerving effect. They spawned continual and proliferating anxiety, causing an epistemic rupture that prevented colonialism and slavery from falling into a normal, taken-for-granted state. Efforts were constantly made to pierce these silences, to bring maroon communities back under control so they could be resilenced in a manner more suited to white interests. Consider, for instance, Moreau de Saint-Méry's account of the efforts made to pierce the silence of the maroon community of Bahoruco. Expeditions were mounted against them in 1702, 1715, 1717, 1719, 1728, 1733, 1740, 1742, 1746, 1757, 1761, 1776, 1777, and 1781. Unable to force the community into an enslaved form of silence, that goal was finally achieved through a negotiated peace settlement in 1782–1785.[80] At the time this attempt to recapture maroon individuals and colonies was viewed as a reassertion of authority and property relations. From a more abstract perspective, however, we can also see it as an attempt to subjugate a freely chosen form of silence and replace it with one controlled by white elites.

In sum, there was a nexus of connection between silence, anxiety, problematization, and incitement. Subaltern silence took two forms in this case: ones that were actively pursued goals of plantation owners and the colonial state; and others that enslaved people pursued as alternatives to the first. In other words, enslavement and marronage each constituted a particular form of subaltern silence. Each obscured the subaltern from view in specific and characteristic ways. As a result, this subaltern became an unknowable source of anxiety. The comings and goings of *petit marronage* were feared to be conduits of plotting and conspiracy. The established freedom of maroon communities was worried about as a supposed base for raids on towns and plantations as well as more sophisticated mischief. Such anxieties problematized colonial life, thematizing aspects of it for worried attention. Such problematization provoked discourse and action: administrative correspondence, maroon notices, newspaper opinion pieces, accounts in books and memoirs, expeditions to the hinterlands, violent crackdowns, torture, and imprisonment. Marronage provided a constant reminder of the instabilities of enslavement. It problematized such practices in a way that prevented them from becoming fully normalized. Silence, anxiety, problematization, and incitement were connected with one another through these channels.

One cannot help but note the circular character of this nexus. Subaltern silence provoked anxiety, which incited practice, which mostly created an even more dire situation for enslaved people, which made them pursue alternative forms of silence (marronage) with an even greater sense of urgency over those enforced on the plantation. These new forms of silence merely provoked greater anxiety among colonial elites. And so on. Subaltern silence, anxiety, problematization, and incitement followed a perverse dynamic that seems to have been poorly understood by the elites driving it forward.

Spivak's insights allow us to see an additional irony of this situation. In both cases silence constituted a form of subordination. Enslaved people who fled operated within a system of constraints that left only better or worse alternatives, but not the ones they ideally would have chosen. Life in a maroon community was better and freer than life under slavery. It was still a life of hardship and anxiety, however, living in remote mountain hinterlands and being hunted.[81] In both cases, silence remained a form of subordination. The issue for the subaltern was one of choosing between its better and worse forms.

PERFORMATIVE ABSENCE

It may seem counterintuitive to talk about subaltern silence in the way that I have. I have argued that maroons pursued a form of freedom with very specific epistemic content. It took the form of a desire to be left alone. By leaving, maroons were not trying to speak in Spivak's sense. Their act of departure was not a form of exit that constituted a form of voice.[82] Rather, it was simply a seizure of autonomy from a pervasive system of control. Fugitive slaves successfully escaped, but it is not clear that they were trying to say anything by escaping.

When marronage was inscribed into the public sphere, however, it became something very different. It served as an incitement to discourse and a source of performative presence for slaves. This performativity was both disruptive and problematizing. It functioned as a form of subaltern speech in ways that we have not previously considered.

Performativity refers to how the actions and public presence of maroons disrupted the sense of normality in the colonies. We can think of it by analogy to Judith Butler's celebrated account of gender. In Butler's account, gender takes on meaning through the performance of a multitude of individual acts. Each of us performs gender in some way. In so doing, we thereby create, modify, and reproduce the meaning of gender, as well as the scripts through which we understand and perform it. Specific manifestations of gender are evaluated against this background of daily, quotidian performances.[83]

Gender norms accumulate as a result of simple, everyday experience. Such norms are not explicit; they are not linguistically articulated. Rather, they form a set of implicit background understandings that we use to embody particular genders. Not every performance of gender reproduces and entrenches gender norms, of course. Some are disruptive: they are performances that stand apart from and thereby challenge these norms. These nonstandard performances reveal a great deal about the pervasive normalization of gender by presenting an alternative vision. Their effect is unsettling, critical, and disruptive.

The disruptive force of marronage can be understood in similar terms. Marronage was, in effect, a performance of freedom and agency. By escaping, enslaved people subverted the legal system that classed them as property and denied the relations of domination in which they had been placed. They thereby performed freedom, simultaneously problematizing the norms that allowed their subordination.

Starting in 1764, marronage was inserted into the print public sphere. Now, when maroons performed their freedom they gained a widespread publicity in addition to the more localized performativity that had already enjoyed. It gave them an official public presence that they were otherwise denied. It named them and described them. Each maroon advertisement bore a form of individuation, one that disclosed a person with a name and distinguishing features. "Here is how you will recognize this person if you find him or her." Along with that was an implicit attribution of agency and autonomy: "These are the ones who defied subordination and escaped." Such people had successfully placed themselves beyond the reach of law and violence. As such, their actions constituted a performative rebuttal to the system that had deprived them of freedom.

There was an additional subtler and more profound performance at work as well. I have already said that the maroon notices inserted enslaved people into the public sphere. To some extent this gave them a public presence: *this* person with *this* name and *these* characteristics. However, and somewhat paradoxically, this presence was expressed as a form of *absence*. The figure of the maroon was an empty placeholder. It marked the absence of a person who was sought. This accounts for some of its performative and unsettling effects. It represented freedom as a form of being gone.

In this sense, marronage amounted not only to the performance of freedom and absence, but also the performance of silence. Maroons had chosen to make themselves free, which meant choosing to make themselves absent. In so doing, they also became unknowable from the perspective of colonial elites. Their whereabouts, designs, plans, activities, ideas, and words were now unknown. In this Spivakian sense, the maroon was silent. The maroon could not speak, because he or she had chosen to leave.

As a result, maroons left it unclear what meaning should be attached to their fugitivity. Fugitivity entered the public sphere as semantically indeterminate. "I do this thing, and leave it to you to figure out what it means." It thereby became all the more unsettling. Rumor and anxiety filled in the blanks where meaning was not clear. The entry of maroons into the public sphere was thus accompanied by a more general discussion of marronage, one that mirrored the problematization created by these underspecified acts.

The dull, prosaic listing of escaped slaves only preserved the aura of silence surrounding them. They were named and described, but otherwise did not speak. As a result, they registered in the public sphere as present but silent: an individualized, nonspeaking, but also noncompliant and subversive multitude. The sheer numbers of maroon notices—multiple hundreds per year—only added to this feeling of multiplicity, silence, and noncooperation. The piling up of numbers, their abundance in the public eye, increased their force.

In this sense, marronage intervened in colonial public imaginaries to unsettle meaning in a variety of subtle, quotidian ways. Unlike the performances that add up to gender, however, those of marronage struck a somewhat different balance between reproducing norms and disrupting them. Gender, Butler argues, is overwhelmingly performed according to a society's standard scripts. In this sense it is pervasively normative and conservative. Marronage, on the other hand, was almost entirely disruptive. It intervened in the public domain as a set of cryptic acts with unclear value. As performative, it did not make claims so much as rupture attempts to naturalize the status quo. Such acts were pebbles in the gears of public communication. Their underdetermination provoked anxiety, interpretation, and an open-ended search for meaning and closure. As a result, they had a problematizing function within the public sphere unlike that of any simple statement or speech act.

The notion of performativity allows us to see the sense in which subalterns were able to "speak" through marronage. The act of flight inserted subaltern subjects into the public sphere. Their acts were disruptive of meaning being created there, simultaneously creating meaning of a different sort. Rather than a pervasive normalization and routinization of slavery, they produced an alternative regime of meaning in which slavery was seen as unstable, problematic, and contested. At the same time, the classification of slaves as productive property was problematized by their presence in the public sphere as contestatory agents. This is precisely the magic of performativity in marronage. It does not say things in the same way that propositions do. Rather, it conveys meaning in less precise and determinate senses that carry great weight precisely because of their imprecision and indeterminacy. In this way, marronage was simultaneously inscribed within a public sphere, a disruption of meaning, an incitement to discourse, and an avenue of subaltern speech.

Of course, the publicity maroons now enjoyed was an ambivalent one. Maroon advertisements interpellated enslaved people as property. They were improper property, property that had stolen itself and needed to be repossessed. This represented maroons as people who could and should be owned. It thereby reaffirmed and normalized the property relations governing the possession of humans, as well as the forms of power and violence used to enforce them.

The disruption achieved by marronage was a similarly ambivalent one. As we have already discussed, it produced anxieties that had a problematizing effect. That problematization ran in all directions, however. In some cases it directly stirred discussions on the rectitude of slavery: whether people could be owned as property. In others, it invited calls to intensify policing, mount military expeditions, and lash out violently against the unsettling phenomenon. The ambivalence of this situation is precisely the kind that arises from subaltern silence. It was a performative silence, one that was therefore all the more anxiety-producing, problematizing, and inciting.

THE PERILS OF PUBLICITY

In this chapter I have returned to the originary scene of the public sphere. We see that this most enlightened of ideals was coeval with that most modern of institutions, globalized capitalism. The slave colonies of the eighteenth-century Caribbean were in many ways an apotheosis of capitalist development, bringing military might and territorial conquest together with enslaved labor in a combination that was wildly profitable. The public sphere was not essential to these developments but a useful technology in their stabilization. When enslaved people resisted, the public sphere became a means of bringing them back under control. The capture of escaped slaves thus became one of the favored uses of this new communications technology in the Caribbean colonies.

Although the public sphere was deployed to contain marronage, that effort backfired in important ways. Marronage exercised a substantially disruptive influence on colonial slavery, one that was propagated and intensified by means of the growing public sphere. It incited discourse in the public sphere and exercised a constituent influence on its development. In so doing, marronage disrupted attempts to create a sense of colonial normality.

My interest here is in the subversive effects of marronage. This is a story of intertwined forms of subaltern publicity and subaltern silence, a complex pattern of action and reaction. It is located in a history of de jure white supremacy, in which property relations and state enforcement mechanisms collaborate with informal brutalities to subordinate a captive population. A crucial part of this subordination was the creation of subordinate identities stripped of public agency, presence, and voice.

Marronage forcefully renegotiated this situation. Maroons gained significant autonomy and freedom compared to their existence as slaves, creating a subaltern silence of their own choosing to replace the one that had been forced upon them. This silence was an achievement, seized from the midst of the other silence of slavery. In an attempt to regain control, planters resorted to publicity, giving maroons a kind of forced public presence that they never had as slaves. The idea was to make them surveyable and identifiable, thus subject to capture and repatriation. However, the performative dimensions of this publicity subverted its own goals.

By publicizing their specific identities, escaped slaves were given a public presence they did not have in the past. The sheer numbers of such advertisements made clear how many people were escaping. The result was a pervasive problematization of enslavement and an incitement to practice around it. The publicity around marronage was not simply an innovation in enforcement but an epistemically disruptive innovation that gave maroons a kind of performative presence. By seeking their own freedom and attempting to restore a whole life of some sort, enslaved people destabilized plantation discipline and colonial rule. They did this in unintended coalition with the growing public spheres of the colonial Caribbean, inciting discourse, promoting anxiety and paranoia, and feeding fears of revolt.

It is important to emphasize the subtlety and ambiguity of this situation. Here subaltern silence was a constant presence, but it was manifested in many different ways. Some of those manifestations look more like freedom and autonomy than others. In no case is this a story of subaltern insurgency in any straightforward sense, however. Nor is it a story of the "weapons of the weak," an undertow of minute subversive acts.[84] The destabilizing effects of marronage were side effects of other practices. Enslaved people sought their own freedom. In so doing, they enacted new forms of subaltern silence that had disruptive consequences. My point here—one that Gayatri Spivak would very much share, I think—is that subaltern silence is a confounding, difficult, and complex situation that poses puzzles both for those submerged in it and for those who try to interpret it. It would be too quick and too much of a distortion to tell a story of heroic self-liberation. That is certainly in play, but it is wrapped in layers of silence, chance, and epistemic confusion. As an interpreter of this archive, I take my task to be one of preserving and conveying that complexity, rather than ... silencing it.

In many ways this story provides us with a counterhistory of the public sphere. It reveals the problematic undertow of this hegemonic Enlightenment ideal, in the form of its ignoble colonial counterpart and the unexpected forces producing it. This counterhistory highlights the substantial abilities of elites to create common sense and the occasional opportunity of subalterns to disrupt it. It is a story of subalterns who could not speak, and the political modalities that they developed in response. It carries lessons about the subtleties of subaltern silence: it can be either an imposition or an achievement; it can exercise uncanny effects on those in power; and silence itself can have a performative aspect that disrupts subordination.

This is not to say that the emergent public spheres of the eighteenth century were purely reactionary. Indeed, many of their continental innovators were also dedicated abolitionists. Thinkers like Brissot and Diderot were dedicated opponents of slavery *and* pioneers in the new technologies of the public sphere. Writers like Raynal and Grégoire used these new technologies to publish widely circulated, influential tracts condemning slavery. All of this simply reveals the complexity of an ideal like the public sphere, in which good intentions and progressive claims travel hand in hand with normalization, depoliticization, marginalization, and exclusion. In chapter 4, we will see some of the wild and unexpected consequences of this abolitionist public sphere.

The mid-eighteenth century marks an important milestone in this genealogy. Subaltern silence became modern in the French Caribbean in 1764. At that point new dynamics were put into play with destabilizing consequences. Even though enslaved people were oppressed and excluded from the colonial public sphere, they managed to exercise a disruptive influence on discourse and practice in the colony. They inserted themselves into the public domain, not as "speakers" in the traditional sense but as being present in the public consciousness. Here the subaltern both achieved silence as a freely chosen project *and* managed to "speak" in Spivak's sense. These subordinated people disrupted the colonial order in deeply epistemic ways and destabilized the conditions of their own subordination.

CHAPTER 3

Unsettling Silences

The Perils of Poison

1682-1758

Colonial domination requires an enormous investment in affect and ceremony and a significant emotional expenditure that few have analyzed until now.

—Achille Mbembe

So far this genealogy has followed subaltern silence across some unusual terrain. Maroons were enslaved people who converted their subaltern status into other forms, seizing freedom under very difficult circumstances. By removing themselves even further from view, they achieved greater subaltern silence as a form of remoteness. The results, I have argued, were rather unexpected. This self-chosen silence problematized colonial practice, disrupting normality among colonial elites who desired above all to normalize the highly prosperous economy they had built on the backs of others.

I have tried to expose the affective core of these phenomena: how this self-achieved silence caused profound disquiet among colonial elites. Maroons were seen as conduits of incitement and dangerous knowledge for the slaves who remained on plantations. They were unknown and uncontrollable, suspected of appearing and disappearing at will and serving as subversive vectors of revolt. Marronage thus added an extra dimension of uncertainty to already existing fears of slave insurrection. This unstable mixture had striking results, provoking an explosion of discourse about subalterns who were thought to be silenced. Here publicity colluded with fear to destabilize the colonial project.

This might seem like an unusual situation, but I believe it is actually a core phenomenon of colonialism. Marronage was part of a much broader dynamic, one in which subaltern silence took multiple forms with destabilizing results. In each case, silence turned out to have profound affective force. It unsettled colonial normality by inspiring fear, anxiety, and paranoia.

TOXIC CONSPIRACIES

In 1682, three years before the Code Noir, Louis XIV issued a decree to regulate magic, sorcery, and poisoning. This marks the beginning of what would become a long and durable association between these offenses. The new decree notes that divination, magic, and enchantment were already banned by much older laws. The lax enforcement of those laws had drawn many "imposters" of such arts into the realm, however, where they "infect and corrupt the spirit of the Peoples." These imposters initially gain people's credulity with horoscopes, pretend magic, and similar illusions. They then pass from simple curiosities to superstitions, then to impieties and sacrilege, and through a series of ongoing engagements, to the criminal extreme of poison to accomplish their evil predictions. The decree notes that "crimes committed by poison are not only the most detestable and dangerous of all, but also the most difficult to discover." As a result, the law now bans poisoning and the unauthorized use of poisons along with pretending to be a sorcerer or magician. This explicitly includes "not only those [poisons] that cause a prompt and violent death, but also those that cause illness by undermining health bit by bit."[1]

Unlike its contemporary the Code Noir, this law is not explicitly aimed at "policing the colonies" or "*la discipline des nègres*."[2] Instead, it maintains a kind of scrupulous universalism: all persons in the French kingdom engaging in sorcery or poisoning will be punished. However, there may be traces of more specific colonial imaginaries at work there. The royal legislators seemed to be thinking of something rather particular when they drafted this decree. Poisoning, sorcery, and magic do not in themselves have an obvious connection. The law, in contrast, suggests a quite narrow and specific association between them: the same people who pretend to be seers and magicians are found later to incite others to use poison. These seemingly unrelated practices are conducted together and in a specific sequence by people coming from foreign lands. In this light, one might speculate that the implicit reference of the law is not to metropolitan France. Subsequent events suggest that the imposters from foreign countries who engage in sorcery and poisoning are coming specifically into the colonies, and specifically from Africa. In that case, this law would be implicitly enunciating part of the racial imaginary that would become explicit in the Code Noir's policing of the *nègre* three years later. That must remain speculation, however. Exactly what the vision of this law is, whom it targets, or why one would see this issue as worthy of a royal edict is nowhere enunciated.

The reasons for antipoisoning legislation may be suggested in subsequent communiqués from the colonies, however. In 1712, the colonial administrator Vaucresson writes that for a long time, plantation owners had been experiencing costly losses of livestock and slaves through illnesses of unknown cause. In this particular instance, a captain of the militia has lost a horse under suspicious circumstances. Vaucresson says that a number of *nègres* are suspected of having poisoned it. He comments that it is hard to get information to verify these suspicions, and the *nègres* claim to know nothing about it.[3]

These concerns continued in midcentury. The governor general of the French Antilles drafted a proposal to reform the Code Noir in 1741. He targets four activities for harsher punishment: poisoning, maroon slaves (*esclaves marrons*) carrying weapons, theft of weapons by *esclaves*, and *esclave* uprisings. Poisoning is first on this list and receives by far the most extended treatment. It is described here as a property crime committed by slaves upon other slaves or livestock. The governor interprets such poisonings as a way of settling grievances with owners or other slaves. His concern to prohibit them is motivated by the costs that such losses pose to planters.[4]

The use of racial language in these communiqués is worth comment. As I noted in chapter 2, the language referring to enslaved people in the French colonies tracks important transformations in racial thinking and its intertwinement with slavery. We see that already underway in Vaucresson's writing of 1712. The casual usage of the day will eventually coalesce around the complex figure of the *nègre*, leaving *esclave* behind. This idea, when fully formed, will combine both a racialized identity and the idea of enslavement. In 1741, however, this imaginary is not yet fully consolidated. The governor general's use of the abstract legal term *esclave* thus stands as a contrast to Vaucresson's more racialized and colloquial *nègre*. The governor general's letter mimics the earlier language of the Code Noir, not unexpected in the context of proposal to reform it. The contrast between the two reveals some of the fluidity in racial thinking at this time.

Ministerial correspondence about poisoning reappears in 1746. It refers to a recent royal decree on "*la discipline des nègres esclaves*" in the French colonies. (The awkward compound "*nègres esclaves*" again reveals a lack of consolidation in racial thinking.) Here the focus on poisoning is more pointed. The ministers express concerns specifically about poisoners: *nègres empoisonneurs*. The damage wrought by poisoning is again reckoned in the loss of people and animals. A plantation owner from Martinique had allegedly lost over one hundred *nègres* to poison. Another had all of his poultry poisoned and in response killed the *nègrette* and *nègre* thought to be responsible. The letter dryly notes that this punishment seems "a bit harsh for some chickens," but it goes on to say that it is not so much the object of the crime that matters, but the fact that poison was allegedly used to commit it.[5]

The letter is a bit more reflective about accusations of poisoning themselves, however. It details the torture methods that had been used for many years to coerce confessions of poisoning in Saint-Domingue. It also notes the difficulty of obtaining accurate information by these means and relates that they have been controversial as lacking a scientific basis and violating religious law. In short, suspicions of poisoning provoke a strong reaction and occasionally a vicious response, but they are never definitively proven. The testimony on which they are based is unreliable and often contradictory, and the whole question seems clouded in uncertainty.

These ambiguities only became intensified in the following decade. A rash of poisonings was reported in 1757 and 1758. Now, however, the targets included plantation owners and overseers. These were thought to be the result of a conspiracy led by the maroon François Makandal. Makandal's particular talent was reputed to be knowledge of poisons, and he was thought to be moving from plantation to plantation, teaching slaves the art of poisoning and coordinating conspiracies among them. He was eventually captured, interrogated under torture, and executed.

The events surrounding this episode are usually treated as historical fact. Seen through this lens, Makandal was an early revolutionary leader, a predecessor of Ogé, Louverture, and Dessalines, and the poisoning conspiracy is seen as an early uprising that presages the Haitian Revolution. The poisonings are typically portrayed as an organized insurgency, one operating through quiet means to attack the apparatus of oppression. For a moment, however, it is worth taking some distance from these reports. Makandal appears in the archives in a rather ambiguous manner. He is surrounded by mythology, bound up with potent fears of poisoning, and subject to extreme affective reactions.

The first newspaper in Saint-Domingue was still some six years in the future, so news circulated through less formal means. A letter written in Cap Français in June 1758 tells one version of Makandal's story. It was subsequently published as a pamphlet, accompanied by a letter from the recipient and a note from the editor confirming the importance of this account.[6]

The letter recounts that Makandal was maroon for eighteen years, during which time he lived in the mountains, infiltrating neighboring plantations and providing the *nègres* with poisons. Some of them were said to kill immediately, while others are not effective for five or six months but then are always fatal. The poisoners were supposed to be those in whom one had the greatest confidence: coachmen, cooks, domestic servants. Whole dinner parties of fifteen or twenty whites could be poisoned by corrupting the tea or soup. As a result, the letter says, "we are terrified to go visit one another, and we do not know whom to trust, since it is impossible to do without the service of these miserable ones."[7]

The letter goes on to provide a detailed narrative of Makandal's execution that could have come straight from *Discipline and Punish*. Foucault's book opens with a gripping account of the execution of Damiens the regicide for his attempted murder of Louis XV.[8] Damiens was sentenced to a grisly, graphically specified death, one that went far beyond merely taking his life. As *Discipline and Punish* vividly recounts, his execution was so far beyond the realm of practicality that it did not work. The executioners found the sentence impossible to carry out and were forced to fumble along as best they could.

Makandal's execution was simpler in concept but seems to have degenerated into a similar tragicomedy. The *lieutenant criminel* of Le Cap conferred a sentence with vividly Baroque styling, similar to the one visited upon Damiens. Makandal was sentenced to be stripped of everything but his shirt and marched to the front door of the parish church, carrying a torch of burning wax weighing two livres, preceded and followed by signs saying "Seducer, Profaner, Poisoner." There, on his knees, he would confess to his impious and profane acts and ask the pardon of God, the king, and the law. He would then be led to the public square, bound to a stake, and burned alive until his body was reduced to cinders, which would be scattered to the wind.[9]

The published account tells us that local *nègres* were brought to observe the spectacle. However, it recounts that when the fire was lit, Makandal struggled so violently, with strength "far superior to the force of a man," that he managed to wrench himself away from the fire. With the spectacle in danger of failing, the audience of *nègres* was herded away. As they left, they shouted that Makandal "was a sorcerer and incombustible, that no one was capable of stopping him, and that as soon as one tried to seize him he would transform himself into a mosquito." In spite of this invocation of supernatural powers, the executioner did succeed in seizing him, binding his limbs, and throwing him back into the fire. The audience of *nègres* was now brought back to witness the falsification of their claims about Makandal's magical powers, and he succumbed.[10]

In this letter, the entire poisoning episode is blamed on a conspiracy with Jesuits. They are accused of openly protecting the poisoners, absolving them of their sins, and threatening them with eternal damnation if they revealed their accomplices under torture. The Jesuits are suspected of doing much beyond this as well, aiming to assassinate all white colonists in order to expand their political dominance in the colonies.[11] In short, there is ultimately a vast, white, European conspiracy behind the sinister black conspiracy unfolding in the colony. European incitement is blamed for the poisonings, rather than any form of subaltern agency or intention.

The letter reports that Makandal's testimony initiated a rash of further interrogations, in which a striking number of *nègres* admitted to having poisoned whites. It cites twenty-four *nègres* and *négresses esclaves* and three *nègres libres* executed since Makandal's death, with nine or ten more arrested as accomplices. Those who were executed admitted to poisoning thirty to forty whites, including their masters and their families. Others claimed to have killed two hundred to three hundred *nègres*, particularly those who seemed too close to their masters.[12]

Indeed, the archives do contain transcripts of such interrogations.[13] However, those confessions were extracted under a regime of torture similar to the one thought to be so problematic and unreliable in the 1740s.[14] As such, they have all the limitations of any testimony extracted under torture. Suspiciously, they also repeat the idiomatic idea first suggested in the Edict of 1682: that sorcery and poisoning have a deep connection to one another. Together, these two facts suggest an uncomfortable alternative hypothesis about Makandal: that he and others may have been interpellated into the figure of the sorcerer-poisoner through torture. Rather than confessing their wrongdoing, they may simply have repeated an idea suggested to them in interrogation, one that had been fabricated in the 1680s and in circulation ever since. Rather than present the facts of the case, this alternative reading suggests that Makandal and his alleged accomplices were merely repeating back what was demanded of them, some version the colonial commonsense of the day, with its fears of poisoning and its exoticized attitude toward the seeming mystical powers of some slaves.

This presents a gruesome variation on the question of whether the subaltern can speak: the subaltern may be willing to say anything to make the pain stop. It would be a form of coerced speech that is at the same time a form of subaltern silence. This is one in which the subaltern is rendered silent by being forced to speak under great duress. We could call it *silencing through coerced speech*. It is an odd form of what Spivak calls ventriloquism—speaking on behalf of the subaltern. In this case, the subaltern is made to speak on behalf of herself or himself, saying something that is forced rather than spontaneous. Whatever the subaltern may have wanted to say is preempted by the things she or he is made to say.

In any case, questions of the accuracy of these accounts seem much less important than their deeper effects in the public sphere. There was an explosion of discourse on the subject of poisonings in the written records of the time. Here white elites' coexistence with the enslaved takes on new notes of urgency, as the more diffuse anxieties surrounding slavery become focused on more specific fears of injury and death. In this reputed poisoning epidemic, the familiar (food, drink, domestic servants) becomes deadly. One's most trusted surroundings become sources of anxiety. It is precisely the seeming innocence of these quotidian situations, combined with their unknowability, that feeds anxiety.

Such surplus anxiety can be seen in Makandal's spectacular execution. Similarly to Damiens's, this attempt at spectacle seems to have been par for the times. Though separated by an ocean, the two events were only a year apart and shared a common sensibility. For Foucault, Damiens's execution is an attempt to represent sovereign power as an awe-inspiring spectacle. I have argued elsewhere, however, that it actually reveals much more about the anxieties of an increasingly delegitimated royal regime.[15] Similarly, Makandal's execution seems to go far beyond a pageant of sovereignty to reveal powerful colonial anxieties. Its intertwinement of vengeance and spectacle says volumes about the fears that colonial slavery seemed to promulgate among those who controlled it.

IMAGINING HARM

The fears animating these reports of poisoning sound similar in many ways to those arising from marronage. This is likely no accident, but a sign of the way they were interconnected in elite imaginaries of the time. To explore those connections, it is worth thinking in more detail about how fear propagated through the colony's public imagination.

Some one hundred years before these events, Thomas Hobbes defined fear as "*Aversion*, with opinion of *Hurt* from the object."[16] This terse phrase describes an anticipatory state of mind in which the harmful consequences of an absent object are imagined as being present in the future. The harmful thing is not present now, but what would happen if it were? For Hobbes, this psychology lies at the heart of politics. It explains actions and motivations that might otherwise seem excessive. He proposes that fear is a natural result of uncertainty, and it drives preemptive action to avoid the potential effects of that uncertainty. People act in anticipation of harm. Because they have no way to understand what risks they might face in advance, they are forced to anticipate potential harms in an unlimited and open-ended way. In this schema, fear has both a hypothetical and a temporal character. It is based on a what-if imagination of the effects of something not currently present, ramified by an imaginary projection of what might be the case in the future, were that harm to be present.

Contemporary psychology implicitly adopts this view but adds a distinction between fear and anxiety. The *Diagnostic and Statistical Manual* of the American Psychiatric Association specifies that "*fear* is the emotional response to real or perceived imminent threat, whereas *anxiety* is anticipation of future threat."[17] This distinction is rather vague both in temporal terms and with regard to the way a threat is perceived or manifested. Sara Ahmed draws a much more precise distinction between the two. Fear, she says, is a response to a specific object that is not present but approaching. Anxiety, in contrast, is a more vague and diffuse reaction that does not have a specific object. Rather, anxiety fixes on one object after another, as one discovers more and more things about which to be anxious. Such anxiety is characterized precisely by its lack of fixity, its open-ended, interminable search to determine which objects might be the most threatening and worthy of vigilance.[18]

From this perspective, we can see that both fear and anxiety have the structure so insightfully identified by Hobbes. They anticipate the unpleasant consequences of potential future states by imagining them to be counterfactually present. They conjure a visceral, affective response that reveals our repugnance and causes us to avoid them in the future. If the object of concern is ambiguous, one might oscillate between the two: fear when the object is perceived as an actual threat, anxiety when doubts about the exact object of concern come to the fore. When it is not clear whether there really is a threat or which object is threatening, it is easy to see that one could shade back and forth between fear and anxiety. In such cases, epistemic ambiguity puts one in a state of emotional turmoil as well. As Ahmed puts it, "The more we don't know what or who it is we fear *the more the world becomes fearsome*."[19]

Imaginaries of potential harm were a signature characteristic of life in the slave colony. Enslaved people had well-founded fears of arbitrary, unforeseen, and brutal treatment. Though denied public speech on almost every occasion, they voice these fears in trial transcripts such as the ones we have examined in chapter 2. Interrogated about their reasons for fleeing the plantation, some narrate vivid fears of torture and death. These narratives voice a small part of the terror that was slavery for those who were enslaved.

In severity and number, this fear was clearly the most prominent affective phenomenon of colonial slavery. For the moment, however, let us focus on a less obvious aspect: the fears that animated the colonial ruling classes. Ann Laura Stoler has catalogued myriad ways in which such anxieties were woven into the fabric of colonialism. These included administrative anxieties about colonial officials and their families going native, miscegenation and the production of mixed-race children, the presence of European paupers in the colonies, "concubinage" between native women and European men, and other forms of moral deviance.[20] Stoler notes the many senses in which the colonial archives are full of "the anticipatory, the foreseen, and the possible"—"what *might yet be*." She characterizes these as fantasies that threatened the political composure of the colonial administration.[21] They constituted disturbances in the fabric of the normal, prompting perpetual self-examination of the colonial order and the people who ran it.

Something very similar seems to have been happening around marronage and poisoning, but with important differences between them. Marronage was a tangible phenomenon: when an enslaved person ran away, he or she was gone. Because maroons were not immediately present, most worries were lodged at the administrative level, seeking to avoid "property loss" (reckoned in human property) and "disorder" in communities adjacent to maroon activity. This was a distant concern for the most part. In strong contrast, much of the anxiety around poisoning seems to have been rooted in its vague, intangible, yet immediate character. It began as a similarly abstract concern in the early and mid-1700s, registered as the loss of slaves and livestock. Things took a dramatic turn, however, when white colonists began to perceive themselves as potential targets. In this era, anxiety became much more visceral and immediate. The forms of poisoning practiced by slaves were reputed to be largely undetectable until it was too late. They were thought to cause a slow, unnoticeable decline that could not be distinguished from a normal state of affairs. It was said to occur in the domestic sphere, typically through food and drink, in the most intimate and familiar domains of daily life. Household slaves were both the most trusted on the plantation and those with the best access to the master's personal routines.

The anxieties of this era were even further intensified when marronage and poisoning were thought to come together. Fear arose that maroons might be infiltrating plantations, conspiring with compatriots who had not escaped, and spreading harmful knowledge. Marronage had remained an abstract concern until it became intertwined with issues such as poisoning. This explains the extraordinary affect surrounding Makandal. His figure combined fears of marronage and poisoning in a vivid way, bringing the diffusely global issues of colonial rule home to individual households, tables, and meals. As a result, abstract fears of marronage became visceral and individual.

AMBIGUITIES OF SUBALTERN AGENCY

Poisoning was unsettling in large part because it seemed so intentional and meticulously targeted. Accounts of the time portrayed it as carefully planned and executed, frequently a result of an organized conspiracy. Moreover, the poison was supposedly undetectable when ingested and able to kill slowly without the victim's awareness. This implies some knowledge and skill to be carried out successfully. Progressive historians of our own time often repeat such attributions of subaltern collective action, intentionality, and skill when discussing these events.

Attributing agency and intention to subaltern subjects can be tricky, however. One of Spivak's chief criticisms of Foucault is that he romanticizes the "subject-in-oppression."[22] This subject is a compound creation, a product of the very investigation that claims to intervene on its behalf. Here the activist intellectual imagines a disempowered and marginalized subject whose voice has been silenced, then asks how the voice of that subject could be made audible. This is a double move of fabrication: first constructing a disempowered subject, then attempting to restore that subject to full agency. Spivak is critical of the productive character of this endeavor, as well as its assumption of a full but silenced subjectivity. As she characterizes it, the romanticized "subject-in-oppression" is implicitly thought to have a full, collective intentionality, and be capable of acting with unanimity, forethought, and a clear sense of purpose. Subjugation restrains this subject from the full enjoyment of its life and capacities, and it becomes the theorist's self-assigned task to intervene in the situation and remove obstacles on behalf of the oppressed subject.

Following this line of criticism, Spivak might look askance at the way Foucault treats the various subjects of his genealogies. The psychiatrized, the patient, and the delinquent are all portrayed by him as unwitting products of particular regimes of discourse and practice. From Spivak's perspective, such analyses may actually have a constitutive force in producing the very subjects they claim to document. If this is the case, genealogy is not a force of desubjugation so much as an exercise of productive power. It summons a subaltern subject and articulates the truths of its condition. For Spivak, Foucault's genealogies risk fabricating the "subject-in-oppression" while claiming to open up spaces of freedom within the apparatus of power.[23] In so doing, they speak on behalf of voices that otherwise may not exist. As she pointedly asserts, "the ventriloquism of the speaking subaltern is the left intellectual's stock-in-trade."[24]

Whether Foucault is guilty of such charges is a question we need not adjudicate here. Spivak's criticisms are directed not just at him, of course, but at "intellectuals and power" more broadly.[25] She raises a whole host of questions about the extent to which one can speak for the silent, liberate silent voices, or enable the subaltern to speak. This includes issues of how we can discern previously excluded voices and perspectives in the historical record, whether we can find signs of subaltern agency, or write "history from below." In her assessment, many such projects risk further silencing the subaltern in their attempts to solicit speech. Investigations of colonialism and postcoloniality thus run the same dangers of positing the objects of their own investigations. This is the sense in which Spivak's work is quite literally *A Critique of Postcolonial Reason*.

All of this brings us back to the topic of poisoning in Saint-Domingue. It raises a double issue: were the alleged poisoners really poisoners, and were they were acting with insurrectionary intent? While approaching these questions we run headlong into broader issues of subaltern agency, the construction of history, gaps of silence within the archive, gaps of silence between past and present, and what it means to do genealogy in this context.

Spivak would be concerned that any attempt to discern subaltern agency in the poisoning episodes might simply construct those subjectivities and intentions. We might worry, for instance, that Makandal's alleged knowledge of poisons was fabricated out of thin air by people desiring to see him as either a hero or a villain. In such a case, the skill and agency of alleged poisoners might actually be an effect of productive power. A history that claims to recognize and celebrate their achievements could actually be fabricating them. This would be another form of *silencing through imaginary unsilencing*: imagining a subaltern who only *seems* to be silent, but who really exercises considerable, but hidden agency. To compound the problem, such an inquiry might also attribute intentions, thoughts, and words to the fabricated subjects, investing them with an oppression that can then be lifted by the sympathetic intellectual. From Spivak's perspective, this would be yet another productive use of power, a *silencing through ventriloquism*. It would reflect the intellectual's agency and intentions, fabricate the subject of that project, invest the subject with subordinated agency, and then proceed to liberate her or him.

Such criticisms might apply to the historiography of the alleged poisoning incidents. Consider, for instance, two celebrated histories of the Haitian Revolution. C. L. R. James's *The Black Jacobins* is arguably the most famous account of these events. It is a bracing, vivid history centered around the exemplary figure of Toussaint Louverture. Arriving in an era when these events were largely unknown, it sparked a great deal of interest in the Revolution among future historians and postcolonial theorists. Carolyn Fick's *The Making of Haiti* was a similarly agenda-setting attempt to plumb the archives of the Haitian Revolution for subaltern agency and subaltern voices. By elucidating the "revolution from below," she explored the archives in a new way that charted a fresh course for Haitian historiography. Each of these books broke new ground and was an important intervention in the literature of its day. Thus they are worth considering precisely for their innovative, influential, and highly sympathetic treatment of subaltern voices.

James and Fick read the episodes of poisoning that I have discussed as instances of insurgent agency.[26] Each sees poisoning as an important strategy of resistance. In these accounts, Makandal capitalized on his botanical knowledge, charisma, and organizational skills to craft a revolutionary conspiracy. Faced with a daunting system of oppression, he made use of the resources at his disposal to strike a blow at the heart of the white colonial slave state. In both accounts, his actions are read as a carefully organized insurgency and an important precursor to the generalized slave revolts that would follow in 1791. James portrays Makandal as a charismatic mastermind. His portrait is animated with personal details that emphasize Makandal's force of personality and unique leadership abilities. In Fick's account Makandal appears as a highly capable insurgent leader. Her history emphasizes the senses in which poisoning could be a way for enslaved people to pursue their own freedom and exert some control over the conditions of enslavement.

Here we have two revisionist versions of the poisoning episodes. Each emphasizes their insurrectionary importance and places them within the context of the Revolution to follow. They recover subaltern agency and "histories from below" that had been ignored. As we have seen, the figure of Makandal was enormously oversignified in the eighteenth century. It was the imaginary of a devious and quasi-magical maroon leader who masterminded a poisoning plot. As such, "Makandal" stood in for a whole cluster of anxieties in the 1750s: secret conspiracies, scheming servants, food that seizes life with no warning. These new interpretations seek to revalue his image. In place of the eighteenth century's treacherous, conspiratorial Makandal, they put forward Makandal the charismatic leader, a person with special knowledge and the organizational skills to make good use of it.

Such interpretations have the virtue of highlighting forms of knowledge, insight, and agency that might otherwise go unrecognized. They suggest that poisoning may have been a highly effective weapon of the weak for those who did not have access to other forms of resistance. However, we must also recognize the risks of such an approach. Postulating subaltern agency in too fulsome a way is precisely what Spivak warns against. It risks inserting the agenda of the interpreter into the interpretation. Rather than noting the ambiguities of the archive, interpreters might instead present a more unified and coherent story, one that corresponds to their own ideas and interests rather than those of the people under scrutiny. Such impositions may emerge as stories of heroic resistance or self-liberation. They may attribute agency and subjectivity to the oppressed in a fuller sense than the archive warrants, failing to note many ambiguities and paradoxes along the way. In Spivak's estimate, this would be another displacement of subaltern voices, another *silencing through ventriloquism*, a case of the subaltern unable to speak because the interpreter is speaking too loudly on his or her behalf.

Such problems can be seen in the accounts of James and Fick. Each writes about the agency of enslaved people in the vivid mode of an eyewitness narrator. To create this sense of verisimilitude, each must flesh out the narrative with added detail. Those elaborations are not declared as such; they are presented as a fully formed picture of what actually happened. James's account of Makandal is animated with many details that are not found in the archive. Like his biography of Toussaint Louverture, this account operates in a heroic mode that emphasizes Makandal's charismatic leadership. Fick is more scrupulous about historical accuracy. She acknowledges some of the uncertainty entailed in saying exactly what happened around Makandal and is aware of the senses in which this history involves conjecture.[27] However, she reads many of the same sources that I have discussed much more credulously, constructing a unified narrative of events by taking their statements largely at face value. In both cases, the resulting narrative conjures a vivid image of Makandal, painting a picture that takes on a reality, subjectivity, and character all its own.

In many ways, these visions draw on the same image of Makandal that they attempt to displace. They reject treachery in favor of revolutionary insurgency and subaltern agency. In so doing, they maintain the image of an active, intentional political agent. Makandal and the other members of his alleged conspiracy act with purpose and direction; it is only the political valence of that action that changes. Such an interpretation revalues the figure of the insurgent poisoner, but also reproduces it.

Such narratives do not reckon with much that seems complex, dubitable, overly convenient, genre-specific, hyperbolic, or too carefully emplotted in this archive. The result is to impose a sympathetic, well-meaning silence over Makandal and the others. Substantial ambiguities surround these figures, but that is foreclosed when they are refigured as engaging in a carefully planned project. Insurgent conspiracy may in the end be the correct interpretation of their activities, but that image could equally well be the product of our own political moment, a moment that seeks to value subaltern agency and discover the unappreciated intelligence of silenced figures from the past. We may inadvertently inscribe these figures in what David Scott calls a kind of emplotment: a genre-specific organization of characters and events to give them a particular direction.[28] It is a tendentious form of history, one that aims at a particular effect by drawing otherwise scattered events into a coherent narrative. The complexities of the situation are blanched away in favor of a simpler story that avoids ambiguities and assimilates details into a common narrative arc. When that happens, the silenced figure is simply resilenced in a new way.

Similarly, attributions of motive, intention, knowledge, and affect to subaltern subjects can have a silencing effect. If these attributions do not have a clear basis in the archive, they risk reflecting the interpreter's agenda instead of the subaltern's. This is the phenomenon Spivak refers to as ventriloquism: projecting one's voice in place of a silent other's. The dangers in such cases are reckoned as artificial foreclosures of problematic questions about subaltern agency. In such cases, we may not know what the subaltern wanted, intended, knew, or felt, yet those lacunae are covered over and become invisible. Again, determinate conclusions and narratives displace the rich profusion of ambiguity around such events.

VEILED PROBLEMATICS

How, then, could one take a more nuanced approach? The question of Makandal and poisoning raises central issues of subaltern silence. It presents us with the epistemic problem that the archive does not simply record events, but also vivid traces of the biases, preoccupations, and imaginaries of its day. It thus constitutes a veil of problematics that obscures and distorts our view of history. This veil is deeply structured into the archive, which was constituted by colonial elites who narrated events and collected evidence in accordance with their own perceptions. The archival residues of those perspectives and actions in turn condition our understanding of what might have happened. That is to say, our access to such events is mediated through the preoccupations of the day, as seen by those who recorded it. In the case of Makandal, poisoning was a highly fraught problematic that provoked substantial fear and anxiety. As a result, it remains systematically unclear to what extent poisoning really was a significant problem and to what extent it seized attention through a contagion of fear.

The figure of Makandal was highly cathected with anxieties and fears at the time, and he was later subject to an extensive mythologization. An account of 1787 advertised itself as "true history," for instance, and asserted seemingly factual details about Makandal along with fictionalized characters, embroidered descriptions, and fabricated dialogue. Those details were partially plagiarized and further fictionalized in an 1814 account, in which Makandal appears in a rogues' gallery of notorious criminals, including a cannibal.[29] These subsequent accounts portray him as a kind of orientalized conjuror or romantic adventurer, adding a further haze of uncertainty around the events surrounding his conviction and death. Already in the nineteenth century he had become an object of extensive mythologization, one that inflected subsequent perceptions of him in powerful and unseen ways.

It is much too late to desubjugate Makandal by peeling back the layers of meaning that have been attached to him. The best we can do now is to divest the *figures* of Makandal and "*le nègre empoisonneur*" from the centuries of interpretation that have mythologized them. This might restore some of the ambiguity to this situation, which, ironically, may get us closer to the truth of the matter.

Hilliard d'Auberteuil, writing two decades after the poisoning episodes, was dismissive of the idea that Makandal and the others had spiritual powers or special knowledge of exotic poisons. He calls this as an "imbecile belief" of the people of the colony, explaining that an apothecary had died and his possessions were sold at auction, including some arsenic and other dangerous chemicals. They were bought by a *nègre libre*, he says, who passed them on to Makandal, who in turn distributed them to others. (Note the changing racial subtext in 1776: *nègre* by this time implicitly includes the notion of enslavement, so it is necessary to specify when this is *not* the case. Thus the compound *nègre libre*: free *nègre*.) D'Auberteuil says there does not seem to have been any conspiracy to poison all the whites or take over the colony. Rather, this poison was used primarily as an instrument of private vengeance, largely on other *nègres*. He is quite critical of what he sees as an overreaction among whites in the colony, noting that for a long time thereafter, any *nègre* accused of poisoning was burned without proof merely on the basis of the accusation.[30]

This opinion was shared by Pierre de Vaissière, who also rejects the idea that the poisons were some form of secret knowledge in favor of the claim that they were arsenic stolen from apothecaries by their servants.[31] Moreau de Saint-Méry is similarly dismissive. Looking back from the perspective of 1796, he claims that most estimates of the number of poisonings were overstated. The deaths attributed to poisoning were mostly the result of the bad climate or other physical causes, he says. He reports that some of the older Africans claim to possess the art of poisoning, but he is skeptical of those claims. On the other hand, he does offer the somewhat surprising report that a quarter of the *nègres* imported from

Africa were sold after being declared sorcerers at home. This claim, however, appears in a catalogue of what he sees as their strange, magical, and naïve views.[32]

In light of the epistemic cautions I have raised, we might say this: The number and nature of deaths that may have been caused by poisoning are unclear to us, and they were likely very unclear to people at the time as well. Our knowledge of these events is filtered through the available archives; theirs was subject to rumor, suggestion, uncertainty, lack of information, selective attention, and collective anxiety. Problematics like poisoning may have loomed larger in people's minds than was warranted by their objective importance. To make things even more complicated, these two problems are interrelated. The archives through which our knowledge is filtered were created by those very people who were subject to rumor, suggestion, and anxiety. The archives do not resolve problems of subaltern silence, then, so much as compound them. As a result, we cannot read subaltern agency directly out of the archive. Instead, we must approach it with epistemic and interpretive caution. If the subaltern might be speaking, it is important to listen carefully rather than speak on her or his behalf.

The truth about Makandal, poison, and insurgency thus remains suspended in interpretive ambiguity. In contrast, we have much more direct access to the veil of problematics itself, the concerns that so vividly play out in the public spheres of the day and condition our understanding of these other events. As a result, we can conclude with much more confidence that poisoning was an important preoccupation of the era. It was a subject of substantial administrative correspondence and talk. There were no newspapers in Saint-Domingue at the time of Makandal, so this publicity could not yet become fully modern as it would with marronage. Yet much the same dynamic seems to be in play. The possibility of poisoning and attention paid to reported cases was very much a phenomenon of the public spheres of the day. They carried a substantial affective charge and occupied an important place in public consciousness. Subalterns like Makandal may not have been able to speak clearly then or now, but the elites of the colony spoke loudly and clearly about the issues that most preoccupied them. The thought that one's soup may be poisoned was clearly one of those issues.

PROBLEMATIZING PRACTICES

What does all of this tell us about the alleged poisoners? Did they mobilize secret herbal knowledge to mount a coordinated insurgency against the people oppressing them? At best, the facts of the matter seem unclear. As d'Aubertueil suggests, it is debatable whether some special botanical knowledge was at work among Makandal and his allies, or whether they had simply chanced on a supply of lethal chemicals. Further, it would be difficult to determine whether such an act aims at revolution or merely at private score-settling. It was even difficult to determine whether poisoning was occurring and to what extent. Was the subaltern acting, and thereby speaking? That seems to have been a very difficult question to answer at the time, and it remains doubly so today.

What *does* seem clear, however, is the perception among colonial elites that such plots were occurring. As rumors and anecdotes of poisoning accumulated over the decades, the whole idea acquired greater tangibility and weight. Conspiracies began to seem more and more real, and the secret knowledge of poisons was inferred with greater certainty. In their anxious imagination, conspiracies of poisoning became a fearsome menace that could be observed nowhere yet seemed a very present possibility.

Rather than a direct insurgency by means of poison, our attention should be drawn to the very obscurity and ambiguity of this situation, which had a profoundly destabilizing effect. The subaltern in colonial Saint-Domingue was unknown because of silence, both as chosen through marronage and as imposed through enslavement. This unknowability fueled speculation, conjecture, rumor, and anxiety. In short, poisoning had a profoundly problematizing effect. Problematization here was an effect of silence. Uncertainty about poisoning caused a perpetual questioning of the status quo and a problematization of colonial normality. In this sense, poisoning was an actually existing, material problematic with real-world results.

Paradoxically, the subaltern was noticed in these instances *as* silent. Silence took on a positive aspect—it was observed, commented on, it led to suppositions and fears. In this sense, we again see a parallel with marronage. In both cases, the careful suppression and silencing of enslaved people had the ironic effect of constituting them as unknowable and thus a potential threat in the minds of those who silenced them.

These practices of problematization constitute a very different kind of insurgency. It was effected not directly through murder or violence but by means of rumor, anxiety, and paranoia. Planters and colonial administrators sat at the top of a vast system of colonial oppression, but they were not immune to fear. Their imaginaries of harm began as anxieties about property crime, including a loss of property in slaves. Those fears became truly existential, however, when the perceived target of poisoning changed. This new perception—always seemingly uncertain—resulted in a much more vivid sense of anxiety because elites could more tangibly imagine how the violence of the system they had established could be visited upon them. The ability of enslaved people to inspire anxiety *that they might be* poisoners seems to have exercised a considerable disruptive effect. This ability of insinuation undermined the stability and self-confidence of the colonial regime.

The very same features of this situation that inspired anxiety in the eighteenth century remain cloaked in silence today. For instance, we don't know the intentionality of the alleged poisoners, the extent to which being able to inspire fear may have been an active project. Moreau de Saint-Méry says that he thinks some of the Africans claiming to possess the art of poisoning were faking it. Consider the rash of confessions after the Makandal incident from this perspective. What if the slaves confessing to poisoning were only *claiming* arcane knowledge and esoteric powers? This could be a different form of agency: playing on elite fears and paranoia by making unexplained deaths look like a sinister and threatening plot. Similarly, we might wonder whether the enslaved audience members at Makandal's execution called him a sorcerer and incombustible in an attempt to speak the truth as they understood it, or to inspire fear, or just to taunt the executioners as a kind of verbal retaliation. We do not know. This array of possibilities holds out some interesting prospects. Each is a different way of reading the interrogation transcripts around the poisoning incidents: not as faithful reports of actual misdeeds but as misleading claims, efforts at intimidation, and deployments of fear and paranoia. These would be unrecognized forms of subaltern agency that should have been understood as strategy, when they were mistakenly recorded as truthful testimony. Here we would be seeing a knowledge of psychological manipulation rather than a knowledge of poison. This is another enticing and plausible interpretation of the archive. Like the others, however, the possibility that inspiring fear was an active, intentional project remains clouded in ambiguity.

Regardless of the intentions or lack of intentions around the poisoning episodes, their effects were clear enough. Poisoning was very much a public problematic. The fear and anxiety of this situation had a very public, intersubjective character. Rumor, supposition, and hypothesis circulated freely within elite circles on the island, and poisoning was the perfect fodder for idle speculation and fearful reaction.

Public talk about poisoning had effects that were arguably more insidious and pervasive than the actual incidents themselves. A mere report of poisoning created an atmosphere of fear and uncertainty. In this context, anxiety often ran beyond merely anticipating potential harms that might arise from colonial domination. The unknowability of the danger caused a more general problematization, a piling up of fearful discourse, that sometimes took on a life of its own. Here we could speak of a kind of public paranoia.

In this sense, poisoning was interconnected with a number of other disquieting themes in the public discourse of the time. Marronage, already viewed as a dangerous destabilization of the plantation, was additionally feared as a potential vector of conspiracy. Word often had it that escaped slaves would come and go at will and spread dissent on the plantations. Jesuit priests in the colony were also thought to be plotters, and now they were suspected of collusion with the slaves in poisoning as well. The public circulation of all these ideas lent itself to free-form speculation unhindered by clear evidence to the contrary, especially when they seemed to form a self-supporting complex of potential menace.

The affective surplus of these events produced a number of important effects. The anxiety around poisoning, like that surrounding marronage, proliferated discourse and destabilized other currents within the public sphere. It became an incitement to action: not necessarily action focused around clear and intentional goals, but a stimulus to activity in a more generalized sense.[33]

This allows us to see the cases of poisoning with greater epistemic nuance. Here the ambiguities of what might be happening had strong practical effects. It need not be the case that slaves were poisoning their masters in a significant enough way to undermine the structure of colonial oppression. Indeed, this likely would have been impossible. Actual cases of poisoning had dramatic but localized effects. However, the problematizing specter of poison entered colonial public spheres with a strong affective charge. In this manner, it was a gnawing, troubling presence that exercised a kind of insurrectionary effect. Its force was tallied in terms of uncertainty and fear. Our uncertainty now about the archival evidence around these events echoes the uncertainty then by colonial elites about what was happening and how dangerous it might be.

In sum, the reports of poisoning in Saint-Domingue present a double problem of subaltern silence. The events were ambiguous at the time because of the silence of those who were alleged to be committing them. As a result, rumor, paranoia, and the preoccupations of the day spoke much more loudly than the alleged poisoners. Today, the historical facts of this matter are obscured behind those same layers of epistemic ambiguity, but now compounded by their incorporation into the archives. It was not clear at the time whether poisoning was a form of resistance or collective revolt. It remains doubly unclear to us today. This is a paradigmatic example of subaltern silence because that silence was not absolute. Rather, it was a subject of avid discussion, debate, rumor, and supposition. The amplitude of elite discourse merely increased the depth of subaltern silence. The events nonetheless remained uncertain and ambiguous.

For all of these reasons, this does not appear to be a clear-cut case of subaltern agency. That, however, is the political magic of these events. Here subaltern subjects managed to create uncertainty, anxiety, and thus disrupt the normality of colonial life. It was precisely this state of suspension and the inability to say what was going on that was so effective.

As a coda, let us return briefly to the question of what it means to do genealogy in this context. Rather than seeking to reveal episodes of subaltern agency, I have parsed out a genealogy of gaps, ambiguities, and silences. Here we see how genealogy, properly conditioned with a sensitivity to those silences, can reveal a certain kind of insurrection at work. This is not a standard story of subaltern insurgency or the "weapons of the weak," but one with more subtly desubjugating effects. Embedding Makandal and his contemporaries in a history of silence makes us attentive to the subtle dynamics of the time: its problematics, its imaginaries, its tendencies toward anxiety about certain topics and the danger of seeing things that may not really have been there. This history also makes us vividly aware that such problematics find their way into the archives. In other words, this genealogical perspective, seasoned with interpretive insights, provides us with the means to peel back the multiple layers of interpretation that have been lacquered over the poisoning cases.

We see, then, that a properly genealogical treatment does not attempt to ventriloquize, reanimate, or liberate subaltern subjects. Rather, it recontextualizes the archive and restores a proper caution to its interpretation. The result is not to make subaltern subjects like the alleged poisoners speak, nor to speak on their behalf. Rather, it pushes back some of the conditions that have silenced them and restores ambiguities that might allow their voices to emerge.

CHAPTER 4

Phantasmatic Public Spheres

The Paranoid Style in French Colonialism

1770–1802

We are all sufferers from history, but the paranoid is a double sufferer, since he is afflicted not only by the real world, with the rest of us, but by his fantasies as well.
—Richard Hofstadter

I have been busily probing the affective underbelly of French colonialism. So far we have observed the complex play of subordination and resistance in the most mature phase of the Caribbean slave system, one that aimed at not only total physical domination but also subaltern silence. I have been interested in tensions and contradictions inherent in that project, ones that created elite anxieties, openings for subaltern agency, and moments when subordination failed to silence. This chapter pushes the genealogy several decades further, observing the intensification of affect around slavery and its consequences for subaltern silence. What we observe is not simply greater problematization and therefore greater repression, as one might expect. Rather, the intensification of fear produces new identities and new phenomena: a whole host of imagined speaking subjects conspiring in an imagined public sphere. The result is new and unexpected forms of subaltern silence. Although these figures are constructed as subordinate and silent, they nonetheless unsettle the colonial project in unanticipated ways.

INCENDIARY WRITINGS

As the eighteenth century wore on and the Makandal affair receded into memory, the focus of anxieties among colonists in Saint-Domingue shifted as well.

Fears of poisoning occasionally resurfaced, and with them, bursts of discourse problematizing slave discipline and "*la police des colonies*." However, other concerns came to dominate the attention of colonial elites.

The movement to abolish slavery was one of the driving preoccupations of the new publicity of the eighteenth century. Abolitionist thought became a primary theme in the salons, the Republic of Letters, and the rapidly developing print media. The discourse about abolition was multilingual and international, drawing strong ties between British, French, and American abolitionists. These strands developed in parallel and often shared an audience with ideas of popular sovereignty. The Enlightenment's democratic ideals had been heavily euphemized under the ancien régime and now emerged as political doctrines to be reckoned with. Abolition had followed a similar path during the ancien régime, rooting its critique of slavery in ideas of suffering and shared humanity rather than politics. Now, however, it could also take a more pointedly political tack.

The Abbé Raynal's *Histoire philosophique et politique des établissemens et du commerce des européens dans les deux Indes* is a prime example of these tendencies.[1] First published in 1770, it would go through several editions and translations into English and Spanish before the end of the century. Encyclopedic in scope, Raynal's work reached ten volumes in those later editions. The book is an often dry study of the minutiae of colonialism: the different administrative styles of colonial powers, the politics and agricultural conditions of particular colonies, sanguine reports of economic innovations, and so on.

The book also includes some striking abolitionist passages, however. Among these is the one that C. L. R. James would claim as Toussaint Louverture's inspiration to become a revolutionary leader: "The *nègres* lack only a leader courageous enough to guide them to vengeance and carnage. Where is he, this great man, whom nature owes to its vexed, oppressed, and tormented children? Where is he? He will appear, without doubt, he will reveal himself, he will raise the sacred standard of liberty. This venerable signal will gather his companions in misfortune around him. More impetuous than the torrents, they will leave everywhere the indelible traces of their just resentment."[2]

Histoire des deux Indes typifies many ideals of free discourse and the open exchange of ideas. Though attributed to Raynal, it was a collaboratively authored document, cobbled together from contributions of several different writers.[3] Much of it seems to have emerged directly out of discussions in the salon that Raynal frequented.[4] He often did little more than supply transitions between the various pieces, so there are frequently jarring shifts in tone and topic. In this sense, the book captures the spirit of the new public spheres of its day while also constituting a kind of internal public sphere within its own pages. It shares this character with the other great collaborative publishing venture of the time, the *Encyclopédie*. The primary editor of the *Encyclopédie* was Denis Diderot, also a principal contributor to *Histoire des deux Indes*—and likely the author of the passage I have just quoted.[5]

Abolition was what David Brion Davis has called "one of the many harmless philanthropic fashions of the late Enlightenment."[6] The "philanthropy" to which he refers was a broad ethos that spanned many individual topics, chiefly focusing on public-minded virtue and love of humanity with a philosophical bent. This backgrounded the Abbé Gabriel-François Coyer's reference to "purity of heart and a universal philanthropy," for instance, and de la Coste's description of falling into a "happy philanthropy" in which an equilibrium of humors raised his moral affections to an expansive benevolence.[7] Like these other enlightened entertainments, Davis sees abolition as a "harmless fashion" because it proliferated a great deal of well-intentioned discourse without actually seeming to change anything.

Although initially broad in scope, "philanthropy" eventually became a specific synonym for abolitionism. In this context it had a biting, satirical edge. Abolition was caricatured as a weak-minded universalism that would wreak havoc on the lucrative colonial economy. This image plays on the increased attention to Enlightenment universalism in general, one that blossomed dramatically in the years of the French and Haitian Revolutions (figure 4.1). It likely reflects the enormous politicization of Enlightenment ideals under the force of political events, both in France and the colonies.

The primary target of attacks on philanthropy was the Société des Amis des Noirs (Society of the Friends of Blacks; note the implicit racial politics in this name, a refusal of the by now derogatory *nègre* in favor of the more neutral *noir*). It was founded in 1788 by Jacques-Pierre Brissot, himself a pivotal figure in the public spheres of the day. Brissot had also founded an influential political journal, *Le patriote françois*, in May 1789, and was a firm believer in public debate and a free press.[8] If that were not enough, he led the liberal-constitutionalist faction of the French National Assembly, often called the Girondins. The Société des Amis des Noirs had many members who were also members of the National Assembly, and thus had unique political traction for its cause.

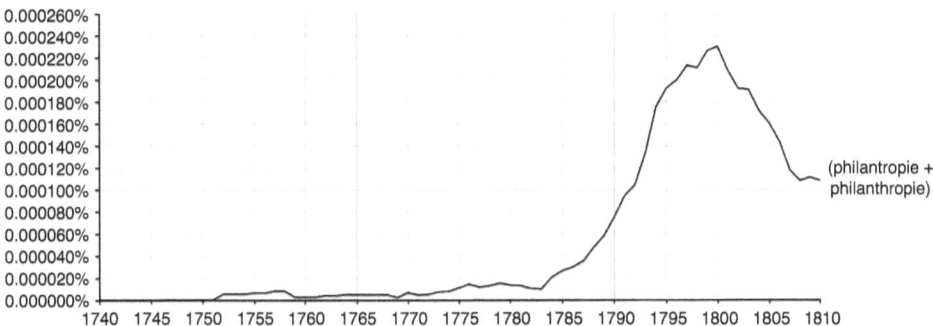

Figure 4.1 Published frequency of "philanthropy" in two variant spellings (*philantropie, philanthropie*) as a percentage of all words published in French, 1740–1810. Google French dataset of 2012, courtesy of Google Labs.

Because of their political power, the Amis des Noirs were singled out for particular abuse. Wealthy white planters organized a countervailing group in Paris, the Club Massiac, as an oppositional base for fighting abolition. They also channeled their energies into a torrent of screeds, pamphlets, and virulent attacks on the Amis des Noirs. In addition, the planters were influential in creating the Committee on the Colonies in the National Assembly, which functioned as a kind of containment device for abolitionism. It allowed them to shunt arguments for abolition out of the main Assembly and into committee, where they could be more quietly disposed of.

This was a striking development. Like the measures of the Code Noir of 1685, it amounted to a *silencing through law*. However, much had changed in the century from 1685 to 1790. Whereas the Code Noir directly silenced individuals by prohibiting certain forms of conduct, the Committee on the Colonies aimed to silence an entire discursive domain by containing it and decoupling it from broader public spheres. This was a more abstract, aggregate approach to enacting silence: it conceptualized discourse as inchoate flows of publicity, rather than as the individual utterances of individual people. It amounted to a whole new epistemology within the strategy of silencing through law.

The papers of the Committee on the Colonies are still held by the French National Archives, and they constitute one of the primary bases of my research for this book.[9] They are testament to a particular kind of silence: a rich trove of written and printed documents that were contained, removed from public debate, and effectively buried in the archives.

A SHIFTING LANDSCAPE OF FEAR

Abolition was not merely a subject of enlightened discourse and vitriol in the public sphere. It had much deeper resonances. Colonial elites began to imagine the effects of abolitionism if it were ever to reach the colonies. Their fear was that abolitionist ideas could cross over from harmless philanthropic fashion to open incitement. Here the anxiety was not so much that slavery might be abolished through legislation, but that abolitionist doctrine could directly incite slave revolts. This was manifested specifically in the fear that the transatlantic public sphere already connecting abolitionists like Thomas Clarkson in England, Jacques-Pierre Brissot in France, and Benjamin Franklin in the United States might reach the Caribbean as well. Attacks on *"philanthropie"* became more urgent as abolitionism became a more serious political force in the 1780s. In this context, it was portrayed as a pernicious doctrine that could spell disaster for the great commercial enterprise of colonial slavery.

Such fears are manifest, for instance, in an open letter written to the National Assembly in 1789. Signed by eighty-four colonial property owners from Bordeaux, the letter was printed for mass circulation in the format of the revolutionary pamphlets also circulating at that time. It clearly aimed at a similar purpose: using the new tools of the print public sphere to mobilize public opinion against abolition. Writing two years before the slave uprisings started in earnest, comfortably situated in Bordeaux at a distance of several thousand miles from Saint-Domingue, the authors describe themselves as "surrounded by the cruelest fear," at "the moment of losing all of our goods," "shaking at the deplorable fate of our families, of our compatriots, menaced like us in their property, in their lives, in their honor." They are "currently terror-stricken by the destructive plagues hovering above their heads," "menaced by fire, iron, poison, afflicted by the terrible future that presents itself to them." Their request of the National Assembly is to be relieved of the "anguish and fears that all of France shares" with them.[10]

Philanthropists are the cause of these afflictions: "Incendiary writings announce every day, from all parts of the colony, that the disorders are ready to begin again. The horrible plot of these monsters is essentially to destroy all the whites by fire, iron, poison, and to spare only our wives to make them the instrument of their pleasures and their servants."[11]

This passage focuses considerable venom on the "incendiary writings" of philanthropists. It does not detail exactly what in those writings is so threatening. It does offer one specific hint about their content, however. The "sole and true cause" of these problems is alleged to be the abuse of the declaration of the rights of man, specifically its extension to blacks (*noirs*).[12] What exactly this means, however, is not given further elaboration. It is consistent with many invocations of "the rights of man" during this time, in which they are cited for the aura of power that they seem to project, with no specific detail about what such rights might actually be. Like other warnings about philanthropy and the Amis des Noirs, the rhetoric is hot, but details are scarce.

The claim that abolitionist writings are "incendiary" remains a metaphor at this point, but it is a prophetic one. In 1791, fire would become the principal means of insurgency during the initial waves of slave revolt. Here, however, two years before the beginning of those uprisings, fire is named along with guns, swords, knives, and poison as the means of enacting philanthropist plots against the whites. This marks a shift from fear of poisoning to fear of generalized insurrection. Poison was still feared, but it now appeared alongside more graphic and violent means of disorder. The sources of anxiety had changed, the landscape of fear was shifting, and imaginaries of potential harm had taken new form.

The municipal officers of Le Havre issued a similar pamphlet in December 1789. Although less melodramatic than the Bordelaise letter, its content was quite similar. Cherished masters have been turned into tyrants in the eyes of the blacks (*noirs*). They face new perils every day and have been obliged to take violent measures to prevent insurrections. The cause of all of this is abolitionist writings. The colonists are "convinced that the spirit of insubordination and revolt that reigns among their *nègres* has its origin only in the multiplied writings and exaggerated declamations of the pretended friends of the blacks; persuaded that this spirit could only be supported by the odious machinations of the enemies of the regeneration of France."[13] Again, the colonies are poised on the edge of disaster, and it is a result of outside agitation and philanthropist incitement from Europe.

Here we see a new set of fears that share features in common with the fear of poisonings earlier in the century. Suspected cases of poisoning were frequently attributed to some secret plot. Maroon slaves were thought to infiltrate plantations and incite trusted servants to murder. Jesuit priests were suspected of conspiring with them, encouraging and facilitating their activities. This was imagined as a matter of quiet whispering from person to person: maroons snuck into the plantations and taught the secrets of poison; Jesuits promised absolution to slaves who used it and damnation to those who did not.

Philanthropy seemed to be a similar vector of danger. Abolitionists now occupied the role of outside agitator. Like Jesuits, they were seen as an international network of talk and association that knew no national boundaries nor racial loyalties and had secret subversive designs. Their conspiracies still whispered, but they now aimed at generalized uprising and wholesale violence. This new imaginary traded above all on the expanded means of publicity available to abolitionists, some three decades after the poisoning episodes. They were based in metropolitan France with its vast revolutionary press and could reach many slaves at once through pamphlets and other publications. Thus elite fears concentrated not simply on the incendiary whispering or rumors of philanthropists, but also on their incendiary *writings*. This was a fear of a thoroughly modernized public sphere.

These fears had a profoundly epistemic dimension. The inherent unknowability of conspiracy seemed to provoke considerable concern. As in the poisoning episodes, colonial elites feared a suspected but unknown association of people dedicated bringing about some bad result. Conspiracies are always hidden; that is a crucial aspect of their threatening character. Now, however, the conspiracy was vastly expanded and extended across two continents.

There were additional objects of fear in both poisoning and abolitionism, however. In the case of poison, the object that inflicted harm was itself unknowable. Poison was a specific, threatening object, but one whose presence could not be detected. Very tangible harms were observed: the unexplained deaths of livestock, slaves, and fellow slaveowners. Those events were explained by the presence of a lethal chemical that would kill slowly without being noticed. In the case of abolitionism, the object was similarly unknowable, but also vaguer. It was a hypothesized domain of publicity extending from abolitionists to slaves. Here the object that might inflict harm was so ephemeral that it could not be observed or verified, nor could its effects be directly noted. It was a specter of people talking to one another, a fear of communication, dialogue, and agreement. Because it could not be observed and its possible effects were only imagined, this object was highly speculative and ambiguous. It may in fact have been imagined out of whole cloth. It thereby provoked even more anxiety.

Here we arrive at the heart of what was so unnerving about suspicions of philanthropist infiltrators. When an object is unknowable and thought to be harmful, it provokes open-ended, chafing anxiety. There is a deep and inherent tension in this situation: a harm is suspected but cannot be verified or denied, faced or assessed. By definition the object of anxiety is absent but could potentially become present. The more vague, intangible, and ambiguous the object, the more it provokes a gnawing sense of potential harm and hyperalertness.

Such experiences fit well with Sara Ahmed's description of anxiety that we discussed in chapter 3. Those tendencies are even further accentuated here, however, in ways reminiscent of Richard Hofstadter's celebrated analysis of the "paranoid tendencies" in American culture. They are fears that go public, taking on a broader social, cultural, and self-sustaining character. Hofstadter notes the role of conspiracy in such experiences. Reviewing episodes of American paranoia in the nineteenth century, he cites fears of secret infiltrators in the United States: Bavarian Illuminati, Freemasons, and indeed Jesuits. The latter were said to be concealed as wandering "puppet show men, dancing masters, music teachers, peddlers of images and ornaments, barrel organ players, and similar practitioners."[14] Like the philanthropists feared to be operating in Saint-Domingue, these practitioners combined invisibility and malign intent in a particularly threatening way.

Hofstadter notes the effects of the mass media in promoting the contagious character of paranoid tendencies.[15] Publicity intensifies one's imagination and propagates anxiety about the objects imagined. This suggests an important difference between poisoning and abolition. In the early years of fear about poisoning, there was no mass media in the French colonies. The first newspaper in Saint-Domingue did not go into print until a decade after Makandal's alleged poisoning conspiracy. The metropolitan news media was still in relative infancy as well. As a result, such anxieties tended to travel a more private route through rumor, correspondence, and written accounts.

It is a striking sign of new developments, then, that the minister of colonies wrote a letter to the Duc de Choiseul, the French foreign minister, in 1767, sending him an article from a Mainz newspaper.[16] The article claimed that a significant amount of Saint-Domingan coffee had been poisoned by slaves, supposedly with a special kind of poison that only manifested itself when the coffee was roasted and brewed. Afraid of the panic that such an article might cause, the minister asked Choiseul to intervene and persuade the newspaper to retract the article. Here we see early recognition of the potential of mass media to stoke fear, anxiety, and paranoia.

These insights were only confirmed as the landscape of fear was taken over by new specters later in the century. Suppositions about philanthropy sometimes tore loose from reality, crossing into an imagination of harms that may never have existed. This kind of paranoia goes beyond fear and anxiety as an imaginative exercise in which seemingly mundane events are interpreted as part of a much larger, more threatening phenomenon. Such a self-created complex forms a system of delusions that takes on greater and greater weight as more observations are found to correspond to it. At this point, it becomes a totalizing, self-confirming hypothesis, in which the preponderance of evidence seems only further to confirm interpretations that support the same hypothesis. Such interpretations are often made to the exclusion of other possibilities and explanations. At this point, the multiplication of fear leads to hypervigilance and overwhelming suspicion.[17] We might characterize this orientation, with thanks to Hofstadter, as "the paranoid style in French colonialism."

There is, of course, some danger in using a contemporary psychological concept such as paranoia to characterize eighteenth-century social phenomena. The danger lies in anachronism: mapping contemporary psychological categories back onto the past in a distorting manner. To avoid this, we must pay close genealogical attention to what it was possible to feel in the eighteenth century. The fact that Thomas Hobbes describes "feare" in terms of anticipation and ambiguity provides us with great assurance that this form of affect was available as early as 1651. Similarly, the term "paranoia" was actually used in the eighteenth century.[18] It had a more general meaning at the time, but the specific characteristics that we now associate with paranoia seem to have been included there as well. In addition, an obsession with conspiracy was a hallmark of the revolutionary period in both France and the United States.[19] Hofstadter is clear that the "paranoid tendencies" he diagnoses are social, cultural, and political phenomena rather than individual pathologies. They are collective dispositions rather than individual ones. The paranoid tendencies of colonial Saint-Domingue seemed to have similar features. They were collectively shared orientations that were propagated through publicity.

SPECTERS OF PUBLICITY

Eve Kosofsky Sedgwick characterizes paranoia as above all *anticipatory*, which means that it seeks to avoid "bad surprises." A "bad surprise" is any harm that was not adequately foreseen and prepared for in advance. Because of its anticipatory character, paranoia exhibits a future-oriented vigilance, a need to seek out potential harms and avoid them now. This gives it a complex temporality, one that "burrows both backward and forward." Sedgwick unpacks this as the idea that "there must be no bad surprises, and because learning of the possibility of a bad surprise would itself constitute a bad surprise, paranoia requires that bad news be always already known." It maintains a future-oriented vigilance so thoroughgoing that any uncertainties become sources of anxiety for the bad surprises they might conceal.[20]

Noting this hyperalertness toward the future, Sedgwick also says that paranoia is built around an imperative of exposure. It is strongly oriented toward having the truth finally be known. The hypothetical existence of some object of fear is what provokes anxiety. Oddly, confirming one's fears seems to dispel them. Fear was built on uncertainty; exposure of the truth brings certainty and ends fear. As a result, Sedgwick theorizes paranoia as a kind of critical capacity, one that drives toward the exposure of new truths.[21]

Sedgwick's observations are astute insofar as paranoia does constitute a will to know, a drive to discover what seems to be hidden. Indeed, this seems to be a core component of the paranoid's obsession. However, Sedgwick misses two key aspects of this phenomenon that seriously undercut its critical capacities. First, the drives that push paranoia forward are not necessarily guided by "truths" in any stable, useful way. Rather, they seek whatever knowledge might have a therapeutic effect on the paranoid's anxious mind. The forms of exposure and knowledge sought by the paranoid are strictly oriented towards release of fear and doubt. They remain narrowly within the ambit of whatever might be worrying the paranoid—however irrelevant, biased, subjective, or detached from reality that object of fear might be. The paranoid tries to pile up confirming evidence in an effort to dispel uncertainty and fear. Thus paranoia does not drive toward exposure of the truth in any straightforward way. Rather, it drives toward therapeutic effect—a relief of symptoms. It is thus prone to inherent distortion and does not constitute critical knowledge, so much as a kind of anxious, insatiable wish fulfillment. The paranoid drive to know tells us a great deal about the mind of the paranoid, but little that is reliable or useful about the world.

Second, Sedgwick fails to notice the substantial ambivalence of the paranoid's will to know. Even while pursing evidence that might dispel uncertainty by confirming her fears, the paranoid's worst fear is the fear of being right. Insofar as there seems to be something to fear, some immanent disaster, the actualization of the object of fear is highly undesirable precisely because... it is feared. As a result, the paranoid wants above all to be wrong. However, being wrong also carries with it the cost of having baseless anxieties, of being on high alert for things that turn out not to be important, therefore of seeming to worry needlessly and furnishing a spectacle of poor psychic calibration. In some odd sense, then, the paranoid would *also* like her or his overbearing anxiety to be appropriate and correct. This is the dilemma of paranoia: being right and being wrong are each simultaneously attractive and undesirable.

As a result, paranoia is plagued by a profound ambivalence. It is by definition a state of uncertainty, one in which fear preys on the psyche as possible outcomes are anticipated and dreaded. At the same time, both of the possible exits from this situation, confirmation and disconfirmation, carry costs and have undesirable aspects. Thus the uncertainty of paranoia is also a state of suspension between two bad alternatives. It does indeed center around a will to know, a will to confirm, and thus a will to forge ahead and end the tensions created by uncertainty. However, there is profound ambivalence about that goal. The paranoid finds both confirmation and disconfirmation problematic in a way that uncertainty is not. Thus all possibilities are painful and undesirable, there is no good path, and the paranoid is suspended in a miasma of bad options. In short, paranoia is fundamentally and painfully ambivalent.

Paranoia's ambivalence leads to a piling up of intense mental and psychic activity without resolution. The result is continual, ongoing attention to the object of fear, a perpetual consideration of its likelihood of existence and its potential effects if those fears are realized. Paranoia's ambivalence holds all of this in suspension, so that the object of fear becomes more and more tangible as time goes on. This only intensifies the fear, while conjuring previously imaginary objects into more and more durable existence. The result is a continual, ongoing provocation. As this happens, the obsession and intense processing of paranoia can spill over into various forms of reaction. Paranoia can thus express itself in an incitement to discourse and/or practice.[22]

We see all of this play out in colonial Saint-Domingue. French planters and colonial elites had the grim satisfaction of having been right to worry. In fact, "incendiary writings" were the least of their problems. Starting in the summer of 1791, a series of well-organized slave insurrections spread into a mass revolt. Much of the colony went up in flames. These events, we recognize in retrospect, were the start of the Haitian Revolution.

A side effect of the slave revolts was a massive incitement to discourse about "philanthropy." It revealed the chafing fear and paranoia that had been simmering just below the surface. The slave revolts seemed to confirm the worst fears of their victims. After the uprising started in earnest, there were waves of interrogations and recriminations that repeated what seemed to have already been the common sense: that philanthropists had been destabilizing the colony and fomenting insurrection. Here the pointed questions of investigators focused again and again on confirming this hypothesis as something that had been true all along. This need for psychic consolation was so strong that all other evidence and hypotheses—the slaves organized themselves and took matters into their own hands, for instance—were more or less ignored. We can read all of this as a manifestation of the paranoid's consolation in at least having been right about the need for vigilance against philanthropist infiltrators. This need to be justified in one's paranoia confirms the ambivalence and psychic ferment that had been stewing for many years before.

In 1791, for instance, the newspaper *Moniteur général de Saint-Domingue* devoted the entire front page of its first edition to a poem, "Ode à la philantropie."[23] This excerpt is typical of the poem's invective:

> What a crowd of rebels
> Rapturously close to carnage;
> The Slave, in his cruel hands,
> Carries fire and death.
> Stop, parricidal tool;
> An invisible and perfidious arm
> leads you to a frightful reversal;
> And the only fruit of so many crimes,
> Will be to mourn your victims
> Under the weight of your new chains.

> Ferocious and bloody mania,
> I recognize you by your traits;
> Under the name philosophy...

Here the rhetoric is quite similar to the indictments of philanthropy before the slave revolts began. The uprisings were tangible and ferocious by 1791, but the presence of philanthropy still remained shadowy. It was "an invisible and perfidious arm" that was recognized by its traits rather than seen outright. Colonial elites were apparently correct in their fear of a generalized uprising, but they only took that as more confirming evidence of their theory that philanthropy was its ultimate cause.

Another such example appears in the manuscript account of a white creole fleeing the slave uprisings. He tells the story of an encounter with a black man whose military dress suggested he might be a leader of the slave revolts. The story is a fraught one. The author gives chase, the man turns and attempts to fire but his powder is damp, the author draws his sword, the man supplicates and flatters him, the author stands down, the man attempts to shoot him again but misses, nearby soldiers intervene, the man resorts again to flattery, the soldiers bind him to a tree, and before he is shot the black man alternates between singing, joking, reviling, and mocking the whites.

After his execution, his possessions are searched:

> We found in one of his pockets pamphlets printed in France, filled with commonplaces about the Rights of Man and the Sacred Revolution; in his vest was a large packet of tinder and phosphate of lime. On his chest he had a little sack full of hair, herbs, and bits of bone, which they call a fetish; with this, they expect to be sheltered from all danger; and it was, no doubt, because of this amulet, that our man had the intrepidity which the philosophers call Stoicism.[24]

This vignette is widely quoted in contemporary literature on the Haitian Revolution and is usually taken to illustrate the connection between abolitionist pamphlets and revolutionary slaves. Indeed, it provides a picture-perfect illustration of the idea that the doctrines of philanthropy inspired the slave revolt. The three items found in the rebel's pocket easily symbolize this: the Rights of Man provide incitement and motive; the African fetish provides spiritual fortitude;

and tinder and phosphate provide the means, fire being the primary weapon of the early revolts.

However, there is much here that strains credulity. I have quoted this anecdote as it always appears in the literature. The rest of the story is always left out: the drama and intrigue of the encounter, the vivid but bizarre characterization of the black man as wearing "regalia," at times charming, at other times wily, treacherous, impudent, or abusive; in the end, rather incongruously pronounced stoic. As I have noted elsewhere, the items allegedly discovered in the rebel's pocket seem overly convenient in their symbolism.[25]

In spite of all that, this story is typically taken as a faithful report.[26] However, that interpretation ignores the circumstances I have already discussed: the substantial paranoia about philanthropist infiltrators that preceded the revolution, the hostility leveled against abolitionists once the revolution started, the psychic payoff of having been right about the danger, now seemingly confirmed in retrospect. All of this seems to play out in the story of the captured revolutionary. Its symbolism is too neat and tidy; its scapegoating too convenient.

Reports of slaves having direct access to the principal tracts of abolitionism are rare. The fears of colonial planters usually focused on less tangible lines of communication between abolitionists and slaves. Félix Carteau's *Soirées bermudiennes* (Bermuda Nights) is a rich confection of conspiracy theory and triumphal paranoia. Its subtitle, "Conversations about the Events that Brought About the Ruin of the French Part of the Island St.-Domingue," clearly stakes out Carteau's position. The book narrates his flight during the early stages of the revolution, fuming about the effects of infiltrators among slaves in the colony. His conspiracy theory is a bit more complex than most, however. He believes that it was royalists, particularly members of the military, who first began inciting the slaves (*esclaves, Noirs, Nègres*) to violence. They were acting in hostility against Jacobins for overthrowing the monarchy, and against mixed-race people (*Mulâtres*), whom they saw as hostile to whites (*Blancs*). This was done out of spite, a much stronger motive than the "philosophical maxims" of the Amis des Noirs. Carteau particularly singles out three officers of the French military in Le Cap, including a lieutenant colonel named Cambefort. We will hear more about Cambefort and the accusations against him in chapter 5. Even though Carteau cites no direct evidence, he claims his accusations are based on a variety of witnesses, reports, and plausible inferences.[27]

Carteau's racial ontology is worth comment. It is an early nineteenth-century development of the racial thinking that we have tracked in earlier eras. As we see, Carteau capitalizes racial terms (though he also capitalizes *Colonie* and *Militaires*). Since *esclave* is not capitalized, it seems to have a different racial status. It would be premature to say that it is unraced, but it seems at least differently raced. Carteau's use of *Mulâtre* is somewhat polemic, though not at all unusual for a white colonist. The mixed-race people of the French colonies preferred to call themselves *gens de couleur*, people of color. Most strikingly, Carteau alternates freely between multiple terms for black insurgents. He seems to prefer *Nègre* when talking about daily peacetime life and *esclave* or *Noir* when referring to insurgency. Thus Carteau seems to imagine the figure of the *nègre* as fully integrating both black and slave in times of peace, but that figure becomes problematized and requires more careful specification during uprising: an uprising of *esclaves*, or a revolt of the *Noirs* against the *Blancs*.

Having pinned the direct causes of the revolts on French soldiers, Carteau still sees the "infernal sect" of the Amis des Noirs as the heart of the problem. He refers to their doctrines as a "democratism" that causes a kind of moral rot, "the gangrene of a false and partial philanthropy, that so corrupted the intellect" of the entire empire.[28] He says that the Amis acted obliquely at the beginning of the uprising, inciting Mulâtres against the royalists. The result was to "humiliate, persecute, and destroy those same *Blancs*; plunder their fortune, uproot their lives, overthrow their towns and burn their edifices and houses." Once the Mulâtres have served their purpose in this venture, the Amis will drop them, and "you will see this perfidious sect finally raise its abominable mask and bring about, along with the general liberty of the *esclaves*, the complete *annihilation* of the colony."[29]

Carteau accuses the Amis of contributing to the uprisings by distributing considerable numbers of pamphlets and engravings among the slaves. He claims to have seen Raynal's work and that of others. He also notes, "Few *esclaves* knew how to read, but it only took one in the workshop who could read to the others when the conspiracy was forming to reveal how much protest there was in France, and how many people there wanted them to throw off the harsh yoke of their pitiless masters."

Besides, he says, most of the Mulâtres and *Nègres libres* (free *nègres*) had learned to read, and they undoubtedly did so for the Noirs (blacks) on such occasions. And then there were images: "As for the engravings, it was only necessary to open one's eyes to understand the interpretation of the subject...." All of this is obvious enough, he claims, and who could have done it except the Amis? Even though he credits the French military with the most active role in the slave revolt, his greatest ire is directed against the Amis, to whom he refers most bitingly as the "society of negrophiles."[30]

Carteau singles out sailors as the actual vectors of distribution for these materials. The sailors, he says, are "nothing but agents of the negrophiles." He claims that they secretly sell abolitionist books and engravings to the slaves. This is particularly true of some officers from Bordeaux who are "imbued with the current fashion of philanthropy, and who profess it quite openly." However, rank and file sailors contribute greatly to the problem as well. They work side by side with slaves in the ports, loading and unloading ships. They are also "nourished by the flaming maxims of the clubs," and as a result, they spread revolutionary doctrines. "One couldn't utter remarks more incendiary and murderous than those that I've heard sometimes from those men," Carteau says. In all of the large revolts, he claims, one always finds some white populist killed on the battlefield or fleeing in retreat. All of this, he says, is a "boiling school of insurrection."[31]

In this regard, Carteau is suspicious not just of captains and sailors but of the clergy as well. He lists a number who were "secret emissaries or conspirators" with the insurgents: the Abbé Osmond, who disappeared around the time of the slave insurgents' attack on Rocou's camp. The Abbé Leblondin, who arrived from France with no known purpose. Father Sulpice, who "came and went freely among the insurgents." The "execrable Abbé Delahaye, *curé* of Dondon, the most ardent apostle of the liberty of the *Noirs*," who is alleged to have written a pro-abolition newspaper under the Jacobin government. And the president of the second Colonial Assembly, who supposedly was seen going back and forth to a plantation owned by "mixed bloods" (*Sang-mêlés*) that was near another plantation where the mass insurrection began.[32]

Writing some eleven years after the start of the uprising, Carteau still locates its origins in a "boiling school of insurrection." What he imagines is not merely quietly subversive conversations on the wharves, however, but a diffuse, far-flung, and potent public sphere. It extends from France to the Caribbean, spreading the doctrines of abolition and revolutionary democracy. Those ideas are propagated in dense but largely hidden connections between slaves and sympathetic whites. They are philanthropist infiltrators who covertly spread the gospel of equality and freedom in the colonies. Or so we have it from Carteau. It is never clear that any such incitement occurred, or even that the relations between these groups had anything like the intimacy they were imagined to have. However, the vehemence of his accusations indicates something of the psychic charge that this specter carried.

In this sense, Carteau's remark that abolitionist engravings can incite people to violence is an interesting one. If true, it would tell us some important things about the interconnections between the relatively elite and privileged discourse of European abolitionists and the covert communications of colonial subalterns. Image-making could be an important way to bridge the gaps of language and understanding between these groups, joining public spheres that would otherwise remain quite separate.

There are relatively few abolitionist engravings prior to the 1790s, but they did have a large impact in the European public spheres of the time. The most widely known example is the celebrated emblem of the Amis des Noirs (figure 4.2). It featured a supplicant slave in chains, accompanied by the legend *"ne suis-je pas ton frère?"*–"am I not your brother?" The emblem was adapted from one devised by English abolitionists in 1787. It was widely diffused in England, and copies were also sent to the United States, earning the praise of, among others, Benjamin Franklin. It became a fashionable way for people to display their enlightened sympathies. The Wedgwood Studio produced a ceramic version, and the emblem adorned snuffboxes and other luxury items.[33] Indeed, the propagation of this image traces the transatlantic public spheres that caused people like Carteau so much concern.

The question, however, is whether such an image might have had the effect he so feared on colonial slaves. The emblem certainly made a powerful statement with its combination of pathos and universal brotherhood. That statement was made not simply by the image itself, however. Rather, its impact derived from the synergy of image and text. The pathos of the figure is given political and philosophical import by the caption citing brotherhood and universal humanity. Here "merely opening one's eyes" would not be enough to create comprehension. French literacy and important cultural information about brotherhood as a metaphor of equality would be required to truly grasp its meaning.

Another image with great impact was Sir William Elford's *Plan of an African Ship's Lower Deck with Negroes in the Proportion of Not Quite One to a Ton* (figure 4.3). It is a potent, minimalist representation of the horribly cramped conditions aboard a slave ship. It shows small, schematic human figures packed side by side

Phantasmatic Public Spheres   117

Figure 4.2 *Ne suis-je pas ton frere?* Title page vignette of Société des Amis des Noirs, *Adresse a l'Assemblée Nationale* (Paris: Potier de Lille, 1790). Library Company of Philadelphia, 1979.O.6.

in a ship's hold. It is not a realist depiction of those conditions but a visceral evocation of their psychological and physical impact.

This engraving was conceived in 1787 by the Plymouth Committee of the Society for Effecting the Abolition of the Slave Trade in England. It was designed to have a powerful impact on the public imagination. Due to the force of its elegantly crafted combination of minimalism and abstraction, it largely succeeded in this goal. The image was widely reprinted in England, France, and the United States.[34] It is a brilliant example of the propagation of images through the abolitionist public sphere, and the complex network of discourse and representation about abolition that connected England, France, and the Americas at this time.

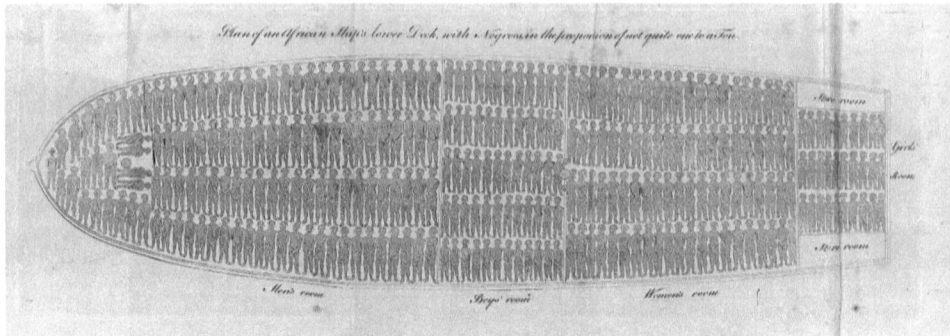

Figure 4.3 Sir William Elford, *Plan of an African Ship's Lower Deck...*, reprinted in *The American Museum; or, Universal Magazine*, May 1789, foldout plate before p. 429. Beinecke Rare Book and Manuscript Library, Yale University.

Cheryl Finley traces the impact of this image in rich detail. She notes that the formerly enslaved person turned abolitionist Olaudah Equiano expressed his appreciation for the image in a letter to a London paper.[35] He wrote, "Having seen a plate representing the form in which Negroes are stowed on board the Guinea ships, which you are pleased to send to the Rev. Mr. Clarkson, a worthy friend of mine, I was filled with love and gratitude towards you for your humane interference on behalf of my oppressed countrymen."[36] Finley shows how these comments echo Equiano's own memories of captivity, as reported in his celebrated autobiography.[37] This might give us cause to think that the slave ship image would be comprehensible merely from its graphic elements in a way that could incite rebellion, even if it was not intended to have that effect.

It is not clear that Equiano's response would in any way typify the reaction of a Caribbean plantation slave, however. Equiano was living in London by this time and had become a campaigner to end the slave trade. His autobiography was published in support of abolition and was widely read in abolitionist circles. In other words, his reaction to the engraving and his motives for praising it were complex. Equiano's voice as a formerly enslaved person was distinctive and respected in the European abolitionist public sphere. From the perspective of someone like Félix Carteau, he would count as one of the people inciting revolt, rather than one of the people susceptible to its incitement. Equiano may not be a good index of the potential impact of abolitionist engravings in the slave colonies, then.

At the opposite end of the representational spectrum is a highly stylized allegory entitled *Soyez libres et citoyens* (Be Free and Citizens; see figure 4.4).[38] It evokes the iconographic language of the French Revolution in its portrayal of a Marianne-like figure giving liberty to the slaves. The image in no way aims at inciting revolt, since liberty is being given rather than taken. It is a somewhat patronizing image, and its portrayal of slaves cowering before a white benefactress could easily be interpreted as *supporting* slavery if one were not familiar with the visual conventions of abolitionism and the French Revolution.

This was the state of abolitionist image-making before the beginning of the Haitian Revolution. The practice took on a much more prominent role several years later, however, as the attention of the Société des Amis des Noirs shifted to the cause of mixed-race equality.[39] Due to the lobbying efforts of wealthy *de couleur* planters like Julien Raimond, the Amis reoriented themselves toward promoting racial equality for mixed-race people. Elites like Raimond defended this cause as consistent with the institution of slavery: it should aim at equality across lines of race between people of the same class. I have commented on the tensions and contradictions of these ideas elsewhere.[40] This effort at *de couleur* equality produced a surge of engravings in support of the cause, leaving the abolition of slavery even less well supported by pictorial representation. The effect of these engravings was very much to redirect the political energies of those viewing them, much as Nancy Luxon has observed in other images of the era.[41] As before, the visual language of these later engravings is highly symbolic and thus dependent upon an understanding of Enlightenment discourses of equality and even masonic symbolism.

The image *Moi libre* (Me Free), for example, is characteristic of an entire genre of identically titled engravings (figure 4.5). The title caricatures the broken French of an enslaved person in the colonies. The figure's headwrap is a style worn by African slaves, but here it is formed into the shape of a Phrygian cap, one of the most iconic symbols of the French Revolution. The figure also wears a carpenter's level as a pendant, one of the so-called working tools of Freemasonry and a symbol of the equality and brotherhood of man. The pendant hangs from a tricolor ribbon, another ubiquitous symbol of the French Revolution. In short, this image relies on a highly codified visual language similar to the abolitionist engravings that preceded it. Such images seem unlikely to provoke mass insurrection among slaves not steeped in the visual conventions of French revolutionary culture. This and the other images we have examined do not suggest a shared

Figure 4.4 Charles Boilly after Pierre Rouvier, *Soyez libres et citoyens*, frontispiece to Benjamin-Sigismond Frossard, *La cause des esclaves nègres et des habitans de la Guinée* (Lyon: Aimé de La Roche, 1789). Library Company of Philadelphia.

Figure 4.5 Unidentified artist, *Moi libre*, Collection de Vinck, no. 6034, Département Estampes et Photographie, Bibliothèque Nationale de France, Paris.

abolitionist/slave public sphere, so much as a lack of connection between those domains. The attention of abolitionists seems to have been squarely focused on achieving public support for legislation in the metropole, rather than inciting slaves to insurrection in the colonies.

In sum, Carteau's remarks about images seem rather hyperbolic in light of what we know of actual abolitionist image-making. The abolitionist engravings of this time were coded in an elaborate symbolic language. Those images required a substantial knowledge to decode and seemed to be directed at white, Francophone audiences that would be familiar with the visual rhetoric of revolutionary France and abolitionist England. Such images were rather unlikely to provide a point of connection between the public spheres of European abolitionists and colonial subalterns. Rather, Carteau's remarks seem more a product of his vivid imagination, particularly his fuming denunciation of a "boiling school of insurrection."

It is possible that there were other abolitionist engravings, oriented more directly at incitement, as Carteau postulated. They do not appear in the archives, however. In this sense, we seem to be in a position similar to that of the colonial elites: we have rumors of such things existing, but no tangible evidence. There seems to be an archival silence that preserves the ambiguity of such practices at the time. The absence of inflammatory images in the archives could suggest that they did not exist, or it could be a product of successful efforts to avoid detection. Carteau could not confirm whether abolitionists were spreading insurrectionary images in the 1780s, and several centuries later, we cannot draw definitive conclusions either.

This is not to say that Carteau's accusations were entirely a product of *his own* imagination. Whether imaginary or not, some of them were clearly shared by others. For instance, the "execrable Abbé Delahaye" is a figure held in suspicion by other colonists as well. Abbé Guillaume Silvestre Delahaye was the *curé* of Dondon parish, which was occupied by insurgent slaves from September 1791 to January 1793. Delahaye was caught up in the midst of the occupation and suspected to be a conspirator in those uprisings. Chris Bongie shows quite lucidly, however, that he was far from a philanthropist plotter himself, and was certainly not the person his reputation made him out to be. That reputation seems to have been a product of several highly tendentious characterizations like Carteau's. In fact, Delahaye's sympathies lay more with plants. He was a member of the Cercle des Philadelphes, a friend of Moreau de Saint-Méry, and was passionate about botany. When Delahaye did express attitudes about slaves and maroons, he was typically quite dismissive. His description as "execrable" seems to have been a product of the highly fractious politics among whites in the colony at this time, as the French Revolution and the prospect of abolition splintered colonial elites into various political factions.[42]

Thus, when Delahaye was later interrogated about his activities during the occupation, there is no particular reason to suspect him of philanthropist bias. Brought before an investigative committee, he was pointedly asked whether the *esclaves* read philanthropist brochures, and if he knew where they got them. "He responded that he had never seen a single philanthropic book in their hands, and the books that he did see them with were the product of pillage, and besides he had never been aware that any philanthropist from France or England had any part in the revolts of the said *esclaves*, and in addition he was very distant from philanthropic principles which he had always shown in his public writings every time the occasion presented itself."[43] In this sense, Delahaye's reputation as a philanthropist agitator is another symptom of paranoia about philanthropy, rather than a verification of it. His interrogation reveals an active concern about outside agitation in the wake of slave insurgency.

Carteau was by no means alone in his hatred of abolitionism, philanthropy, and the Amis des Noirs. An undated manuscript of the time, collected in the papers of the Committee on the Colonies, directs a sharp invective against the Amis.[44] The document is addressed to the National Assembly and is clearly a rough draft of a tract that would be typeset for publication. It is formatted to mimic a legal case against the Amis des Noirs, drawing up articles "In Point of Fact" and "In Point of Law." The author indicts the Amis as "fanatical writers," "guilty of the assassination of colonists." He quotes them as claiming that their doctrines formed a "catechism for the *noirs* and *gens de couleur*" that would "serve as an alphabet for the *noirs* like it had for the *mulâtres*" (22, 19). At another point, he refers to the "pastoral instruction of the Amis des Noirs," including their pamphlets. They justify allegations with other false allegations, putting illusions in the eyes of the people like a magic lantern (23). They invoke the freedom of the press, saying they are not to blame for the consequences of their ideas and writings. But, says the author, if you own a dangerous weapon and it injures someone, even accidentally, you are still responsible (24). In short, the Amis des Noirs are "putrefying protuberances" and "a malignant growth upon the globe" (25).

124 *Innovations in Subordination*

A dramatic poster printed during the slave insurrection bears a similar indictment. It is a broadsheet listing all sugar plantations known to be burned as of September 30, 1791 (figure 4.6). The destroyed establishments are listed in tabular form, region by region. Interestingly, the list includes "Bréda," the plantations of the Marquis de Noé that had been the home of Toussaint Louverture.

TABLEAU
DES
SUCRERIES INCENDIÉES A S^T.-DOMINGUE,

Dont on a eu connoissance jusqu'au 30 Septembre 1791.

QUARTIER DU PORT-MARGOT.	QUARTIER DU LIMBÉ.	QUARTIER DE L'ACCUL.	QUARTIER DE LA PLAINE DU NORD.	QUARTIER DE LA PETITE-ANSE.	QUARTIER MORIN.	QUARTIER DE LIMONADE.
Bayeux.	Chabaud.	Saint-Michel.	Robillard.	Walch.	Bonamy.	Durcourt.
Novion.	Des Grieux.	Ladebat.	Ruotte.	Baubert.	Dufay.	De Reynaud.
Thebaudieres.	Frémont.	Debergue.	Galloy.	Devort.	La Combe.	Bulet.
Chabert.	De Russi.	Dufour.	Tsunst.	De Sédieres.	Grandpré.	Brémont.
Puyon.	Bargues.	D'Agoult.	Lisladam.	DeCourt de la Tonnelle	L'Héritier.	Butler.
Le Gras.	Bonneau.	Bernon.	Menou et Coutances.	3 habitations Galliffet.	De Cadach et Barré.	Charitte.
Gouy-d'Arsy.	Cabot.	Pillat.	Fauheau.	Montalibor.	Darans.	Castelanee.
Trainier.	Reynaud.	Caignet.	Bréda.	Le Bral.	Fournier de Bellevue.	Lescarmoutier.
	La Corée.	Sacanville.	La Sote.	Desportes.	Gradis.	De Réal.
	Fournier de Bellevue.	Macarti.	Pasquet.	Le Bourday.	Rocheblave.	Du Mesny.
	De Cabour.	Dupati.	Poupe.	Baubert.	Tauzin.	Tauzin.
	Bacontis.	La Plagne.	Daux.	La Rivoire.	Beaujeau.	Destouches.
	Joubert et Canivet.	Molines.	Boulin	Archambaud.	La Lande-Gayon.	Walch.
	Desgouttes.	Jolly.	Butler,	Millot.	La Molaire.	La Chevalerie.
	Borrie.	Flaville.	Le Normant.	Dubreuil.	Carré.	Chabanon.
	Mondyon.	Gaudin.	La Glaise.	Berard.	Guillodeu.	Narboone.
	Dupetit-Houars.	Dutil.	La Rue.	Laugardiere.	Lefebvre.	La Belinaye.
	Fages.	Denoé.	Gruel.	Le Curieux.	Daux.	Veuve Miniac.
	Le Normand.	Guilmanson.	Menou.	Montégût.	Duplat.	Fournier de Bellevue.
	Lavaud.		Gaudin.	Brossard.	Chetenoye.	La Chapelle.
	Belin.		D'Hérincourt.	Gabriac.	Destreille.	Tressein.
	Bayon.		Vaudreuil.	D'Agoult.	Charitte.	Du Reau.
	Guillotin.		Bréda.	Les Péres de la Charité.	Fortelance.	La Baronie.
				Bongars.	Briard.	Tabary.
				Choiseul.	Macnémara.	De Parroy.
				Lefevre.	Demenou.	Fontenille.
				Duston.	Aubert.	Parroy de Bellevue.
					Bois-Himont.	Duhourg.
					Des Glereaux.	Le Manteaunoir.
					Mazeres.	Froger.
					Clerisse.	
					Choiseul.	

Les noms des douze cents Caféyéres incendiées, ne sont point encore connus : la destruction des ces Propriétés est évaluée à 600 millions. Ces pertes sont moins affligeantes, que celle de plus de mille Colons égorgés, et environ quinze mille Nègres tués.

Voilà, Français, les effets qu'ont produits les Écrits des amis des Noirs.

Figure 4.6a *Tableau des sucreries incediées à Saint-Domingue*, September 30, 1791, Archives Privées de Paroy, Archives Nationales d'Outre-Mer, Aix-en-Provence.

douze cents Caféyéres incendiées, ne sont point encore connus : la destruction des ces Propriétés est evaluée a 6(
ns affligeantes, que celle de plus de mille Colons égorgés, et environ quinze mille Nègres tués.

Voilà, Français, les effets qu'ont produits les Écrits des amis des Noirs.

Figure 4.6b Detail of 4.6a: "There, Frenchmen..."

Beneath the list, the broadsheet intones, "The names of the twelve hundred burned coffee plantations are as yet completely unknown. The destruction of these properties is valued at 600 million. These losses are less distressing than those of more than a thousand butchered Colonists and approximately fifteen thousand killed *Nègres*." At the bottom in large print is the slogan, "There, Frenchmen, are the effects of the writings of the Amis des Noirs."

Was it accurate to blame the "incendiary writings" of the Amis des Noirs and other philanthropists for the actual *incendies*? It is impossible to say. The philanthropists certainly were blamed, however. This was more likely a function of the effects of phantasmatic projection itself than anything coming from France. Colonial elites had so thoroughly conditioned themselves to *expect* slave revolt as a result of the activities of the Amis des Noirs, that it must have seemed entirely natural to blame them. Whether this was warranted is, however, an entirely different question.

The actual facts are not particularly germane to understanding the effects of this speculation. It is not terribly important to decide whether there were philanthropist infiltrators in the colonies inciting slaves to rebellion. Nor does it ultimately matter whether the Abbé Delahaye was in fact a collaborator. What matters is the feverish speculation, the conjectures drawn with little or no evidence, the postulation of causes, the efforts to assign blame, the highly cathected and affective response that was turned in a vague and nebulous direction. True, the Société des Amis des Noirs was singled out for unique hatred by planters and anti-abolitionists. The object of fear, anxiety, and paranoia was not them, however. Similarly, there was great fear of a slave revolt, but it was only the imagined end point, the ultimate consequence of the thing that truly inspired anxiety without end.

The ultimate object of anxiety was the prospect of *public spheres* connecting abolitionists to slaves and free blacks in the colonies. People fearing these lines of communication imagined publicity in a new form. They imagined what it might look like to extend the well-established abolitionist public spheres from Europe into the colonies. Such ephemeral veins of publicity were imagined around a set of figures: "philanthropist infiltrators," sympathetic sailors and priests, and enslaved people who were ripe for incitement. These new subjects were imagined as endowed with revolutionary intent and revolutionary agency. They enacted those characteristics through speech, specifically by propagating dangerous doctrines. Their suspected communication would constitute an unknown public sphere focused on menacing themes. It was the possibility of such communication itself, especially the communication of dangerous European doctrines, that was most feared by colonial elites.

PHANTASMATIC PUBLIC SPHERES

Fear and anxiety shade into paranoia when the cascade of apprehension becomes so pervasive that one starts imagining things that are not even there. The reaction surrounding poisoning was a classic case. It was generated by the uncertainty of something that might possibly happen in the future. One never really knew right now whether one was entering that path, whether the actions and choices one was about to take might have disastrous consequences. (Trust the servants? Eat the soup?) As a result, the existence of arcane African knowledge, secret maroon visitors, and toxic conspiracies began to take on a life of its own, free from fact and verification.

This piling up of the imagination is what Richard Hofstadter refers to as "the characteristic paranoid leap into fantasy."[45] He describes the paranoid as having "a vast theatre for his imagination, full of rich and proliferating detail, replete with realistic cues and undeniable proofs of the validity of his suspicions."[46] As a result of this feverish activity, Hofstadter notes, "the paranoid spokesman sees the fate of conspiracy in apocalyptic terms—he traffics in the birth and death of whole worlds, whole political orders, whole systems of human values."[47] This can be just as true of collectives as individuals. Paranoia can easily become the stuff of public, shared imaginaries. In this case, whole worlds and systems of values are collectively imagined into existence, becoming a shared, self-sustaining reality.

Something very similar seemed to be happening around philanthropy in Saint-Domingue. The fear of connections between European abolitionists and Caribbean slaves conjured whole worlds into existence, regardless of whether they were really there. Paranoia around visions of abolitionist conspiracy developed to a high level of complexity and abstraction. The fevered imagination was not content to anticipate negative outcomes but also remained alert for currently existing, unknowable entities that could bring about such outcomes. It imagined a public sphere inhabiting the penumbrae of the slave colony in unknown and threatening ways. We could call this shadowy specter a *phantasmatic public sphere*.[48]

The spectral presence of an imagined public sphere has a complicated epistemology. It is layered with suppositions, feared conspiracies, and postulated but unobserved events. Here we see all of the ambivalence, piling up of anxiety, and obsession with the object of fear that I drew out of my engagement with Sedgwick earlier.

The phantasmatic public sphere is a source of great ambivalence. It is an object that might exist, is feared to exist, and would be bad if it existed. It is postulated to exist, but the paranoid sincerely hopes that it does not exist. The postulate of its existence is a fallback position, a less favorable option, but one that must be considered out of fear of the consequences of not doing so. The hope is that such fear will be relieved by being shown to be baseless. This would be the best outcome. However, because the object is an hypothesized one that has not been or could not be observed, this solace is perpetually off-limits. The object of speculation is conjured into existence out of fear, and as such cannot be verified. It is a nonobject that results from projection; it is therefore rooted in uncertainty. Fear, anxiety, and paranoia generate the motivational energy to gin up the projection itself. As a result, the phantasmatic public sphere causes a perpetually unrelieved state of anxiety that continually chafes and problematizes, furnishing the affective basis for further acts of imagination. The object of fear is perpetuated as an object of obsessively fearful attention.

In this way, the object of fear comes to seem more and more real. Obsession and constant psychic processing project an ambiguous object into an imagined but ever more real existence. A suspected public sphere becomes more tangible as it becomes more and more the focus of anxiety. Here publicity is rendered autonomous, free-floating, and threatening.

From our more distanced perspective, it is not clear whether there ever was a public sphere connecting abolitionists and colonial subalterns. Nor is it clear whether paranoia about philanthropist infiltrators was justified by any actual subversion in the colonies. That in itself is the point. It was a projection, a shared imaginary, rooted in fear. The phantasmatic public sphere was a hypothetical object or a nonobject: the phantasm of abolitionists and their ideas and pamphlets potentially exercising some influence on slaves in the colonies.

Fevered imaginings and phantasmatic projections would not have been foreign to European audiences of this time. The Freemason Johann Georg Schröpfer was a famed practitioner of necromantic ghost spectacles in Leipzig in the 1770s. He apparently used hidden magic lanterns to project images of phantoms onto smoke in a darkened room.⁴⁹ This is the same magical technology that one of the authors above used as a metaphor for the deceptive ideas of abolitionists. Schröpfer's success was copied in Paris and Vienna by "the physicist Phylidor" in the early 1790s, who used the term *phantasmagorie* to advertise his shows. Étienne-Gaspard "Robertson" Robert, the "physicist-balloonist," was another celebrated impresario, staging his seances in Paris in the late 1790s.⁵⁰

Phantasmagorias were elaborately staged productions (figure 4.7). They were held in blackened rooms, with a complex apparatus of hidden projectors that worked their effects by means of mirrors and lenses. The ghosts themselves were hand-painted onto glass slides, and those images were projected onto smoke to enhance their disembodied and three-dimensional appearance. The projectors could be moved forward and backward to make an image advance and recede or appear to change shape. In more sophisticated cases, one could even order up a seance with a departed loved one, whose image was secretly obtained and painted onto a custom slide. Phantasmagorias were booming during the time of the Haitian Revolution and remained popular through the gothic years of the early nineteenth century, no doubt due to the public fascination with monsters and the supernatural of all kinds (figure 4.8).⁵¹

Figure 4.7 *Fantasmagorie de Robertson dans la Cour des Capucines en 1797*, frontispiece to E. G. Robertson, *Mémoires récréatifs, scientifiques et anecdotiques*, vol. 1 (Paris: Privately printed, 1831).

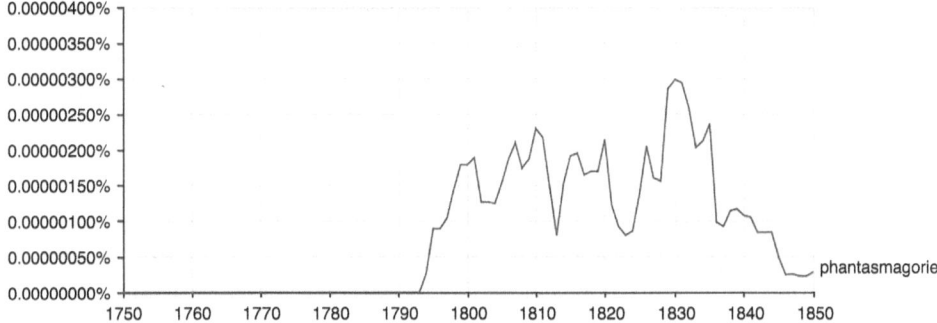

Figure 4.8 Published frequency of *"phantasmagorie"* as a percentage of all words published in French, 1750–1850. Google French dataset of 2012, courtesy of Google Labs.

Phantasmagorists went to great lengths to conceal their trade secrets. At the same time, they were fairly candid about the fact that they were peddling in illusions. As far back as 1770, Edmé-Gilles Guyot described some of the techniques used to create phantasmagorias in his *Nouvelles récréations physiques et mathématiques*.[52] Guyot's book was a do-it-yourself manual for building scientific curiosities, including magic eyeglasses, an electric spider, and the *aurora borealis*. Among these were the mechanisms of smoke and mirrors that could be used to create phantasmagorical illusions—perhaps a clue to the origins of our own expression for devices of mystification. *Nouvelles récréations* apparently sold well, since it went through a number of editions by the end of the century. In a similar spirit, several famous phantasmagorists of the 1790s advertised themselves as men of science who were dedicated to dispelling myth and superstition. Robertson, for instance, once wrote that the government "has recognized the need to encourage the physicist-philosopher, whose works tend to destroy the enchanted world which only owes its existence to the wand of fanaticism."[53] These words should be taken with a grain of salt, since Robertson was a consummate self-promoter who claimed to have invented techniques that he actually stole from others. Nonetheless, the optical marvels underlying the phantasmagorias were still being revealed to an eager public a century later.[54] In this sense, the phantasmagorists manufactured a fear whose artifice was widely understood. Audiences could be drawn into the fearful illusion with a reassuring knowledge of its artificiality.

The phantasmatic projections of colonial elites seemed every bit as real as the ghosts of Robertson and Phylidor, but in contrast, they were not staged in public spectacles and there was no reassurance that they were mere illusions. Instead, these phantasms were the much less tangible product of nagging doubts and fearful imaginations. Lacking any reassurance that these specters were only illusions, visions of communication between slaves and philanthropists elicited a real and visceral reaction, one that seemed only confirmed by the subsequent outbreak of slave revolt. This fear was bivalent: it was a fear of subaltern speech that was seemingly confirmed by subaltern *silence*. The apparent *lack* of philanthropist infiltrators seemed only to heighten anxiety about a successfully concealed conspiracy. Suppositions of what might become, along with rumors of what might be, created a continual vigilance and anxiety about what might happen if the apparently silent subaltern were not really silent. Here a powerful specter was projected in the imagination, but there was no Guyot to reassure the slaveowner that it was all just an illusion.

Metropolitan phantasmagoria and colonial paranoia might seem worlds apart, but they were very much of the same world. Robertson, the peddler in illusions who also claimed to dispel them as a man of science, had fairly close ties with colonial elites. He was tutor to the son of a former governor of the French Caribbean colonies named Chevalier. He was also close to the Comte de Paroy, who had substantial plantation holdings in Saint-Domingue. Paroy advanced the doubtful claim that it was actually he who gave Robertson the idea of staging phantasmagorias with a magic lantern, and invented the moving projector technique that gave it such verisimilitude.[55] Either this very Paroy or his father, the marquis, collected the broadsheet *Tableau des sucreries incediées à Saint-Domingue* that we examined earlier, which lists several of their properties among those burned in the slave revolts. In chapter 6 we will see a beautiful watercolor map of one of those properties, also from their collection (figure 6.1). The Paroy family papers are now in the French colonial archives in Aix-en-Provence, though apparently without further mention of Robertson, magic lanterns, or phantasmagorias. It is nonetheless worth noting that some of the people most exercised about colonial slave revolts were also avid consumers of phantasmagoria.

SUBORDINATION, DISPLACEMENT, SILENCE

The phantasmatic public sphere is a striking case of subaltern silence. It illustrates many of the dynamics I have been tracing through the colonial archives, but also reveals some new and unexpected ones. We can distinguish four distinct entities in this imaginary, each imagined in its own way. Together they populate the landscape of a particular, anxious vision of the colonial order.

> *The figure of the silent slave.* Enslaved people, free blacks, and *gens de couleur* were forcibly silenced in various ways by white colonial planters. This includes the legal exclusion and subordination of colonial laws, well-known forms of violence and intimidation, and more subtle forms of subjectification.
> *The figure of the European abolitionist.* Abolitionists tried to speak for the subaltern. This effort was manifested in an international network of communication and cooperation, and in the paranoid visions of some colonists.
> *The phantasmatic public sphere.* A very abstract entity, imagined as a domain of publicity. It is the hypothetical and fearful postulation of publicity connecting slaves and abolitionists. Colonial elites projected the highly developed abolitionist public sphere of Europe and the United States back into the colonies and supposed that slaves might have access to it. It is populated by speaking subjects, both the European abolitionist and a new subaltern figure:
> *The figure of the incitable, potentially insurgent slave.* This vision postulates subalterns who were meant to be silent, and who seem to be silent, but who have actually become participants in the abolitionist public sphere. This is a reversal of subaltern silence. It conjectures the figure of an enslaved person with agency, susceptible to incitement, and having intentions to do harm.

The first and second of these figures illustrate classic tendencies of subaltern silence. The first is a straightforward example of the kinds of silencing we have already discussed in chapter 2. Enslaved people in the Caribbean occupied the most subaltern of positions: they were classified as property, denied legal personality, excluded from the formal legislative and journalistic public spheres of the colony, and refused education and literacy. Their silence was enacted through law and violence.

The European abolitionist is a self-ascribed identity that attempts to rectify these wrongs. Responding to the severe cruelties of slavery, abolitionists tried to speak on slaves' behalf. They appealed to public sympathies about the humanity of enslaved people and the frightful treatment to which they were subject. They also pointed out the hypocritical application of Enlightenment ideals, existing laws, and French revolutionary doctrines. While their legislative successes were inconsistent, those efforts did have desirable political effects. As we have seen, abolitionists' attempts to speak for the subaltern often threw their contemporaries into spasms of anxiety.

Nonetheless, abolitionist discourse is a classic illustration of the dangers that Spivak identifies. Abolitionism was a well-meaning attempt to liberate subaltern subjects by speaking for them. It adopted the form of representation that Spivak refers to as *Vertretung*. This is an attempt to represent the interests and positions of others. At best, it can be an effort to speak on behalf of someone who cannot. At worst, it risks a ventriloquism of subaltern voices, in which the interests, hopes, and fears of the subaltern are postulated because they cannot be directly presented. This substitution can constitute silencing in itself, a displacement of subaltern speech by the very effort to speak on its behalf. The result is to misunderstand, misrepresent, occlude, or ignore what the subaltern might have wanted to say. It is a *silencing through ventriloquism*.

All of this is relatively straightforward from the standpoint of subaltern silence. In contrast, the third and fourth figures—the phantasmatic public sphere and the incitable slave—generate rather novel dynamics. Specifically, they create new mixtures of unknowability and affect. The idea of the phantasmatic public sphere expresses great anxiety about subaltern speech. It is anxiety that the subaltern has not been completely effaced and may have access to publicity that is unknown and powerful. In that sense, this is a fear of subaltern agency, a fear that the silent subaltern has become an incitable, potentially insurgent one.

In these ways, the phantasmatic public sphere reveals relatively unmapped dimensions of subaltern silence. It vividly expresses the ambiguities of presence, agency, and speech that plague the subaltern. It displays the powerful affective bases of subordination. In this vision, concerns about subaltern speech are inverted: rather than worrying about the aporias of discovering or liberating subaltern subjects, this is a concern about failures to *silence* them. In this sense, the phantasmatic public sphere represents a fear of the failure of subaltern silence.

The phantasmatic public sphere illuminates a side of subaltern silence that is highly complex and rarely observed. It imagines unknowable but dangerous speech, and in so doing, illustrates the core epistemology of subaltern silence. The (apparent) silence of the subaltern might be a result of *unknowability* rather than subordination. This subaltern may not be silent to everyone, but only to the self-identified potential victim—the paranoid. The ambiguity and unknowability of subaltern speech become a source of fear. The subaltern could be unknown and speaking: speaking to someone else, about dangerous topics.

The reaction to these fears creates issues of subaltern silence in a rather different register. It is not a representation or ventriloquism of subaltern voices, but a fevered imagination of what they might be saying and doing. It is the imagined unsilence of the subaltern—which again, has the effect of an *imaginary unsilencing*. It attributes agency to the subaltern, but then cloaks it in silence. This is a speaking agency that is silent only to the paranoid, however. As a projection that inspires paranoia, its great force lies not in what is said, nor in claims about the rights of man or the horrors of slavery. Rather, its force lies in problematization itself. It causes a great unsettlement of the colonial sense of order and a paranoid derangement of the colonial apparatus of power.

In the end, much paranoid ambivalence of colonial elites seems to have been relieved by the slave revolts themselves. The actual insurrections were taken as confirming evidence (in a darkly self-satisfied way) that paranoia had been justified all along. The suspicions of incitement seem to have been realized, and as a result, the worst fears of the colonists were now confirmed as well. We can imagine that this release from ambivalence may have actually been some relief; though of course, it was the pyrrhic relief that comes from having feared the worst and been right. Paranoid ambivalence toward discovery is replaced by self-satisfaction at having been right to worry. Of course, this self-congratulatory interpretation of the slave revolts proves nothing. It merely interprets those events as a confirmation of prior suspicions. It is a failure of self-reflection, rather than evidence of having been right all along.

In any case, this very sense of confirmation creates yet another form of subaltern silence. The idea of a phantasmatic public sphere blames European philanthropists for inciting rebellion in the colonies. It was supposedly they who formulated toxic doctrines, printed pamphlets and engravings, spread them through the colonies, and whispered seditious ideas in the ears of slaves. The privilege accorded to the European conspirator in this anxious imaginary constitutes new forms of invisibility, silence, and subordination for the enslaved people alleged to collaborate with them. It is a *silencing through substitution*, attributing agency and intention to someone else, rather than the subaltern. Here the causes of the Haitian Revolution are attributed to French revolutionary conflicts. The blame for revolution is not pinned on the brutal, calculated cruelty visited on enslaved people, on the discriminatory racial codes placed on blacks and *gens de couleur*, or on the racist culture of the colonies. Rather, the paranoid imagination locates agency and revolutionary zeal in what Félix Carteau called "democratism": the leveling doctrines of French Jacobins who would destroy colonial commerce to advance their principles. Paranoia about philanthropy is the driving force of this vision. It devalues the agency and intentionality of those who planned the slave revolts, postulating that those acts must have been the work of white agents operating in secret.

This kind of substitution is another form of what I earlier called *silencing through displacement*. It is another way of reconstructing subaltern identities and draining them of significance and agency. The paranoia surrounding the phantasmatic public sphere functions as a form of racialized displacement. It creates an imaginary in which bold revolutionary projects are launched by white Europeans, thereby silencing the slaves and other racialized subjects who actually launched the revolution and fought for independence.

In all of these ways, phantasmagoria is an apt metaphor for the production of subalternity in the colonial regime. The apparatus of publicity functioned very similarly to Johann Georg Schröpfer's magic lanterns. It aimed to cast light on the important phenomena of the day. When that light was passed through the smoke and mirrors of colonial common sense, however, the result was a set of ghostly apparitions that turned back to frighten their unwitting audience. They were shadowy figures of an abolitionist public sphere, with its vividly imagined philanthropist infiltrators and incitable slaves. In retrospect, we can see that this also amounted to a substantial reconfiguration of the revolutionary landscape. Imagined European conspirators were given vivid presence and key roles, while real, acting enslaved people were displaced to a spectral netherworld. They were subordinated and silenced as mere reflections of active revolutionary subjects.

In short, the phantasmatic public sphere lays bare some of the mechanisms that underlie subaltern silence. It reveals the senses in which the forces of domination sometimes run away with themselves, creating dangerous and undesirable side effects. The phantoms that populated the elite imagination were largely self-imposed. They were surplus effects of power circling back on those who wielded it.

All of this reveals limitations in a romantic ideal of "the weapons of the weak": subalterns who fashion devious means to subvert the power exerted upon them. It also goes well beyond Spivak's original notion of a subaltern subject who is condemned by history and misunderstanding never to speak. Instead we see a much more complex picture of subordination, erasure, self-assertion, slippage, uncertainty, vagueness, and unintended effects. Even the successful imposition of subaltern silence—as had been exercised on enslaved people in the colonial Caribbean—can take on a threatening emptiness when the elites who imposed it become uncertain of their achievement. The question whether the subaltern can speak has an ominous aspect here, made all the more ominous by the fact that the people who most wanted to know the answer were those with a concrete stake in achieving subaltern silence. In these cases, the flip side of silence and subordination is unknowability and uncertainty. The silent subaltern becomes a phantasmatic and troubling presence, a self-problematizing object of power. Or perhaps not really a silent subaltern at all, but only the deceptive appearance of one ... until it is too late to do anything about it.

CHAPTER 5

Disruptive Object

The Tricolor Cockade and the Fear of Black Jacobins

1789-1791

No ideas but in things.

—William Carlos Williams

Abolition was not the only explosive doctrine of the late eighteenth century. For several decades it had traveled hand in hand with rumblings about natural right, equality, and popular sovereignty, political themes that were becoming more and more prominent as the French monarchy was increasingly called into question. An intense regime of censorship had kept a lid on this talk for several decades, forcing it into various other channels. All of that changed in 1789, however, when a series of miscalculations by the crown resulted in open revolution. Now the revolutionary talk and action that had been quietly incubating could come out into the open. This resulted in the iconic events of the French Revolution, as well as a massive efflorescence of discourse about revolutionary themes.

News of the French Revolution began to arrive in the colonial Caribbean in late 1789. With this turn of events, colonial planters now had a whole new set of worries. Abolitionists had argued for the end of slavery based on its cruelty and disrespect for the basic dignity of all people. To this could now be added equally potent arguments about equality and the rights of man—arguments that were having wide uptake and sweeping effects in metropolitan France. In addition to fretting about abolitionist doctrine spreading to the colonies, planters now had to worry about the ideological underpinnings of the French Revolution spreading there as well.

As news of the revolution began to arrive in colonial Saint-Domingue, we find small, odd fragments of suggestion that something new was afoot. The archives of this time make occasional references to slaves and free blacks wearing the tricolor cockade. This was the rosette ribbon, in concentric circles of blue, white, and red, that was an omnipresent symbol of the French Revolution (figure 5.1).[1] Some of those people were enslaved, some were free, but none left records explaining why they wore the cockade or what wearing it meant. The ornament apparently had some meaning for the white elites who ruled the colony, however. A series of local laws sprang up banning blacks and *gens de couleur* from wearing the cockade. Again, we don't know why. They seem important, but cryptically so. Local legislatures kept scant records, and any that existed are now lost to us.

The reactive behavior of colonial lawmakers, banning the display of a symbol by particular racial groups, is rather striking. Its affective dimensions are similar to reactions we have seen before, suggesting new forms of fear, anxiety, and paranoia. This concern about the symbols of the French Revolution seems to mirror worries about the phantasmatic public sphere: the potential for dangerous ideas to be communicated into the colonies with potentially explosive results. Yet abolition and the phantasmatic public sphere were a rather different situation. Fear in that case was largely centered on discourse as a means for propagating ideas. To be sure, it was discourse communicated in material form: the whispers of philanthropist infiltrators, the idle chatter of dockhands and slaves on the wharves, printed tracts and pamphlets from France, and even abolitionist engravings that "could be understood merely by opening one's eyes." As material and vivid as those practices were, however, the danger lay not there but in their communication of dangerous ideas.

The tricolor cockade represents something rather different: concern over a symbol and the material practice of displaying that symbol. It hearkens back to some of the things we have examined in earlier chapters. We have seen how various forms of material practice had an unsettling influence on colonial domination in the early decades of the eighteenth century. Maroons and suspected poisoners did not articulate claims or issue manifestos. Instead, they engaged in practices that disrupted the silence imposed upon them. The materiality of those practices was an important opportunity for subaltern subjects. Even when they could not speak, their actions sometimes had unsettling effects. Such practices tapped into the internal tensions of enslavement and colonialism, creating instabilities and

Figure 5.1a Dominique Doncre, *Le juge Pierre-Louis-Joseph Lecocq et sa famille*, 1791.
© Collection Musée de la Révolution Française, Département de l'Isère, MRF 1984-263.
Photograph by Rama, Wikimedia Commons, Cc-by-sa-2.0-fr.

Figure 5.1b Detail of 5.1a: The tricolor cockade.

new openings for subaltern agency. The tricolor cockade could be operating in a similar modality: as a form of material practice with unsettling consequences.

However, the cockade was not just any symbol, but a *revolutionary* one. This created additional ripples of complexity in its display. Because of its significance in revolutionary France, the cockade had a strong ideational connection with the ideologies and doctrines of that revolution. In this sense, wearing the cockade had more in common with the phantasmatic public sphere and its paranoia about the communication of dangerous ideas.

In short, the tricolor cockade seems like a striking convergence of strands that we have been tracking in previous chapters. The affective response to it seems to be driven by a fusion of discourse and material practice. But this is all just preliminary speculation.

In what follows, I will try to peel back the layers of silence packed into the scattered mentions of the cockade. A careful interpretation of these fragments reveals important traces of political action and agency under conditions of pervasive silence. The subaltern was not allowed to speak under slavery in the colonial Caribbean. When normal forms of speech and action were blocked, however, more subtle dimensions of subaltern politics came to the fore. Those included practices of signification featuring missed communication, opaque meaning, paranoid projection, and creative, self-reflexive misinterpretation. In this context, the tricolor cockade constituted a distinctive response to the imposition of silence: a disruptive act that was at once highly visible and unnervingly silent. It had revolutionary significance in excess of whatever people may or may not have been trying to communicate through its use. The cockade reached across substantial fissures of race and epistemology to pose an internal critique of French revolutionary ideals. It did this with no propositional content, no political manifestos, and without making any discernible claims. It was, in a literal sense, silent. However, the cockade nonetheless exerted potent political effects. It managed to speak in a sideways, disruptive sense even while the subordinated subjects wearing it were silenced.

SHARDS OF HISTORY

We have already seen how the threat of abolition created disquiet among colonial elites. Starting in the late 1780s, however, the character of abolitionism began to change. There had been striking rhetoric going back at least to Raynal-Diderot's infamous 1770 statement about the immanence of a slave revolt bringing "vengeance and carnage."[2] Such statements remained mere words under the ancien régime, however. Abolition took a notable turn with the democratic ferment leading up to the French Revolution. Groups such as the Société des Amis des Noirs were composed largely of French Revolutionary thinkers and political operatives. This promoted an increasing fusion of abolitionist ideas and revolutionary thought, drawing comparisons between the plight of the French people and that of the enslaved people of the colonies.[3] As these revolutionaries gained political traction, they also developed increasing leverage to abolish slavery. They began moving forward with concrete legislative proposals rather than mere pamphlets and treatises.

Notions of liberty, equality, popular sovereignty, and national unity animated the French Revolution and continued to be debated during the formation of the new republic.[4] Although they often took more specific form—a commitment to end status distinctions and inherited privileges, for instance, or calls for virtue and self-sacrifice—these revolutionary-republican ideals were broadly shared across the revolutionary political culture. Like abolitionism, they were the common currency of the salons, *sociétés de pensée*, National Assembly, popular press, learned tracts, pamphlets, broadsheets, public oratory, and a wide variety of other fora.[5] These ideals caused fear in many European capitals, where their potential disruptive effects could easily be imagined.

Similarly, fears of abolitionism in the colonies began to be intertwined with fears about the spread of French revolutionary and republican ideals. Médéric-Louis-Elie Moreau de Saint-Méry, now a deputy in the French National Assembly, noted the increase in revolutionary rhetoric and what he saw as incitement to revolution. He complained that the same people tasked with writing the constitution have put forth "a pile of writings where they preached, advised, and desired slave revolt; where they vomited out the most horrible curses against the colonial planters and merchants, and sought every means to spread a doctrine that incites thousands of men to slaughter one another, that tends to depopulate entire islands, and whose only end can be the ruin of empires."[6] In other words, the new rhetoric favors not merely ending the slave trade but violent insurrection in the manner of the French Revolution. These traces of revolutionary thought were also vivid in the Amis des Noirs' response to Moreau de Saint-Méry's diatribe. They accused him of treason against both the rights of man and his brothers, by which they meant the African slaves.⁷ In other words, he was violating fundamental values of liberty and equality. The Amis thereby invoked republican virtues in defense of abolition.

A similar version of this fear shows up in the anecdote that I discussed in chapter 4 about the black insurgent who was captured with three highly symbolic objects in his pocket: "pamphlets printed in France, filled with commonplaces about the Rights of Man and the Sacred Revolution," fire-starting materials, and an African amulet.⁸ Even though he was a participant in a slave revolt, the insurgent was traveling with texts advocating not abolition but *revolutionary republicanism*. The fear, of course, was that the spread of notions of equality could destabilize the racial order on which enslavement was based, and doctrines of freedom could promote violent revolt.

This is something of the context in which the tricolor cockade starts to appear in Saint-Domingue. Joseph-Paul-Augustin Cambefort, a French colonel, says he introduced it into the colony (figure 5.2). This claim is somewhat suspect, however, since it appears in a brief in which Cambefort defends himself against charges of undermining the spirit of the French Revolution. These include charges that he aided the slave revolt in Saint-Domingue and that he showed counterrevolutionary tendencies by continuing to use the title of baron and avoiding the cockade.⁹ Defending his patriotic credentials, Cambefort protests,

> The Commissioners additionally accuse me of having shown repugnance at wearing the tricolor cockade; they cite a case where, if one believes them, I felt some discomfort in this regard.
>
> In my interrogation I demonstrated the falsity of this double accusation. It was I who wore the first sign of liberty in the Colony, who distributed it to officers and soldiers; it was my example that caused it to be worn by citizens in the Northern, Southern, and Western provinces; and it was to my eagerness at adopting this revolutionary sign that I attribute the tricolor ornaments that decorate the flags of the regiment that I commanded, which were given to me by the civil authorities with the greatest solemnity.¹⁰

This is the same Cambefort who was accused by Félix Carteau of aiding the slave revolts in chapter 4.¹¹ Given Cambefort's eagerness to please the Jacobin authorities, his claims of patriotic zeal cannot be taken at face value. It is rather unclear what his role might have been in introducing the cockade into the colony.

Figure 5.2 Charles-Étienne Gaucher, after Claude Bornet, *Portrait de Joseph-Paul-Augustin Cambefort*, Château de Versailles, LP83.79.4. © RMN-Grand Palais/Art Resource, New York.

Moreover, his account of how the cockade spread from his fine example seems conveniently self-serving for someone on trial. What does seem significant, in any case, is Cambefort's invocation of the cockade in particular to leverage his claims of patriotism.

In this regard the correspondence of Julien Raimond is also relevant. Raimond was an influential member of Haitian society. He was an *homme de couleur*, a man of color, born in Saint-Domingue. Raimond was also a wealthy plantation owner who possessed some one hundred slaves.[12] He spent many years in France lobbying for the rights of mixed-race citizens in the colonies and had close contacts in the French National Assembly and the Société des Amis des Noirs. Raimond is often credited or blamed, depending on one's perspective, for turning the agenda of the Amis des Noirs away from the abolition of slavery and toward equality for free, mixed-race *gens de couleur*.

Not surprising for someone in his position, Raimond is ambivalent about the French revolutionary legacy. He is supportive to the extent that revolutionary ideals could expand the rights of *gens de couleur* but opposes it to the extent that these ideals might entail the abolition of slavery.

This ambivalence plays in the background of a French government investigation of Raimond's activities in 1793.[13] In the dossier compiled against him we find excerpts from a letter by Raimond's brother François, dated October 1, 1789, updating Julien on events in the colony while he was living in France. The investigators copy selected parts of the letter and intercut them with their own commentary (in italics below):

> [F. Raimond:] The troubles of France have now arrived here; the whites [*blancs*] have put on the cockade. That hasn't happened, as you can imagine, without some trouble and blood spilled between them, etc.
>
> [Investigator:] *This is a calumny. Note in addition how he qualifies as troubles the revolution that was accomplished in France. Note further that it was the whites who first put on the tricolor cockade.*
>
> Everything is in order.
>
> *How to reconcile that with the blood spilled among the whites.*
>
> But the most terrible are the blacks [*noirs*] who, understanding [*entendant*] that the cockade is for equality and liberty, wanted to revolt.
>
> *This is false. There was absolutely no slave insurrection before the month of August 1791.*[14]

The interplay between Raimond's remarks and the investigator's commentary reveals a great deal about racial and metropolitan-creole tensions in this era. They are compactly telegraphed on the cover of the dossier, which characterizes its contents as "pieces collected by the Committee [of the Navy and the Colonies], concerning Julien Raimond, creole mulatto [*mulâtre créole*], conveyed to the Revolutionary Tribunal."[15] Even though Raimond was a well-known figure in the political circles of Paris, the authors of the report still take pains to make his racial and colonial identity explicit. In this context, the fact that the (clearly white) French investigator attaches such importance to a remark about the tricolor cockade says volumes. François Raimond's characterization of the cockade as reproducing the French "troubles"—a word that he underlines in the letter—was thought important enough to merit the attention of a criminal tribunal. It seems to be interpreted both as antiwhite and antirevolutionary sentiment that might be shared by his brother.

Also striking is the investigator's strenuous denial of blacks' understanding of the cockade. He says bluntly that Raimond's statement is false. It is not clear in exactly what sense he contests this statement, however. Most obviously, he denies that any revolt took place based on the cockade. In this regard, we should note that Raimond claims only that blacks *wanted* to revolt, not that they did: "*les noirs . . . ont voulu se soulever.*" It is not clear whether the investigator's denial extends further to the claim that the blacks understood the cockade to represent equality and liberty. It would be very useful to understand better what he thought about this, but his statement is too terse to be read clearly one way or the other.

We find a similarly brief and cryptic mention of the tricolor cockade in a series of letters written by the colonial officials the Comte de Peynier and the Marquis de Barbé-Marbois. The first is from September 27, 1789, showing that there was some awareness of the French Revolution in the colony. "Up there [in northern Saint-Domingue?] the *nègres* all agree on an idea that struck them as though spontaneously, that the white slaves [*blancs esclaves*] killed their masters and, now free, govern themselves and regain possession of the goods of the earth." In a subsequent letter on October 10, 1789, they relate this idea to the tricolor cockade, saying that "the blacks [*noirs*] called this cockade the sign of the liberation of whites [*blancs*]."[16]

There is a certain verisimilitude in these observations, yet also overstatement and hyperbole. They are short observations that are reported as fact, but in an overgeneralized form. They provide a loose idea of what slaves and free blacks might have thought the cockade meant. But this is also an elite interpretation, and it is unclear whether its sources were supposition, rumor, paranoid projection, or overgeneralization of a more specific observation.

Finally, we can see something of the cockade's significance in the legislative reaction to it, a sort of action at a distance. We have reports of local laws being passed in Saint-Domingue that ban *gens de couleur* and blacks from wearing the tricolor cockade. For example, a brief reference appears in an unsigned, undated manuscript by the "Citizens of Color of St. Marc." It presents itself as an account of recent crimes committed by whites against *gens de couleur* in Saint-Domingue. In the midst of a horrible list of complaints—assassinations, house burnings, and executions—we find a brief mention of the tricolor cockade: "What did [the *hommes de couleur* and *nègres libres*] not have to fear in a town that contained so many factious people, in which they have suffered so many injustices and atrocities since the revolution based on simple suspicions and false reports, in which they were prohibited from wearing the national cockade as though it were a crime?"[17] Here we discover that *gens de couleur* and free blacks were forbidden to wear the cockade under criminal law. It would be nice to know more: why the prohibition came into effect, what its authors were thinking, why they singled out this practice for attention. Unfortunately no more is said about that here. We do know that the Citizens of Color of St. Marc saw this as a grave enough affront to mention it in a list of horrendous offenses.

The location, St. Marc, says something about these events. It was the site of a white creole independence movement in 1790, an anticolonial movement that briefly established its own legislative assembly with thoughts of separating from France.[18] This movement was accompanied by vivid rumors and fear of another rebellion that might preempt their own, a slave revolution sparked by infiltration from French abolitionists. While these fears of subversion were largely unfounded, they resulted in paranoid rumors of slave armies on the march and efforts to uncover abolitionist plots—exactly the phenomenon we examined in chapter 4.[19] In this environment one can imagine the psychic roots of ill treatment for blacks and *gens de couleur*. This still does not answer the question why such psychic energy would be channeled into a prohibition on wearing the cockade, however.

This, then, is the enigma of the tricolor cockade in the revolutionary Caribbean. These remarks do not settle the question of what the cockade "meant," so much as *pose* that question through layers of epistemic uncertainty and ambiguity.

EPISTEMOLOGIES OF AMBIGUITY AND SILENCE

The rich historical record of the French Revolution gives us a fairly clear idea of the tricolor cockade's complex significance as a revolutionary symbol. What it might have meant in prerevolutionary Saint-Domingue is, however, a very different question. The accounts that we have are spotty, terse, and occasional. Their brevity and scattered character only highlight the gaps and silences in this archival record. To piece together some idea of the Caribbean cockade's "meaning" requires us to look for scraps of meaning in the gaps within the archival record. At the same time, we must be careful not to impose an artificially determinate significance on practices that may, in the end, be inherently ambiguous. This is a delicate act of interpretation, striving to see that which is not visible while avoiding projections and hallucinations.

Approached in this way, the scattered archival remarks on the tricolor cockade become an interesting moment of political epistemology. We must ask whether the silences here are characteristics of the archives or of the practices themselves. Are they silences in what we can know about this culture based on the fragmented remains handed down to us, or are they inherent ambiguities in the practices we are interpreting? These are issues that we have faced in previous chapters as well. Subaltern silences register in multiple ways. We observe their effects in the archives now, but we also face the question whether that is a problem of our own biases and agendas, a problem of historical documentation and preservation, or a real effect of some other silence in the past. Of course, this is not an either/or situation. The answer could well be "all of the above," since such silences can have shared roots and ramify over time.

Disaggregating these forms of silence presents two interpretive puzzles: the historical-epistemological puzzle of interpreting the archival fragments on the cockade in the revolutionary Caribbean, and the political-epistemological puzzle of what the cockade "meant" to its own contemporaries. These are problems of interpretation in which the criteria of success are not clear, and it is quite possible to overreach and overinterpret, arriving at a falsely determinate result. It is not clear in what sense the cockade might have meant something, and it is not clear to what extent meaning was shared across the lines of race, class, ownership, and nativity in the colony. Ignoring these ambiguities risks imposing false closure on a question that may be inherently open and unanswerable. In retrospect, we can see that similar problems have been playing out in our previous discussions as well.

The first form of silence, *archival silence*, is one described by Michel-Rolph Trouillot in his insightful investigation of bias and distortion in our understanding of Haitian history.[20] Trouillot traces how silences are actively produced as part of the selective attention that is required to construct history. Such lapses are never neutral, of course, but reflect underlying power dynamics. The "differential control of the means of historical production" by elite groups biases what is said, how archives are assembled, and what interpretations are made.[21] Trouillot highlights some of the ways in which subaltern voices have been silenced in Haitian history, vividly demonstrating the need to ask what was excluded, ignored, or left aside in the formation of the archives.

The observations I have collected about the tricolor cockade tell a one-sided, problematic story similar to Trouillot's. This topic suffers from a kind of minuteness, almost escaping attention and only being mentioned in connection with other things. This should put us on notice. In the metropole during the French Revolution, the cockade was subject to high emotions and thorough documentation. While not well documented in Saint-Domingue, the reaction to it there also seems to have had some emotional urgency: laws were passed explicitly banning its use by members of certain races. This is not the story of a trivium scarcely worthy of attention. Something else must have been going on.

In the colonial context in which the cockade appears, silences are not just accidents of archival loss; they are to some extent political. The fragmentary observations I have gathered come from a count, a marquis, and a baron—all white and French—and one of the wealthiest *gens de couleur* in Saint-Domingue, a man with extensive ties to France and extensive financial interests in slavery. The count and the marquis are members of the colonial administration; the others are defending themselves against criminal charges. The people leaving these accounts have interests quite opposed to the liberation of slaves. In addition, each of them writes from a defensive position of self-justification. All of this poses substantial problems of narrative reliability, to say the least.

The silence of blacks about what they "meant" by wearing the tricolor cockade is likely not accidental, then, but a form of silencing like those excavated by

Trouillot. As we have seen, the tricolor cockade was legislatively prohibited for blacks in the public spheres of Saint-Domingue. We can view the archival silence about this practice as a similar kind of erasure, an exclusion from the documentary record of possible explanations about what was meant. It was a systematic failure to record points of view that might explain what the cockade meant to the people wearing it. Their nonexistence constitutes a form of silencing, a preemptive erasure of the opponent's ideas from posterity.

This is quite different from many of the other practices of silencing we have examined. It is not a direct silencing of individuals through law or violence, nor is it a form of displacement that operates in a symbolic, cultural domain to reshape identities or revalue their voice and actions. Rather, it operates in a simpler, more direct way to deny people access to documentation. Following Trouillot's line of thought, we might call it *silencing through exclusion*. This name highlights the simple and direct character of this form of silencing. By contrast, it also reminds us that silencing is so often *not* simply a matter of exclusion, but of something much more subtle: convoluted forms of inclusion that still have a silencing force.

Now let us move from the archive to these silencing practices themselves. The tricolor cockade is silent in the most literal sense. It says nothing, at least not in the narrowest meaning of that phrase. It has no propositional content; it asserts no fact or value that can be affirmed or rejected. The silence of the cockade implies a corresponding silence in the practice of wearing it. The physical display of the object seems to imply meaning or intent—it is a ruffled, circular ribbon in bright, primary colors, worn as a decoration—but it is not prima facie clear what that meaning or intent might be.

To the extent that the object has meaning, it is determined against the background of an interpretive context. An object like the cockade takes on meaning through attribution, by being associated with other concepts, ideas, and practices through an act of interpretation by those viewing it. To determine an object's meaning we place it within a context and through this interpretive act decide what minima of signification, communication, and/or political action it implies.

Because this interpretive process is a complex one, there are many ways it could go awry. We can imagine an object that is awkwardly placed within some interpretive context so that the connection between them seems loose and problematic. An interpreter has much less to go on in this case. Since there is no right answer, no correct application of background knowledge, and no objective meaning for the object to disclose, interpreters have to forge ahead with the information they have and see what happens. Here differences in cultural background, language, and life experience can lead people to quite odd conclusions about one another's practices. They may use the same words, engage in the same actions, view the same symbols and events, yet not understand them in the same way. Their interpretive horizons are partially decoupled in ways that lead to misunderstandings and erroneous conclusions. Moreover, such gaps may be mystified—they are not necessarily apparent to those between whom they occur.

REVOLUTIONARY RIBBON

What then can we make of the tricolor cockade in colonial Saint-Domingue? Given the precarity of subaltern speech and the silencing of subaltern voices, it would be a mistake simply to accept the interpretation of colonial elites, that slaves and free blacks wore the tricolor cockade as a sign of allegiance to French republicanism. This interpretation would prematurely foreclose other possibilities in favor of an unreflective Eurocentrism. It would be another form of silencing through substitution. In this case, the Eurocentric reflex would silence other, different meanings that Caribbean subalterns may have attached to the cockade. To avoid this interpretive distortion, I will bracket the assumption that the tricolor cockade in colonial Saint-Domingue derived its meaning from revolutionary France. We must consider other possibilities: that the cockade was understood by slaves and free blacks in unique ways that are not reducible to European precedents, or that it was understood in different ways by the different groups involved. Here we cannot presume that the colonial subjects wearing the cockade were representing themselves as republicans in the European sense. That is only one of the hypotheses under consideration.

The situation of the cockade favors more subtle and complicated interpretations over the simplistic one of the colonial elites. It seems to have been characterized by misunderstanding and incomprehension of a kind that reveals epistemic gaps between the various parties involved. Consider, for instance, the great potential for gaps of meaning along the metropolitan-creole axis, even among whites or *gens de couleur*. Those present in France during the revolution would have a very particular interpretive context for understanding the cockade. This would include a fairly detailed understanding of the cockade's complexities, but as they played out in France.

The French Revolution was rich in symbols. That most enlightened of political movements had elaborate iconographies and semiotic codes. There is the well-known figure of Liberty as a woman named Marianne.[22] The guillotine was also represented as a female figure, Mme. Guillotine, and it was further associated with the justice of the people as "the popular ax" and the "scythe of equality."[23] There are well-known garments like the culotte, the silk knee-breeches of the upper classes, and the Phrygian or "liberty" cap of revolutionary insurgents. As Ronald Paulson notes, this proliferation of highly cathected symbols is not surprising. The French Revolution was a series of shocking and unprecedented events for which there were no conventions of representation. To some extent, all of this was an attempt to represent the unprecedented.[24]

In this milieu, no symbol was more wildly popular than the tricolor cockade. Ferdinand Pouy describes it as an "electric and magical fashion," recounting its development from the decorative plumes that soldiers wore in their hats.[25] The term "cockade" (*cocarde*) was thus derived from the feathers of a cock (*coq*). It went on to become an official part of the French military uniform in various colors by the mid-1700s. A green cockade was briefly adopted by French revolutionaries in July 1789 so that they could recognize one another. It was modeled after a tree leaf, supposed to be the color of hope. The next day it was replaced by a red and blue cockade, the colors of the city of Paris. It is said that the Marquis de Lafayette, upon becoming commander of the National Guard, added royal white to this design. Evidently satisfied with his creation, he is reputed to have claimed, "I give you a cockade that will travel the globe."[26]

By October 1789 the tricolor cockade was being debated in the National Assembly. A member declared that anyone not wearing it was not proud of being a citizen and should be excluded from the Assembly.[27] It had become a visible way to declare one's allegiance to the revolutionary project. That same month, rumors of soldiers trampling on the tricolor cockade at Versailles caused a women's protest march.[28] Less than two years later, a letter writer from Bordeaux enthuses about a parade of more than ten thousand women wearing the "national cockade" on July 14. He goes on to note a general explosion of pride in the "national colors"—blue, white, and red—from ribbons to the edges of book pages, ceramics, Masonic documents, and mortuary drapes.[29]

The tricolor cockade was a highly cathected symbol in many ways. In general, it represented adherence to revolutionary-republican values. To wear the cockade was to be in favor of the new ideas and the new nation, new society, and "new man" they described.[30] Symmetrically, rejection of those values could be symbolized by wearing a cockade of some other kind: the white Bourbon one or the black of the counterrevolution. These were seen as direct affronts to revolutionary ideals, so wearing them provoked conflict. Similarly, sarcastic articles about the wearing and sale of tricolor cockades became a staple of the antirevolutionary press. Reports on the widespread trade in cockades on street corners by poor women were used to parody the revolution as a movement of the plebian and the unwashed.[31]

As time went on, the tricolor cockade came to stand not just for adherence to the revolution but more narrowly for a certain conformity of representation. Efforts were made to police and discipline the wearing of the cockade. For instance, complaints arose about variations in color and design that were seen as suspect and a sign of the "enemies of the public good." Similarly, arrest reports of deviant or unpatriotic behavior began to include details about the improper forms and displays of the tricolor cockade.[32]

In July 1792, as an attempt to impose ideological conformity during the war on Austria, it became obligatory for all men to wear the cockade.[33] While this law was designed to foster patriotism in a militarist vein (since the cockade was originally a military ornament), it had other consequences as well. By making the cockade compulsory the law vastly increased demand for cockades relative to supply. By 1793, people were complaining of elevated prices and speculators were rushing into the market.[34] Later that year the movement for conformity and legalization went further by passing a law requiring women to wear the cockade.[35] It was thereby entangled in opposing imperatives to promote women's patriotism, suppress their political participation, end distinctions in dress, and maintain gender differentiation.[36] In all of these senses, French citizens would have been familiar with the cockade not only as an emblem of revolutionary republicanism but also as a tool of ideological discipline. It was a point of insertion for policies aiming to control ideological allegiance and gender identity.

All of these events, controversies, and shades of meaning would have been vivid to those who witnessed the French revolution and its aftermath. They would have been aware of the cockade's complex and countervailing significations in this context. They would have observed the struggles of representation and political power that played out in the cockade. They would have been broadly familiar with the multiplicities of meaning and range of significations that the cockade was held to have by various people. They would have been equally familiar with later attempts to discipline this meaning, to enforce a revolutionary orthodoxy by regulating the cockade's appearance and requiring people to wear it. They would have understood the futility of this legislation while also observing firsthand the strong emotional cathexes that were attached to the cockade in various ways.

French expatriates, creole whites, and creole *gens de couleur* living in Saint-Domingue had a much less direct experience of this context. The ideas of revolutionary republicanism were reported in the colonies, so its language and commitments were not entirely foreign to colonial elites. The *Moniteur général*, for instance, a prominent Saint-Domingan newspaper, often employed language and ideas of revolutionary France. It advocated a free press in the name of "regenerating the people" and safeguarding its rights and privileges. It talked about the "new order of things" and proposed itself as the means for the "propagation and communication of the enlightenment of which a new people has a constant need to be surrounded."[37] In this sense, the Saint-Domingan press showed an awareness of revolutionary-republican language and ideals. These concepts were received in a local idiom, however, being used to justify the sovereignty of a white separatist movement and oppose the abolition of slavery.[38] We see, then, that the understanding of revolutionary republicanism was mediated by cultural, temporal, and physical distance, the print media, and hearsay.

Because expatriates and creole elites had an approximate, mediated, and personalized reception of the ideas of the French Revolution, we cannot assume that what the cockade meant in France it also meant in the French colonies. They did not experience the events and controversies surrounding the cockade in France directly, so their understanding would have been an indirect one at best, interpreted through local needs and agendas. We can conclude that colonial elites understood some of the cultural background that shaped the cockade's reception in France, but we cannot assume that their understanding was accurate, complete, or identical to that of people in France.

In this light, consider the sizeable epistemic gaps between colonial elites and the majority of slaves. Most enslaved people in Saint-Domingue did not speak French, and most of those who did, including a preponderance of the revolutionary leadership, were illiterate.[39] An estimated 60 percent of the enslaved people in the colony at this time were born in Africa, mostly in the Kingdom of Kongo. Their beliefs were strongly influenced by a number of Central African sources, adapted into the conditions of slavery in the Caribbean. This included notions of community comprised of both the living and the dead, in which departed ancestors took an active interest in the affairs of the living; notions of multiple souls that had different characteristics and functions; and the idea of an ancestral homeland in Guinea to which souls returned after a person's physical death.[40] Most notoriously, it included the practice of Vaudou. While this was considered "fetishism" and "sorcery" by European observers, it provided powerful forms of protection to those on whom coercive and cruel labor was imposed.[41] It also gave enslaved people the means to ritually repossess their commodified, appropriated bodies.[42]

These differences in cultural background produced quite different understandings of shared political realities. Revolutionary slaves interpreted the unfolding political situation in terms of their own constitutional struggles in the Congolese civil war and their own understanding of European religion. This is seen, for instance, in the unique political theology of the revolutionary leader Macaya, who saw himself as beholden to three overlapping sovereignties: "I am the subject of three kings: of the King of Congo, master of all the Blacks; of the King of France, who represents my father; of the King of Spain who represents my mother. These three Kings are the descendants of those who, guided by a star, came to adore God made Man."[43] It is not clear what Macaya meant by this, but it illustrates at least the potential confusion of mixing European and African political idioms.

For these reasons and many others, it is a mistake to assume that the events surrounding the Haitian Revolution were simply a reenactment of French revolutionary ideals.[44] Similarly, it is quite problematic to claim that Saint-Domingan slaves and free blacks wearing the tricolor cockade were representing French revolutionary ideals in any way that the French would have recognized. They had no direct experience of the French Revolution or the French revolutionary culture of the metropole; at best their knowledge of revolutionary ideas and events would be based on a kind of mediated, indirect experience. They had their own understanding of the cockade's significance, one that was separated from metropolitan French significations by space, social distance, and cultural difference.

In general, it seems clear that these lines of social differentiation led to communicative disjunction. Lines of class, property, race, and nativity created forms of group differentiation that also differentiated lines of communication, discursive codes, and horizons of understanding. This occurred in the senses described by Pierre Bourdieu, in which communication and social distinction go hand in hand in a self-reinforcing system.[45] In this context, there was minimal discursive calibration between various ideas about the cockade's significance.

In these ways, the cockade serves as a measure of the cultural and epistemic distance between Paris and Saint-Domingue. The local understanding of this decoration was not identical to that of French republicans. Colonial elites would have understood its meaning as an element of the revolutionary events in the metropole, but in an idiomatic way not identical to the understanding of metropolitan French. Some Caribbean slaves and free blacks adopted its use, but it is even more problematic for us to come to any determinate idea of what this "meant" for them. Their use of the cockade seems submerged in a substantial silence.

PARANOID PROJECTION

Because of gaps in the archival record and the silencing of subaltern voices, we do not know why slaves and free blacks took to wearing the cockade. We cannot attribute particular goals and intentions to this practice, and we cannot say that wearing the cockade was an attempt by enslaved people to "say" anything in particular. Chastened by the insights of Spivak and Trouillot, we must be careful about filling in the blanks of meaning that we find here, attributing voice, subjectivity, agency, and intentionality to colonial subalterns where such attributions are problematic. To do so would constitute silencing through both ventriloquism and substitution. It would write over the unknown and perhaps unknowable workings of the tricolor cockade in the revolutionary Caribbean, substituting something more familiar, a European republicanism transplanted to an exotic location. To avoid such damaging shortcuts, we will have to find meaning in this situation without those familiar interpretive crutches, thinking carefully about its epistemic and communicative characteristics and how the cockade functions within them.

The two forms of silence I have traced, archival silence and silent practices, are joined here in important ways. They come together when we ask about the political meaning of the cockade in colonial Saint-Domingue. I believe that the first set of gaps helps to explain what was happening within the second.

Most strikingly, we see an isomorphism between the white elites of the era and us. The elite reception of the cockade mirrors our own efforts at interpretation in many ways. Theirs were based on insufficient information and lack of a proper context. They were troubled by gaps similar to those in our current archive. Cockade wearers obviously had some idea of what they "meant" by wearing the cockade. White and colored planters and colonial officials clearly had some idea of what it "meant" to see the cockade being worn. But all of that seems to have been ambiguous at the time, and with the passage of several centuries it is even more so today. Therefore, we are left with layers of clues and observations, covered over by the patina of time. Their situation must have been rather similar. It seems to have been characterized by misfired communication and interpretations made without adequate basis but acted upon nonetheless.

There is an inherent gap between intention and reception here, one created by communicative disjunctions and the very silence of the object itself. Lacking the rich tapestry of significations available to a French metropolitan, wearing the cockade in the Caribbean was a semantically ambiguous act. Thus we can say that the two forms of silence are connected. Because colonial elites failed to understand the significance of the cockade for slaves and free blacks—because they failed to hear the subaltern speak—their accounts of it are awkward, one-sided, and incomplete. When those elites recorded their observations in letters and memoires, they also immortalized the silencing of the cockade. What started as social distance and cultural incomprehension was incorporated into the archives as a silence of subaltern voices.

We can call this *silencing through interpretation*. It posits particular meanings and truths about the subaltern in conditions of ambiguity. Such misunderstanding is matter of assuming that one has understood and attributing meaning to subaltern others on that basis. When one has *not* truly understood, such attributions constitute a form of silencing. Whatever the subaltern may have been saying, thinking, or doing is further obscured by the attribution of some other meaning. As such, this is yet another form of displacement. Rather than displace one identity with another or one form of agency with another, however, it forecloses ambiguous possibilities with premature determinations.

Such forms of silencing are similar to ventriloquism, but they are not the same. Interpretation claims to have understood something important about a subaltern other, while ventriloquism is a form of advocacy or speaking on behalf of the subaltern. The two forms are often intertwined, however, and in some cases it is not possible to cleanly distinguish one from the other. Ventriloquism frequently starts from the attitude of having understood something about the subaltern and proceeds to represent this truth on the subaltern's behalf. In this manner, silencing through interpretation can become a precursor to silencing through ventriloquism. Similarly, ventriloquism can be rooted in interpretation, folding two forms of silencing together in certain cases.

Although the tricolor cockade became a nexus of silence in complex ways, it did have clear political effects. A small and innocuous ornament, it still drew pointed attention and blunt legal responses from white elites on Saint-Domingue. I believe that the cockade's impact in anticolonial politics was created precisely by its ambiguity. Above all, the cockade in the revolutionary Caribbean was an *equivocal* object. It equivocated on values and propositions that may have been attached to it, appearing to connect with various interpretive contexts without confirming or denying assertions about its "meaning." In the remarks I have surveyed, for example, elites posit various theories about the meaning that slaves and free blacks attribute to the cockade. Lacking a clear indication of the cockade's meaning for the people wearing it, those elites drew their own conclusions. They relied on their experience of the events, ideology, and iconography of the French revolution to provide an interpretive context for understanding the Caribbean cockade. As we have seen, however, this was an interpretive leap over a significant epistemic gap. There was no unified background to support interpretation nor robust enough discursive means to create one.

Thus, the cockade was interpreted in terms of a somewhat alien context, one familiar to white elites but not necessarily appropriate to the people whose actions were being interpreted. It came to symbolize the values that these elites most feared if they were to spread to the colonies: the doctrines of equality and liberty that were the foremost elements of revolutionary republicanism. There was widespread paranoia about abolitionist infiltrators from France or England and printed materials that might spread these doctrines. Elites seemed to see the cockade very much as part of this picture. They seemed to attribute an understanding of French revolutionary ideals to slaves and free blacks that ignores the intervening silences and epistemic gaps.

The tricolor cockade appears here as a screen on which fears and anxieties are projected. Its lack of propositionally specific claims lent it a kind of paranoid versatility. Whatever most troubled white plantation owners about slavery, colonial race relations, or the inconsistent application of republican ideals could be read into this symbol. It could thus stand for the most inconsistently held values in the heart of the white conscience, without anyone else needing to know what was troubling that conscience. By constituting a domain of possibilities and a screen of projection, it tapped into white anxieties in a flexible and individualized way.

Here, I believe, we find the political genius of the tricolor cockade. It functioned as a kind of mirror to the elite understanding of the ideals of the new French republic. White elites brought French republican ideals to bear as an interpretive context, and in so doing, simultaneously problematized them. By projecting them onto a highly racialized colonialism, they were forced to confront the tensions within their own ideals and practices.

This tension is mutely symbolized by what we might call "the black republican": the figure of a slave or free black displaying the iconography of revolutionary France. (In homage to C. L. R. James, we could also use the term "black Jacobin.") By openly displaying republican symbols, blacks seem to have been interpreted as making a republican statement. In the paranoid imagination of colonial elites, that statement was something like "I also believe in liberty and equality, and that includes extending those values to people like me." Any dissonance the viewer might have seen between the symbol and the person wearing it highlighted the implicit silence of revolutionary republicanism on issues of race. It revealed the racially unmarked character of republican ideals, the way they postulated universal liberty and equality for all people while implicitly imagining those people as white. When the cockade was worn by blacks, their exclusion could no longer pass silently and must now be openly justified as an exclusion. This open challenge to the racial order may explain the adoption of explicit, legal prohibitions on slaves and free blacks from wearing the cockade. Losing their ability to finesse the inconsistent application of republican ideals, white colonists had to make those exclusions explicit. They did so, interestingly, through similarly symbolic means, forbidding nonwhites from representing themselves as revolutionary republicans. This shows how easily the revolutionary-republican ideals symbolized by the cockade could be adapted to a new set of struggles and how difficult it was to contain their meaning.

In these circumstances, the object acquires a kind of primacy, with a moment of independence from the agendas and intentions of the people surrounding it. It has, as Jane Bennett says, a particular force as a thing.[46] Because of its complex epistemic situation, because of the ease with which it accommodated alternate interpretations of its meaning, the tricolor cockade constituted a potent form of immanent critique. In the revolutionary Caribbean it functioned as a disruptive intervention, a purely political object that became a pebble in the gears of political domination. Through a series of interpretive missteps, it caused the bad conscience of the colonial elite imagination to turn back on itself. By tapping into visceral fears in conditions of interpretive uncertainty, silence, and epistemic rupture, the tricolor cockade criticized the dominant culture in the terms of its own republican ideals. It caused a backlash precisely because of elite fears of what their own moral code might have to say about colonialism. In this sense it provides an example of political action that is performative, indeterminate, and critical. It is one generated out of subaltern silence itself.

The visceral force of this critique is provided by fear, rumor, and paranoia. It is surplus anxiety about the true universalization of republican principles, created by the inconsistency of their application. As Charles Mills has argued, the concept of race was a device for reconciling universalism with domination.[47] It provided psychic relief from the tensions between political doctrines of liberty and equality on one hand and the brutalities of colonialism and slavery on the other. Here we see that race was not enough, however. It did not resolve the tensions between universalism and domination, as the fear of white elites attests. This fear was all the more effective as a mode of critique because it so thoroughly animated the minds of the oppressors.

ELOQUENT OBJECT

The silence around the tricolor cockade in revolutionary Saint-Domingue was a highly resonant one. We can excavate rich layers of meaning from the comments about it that are scattered through the archives. They reveal a great deal about the epistemological complexity that comes from mixing race and slavery with revolutionary politics. Wearing the cockade was a form of expression in one of the most cosmopolitan public spheres of the eighteenth century: the Caribbean port cities and coastal towns where sailors, soldiers, traders, and workers mixed from around the globe. It was, as Spivak would say, an attempt to speak. Yet the cockade had no propositional content. It meant something without saying anything. Thus it became a screen of projection for all kinds of ideas, including the paranoid fears and guilty conscience of white slaveholders. It could thus probe the tensions implicit within their most inconsistently held values, without anyone needing to know exactly what those values were or why they were in tension. The uncanny ability of this material object to access the innermost fears of powerful people explains the psychic violence manifest in the legal restrictions placed on "republican" slaves. It also shows us a great deal about internal tensions within the white colonial conscience and reveals important things about the performative character of subaltern silence. The enigmatic, silent nature of the cockade gave it unique political potentialities in the public sphere, even without "saying anything."

This reveals a further permutation of subaltern silence in colonial Saint-Domingue. In this slave colony the subaltern was systematically and forcibly prevented from speaking. Enslaved people in the colonies undoubtedly had public spheres of their own, covert spaces of communication through clandestine meetings and marronage, and perhaps even the lines of communication with "philanthropists" that white elites so feared. They were, however, denied the epistemic and communicative space to make claims about the injustice of their situation. In Spivak's broad sense, the subaltern could not speak.

The tricolor cockade reveals a subversive dimension of this situation. It makes no claims; it expresses no doctrine. It does something with political significance that cannot be theorized as a form of propositional speech. Rather, the object exercised a potent force of its own by existing in a context of communicative disjunction, accompanied by overly hasty attributions of meaning and intention. The political effects of the tricolor cockade were not exactly accidental, but they cannot be theorized as the intentional enactment of a revolutionary theory with intent to bring about specific goals. Nor can they be seen as raising propositionally differentiated claims about the injustice of colonial practices. They do not fit our standard conceptions of revolutionary or discursive politics. Rather, they were unspoken and elliptical, examples of revolutionary politics without discursive claims or an explicit theoretical apparatus.

This moment of subaltern silence displays a striking conjunction of ambiguity, interpretation, epistemic distance, subversive signification, and problematization. The object has a disruptive force because of the uncertainty about what it signified. Its indeterminate character gave it a distinctive political power, different from that of a propositionally differentiated claim about justice or rights. It did not aim to establish the truth of any particular proposition. It did not ask for the realization of any theoretical doctrine. Rather, it disrupted attempts to pave over existing instabilities in belief. It provides an example of subaltern politics when "speech" in the narrowest sense is prohibited. We are forced instead to focus renewed attention on the performative dimensions of silence, the material aspects of action, and the epistemologies that surround it. The cockade provides us with an epistemologically rich example of subaltern silence that provokes the explosive potential of epistemic gaps, imaginary ideals, implied meanings, and false projections. This is precisely its power: the cockade was a disruptive enigma well suited to the subversive needs of people not allowed to speak.

INTERLUDE

The Shifting Horizon of Modernity

Placide Camus, Apprentice Printer

1791–1804

Then begins an epoch of social revolution.

—Karl Marx

Citizen Placide Camus, apprentice printer, was arrested in Nantes on October 26, 1794. He had just disembarked from a ship sailing from Philadelphia. Camus's arrest dossier tells a story that was typical of his turbulent times. It recounts his birth in Chartres, his journey from Paris to the coast, his departure on a ship sailing from Le Havre to Saint-Domingue, his apprenticeship in a printing shop there, his flight from Saint-Domingue to Philadelphia during the Haitian Revolution, his return to France, and his arrest.[1]

In the course of this circuit, Placide Camus passed through some of the most worldmaking events of his day. Paranoia over the spread of abolitionism and republicanism in Saint-Domingue had been overshadowed by much more tangible concerns. Widespread slave revolts erupted in the north in August 1791. They marked the beginning of what was to become a successful revolution against French colonialism, resulting in the independence of the new Republic of Haiti in 1804.

None of this seems to have been apparent when Camus signed his apprenticeship papers in Paris in January 1792, however. His contract shows no sign of expecting that colonial life would be profoundly altered. The contract carefully specifies, for instance, that the owners of the print shop in Saint-Domingue have the right to train as many of "their *nègres*" to work in the press as they see fit. Slave revolts were turning the colony upside-down at this time, but the Parisian partner of the print business seems to have unaware or unconcerned about their ultimate effects.

He was obviously wrong, however. The revolts forced colonial administrators to take measures that had been unimaginable several years before. On August 29, 1793, the colonial administrator with the happy name of Léger Félicité Sonthonax issued a proclamation freeing all slaves in the northern province of Saint-Domingue.[2] Two more proclamations would follow over the next six weeks, emancipating slaves across the entire colony. They formally confirmed the process that enslaved people had initiated by seizing their own liberty. This also gave those colonial subjects an odd sort of publicity, through the mixture of horror, outrage, and fascination that the revolution occasioned in media audiences across the globe. These events initiated a new stage in renegotiating subaltern silence, one that entered uncharted territory with the abolition of slavery and the new challenges that followed.

Three weeks after Sonthonax issued his emancipation proclamation, he also signed travel documents giving Placide Camus permission to leave the colony. Camus had completed only half of his three-year apprenticeship. His papers did not state why he was leaving, but presumably the revolutionary upheaval had much to do with it. He was part of a general exodus of whites from the colony. Many, like Camus, resettled in Philadelphia or other parts of the United States while preparing to return to France.

Camus stayed in Philadelphia for a year. While he was there, the French government abolished slavery in all of its colonies. Meanwhile, the revolutionary Terror reached its peak in France, with the Committee of Public Safety increasingly providing a power base for the Montagnard faction to eliminate their political enemies. By the summer, however, all of this was over. The Thermidorian Reaction had ended the Terror and calmed the country. Placide Camus enters this scene in a small way with his return and arrest. None other than the all-powerful Committee of Public Safety reviewed his case and released him. The unsigned ruling from the Committee noted that Camus had asked for his liberty so he could return to work as a printer. Since it was unclear why he had been arrested in the first place, Camus's freedom was a matter of "justice that he has the right to expect in a free country."[3]

Placide Camus traversed the shifting horizon of modernity in a way that reveals much about his times. He was a sort of Zelig in the revolutionary politics of the day, always seeming to appear in the midst of some world-historical event.

He also participated in some of the most revolutionary new technologies of his era. Camus came to the colonies as a junior representative of the European public sphere, part of an explosion of print culture in France that spread rapidly to the colonies. This socio-technical revolution began on Saint-Domingue in 1764 with the establishment of the *Gazette de Saint-Domingue*. Camus entered the picture several decades later, as it was dismantled in the chaos of a very different revolution.

Camus's dossier reveals much about the underlying social dynamics of the colonial press, its relation to metropolitan Europe and the United States, and the ways discourse spread back and forth across the Atlantic through complex, interconnected lines of communication. This was a set of publics that spanned two continents, disseminating metropolitan European innovations to the colonies and colonial ones to the metropole. People avidly read one another's newspapers around the Caribbean and across the Atlantic, and Camus's short career illustrates the transnational connections that made this possible.

We have seen that this story of Euro-American print publicity is deeply intertwined with subaltern silence. Law and violence had been used to silence enslaved people for decades. That project of silencing became more complicated when the new technologies of publicity were pressed into its service. These innovations improved the efficiency and scope of subordination, but they also exposed long-existing tensions and contradictions in colonial society. The new, more efficient public sphere stoked rumor and paranoia as much as it allowed for the more efficient tracking and repatriation of fugitive slaves. Placide Camus and his contemporaries were at the forefront of these changes, constituting the technical arm of a public sphere that was being reshaped by the subaltern silence that it had helped to create.

Sites of resistance were few within the colonial slave system. Nonetheless, we have observed some singular and unexpected moments of subaltern agency, publicity, and voice. Their subtlety and evanescent quality stand out against the stark power of the system they opposed. Some of these opportunities were created by fugitive slaves seeking their own freedom. That undertaking had collateral effects that may not have been anticipated, but they tapped into the very machinery of control in a way that aided the cause of enslaved people. Similar things can be said of poisoning. It may or may not have aimed at open revolt, but its effects reverberated through the power structure of the colony in uncanny ways. The tricolor cockade was a more purposive effort at communication, but it too created problematics that its wearers may not have anticipated. The most extreme case is that of the phantasmatic public sphere, in which merely the thought of subaltern agency hidden behind silence caused consternation. In each of these cases rumor, paranoia, and the ambiguities of subaltern silence served to unhinge legally entrenched forms of subordination. All of these instances propagated anxiety and paranoia about subaltern figures who were thought to have been silenced. The apparatus of publicity, and its propagation of affect, created new forms of presence for people who were otherwise silenced.

This investigation reveals some of the fine texture of colonial subordination: its internal tensions and contradictions; the ways colonial practices were heavily riven by affect, the propagation of fear, rumor, and other unsettling phenomena; and the ways this could be exploited by those otherwise denied voice. All of this opened up cracks in colonial practice. It disturbed the routine mechanics of subordination, unsettling their hold and creating moments of subaltern action and voice in the midst of silence.

I have tried to expose these subtle dynamics to view while being wary of the interpretive dangers that could be encountered along the way. We must be careful not to celebrate subaltern agency uncritically. Such attributions are always viewed through the archive, which is itself highly conditioned by the preoccupations of its time. We must therefore be careful to take account of all that is ambiguous and problematic there. Did the reports of poisoning disclose organized insurrection, a quiet attempt at revenge, or a set of isolated incidents compounded by rumor and amplified by fear into something that appeared organized and sustained? The paranoias of the age may see agency in places where it had been effectively foreclosed. I have tried to show that ironically, that very misattribution of agency can constitute yet other unexpected and unrecognized forms of agency. In the midst of de jure subaltern silence, we find cracks in the system that created openings for subversion.

Michel-Rolph Trouillot famously claimed that the Haitian Revolution was inconceivable.[4] The elite reactions that I have examined suggest otherwise. They seem to show that insurrection was *constantly* conceivable, that colonial elites saw menace all around themselves in a variety of ways, and that potential calamity was often a source of nagging anxiety. The possibility of a free Black republic may not have been thinkable, but violent upheaval certainly was.[5]

Placide Camus's story occurs as the horizon suddenly shifts in the colonial Caribbean. The always too conceivable vision of a slave revolution had come to pass in the worst possible way from the perspective of colonial elites. As I noted, many departed in haste for American cities like Charleston and Philadelphia, where they set up expatriate communities. Some people settled there, while others like Placide Camus awaited favorable winds and eventually departed for Europe. There are many vivid accounts of white elites fleeing the chaos, several of which we have already examined. The reactions and accusations of these privileged few are well documented, unlike the opinions of the enslaved people who initiated the Haitian Revolution and pushed it to its conclusion.

This worst of times for colonial planters was not exactly the best of times for those who had recently liberated themselves. The Haitian Revolution marked a striking new chapter in an era of revolutions. However, Haitians now faced all of the challenges of going forward in a world largely hostile to their freedom. Placide Camus was safely home, but many challenges remained ahead for the black and *de couleur* people of Haiti.

I will not dwell on the details of the revolution except to note that it was an extraordinary reversal of subaltern silence. The enslaved capitalized on the contradictions of colonial slavery and overcame them. In every way imaginable these events seem a rupture with the past and a termination of subaltern silence. If ever there was a case for historical discontinuity, the Haitian Revolution would seem to be it. It marks an amazing disruption of slavery and colonialism. It constituted a radical desubordination of subaltern people, one that created vast new possibilities as compared with their previous lives of enslavement and subordination. As they set about drafting constitutions and establishing a government, Haitian lawmakers displayed an acute awareness of the unprecedented character of their enterprise. At times they tried to become a beacon of freedom for other subordinated peoples, devising wildly novel measures to uphold these principles.[6]

Questions of rupture and continuity have troubled genealogy for some time. At one point Michel Foucault characterized his work as "much more willing than the history of ideas to speak of discontinuities, ruptures, gaps, entirely new forms of positivity, and of sudden redistributions."[7] He was anxious to separate himself from all of the monotonous attributions of continuity that attenuate and tame "the wild fact of change."[8] After providing nuanced accounts of the ways in which he was avoiding abstract conceptions of both continuity and discontinuity, he was alarmed to be characterized nonetheless by a French dictionary as "a philosopher who founds his theory of history on discontinuity."[9] As a result,

Foucault returned to this theme many times, insisting on "the diversity of systems and the play of discontinuities" within his work.[10] He emphasized that history has a complex texture and cannot be reduced to any single principle. When one does see sudden shifts of discourse and epistemology, he says, they are typically connected to moments of political change. Such formations of power often govern what can be said and how discourses are formed. Rupture is thus an effect of power, but each manifestation is unique and cannot be reduced to uniform, universal ideas of change.[11]

These insights are helpful for thinking about the moment of rupture traversed by Placide Camus. Haitian independence was characterized by lines of rupture and continuity, radical innovation, and adoption of Euro-American precedents.[12] Even while they engaged in an extraordinary rejection of past institutions and practices, the new Haitian founders did not completely overthrow of all that had come before. Perhaps as a kind of conceptual economy, they also adopted certain recognizable conventions of the modern nineteenth-century nation-state. Among these were constitutionalism, republican government, and empire.[13]

More darkly, we will see that this was also not the end of subaltern silence. Neither subalternity nor silence disappeared with colonial slavery. Instead new problems emerged, accompanied by new tensions and new forms of subordination. Emancipation and postcoloniality had their own contradictions, creating new forms of subaltern silence. In other words, the revolution did not mark a complete rejection of the past, and certainly not a complete realization of freedom out of the rupture with slavery and colonialism. There were fresh permutations of practices that had existed under colonialism, including ones that now silenced members of the new society.

Even when thinking about moments of rupture, it is important not to think of the Haitian Revolution as the *sole* point of inflection between old and new. There are other moments of rupture, discontinuity, and sudden change in this history that do not coincide with the revolution. We have already seen, for instance, that the institutions and practices of print publicity changed radically in 1764, setting in motion new dynamics that broke with what came before. Placide Camus's exit from Saint-Domingue marks a temporary suspension of the colonial press, but it will resume quickly enough and continue to develop in the nineteenth century. We will see these institutions and practices undergo striking transformations. Here the decisive moment of sudden change occurred some three decades before the Haitian Revolution, and it spun out a long tail of consequences that extended well after.

Other aspects of the story vary in a more continuous manner. Race relations will continue to be fraught in Haiti, even as black and *de couleur* citizens now control the state. The racist culture of the old colonial society will continue its development, generating new forms of racial distinction and governing relations between metropole and the postcolonial Caribbean. All of this will create novel forms of subordination and silence. It will be put in place by new techniques that are more efficient, subtle, and diffuse. Yet all of these developments display a certain continuity of the basic dynamics of subaltern subordination. In short, subaltern silence remains a continuously permuting problem. However, it will start to take on surprising and characteristic new forms in the postcolonial era.

To some extent, these dynamics will mark changes already in progress under colonialism. As the apparatus of colonial slavery is forcefully torn out, publicity gains increasing dominance as a form of subordination. Rather than function as an adjunct to more directly violent and physical forms of subordination, the public sphere itself now becomes a principal site and means of subordination. Subaltern groups are still maintained in obscurity and silence, but increasingly through more subtle means dissolved into the fabric of publicity. Physical terror and violence had been principal means of subordination under colonialism. With the transition to postcoloniality, subaltern groups are not desubordinated so much as articulated on new national or regional scales, through new and more subtle means. Tracing that sometimes phantasmagorical evolution is the task of the chapters to come.

Ironically, the same disruptive technologies that so unsettled the colonial matrix of power would now provide the basis to reconstitute it in new form. These were the *dispositifs* of publicity that were developed to oppose the concentrated power of the absolutist state. They now coalesce into a new nexus of subordination, one combining publicity, postcoloniality, and racist culture in a potent new blend. The result is new but oddly familiar forms of subordination. These changes mark a shift in the horizon of modernity, taking on forms that are still familiar to us today.

PART II

Postcolonial Transformations

CHAPTER 6

Times of Exception

Subaltern Silence in the Revolutionary Caribbean

1770–1805

Freedom did not abolish the lash.

—Saidiya Hartman

Of all the events in Haiti's event-filled history, the Haitian Revolution receives by far the greatest attention. It marked a dramatic break with the colonial past, creating a new sovereign nation out of a former slave colony. These events exercised an influence on world history that continues to be felt today. However, even this epochal victory against slavery and colonialism came at some cost, including costs that are not often recognized as such.

Over the next three chapters I will tally up some of the collateral damage of this justly celebrated revolutionary project. It can be reckoned in the production of subaltern subjects who were repeatedly silenced in a variety of ways, yet periodically managed to claim some voice. I will trace their struggles through shifting forms of subaltern silence from the end of the Haitian Revolution in 1804 to the mid-nineteenth century. During this postcolonial era, we can discern a set of erasures, foreclosures, barely heard utterances, and silences. They are articulated in the midst of conflicts over national independence and the aftermath of slavery, incomprehension between sides of a revolutionary conflict, the development of transatlantic public spheres connecting the Americas and Europe, the nation-building projects of the new Haitian Republic, and ultimately, the silencing effect of caricature, a popular new print genre of the mid-nineteenth century with profound effects in this postcolonial context.

This postcolonial phase of the genealogy traces shifting tensions and struggles between different strands of the Haitian revolutionary project. Dominant in this picture is the imaginary of a black republic, with all of its national intrigues and imperial ambitions. I will try to show, however, that threaded alongside it is a quiet subaltern voice that appears and disappears, much more associated with subsistence, autochthonous tradition, and rural life. It presents a view of independence quite different from the concerns of the Haitian republican project—but it is also one that is ineffable, fragile, appearing and disappearing under the pressure of other currents. In the end, my efforts to follow these traces will emphasize the multifarious and ambivalent character of Haitian independence. What seems like a victory for subaltern subjects also produces new forms of subaltern silence. In the end, the victorious republican project is itself subordinated and silenced—reduced to the status of those whom it had silenced—by broader movements within the transatlantic public sphere.

This genealogy illustrates my motivations for focusing on subaltern silence rather than subaltern "speech." This is not a history of grassroots agency but a critical analysis of that project's blockages, blindnesses, and opacities. Subaltern silence can be created in many different ways. Because it is ultimately an epistemic phenomenon, I try to broaden attention to the full array of performative, symbolic, and material registers in which subordination occurs: not just literal speech but a wide variety of material, representational, and discursive practices. Here we will see why it is best to leave talk about subaltern speech behind and focus more broadly on subaltern silence.

This story also provides a vivid demonstration of the usefulness of genealogy. It traces shifting qualities, forms, and conditions of subaltern silence, observing intertwined dynamics of subordination and desubordination and showing how misleading it can be to think of this changing scene in terms of liberation, emancipation, exclusion, or marginalization. Instead, this genealogy reveals the continuously productive character of subordination. It illustrates how the success of a progressive revolutionary movement can subordinate others in turn. However, the genealogy also shows that this phenomenon can itself produce its own creative opposition. A critical history of subaltern silence paints a vivid tableau of its many complexities, revealing much that might otherwise escape notice.

WHISPERS OF SILENT VOICES: "THREE FREE DAYS"

The bold, world-historical events of the Haitian Revolution captivate our attention for good reasons. Well-organized slave revolts defeated one of the world's dominant colonial powers, creating a free black republic in the midst of the colonial Caribbean. These events served as a striking example of a new form of anticolonial revolution and a new way of being free in the world. It is no surprise that this revolutionary legacy is now being appreciated as a profound contribution to political modernity.

When we parse out the fine details of these events and the archives they left behind, however, there is reason to think that there are other sides of the story. During the early days of the uprisings, insurgent slaves did not demand a free and independent republic, the abolition of slavery, or even the enforcement of rights that were already accorded to them under the Code Noir. Instead, their demands were consistently for three days per week free from the regimen of slave labor. These demands were made when insurgents had the upper hand and were in a position to advance their interests.

Mentions of the idea appear fitfully in the archives. Carolyn Fick insightfully traces a number of them through the scattered records of the early slave rebellions.[1] She notes that such demands were made even before the start of the revolution. In January 1791, a small insurgency erupted in Port-Salut, in the south of Saint-Domingue. It was put to an end fairly quickly and some of the insurgents were arrested and interrogated. In the record of this inquiry we find "a slave named Antoine... interrogated on the purpose of the slave gathering." The interrogation transcript recounts his testimony:

> In the name of the slaves on the plantations of each district, the said leaders were to demand of their masters three free days per week.... The declarant stated that Jean-Claude Lateste is supposed to have said on Sunday at M. Masson Duhard's place that the king had granted the slaves three free days per week, and that the said Jean-Claude is supposed to have said that the mulattoes were saying that the whites were the only obstacle preventing the application of this decree.

A bit later, the record circles back to this theme:

> The said slave Antoine, while making his declaration, had one of the members of the municipality called to the bar, and declared before him that, prior to reaching their camp, the mulattoes had assured the blacks that they were going to fight the whites to obtain three free days per week; that the blacks of the Plaine-du-Fond had offered to join their camp; and that they had refused this offer for fear that some harm might befall them.
>
> He also declared that when the mulattoes had abandoned their camp, they had told the blacks that if the whites accorded them three free days per week, they would also accord three free days per week to the blacks; but that it was their concern to act on their own behalf; and he declared that the black slaves of each particular plantation had thereafter resolved to present their demand on one day this week, and that if the whites refused to grant their demand, they would attack and slaughter them.[2]

Here the idea of three free days seems to operate as a primary focus of rebellion. This occurs in a number of ways. On one hand there seems to have been a rumor among slaves that the king had already granted them three free days and their masters were preventing its implementation. There is no evidence that the king had even contemplated such a measure, however, so the rumor may have simply been wishful thinking. On the other hand, the idea also seems to be inscribed in the complex politics between *gens de couleur* (the "mulattoes") and blacks in struggling for their freedom. Here it seems to be a recruitment strategy on the part of *gens de couleur*, soliciting slave support for a revolt while not entirely welcoming their participation. In this sense, the idea of three free days could have been a fabrication designed to foment hostility toward the white masters and leverage participation in an uprising. In any case, the idea seems appealing enough that it is put forward later as the central demand of the rebellion.

Another mention of three free days occurs in a retrospective account of the "troubles" of Saint-Domingue commissioned by the French government:

> Soon [Thiballier] was reduced to negotiating with the *esclaves*, as he already had with the *hommes de couleur*, who had promised freedom for a number of slaves and who insisted on the execution of that measure. A memoir written in the parish of Trou states, "that the *hommes de couleur* had forced the plantation owners of the neighboring parishes to declare in a written memorandum that they would give their slaves two days per week, and that the other

days, if they wanted the slaves to work, they would." The *nègres* assembled on the Plaine du Fond and the neighboring hills wanted more favorable conditions from the Southern Assembly.... They demanded for all *nègres* in general three free days [*trois jours francs*] per week, which had been the avowed object of their insurrection from the beginning.[3]

This account focuses on the same area and time period as the previous one. It is taken from a secondhand account of the "troubles," one written at a removal of several years and working from other documents. Nonetheless, it seems to substantiate the idea that three free days functioned as a key demand of the rebellion. Again, *gens de couleur* are reported to be advocating for the slaves, but seemingly insufficiently. The slaves extend their demands to a full three days for everyone.

Demands for three free days show up elsewhere in a similarly oblique fashion. A somewhat different reference appears in a letter by a Captain Henry of a ship registered in Nantes, waiting to leave port to escape the slave uprising.[4] Henry provides an account of the dramatic events in the colony to his associates back in France. He indicates his interests as lying chiefly in the commercial aspects of the colony, though he is also clearly concerned by the loss of life on all sides of the uprising. He is quite sympathetic with the cause of the *gens de couleur*, arguing that they should not be blamed for the slave revolts and saying that the prejudice against them is unfair and would take a century to extinguish. He is unsympathetic to the arrogance of the separatist movement among the white planters on the island. His account of the slave uprising is triangulated in the midst of all this. He claims that the *gens de couleur* and some whites in the Northern Province raised up the plantations as a tactic in a struggle against white planters. The results were a disaster: "In an instant several parishes were in flames. Their rallying cry is *liberty*. Someone told them that the King gave them three free days per week and the other three for their master earning three *livres* per day, they seized the cannons and arms of various burned parishes."[5]

Similar to what we have seen before, the implication seems to be that three free days was a way of leveraging the slave revolt on the part of *gens de couleur*, telling slaves they had already been given something by the king that was not being honored by their masters. In this case, the claim is further embroidered with the promise that the remaining three days would earn a daily wage of three *livres*, another enticement that seems not to have been true.

The mention of three free days is tantalizing here. We must remain suspicious of the details, however, because of other ambiguities in Henry's account. He is writing about the slave uprising in the North, the one that blossomed into full-scale revolution. He claims that these uprisings were solicited by subordinate whites and *gens de couleur*. This does not fit other accounts of those events, however. The received wisdom is that the uprising in the North was a self-initiated, self-planned, carefully executed project.[6] In this sense, Henry's account seems either to confuse events in the North and South, or to map one onto the other as a way of understanding the first in terms of the second. All of this reminds us that Henry himself was likely operating on hearsay, giving too much credence to the tendentious rumors and theories of others even while arguing against them. He was, after all, an occasional visitor to the colony who was quite anxious to leave.

Together these three fragments provide a provocative glimpse of what is being imagined within the early slave revolts. The ideas of colonial secession or national independence are nowhere on the table. Instead, we have an attempt to renegotiate the terms of servitude, to carve out more free time within the structures of slavery. It is not immediately clear what sense one might make of the idea of three free days itself, however. Was it a fabrication of colonial elites, used to solicit slaves' complicity with other political agendas? The idea may have been developed in this context but was then later taken on by insurgent slaves as a demand. Alternatively, the idea that the king had conferred three free days could have been a fabrication of the slaves themselves—perhaps a rumor or wishful thinking that took on more concrete reality as it circulated. Or reports about the king could have been idle chatter on the part of elites, while the idea of three free days was a concrete demand of insurgent slaves. In any case, we seem to wind up at the same point in the end. Regardless of its origin, three free days had an appeal and a logic of its own as a freestanding demand.

FAILURE OF THE IMAGINATION?

Commentators on the Haitian Revolution have expressed puzzlement or contempt toward such demands. Seeing them within the context of the revolution, most interpret these demands as a failure of the imagination. Some see the slaves as so beaten down that they could not imagine themselves being able to demand an independent, sovereign nation-state. Pamphile de Lacroix exemplifies such a view. Writing a decade after he commanded French troops attempting to suppress the revolution, Lacroix characterizes the heads of the revolt as "too barbaric to conceive the idea of the general liberty of their color."[7] Eugene Genovese frames such opinions more charitably. He sees them as a restorationist impulse that tries to reconstruct elements of African tradition in the New World. The early slave rebellions looked backward toward the life that had been taken from them when they were enslaved, he argues. Their efforts to recreate this existence in Saint-Domingue ended only when they were exposed to the revolutionary ideals of France and America. When Saint-Domingan slaves came in contact with the more forward-looking doctrines of white, bourgeois revolutionaries, Genovese argues, they revised their own goals accordingly.[8]

In agreement with Genovese, one could imagine a more epistemically oriented and sympathetic variant of this failure-of-the-imagination trope, taking its cue from Michel-Rolph Trouillot. Trouillot claims that the Haitian Revolution was literally inconceivable.[9] Before the revolution, there was a rich discussion of the merits of abolition, but it would have meant slavery being dismantled by Europeans and some new colonial arrangement being established. Of course there was also substantial fear that *talk* of abolition could provoke a slave insurrection. All of that notwithstanding, the idea that such an insurrection might mature into decolonization and a free, black republic was nowhere to be found. There was no precedent for such an outcome and no public discussion of it. Here we might claim, along with Trouillot, that insurgent slaves could not imagine national independence because such an idea was literally unimaginable. There was no precedent for the self-conversion of a slave colony into an independent state, so their imagination did not fail so much as express what was epistemically possible at the time. In this view, three free days would be the limited vision that *was* imaginable. As events changed, the horizons of imagination did as well, and the earlier vision was abandoned for others that were previously inconceivable.

In all of these interpretations, the relation between three free days and national independence becomes a story of epistemic innovation. Pushed forward by the onward rush of events, insurgent slaves were later able to imagine themselves as a national people in ways they had not before. As a result, the stunted vision of three free days was set aside or evolved into a new one envisioning Haitian independence.

From the perspective of subaltern silence, there is much to give us caution here. First, these interpretations view the history of the revolution in hindsight from the perspective of its ultimate end. All of the various movements, visions, and imaginaries of the decades preceding 1804 are evaluated from the standpoint of national liberation. They thus become early, crude precursors of something that reached maturity with the declaration of independence. This is a Whig history, a form of reverse teleology that interprets the past as progression toward the present. Second, such interpretations also make the error of privileging Westphalian national visions and national liberation as natural end states, framing other ideals as incomplete or misguided. From this perspective, visions of liberation not imagined as national in scope are rudimentary precursors of those that are. Third, these interpretations adopt a crude avant-gardism about reform versus revolution. Visions such as three free days are seen as reformist in the sense of working within an oppressive system but not transforming the underlying structures of subordination. Such reformism is seen as retrograde, ideological, and insufficient compared to the radical and transformative character of revolution.

These perspectives create substantial distortions when used to interpret subtle movements against subordination in the revolutionary Caribbean. Each represents a tendency to read the claims of Haitian revolutionaries through the lens of European categories. Privileging ideals of national liberation and the Westphalian state maps categories of European modernity onto perspectives that may have had very different orientations. "Reform" versus "revolution" carries forward an outdated dichotomy from Second International socialism. Neither term corresponds to a discrete social reality; rather, they are elements of a language for evaluating social change that is highly charged and deeply unclear. They are politicized labels used to valorize or discredit political movements rather than informative ways of describing characteristics inherent in them.

What, then, would a more epistemically and historiographically nuanced interpretation look like? The demand for three free days is at the same time both clear and ineffable. It is put forward quite unambiguously, but without explanation. The demand itself is forcefully articulated, but the ideas that animate it remain obscure. In this sense three free days has both an odd positivity and an ambiguous hint of something not fully said. These voices were heard and registered, yet their underlying motives were not recorded. Similar to the mysteries of the tricolor cockade that I discussed earlier, those voices seem to remain largely silent today, across the span of some two hundred years and through archives that are problematic, incomplete, and unreliable.

This is a textbook case of subaltern silence. We do not know what these subaltern subjects might have meant because they left no indication of their thoughts and visions. We are confronted, then, with all of the paradoxes and ambivalence that subordination presents. I am too chastened by Spivak's insights to think that my own observations could arrive at a "correct" view of what the subordinated voices of these enslaved insurgents intended. Instead, I will piece together a more tentative interpretation that tries to refrain from false confidence about its own correctness. It is guided by the idea that insurgent slaves were aiming at something specific in their bargaining demands, part of a distinctive political imaginary that was largely obscure at the time and is even more obscure to us today.

SILENCE AS AN ACHIEVEMENT: TIMES OF EXCEPTION

Implicit in the idea of three free days seems to be a broader imaginary of freedom. It takes the form of a limited, particular exception from plantation slavery. The content of that vision—what would be done with such freedom—is not specified, however. The desirability of this ideal seems to require no explanation on the part of those articulating it. It has the appearance of an idea that already has common currency.

To trace out the threads of this unspecified vision, it is useful to note similarities to other ideas and practices of the time. In the plantation system, garden plots and provision grounds were often carved out of unused land and allocated to slaves to grow their own food. In the plantation map in figure 6.1, for instance, the buildings marked "L" are slave quarters, and the lands around them marked "M" are garden plots allocated for subsistence agriculture.

This practice of allocating land to slaves relieved slaveowners of providing food for them. In larger colonies such as Saint-Domingue and Jamaica it was often enslaved people's only source of food. In the *Histoire des deux Indes*, first published in 1770, Abbé Raynal explains, "The state of slaves, although everywhere deplorable, shows some variation within the colonies. Those with extensive lands [such as Saint-Domingue] give them a communal plot of ground to provide for all of their needs. They can work this land during a part of Sunday

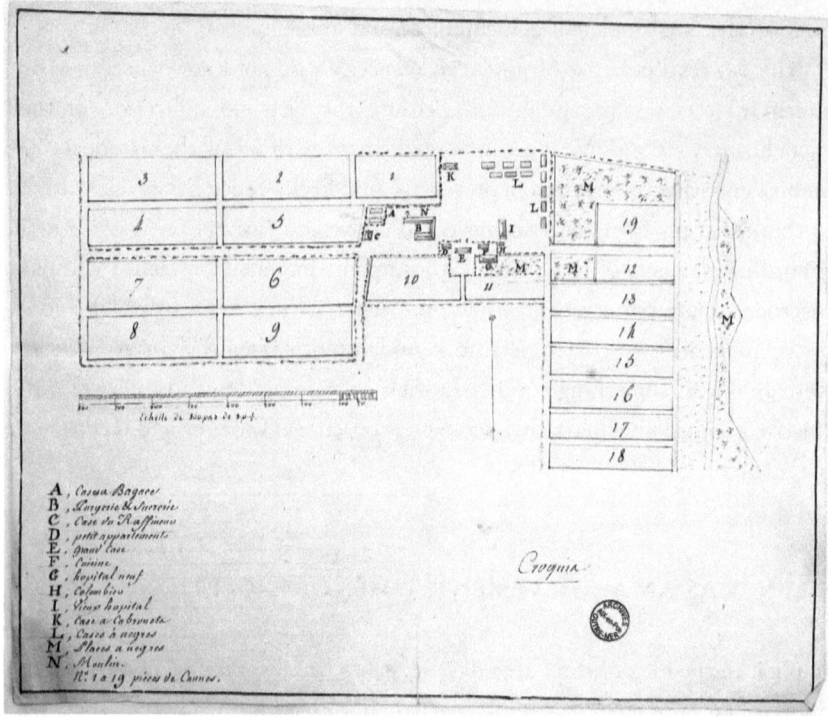

Figure 6.1 Map of the Paroy plantation "Croquis," near Limonade, Saint-Domingue, artist and date unknown. Archives Privées de Paroy, Archives Nationales d'Outre-Mer, Aix-en-Provence, France.

and the few moments they can steal from other days during meal times."[10] Marcus Rainsford provides additional details in his account of 1805: "They had gardens which produced the necessaries of life; pigs, poultry, and even horses; and were sufficiently clothed, agreeably to the climate; but they were considered and treated, as much beneath, the ordinary class of human beings."[11] In other words, the allocation of land for subsistence farming was never a product of generosity. It was a cost-saving measure, relieving plantation owners of the need to feed an ever-growing slave population.

An account from 1790 in Jamaica paints a vivid picture of these practices. Writing on the neighboring island during the time that the slave revolts in Saint-Domingue were beginning to intensify, William Beckford describes similar practices: "All kinds of ground provisions and corn are, as well as the plantain, successfully cultivated in the mountains; but as this is done by the negroes in their own grounds, and on those days which are given to them for this particular purpose, it does not enter into the mass of plantation-labour; it may be however noticed, that some idea may be conveyed of the manner in which they consume or employ that time which is given to them either for relaxation or profit."[12] Beckford describes subsistence farming on Jamaican plantations that is quite similar to that practiced in Saint-Domingue. Like Raynal and Rainsford, he takes special note of the temporality of this practice: the way subsistence farming is separated out of the temporal division of labor within the work week. It is to be done during time that is not devoted to plantation labor. Beckford seems to imply that this time is left to the discretion of slaves to grow their own provisions or occupy themselves in other ways, as they see fit. In other words, subsistence time is also a time of self-direction.

Beckford estimates the slave's free time as "every Sunday throughout the year to himself, every other Saturday out of crop, two or three days at Christmas, many days in the rainy seasons, and afternoons at other times besides; and he is frequently laid-up for days, by imaginary illness; and in which he is perhaps too often indulged."[13] This is part of an enumeration in which he states that English manufacturers, artisans, and mechanics have no time they can call their own, whereas a slave has "many weeks, nay months, that he can apply according to the bent of his inclinations, and for which he is not accountable to any one."[14] Having said that, Beckford also notes the considerable amount of work that must be accomplished during this time: "They prepare their land, and put in their different crops on the Saturdays that are given to them, and they bring home their provisions at night; and if their grounds be at a considerable distance from the plantation, as they often are to the amount of five or seven miles, or more, the journey backwards and forwards makes this rather a day of labour and fatigue, than of enjoyment and rest; but if, on the contrary, they be within any tolerable reach, it may be said to partake of both."[15]

Saturdays, then, are allocated to subsistence farming. If conditions allow it, however, a bit of "enjoyment and rest" can also be worked into the schedule. Sundays, by extension, were dedicated to the market. Here, Beckford says, slaves were sometimes able to earn money by selling spare produce: "When a tract of negro-provisions is regularly planted, is well cultivated, and kept clean, it makes a very husbandlike and a beautiful appearance; and it is astonishing what quantities of the common necessaries of life it will produce. A quarter of an acre of this description will be fully sufficient for the supply of a moderate family, and may enable the proprietor to carry some to market besides."[16] The extra produce would become a source of cash in the marketplace. Beckford reports the enthusiasm around this market participation, saying that slaves would walk sometimes ten or more miles from the garden plots to the market, "and it is astonishing what immense weights they will carry upon their heads at this extended distance, with what cheerfulness they will undertake the length, and with what spirit and perseverance they will overcome the fatigue, of the journey."[17]

As Raynal noted, such subsistence farming was a common practice in the larger Caribbean colonies. Some of the details seem to differ from place to place, but Beckford, Raynal, and Rainsford provide similar accounts of the temporality and spatiality of these practices. Particularly important is the demarcation they note between compulsory labor time and free time. Free time seems largely left to the slaves' discretion. It is to include subsistence farming, but also leaves personal discretion for other unsupervised activities.

The language of three free days echoes this practice in simple but striking ways. It demarcates periods of freedom and servitude in terms of time, and it attempts to renegotiate the distribution and control of that time. Specifically, it is a demand for unsupervised time, time that can be used for purposes determined by the user. Rooted in the distinction between compulsory labor and free time, it carves out greater independence and a different rhythm of life from within the plantation system. It is a *politics of time* that is also a *politics of freedom*.

In these senses, the inner logic of three free days seems to parallel that of subsistence farming already practiced on the plantations. This is not to say that slaves were necessarily demanding more free time for farming, only that both share a logic of time and indetermination. From this perspective we can speculate about the broader significance that three free days might have had for insurgent slaves. The demand for free time seems to hollow out a space of freedom from within the work regimens of the plantation. This could be freedom to engage in labor that is directly related to one's life and needs; freedom to labor or not, as one sees fit; freedom to pursue a variety of other activities—religious observances, social activities, visiting friends and relatives; or freedom to direct one's own time in general. It could also be seen as access to money: more time spent in subsistence farming would produce a greater surplus, leading to spare cash in the market. We know that cash and freedom were often connected for slaves: they were sometimes able to buy their own freedom, and money for this could come from small-plot farming. The slow accumulation of capital could serve as a way of legally escaping from slavery.

In any case, the specific motivation for three free days remains obscure. We can say that it seems to have been connected to a broader conception of free life, however, whatever that might have entailed. Three days per week might constitute a partial realization of this vision, which could then simply be scaled from three free days to seven. Whether this would have been the totality of the motivation for such a demand remains obscure. The archive is ultimately silent about the form of life that was envisioned during its intervals.

At the time, some European observers drew parallels between independence and subsistence farming similar to the interpretation I just outlined. Already in 1770, Raynal had offered additional reflections on such agricultural practices in the infamous abolitionist sections of *Histoire des deux Indes*.[18] He, or more likely Denis Diderot, who is thought to have ghostwritten those passages, recommends phasing out slavery and freeing slaves for self-sufficient farming.[19] The newly freed citizens would be given a hut and a piece of land large enough to sustain themselves. The clever ones might go beyond this, selling extra produce for their own profit. They would have the incentive of benefiting from their own initiative and providing the means for enhancing their own lives, and the colonies would benefit from their entrepreneurship, now buried in the pains of slavery. In this vision, small-plot gardening becomes an alternative means of sustenance and a source of independence. It is thus an alternative political vision and a replacement for the slave economy.

There is no indication that Raynal-Diderot understood this proposal to be the vision of Caribbean slaves. For them it was a relatively straightforward effort to speak on behalf of the subaltern, to describe an alternative to slavery and use it as leverage against social injustice. The proposal is quite similar to the one John Stuart Mill would advance as a solution to the Irish Potato Famine seventy-five years later: land reform and individual initiative as a solution for domination, servitude, and misery.[20] That vision shares the happy self-confidence of enlightened liberalism that we also see in Raynal-Diderot.

The agrarian vision of *Histoire des deux Indes* was formulated as a way of imagining emancipation while slavery was still in full force. As we saw in chapter 4, such ideas were a formidable battering ram for abolition. And in fact, something like that vision did come to pass. Slaves moved out of the plantations and set themselves up on small farms after emancipation, validating the ideas of

Raynal-Diderot to some extent. At the same time, we cannot suppose that the passage in *Histoire des deux Indes* describes the understanding of subsistence farming that enslaved people themselves might have had.

Today it might be similarly tempting to compare the demands for three free days to other celebrated rebellions against the capitalist commodification of time and labor. For example, one might see parallels with agrarian populations in Europe who rebelled against the standardization of time because it was a means of exploiting their labor.[21] However, we must be attentive to the specificities of this situation and not reduce it to phenomena observed in Europe. Three free days was part of an agrarian economy, but it was an economy of enslavement organized in a very distinctive society in a different part of the world. The relevant notions of freedom were rooted in these specific forms of life.

We might see these instead as more specifically creole and Afro-Caribbean ideas and commitments. Viewed from a more abstract perspective, three free days essentially demanded a *time of exception* from the structures of colonial capitalism. It was above all an exception from the practices, rules, and laws of the slave economy. It demanded exceptionality in a legal and temporal sense: contractually encoded times of self-determination. The point may well have been to establish a time period free from discipline, agenda, or having to account for oneself. Freedom from scrutiny, freedom from giving an account, all of this implies the ability to do as one wishes within the confines of the exception, without having to explain or articulate what that is.

If we go further to read three free days as connected with small plot farming, then it becomes an idea of *spatial exception* as well. It demands a legally encoded time during which one could range freely in space and use specific spaces freely for self-determined purposes.

Exceptionality in this case is not simply temporal, spatial, and legal, however. It would create an *epistemic exception*, an epistemically free period of time. This takes the form of a time in which no account needs to be given, in which actions have no publicity because they are released from control for a specified period. This time is epistemically free in the sense that actions and decisions no longer need adhere to the range of options imposed on enslaved people by the capitalist modernity of the plantation. Within the temporal and spatial confines of three free days, they would be able to engage in other forms of life and other practices. These need not be legible or coherent to European eyes, because no accounts need be given. This is another possibility that three free days would have opened up. Whether it was the motivation of insurgent slave demands is a question we cannot answer, precisely because their demands were epistemically opaque. Some two centuries later, the same opacity seems to shield those ideas from the comprehension of interpreters sifting through the archives.

In this case, subaltern silence may not be the result of a gap in understanding, or a lack of legibility, or archival loss, or power deployed in the archives. Subaltern silence may in fact *be* the point, a goal successfully achieved as a demand to be left alone. That is to say, the aim may have been to shield the subaltern from having to have a voice, from having to interact, interpret, give an account, say or do anything that is publicly legible in terms of dominant spheres of publicity. On this interpretation, three free days demands a period of exception which intentionally creates a space of subaltern silence. It holds out the prospect of subaltern silence as goal, strategy, demand, and desideratum. What seems like a lapse of understanding between sides in negotiations could actually be a deliberate refusal to specify the reasons for one's demands. It could be subaltern silence as an achievement rather than an effect of oppression or marginalization. Similarly, what seems like silence in the archives could simply be the nonexistence of traces of something that was never there to be recorded.

This interpretation draws lines of continuity between marronage and three free days along the lines I laid out in chapter 2. There I speculated that marronage could actually have been a form of silence as achievement: *self-silencing through opacity*. Fugitives were certainly seeking a space of exception from plantation life, but this exceptionality may have extended to silence as well. This would constitute a reversal of our typical view of subaltern silence. Being forgotten, ignored, or pushed to the side would not be a problem here. Rather, it may have been desirable. Rather than see silence as a characteristic of subordination, in this case we would have silence as an active pursuit, a self-chosen condition, an achievement, and a way of *undoing* subordination.

We can see elements of a similar vision in three free days, but in a more abstracted and explicit form. Like marronage, three free days includes a spatial element which is a similar removal from the plantation. In addition, we see similarities in the form of opacity it seems to aim at. This is a refusal to account for oneself, seeking out a state in which there is no need to do so. Three free days goes even further than marronage, however, by using temporality as a way of defining and creating exceptionality. Marronage was effectively infinite in its temporal extension. Many maroons remained fugitive for the rest of their lives.

However, it was also a highly precarious state. The effective open-endedness of its temporality applied only until the *maréchaussée* invaded one's community. In contrast, three free days uses time to delimit a more structured zone of exception, one that is temporal, epistemic, and potentially spatial as well. Here self-silencing through opacity takes on new forms, ones that use time, space, and contractual limitation in creative new ways.

In light of Spivak's cautions about speaking for the subaltern, we must be clear about the limits of this interpretation. I have laid out several alternative possibilities. Three free days may have been an attempt at autonomous self-direction, trying to establish oneself as an independent decision maker. More narrowly, it may have been an economic calculation in which a desire for cash motivated side work in addition to that demanded by the plantation. At the limit, this could even amount to a relatively radical attempt at decommodifying the person of the slave by working within the structures of the market. It would operate within those strange institutions of capitalist modernity that commodified people, using the forces of the market and private property to decommodify them. More radically, three free days could have been an effort to move beyond capitalism and colonial government in an epistemic sense, demanding a right not to account for oneself.

These alternatives display a wide array of attitudes insurgent slaves may have taken toward the modernity of colonialism. That may have included working within its structures, seeking piecemeal exception from it, or demanding silence as a goal. This raises the question of the relation between insurgent demands and the cognitive, symbolic, and institutional structures of colonialism. As David Scott might phrase it, it causes us to ask how insurgent thought and practice may have been conscripted by modernity, and how it aimed to oppose such foreign perspectives.[22] This is a difficult, perhaps impossible interpretive puzzle. Some notion of freedom seems to be implied in three free days, but we know not exactly what. Some attitude toward the plantation and the colonial apparatus also seems to lie there, but the details remain conjectural. Some hints of a grander strategy might be in operation, some aim that would use three free days as a first step in a broader liberation, but this is speculation. Some orientation toward modernity is implied (rejection? immanent unworking from within?), but we would overstep the limits of interpretation to say what that is.

In short, the events we have been examining are paradigm cases of subaltern silence. They are situations in which subaltern subjects make clear statements that are nonetheless filled with ambiguity. Subaltern speech makes demands here but does not explain the broader imaginaries that animate them. A politics of time seems to be used to enact goals that are potentially quite radical, but nonetheless they remain obscure to us.

THE CREATIVE MODERNISM OF HAITIAN INDEPENDENCE

In any case, the visions of three free days and agrarian independence seem to have been displaced by other concerns. Starting in 1791, well-organized slave revolts broadened into a full scale insurrection. The slave uprising was well planned, but the twists and turns of insurgency that followed it over the next decade were very much improvisational. Alliances were made and dissolved, new aims formed, and the eventual result, the declaration of the Republic of Haiti from the ruins of a slave colony, was both unprecedented and unanticipated. As Trouillot has argued, this event may have been literally inconceivable, completely outside the bounds of what could be imagined.

As a result, the declaration of Haitian independence in 1804 was the consummation of a military victory, but only the beginning of an effort at new thinking. The means for understanding independence were improvised in the doing. Perhaps because of the inconceivable character of what they had done, Haitian revolutionaries adopted certain conventions that had been established in other recent revolutions. The American and French Revolutions provided a nascent script for conducting a modern revolution. Chief among its features were ideals of *justification*, *rupture*, and *publicity*.

The American Declaration of Independence asserts that when a people dissolves the bands that have connected them with another, "a decent respect to the opinions of mankind requires that they should declare the causes which impel them to the separation." Aiming to "let Facts be submitted to a candid world," it undertakes such a justification with a long list of complaints. These passages try to make good on the claim that revolutionary acts should be explained and justified. The Haitian documents announcing independence adopt this expectation as well. They do so in unique ways, however.

There are two documents of Haitian independence. Both were issued on January 1, 1804, by Jean-Jacques Dessalines, commander of the revolutionary army, and written by his secretary, Louis Boisrond-Tonnerre. The legends surrounding these documents tell us that the general had a close role in dictating their content. Thomas Madiou, an eminent mid-nineteenth century Haitian historian, tells us that Dessalines rejected an earlier draft of a proclamation by a different writer as being too similar to the American Declaration and too dryly jurisprudential. The project was next proposed to Boisrond-Tonnerre, who said that he understood Dessalines to be asking for a proclamation written with "the skin of a white for parchment, his skull for a writing desk, his blood for ink, and a bayonet for a pen." This prospectus received Dessalines's enthusiastic approval, and Boisrond-Tonnerre was given the task.[23] The two documents that he produced have an interesting relation to one another. They are a strange pair of mismatched twins: one is oddly indirect, the other inflammatory and forceful.

The Haitian "Act of Independence" declares independence in a rather elliptical way. It tells the story of a meeting between Dessalines, general in chief of the "native army" (armée indigène), and its generals. At the meeting, Dessalines announced his intention "to make known to foreign powers the decision to make the country independent and enjoy a liberty consecrated by the blood of the people of this island." After having gathered the generals' opinions, he asked each of them to renounce France forever, die rather than live under its domination, and fight to their last breath for independence. We are told that the generals were greatly moved by these "sacred principles" and gave their unanimous oath "to posterity and the whole universe" to support independence and renounce France in the manner Dessalines had described.[24]

Although it is an "act of independence," this document is rather ambiguous about independence itself. Dessalines tells a story about informing the generals that he has an intention to publicize a decision. There is no actual declaration that Haiti is now independent. The only indications of this are the title "Act of Independence" and the signatory statement at the bottom: "Issued at Gonnaïves, January 1, 1804, the first day of Haitian independence."

All ambiguities are dispelled in another document issued on the same day. This is a proclamation by Dessalines to the people of Haiti, explaining and justifying what had just occurred.[25] The proclamation is vividly polemic and explicitly racial. Its rhetoric is powerful and direct. The document derives a formidable normative punch by evoking moral outrage at the horrors of slavery and colonialism. It reveals Boisrond-Tonnerre to be a writer equal to Thomas Jefferson in prose stylistics and rhetorical force.

Here the justification for independence is unambiguous. Boisrond-Tonnerre writes, "The name French still saddens our land. Everything here reminds one of the cruelty of this barbarous people: our laws, customs, towns, everything still bears the French imprint."[26] He asks how the Haitians can even breathe the same air as the French, who are characterized as vultures, tigers, and executioners. The justification provided here is simple and straightforward, unlike the long list of grievances in the American Declaration. French colonialism was awful, cruel, and inhumane. Haitians are fully justified in taking vengeance on the French, and independence is long overdue. The horrors of colonialism and slavery motivated the current state of affairs, and they fully justify the actions being taken.

The Haitian proclamations not only justify national independence but above all make an emphatic break from the past of French domination. Admittedly, this rupture is complex. The Act of Independence is highly indirect. We are told that Dessalines had recently made known his intention to declare independence. Recently, too, the generals acclaimed this intention and swore themselves to it. Independence in this case consists of telling a story about the intention to become independent, in a document that declares itself to be an act of independence. Independence here has an odd temporality: "By recounting my past intention to do this thing in some indeterminate future, I hereby imply that I am now doing it." The actual constitution of an independent nation is purely performative, then, in the soft sense that the document's title implies that the moment has now arrived. Independence is not explicitly declared, but performed by publishing a document called an act of independence and marking its temporality as the first day of independence.

The odd temporality of this document may reflect the fact that it comes at the end of a revolution rather than the beginning. As Trouillot points out, the Haitian Revolution was already accomplished when this document was issued.[27] It is unlike the American Declaration, which initiated the break rather than pronouncing its accomplishment, and unlike the French "Declaration of the Rights of Man and Citizen," which was issued while the revolution was still very much under way. This is the sense in which Haitian independence is most truly performative. It preceded its own justification, which only came later, and ambiguously at that.

Here the Haitian Revolution goes well beyond its French and American predecessors. The American Revolution, as Hannah Arendt notes, drew strong lines of continuity between colony and independent republic.[28] The French Revolution, in contrast, advertised itself as making a sharp break with the past. It emphasized this novelty with a new calendar and ideologies of a "new man" who would result from epoch-making political change.[29] Historians have often taken the French claims of novelty at face value, but in reality this novelty was a studiously pursued achievement. The celebrated artist Jacques-Louis David was hired to invent a national costume. The government set about organizing national festivals aimed at patriotic unification. But in the end, as Alexis de Tocqueville pointed out, there was a great deal of continuity between past and present despite the revolutionary ideology to the contrary.[30]

In Haiti the break was much more complete. The proclamation executes a decisive rupture with French colonialism in stirring language:

> It is not enough to have expelled from our country the barbarians who bled it for two centuries. It is not enough to have curbed the continually recurring factions that made a joke of the phantom of liberty that France held out to you. We must, by a final act of national authority, assure forever the empire of liberty in the land of our birth. We must deprive the inhuman government that held our spirits in the most humiliating torpor for so long all hope of reenslaving us. We must finally live independent or die.[31]

The rhetoric of the proclamation makes it clear that independence is the only option. It would be a dishonorable absurdity, Boisrond-Tonnerre writes, to win the war and wind up slaves in some other form. This is what happened to the French, he implies, who fought a revolution only to become imperial subjects of Napoleon. Instead, Haitians must be willing to choose death rather than subjection. Therefore, by a final, decisive act, foreign rule will be thrown off forever. Haitians are exhorted to take the name "French" as anathema and maintain eternal hatred toward France. The rupture will be complete, final, and absolute; there is no return.[32]

Above all, it is clear that these founding documents of Haitian independence were designed to perform a public function. Even though the longest and most forceful of them is addressed to "the Haitian people," its audience clearly seems to overshoot that designation. It was written in French, which was not by any means the language of the Haitian people at this time. The audience was intended to be an international one. This was, in sum, an effort at publicity: articulating arguments and reasons for revolution to "a candid world." In the case of the American Declaration of Independence, Congress had ordered copies to be printed in newspapers and broadsheets, both domestically and in Europe.[33] A similar practice was pursued for the Haitian documents, especially in American newspapers. Dessalines seems to have been particularly interested in courting favor with the United States after the Revolution. Like Haiti, the United States had also thrown off a colonial oppressor, and it could be a beneficial ally of the new republic. Thus documents from Haiti began appearing in the American media as soon as the revolutionary war ended. Deborah Jenson documents Dessalines's careful courting of the American media. She shows, for instance, that even before the formal declaration of independence, an earlier declaration was widely distributed in the United States and printed in some thirty-six U.S. newspapers. The actual proclamation generated similar attention several months later, followed by widespread publication of a further series of official proclamations on related topics.[34] Dessalines was clearly courting American public opinion, and there was obviously a large audience for news about the Caribbean revolution.

While aiming stirring rhetoric against French colonialism and in support of Haitian independence, Dessalines simultaneously discouraged his followers from spreading the Haitian Revolution to other colonies. He suggested that "the spirit of proselytization" should not cause Haitians to lose track of their own purpose. They should leave their neighbors in peace, not becoming revolutionary firebrands nor setting themselves up as legislators for the whole Antilles. The causes that have impelled Haitians to revolution are not necessarily shared across the region: the other islands have not been "watered in the blood of their innocent inhabitants." There was of course widespread fear that Haiti would become an example of contagious uprising, serving as a model of insurrection for other slave-owning states. Here Dessalines's remarks seem largely aimed at the wider American-European public sphere as a reassurance to the contrary. Although the proclamation is addressed to his fellow citizens, these parts of it seem clearly aimed at the colonial powers and particularly the United States. Again, publicity and justification to the wider world seem to be an important function of the document.

In all of these ways, the Haitian Revolution initiated a public project of conceptual innovation and novel political action. While Haitian revolutionaries adopted nascent genre conventions governing the form of revolution, their particular version of them was unique. Their actions in turn helped shape the new revolutionary imaginary forming at the time, one that would be highly influential in the nineteenth-century "age of revolutions," particularly as the nineteenth century wore on and many other peoples contemplated anticolonial rebellion. They thereby became full-fledged actors in devising the modern script of revolution.

The modernity of the Haitian Revolution takes other forms as well. Its focus on rupture is modernizing by marking a decisive break with the past in favor of some indeterminate future. Haitian revolutionaries aimed at displacing other, preexisting imaginaries in an attempt to create something new. In ways similar to but also quite different from the French Revolution, there was a concentrated effort to make a break from the prior order. The Haitians executed a deliberate rupture with the past in favor of postulating something unprecedented. They propagated these ideas using the cutting-edge technologies of the day—the print media—and the conventions of justification that were forming around them. This is an autochthonous modernism, one that proceeded on its own unique terms and negated history to aim at a better future.

Unlike the aesthetic modernisms of the twentieth century, this one did not aim at originality for its own sake.[35] It was not wearing avant-gardism as a badge of honor. Rather, it was flung into this position by the sweep of events and found rupture necessary because of the pervasive, corrosive influence of French colonialism and French ideals. This was made clear by Boisrond-Tonnerre in the Proclamation: the damage of slavery and colonialism was not simply physical and political, but psychic and epistemological as well. He refers to "the phantom of liberty that France revealed to our eyes" and says that Haitians have been "victims for 14 years of our credulity and indulgence."[36]

We might be inclined to view all of this as an Arendtian new beginning, an effort to articulate new and unprecedented ideas based on shared political realities. However, this is not a new beginning built on the optimism of a shared project, but one pushed along by necessity in which the unity of the cooperators and the character of the project is substantially in doubt. Independence, the nation-state, and eventually empire are adopted as organizing principles, but there is no clear direction on the path going forward.

CONSTITUENT DISPLACEMENTS: THE AGRARIAN PROBLEMATIC

In the account I have just given, we can see why the Haitian Revolution is so widely celebrated. It combined unprecedented, world-transforming events with highly inventive visions of sovereignty and independence. Those events and imaginaries drew on precedents from the metropole, but in creative ways that provided a basis for anticolonial revolution and a new vision of a postcolonial republic.

A number of insightful commentators have explored the modernity of the Haitian revolutionary project. Laurent Dubois, Lynn Hunt, and James Martel see Haitian independence as an overdue, rectifying realization of the Rights of Man and other aspects of European Enlightenment thinking.[37] Adom Getachew, Nick Nesbitt, and Massimiliano Tomba emphasize differences rather than continuities, characterizing Haitian revolutionary doctrines as unique forms of non-European universalism that challenge the limits of the European tradition.[38] Sibylle Fischer and David Scott are much less sanguine than either of these groups, noting the tensions, paradoxes, and contradictions within the Haitian project.[39] We have, then, a spectrum of positions: from Haitian independence as a realization of modernity to Haitian independence as an articulation of countermodernity and as a tension-filled practice making difficult compromises in fraught circumstances.

In a certain sense, I am most closely allied with those who see Haitian independence as a countermodernity. I particularly appreciate the creative invention manifest in this project and the way it explicitly aims these innovations at Euro-American powers. All of this speaks of countermodernity rather than a continuation of Euro-American legacies. However, I am also quick to note that this project often operates by coopting and refashioning practices central to European modernity itself, especially European *political* modernity. This is particularly true of the emerging genre conventions around revolution, ones that developed new revolutionary scripts around justification and rupture. The Haitian Revolution also includes an enthusiastic embrace of the public sphere as modernity's arena of justification. There is, then, a kind of deft repurposing of modernity to turn it back on itself: a creative, modern countermodernity.

There is also a strong sense in which, having said all of this, I join Fischer and Scott in noting the tensions, paradoxes, and contradictions of this countermodern project. I am especially concerned to emphasize what is lost here. There was a great deal of heterogeneity within "the" Haitian Revolution, and those unresolved tensions prevented it from settling into any one doctrine or position. Commentators typically fail to distinguish the multiple voices of Haitian independence, losing sight of the contestatory politics, relations of power, hegemony, and domination among its component factions. The cost is a lack of attention to the fragile inaudibility of silenced voices.

In this light, it is striking that we see no more mention of "three free days" in the years leading up to Haitian independence. At some point the struggle took a different path, imagining freedom as an end of slavery, a rupture with French colonialism, and the formation of an independent state. This poses the question of how the famous doctrines of Haitian independence relate to the ideas of "three free days" that had come before.

As a working hypothesis, I suggest that the vision of freedom in three free days was actually silenced by national independence rather than sublated into it or abandoned in favor of it. The operative category here is one of displacement: the subaltern vision of three free days was pushed out of the way by a louder, better publicized, and institutionally victorious vision of national independence. Again, this constitutes a form of *silencing through substitution*. It is a modification and evolution of that form, however. Substitution operates here not by privileging *European* voices and actors over Caribbean subaltern ones. More subtly, it displaces autochthonous visions like three free days by privileging the Euro-inflected project of Haitian independence. In this interpretation, three free days does not go away so much as become subordinated by the other view. Rendered in more explicitly social terms, one might suppose that there was still a constituency among insurgent slaves for the vision of independence represented by three free days, but they lost the ability to give voice and publicity to that vision. In other words, this is not a question of new and better concepts replacing cruder, earlier ones but rather of specific, evolving forms of subaltern silence.

There are reasons to suspect this might have been the case. An important illustration appears in the documents of independence themselves. Even though the proclamation was addressed "to the people of Haiti," it was written in French. Various African languages and Haitian Kreyòl, a fusion of French and African elements, were the primary languages of most people in the new nation.[40] This indicates that the audience of the Haitian independence proclamations was not

Haitians so much as the "candid world" to whom revolutions must be justified—France, the United States, and the other world powers. Official proclamations had been translated into Kreyòl under French colonial administrators, but these were not.[41] In this sense, the shift to French marks an attention to other audiences and a displacement away from the linguistic realities of the Haitian population. The official use of French marginalized the rural population and created barriers between what was official and their lived experience. As a result, to render their ideals legible required additional work of translation, both literally and epistemically.[42]

In contrast to "three free days," the Haitian revolutionary project did not create a space of exception from modernity. Rather, it entered into modernity in a complex manner that required constant negotiation. It staked out a bold new vision of independence, one that has been rightly celebrated for its strong repudiation of slavery and colonialism. However, we realize here that there was collateral damage along the way. The bold, muscular, countermodern project swept out of its way other visions of freedom and autonomy, ones that *were* aiming to create spaces of exception from modernity. A new group of subalterns were silenced in this case: those who saw liberation as something different, something they were scarcely able to articulate and were subsequently prevented from doing so.

LIBERTY AND SUBORDINATION

History is often read backward from end to beginning, typically with an aim to make beginnings presage the end. In such a reading, a Haitian revolutionary subject should have formed out of slavery and the plantation system, aiming at full and complete self-determination. In the revolutionary vision of 1804 this would look something like claims for an independent nation-state and shortly thereafter empire. The Haitian Imperial Constitution of 1805 would seem to further cement this vision, with its ideals of citizenship and radical conception of racial unity: Haitian citizenship was consolidated around black racial identity, and Haitians were declared to be brothers, living under a regime of equal legal treatment.[43]

However, the history I have sketched is more fraught with difficulties. The multitude of meanings that can be read into "three free days" and the agrarian problematics that followed the revolution are suggestive. They point toward a tension between slave revolt and revolution. The emerging Haitian sovereign imaginary of the early 1800s—the one that concluded the revolution—seems to have displaced other currents of insurgent thought and autochthonous practice, ones emerging from earlier slave revolts. The consolidation and publicity of the revolutionary imaginary of 1804 may have obscured other projects and ideals that were already in circulation. Those other unique visions may have been silenced, suppressed, or lost in this effort of renewal.

This suggests the subordination and de facto suppression of a distinctive vision of post-slavery independence. The agrarian imaginary and the vision of autonomous life and sovereign community that went with it seem to have been silenced, misunderstood, or pushed aside in favor of the Haitian revolutionary vision. The reasons for this may have something to do with the relative legibility of the two visions. Although the ideas of the Haitian Revolution were radically novel and conceptually unprecedented, they were put forward within a revolutionary idiom that felt comfortable to European intellectuals celebrating the novelty of the American and French Revolutions. Even Euro-American politicians and press who were horrified at the news of an anticolonial revolution and black republic found its points of reference familiar. It fit the script of the revolutions that preceded it. The agrarian imaginary, in contrast, never fit the model of modern revolution. It did not have an elegant rhetorical elaboration, nor did it correspond to the emerging ideal of national self-determination through armed revolt. As a result, it slipped into obscurity.

I want to insist on the irreducible particularity of these seemingly silenced voices and their inherent ambiguity. We must note the minute positivity of the traces that still connect us with them not as part of some grand narrative of Haitian history, but as irreducible ciphers that invite interpretation. I note their obscurity and ambiguity as specific evidence of what might have come before: erasure, displacement, and silencing. This is my primary point of departure, for example, from Carolyn Fick's highly laudable treatment of "the Saint Domingue Revolution from below." We must take obscurity and ambiguity as positive phenomena here rather than as something to be explained away in a more unified and seamless account.

Here we are traversing terrain very similar to what I have explored in earlier chapters. While trying to gain understanding from the archive of politics, we find those understandings already inflected by the politics of the archive. We witness the traces of past practices, which we experience through the assembly of what is preserved, the political agendas of contemporary accounts and the selectivity of what was recorded. All of this is worth a fine-grained epistemic and political analysis, one that preserves traces of these capillary movements rather than hypostasizing or paving them over. In short, my discussion is not an attempt to retrieve lost voices from silence. Rather, it aims to track their occasional episodes of appearance, as well as the circumstances that result in their resubmersion in silence.

This interpretation suggests that the dominant strand of Haitian revolutionary thought and practice constituted a potent form of subordination for other people and practices. Even as the Haitian project was a highly creative countermodernity, it was also one with constitutive exclusions. For all of these reasons, I am inclined to conclude that the celebrated Haitian Revolution produced new regimes of subalternity within the republic. The liberation of some produced the subordination of others. There was a silencing of the ideas and speech of many rural Haitians who did not imagine their freedom on the scale of national independence. We have tantalizing glimpses of a different notion of freedom and independence here, one secured through agrarian self-sufficiency. Unlike the widely celebrated legacy of the Haitian Revolution itself, this vision seems to have been silenced in favor of claims and ideas aimed at national independence, the Euro-American public sphere, and the developing script of modern revolution.

This produces a vision of the Haitian Revolution that is perhaps surprising. That revolution is rightly celebrated for its history-making reversal of slavery, its unique thinking about national independence and constitutionalism, and its exemplary place as a striking pioneer in the project of postcoloniality. We also see, however, another side of that project: the sense in which the creation of freedom can have unanticipated costs and damages. These collateral effects can go unnoticed when they are reckoned in terms of subaltern silence. This can even occur through the proliferation of discourse for some, producing silence for others. Here the busy energies of the revolutionary project silence that other vision of exceptionality and the desire to be left alone. Silence can also be created through the performative enactment of liberty—of one vision of liberty at the expense of others. A vision of liberty at the national scale receives the military backing of the revolutionary army, which coalesces into institutional materialization in the new republic. Three free days and its vision of agrarian independence have no such material embodiment and thus remain ineffable and subject to silence. Finally and most surprisingly, we may be seeing subaltern silence as a positive achievement, a demand for exceptionality or a demand to be left alone. This would be an unusual case, one that claims back a small amount of agency within a broader regime of subordination. It is unclear that this is actually the claim being made in three free days, but it is a tantalizing hypothesis.

All of this suggests some more general conclusions about subaltern silence. It suggests that even a well-intentioned, progressive movement can create forms of subordination. The very innovations of the Haitian revolutionary project and the energy it marshaled to overthrow French colonialism had the unanticipated effect of subordinating other visions of independence. A successful movement to oppose the silencing effects of slavery and colonialism in turn silenced other such visions. Ironically, a successful attempt to overcome silence and subordination became a new source of silence and subordination. Here we see that these movements had a productive character: their creative energies opposed subordination and in turn reproduced it. There was a surplus of effect, one that overspilled the bounds of what was intended and perpetuated silence and subordination in other ways.

This, of course, is a conclusion drawn from a very specific context. It poses more general questions about subaltern silence and its opposition, however—that is, whether opposition, resistance, and successful revolution are always productive in this way. Whether the effort to rectify one problem merely reinscribes it in new form on a different register. Whether, in cases of subaltern silence, everything is dangerous.

CHAPTER 7

Revolution Within a Revolution

Postcolonial Liberalism and the Army of Sufferers

1793–1844

It will be evident in these proceedings, that those who projected this movement, were not sufficiently advanced themselves, to see that the means by which they proposed to reform abuses, were themselves the greatest and most ruinous of abuses.

—M. B. Bird

We have seen how subaltern silence changes form as Haiti enters its postcolonial years. The legal and institutional silence of enslaved people under colonialism is now replaced by more subtle and differentiated forms. The dynamic energies of the new Haitian Republic submerge other voices into a silence so profound that it largely escapes notice.

In this chapter I will continue to trace those postcolonial tensions, showing how they erupted into conflict in midcentury. This is a tale of two revolutions. Both occurred in the early 1840s, the second an immediate response to the first—a revolution within a revolution. The first one took political modernity to new and striking forms. It was organized around liberal democratic precedents but was highly innovative in both form and content. It creatively adapted European revolutionary ideals while developing striking new forms of constitutionalism and citizenship. It also drove forward the modern project of revolutionary self-justification, using the nascent public sphere as a principal means of revolutionary activity. The second revolution was a diametric negation of the first. It rose in reaction to the first revolution and all that it implied. It was a more inchoate movement, one that struggled to be heard, struggled to justify itself, struggled to make sense as it pushed back against its revolutionary competitor.

I will argue that each of these movements drew its considerable energy from subaltern subordination. The first, I will claim, was deeply shaped by how Haiti had been subordinated and silenced on the world stage since 1804. It sought greater legitimacy and recognition for the Haitian state. As innovative as it was, however, this movement had the perverse consequence of subordinating other members of the Haitian populace. What seemed like a promising set of postcolonial developments had the ironic result of creating subaltern silence. The second revolution, I will argue, was the product of that silence. It was a revolt of those swept aside and silenced by the emerging project of Haitian postcolonial modernity.

My fascination with these nested revolutions comes partly from how they continue the line of argument of the previous chapter. The contrasts between them are similar to the ones I have already observed during the Haitian Revolution at the beginning of the century. On one hand, we have a talkative, modern, highly discursive political movement. On the other is a movement of rural people who seem to envision their freedom quite differently and seem correspondingly less interested in national and international politics. Their silence is difficult to interpret, but it may represent a freely chosen form of refusal, in contrast to the busy discursive energies of the other movement. These revolutions represent two very different responses to subaltern silence: one through a proliferation of discourse, the other by choosing silence as an achievement. They are not merely different from one another, but in substantial tension with one another, both politically and epistemologically.

These events take on special significance within the genealogy of subaltern silence. They reveal the appearance of something that seemed to have vanished: the voice of a long-silent rural agrarian population, suddenly reappearing to "speak" in some cryptic manner. This phase of the genealogy is a study in contrasts: of fertile postcolonial projects that are fraught with problems and subaltern silences that suddenly come into focus in surprising and subtle ways.

DISCURSIVE FERMENT OF THE LIBERAL REVOLUTION

The year 1843 was a turbulent one in Haitian history. The long presidency of Jean-Pierre Boyer was ended by an elite, bourgeois revolution. This rebellion was striking in two important ways. It was based on liberal principles, largely inspired by strands of the American and French revolutionary thought, and it was accomplished partly through a huge proliferation of discourse: talk, writings, manifestos, and pamphlets. These two features place the movement against Boyer, which I will call the Liberal Revolution of 1843, squarely at the center of an emerging modern script for revolution. It is one in which revolution was accomplished as much through principles and publicity as through weapons and warfare. In this emerging paradigm, conflict and mobilization occur importantly in the public sphere. They are fought out discursively, in parallel with more widely noted forms of armed conflict.

Boyer was brought down by members of his own ruling class, affluent mixed-race elites who had dominated Haitian politics for several decades. Their disaffection became more and more tangible in the early 1840s, giving rise to quiet forms of political organizing and increasingly direct criticism of the president. An early venue for this activity was an opposition paper called *Le Manifeste*—"Manifesto"—founded in 1841 (figure 7.1).

Le Manifeste published a steady stream of discussion about governmental reform, constitutional amendment, election law, public education, and the regeneration of Haitian society. Its contributors saw themselves as democrats and constitutionalists. They aimed to create a liberal reform movement in opposition to Boyer's increasingly autocratic tendencies.

The Liberals often looked to the United States as an example of what they hoped to achieve in Haiti. They were particularly impressed by "the genius" of American institutions. The Americans used good laws to foster an admirable public spirit, industry, patriotism, and public morality.[1] Their laws established communal institutions staffed by locally elected officials. These officials did the community's daily business; they were the assessors, collectors, constables, surveyors of the poor, commissioners of schools and parishes, and road inspectors. Such officials were overseen by a mayor and a communal council; their initiatives were guided by town meetings. The Liberals viewed this communally embedded, carefully structured, democratic government as a good model for reform in Haiti.[2]

The source of such insights was most frequently Alexis de Tocqueville. The two volumes of his *De la démocratie en Amérique* had just come into print in 1835 and 1840.[3] This book provided a detailed source of information on American institutions and political culture. The Liberals' fascination with America gave them a broader ideological affiliation with Tocqueville as well. They especially

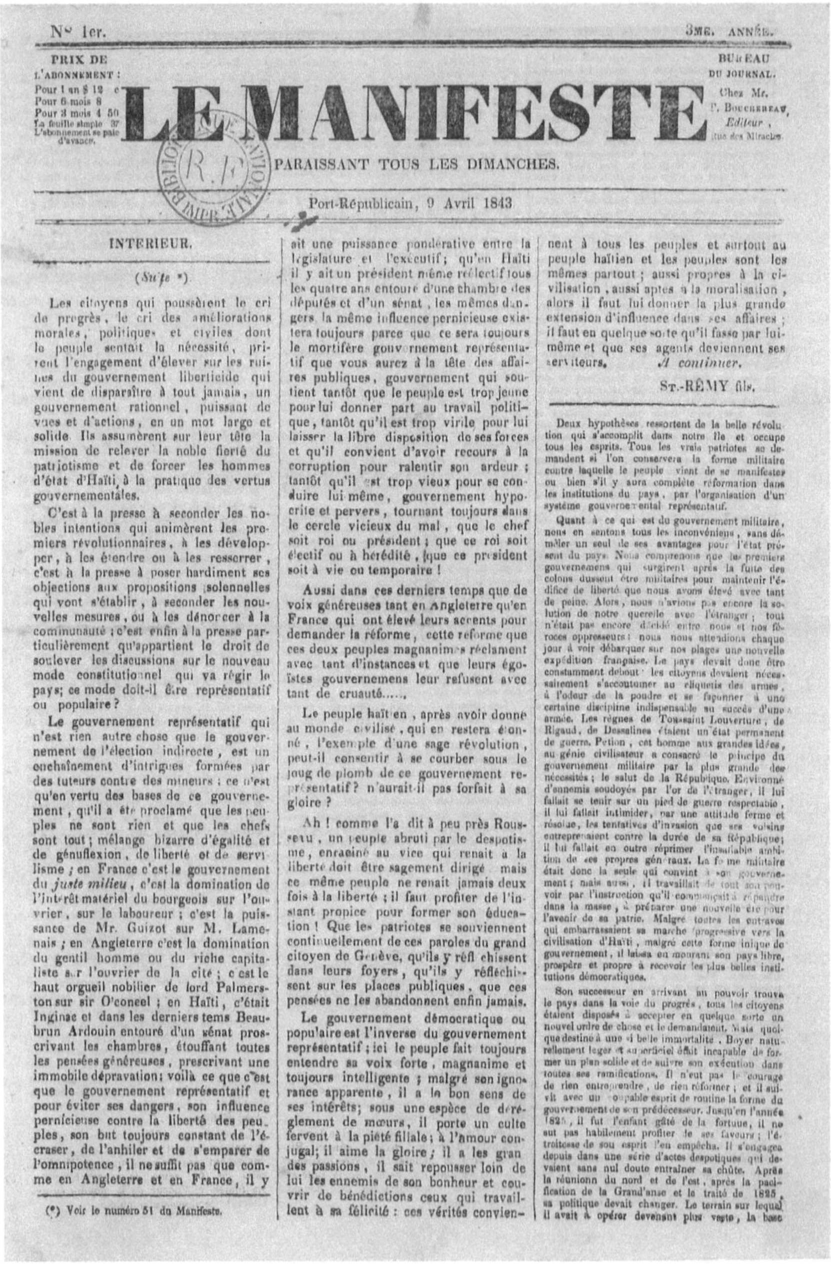

N° 1er. 3me. ANNÉE.

PRIX DE L'ABONNEMENT : Pour 1 an $ 12 c Pour 6 mois 8 Pour 3 mois 4 50 La feuille simple 37 L'abonnement se paie d'avance.

LE MANIFESTE

BUREAU DU JOURNAL. Chez Mr. P. Boucherreau, Editeur, Rue des Miracles.

PARAISSANT TOUS LES DIMANCHES.

Port-Républicain, 9 Avril 1843

INTERIEUR.

(Suite *).

Les citoyens qui poussèrent le cri de progrès, le cri des améliorations morales, politiques et civiles dont le peuple sentait la nécessité, prirent l'engagement d'élever sur les ruines du gouvernement liberticide qui vient de disparaître à tout jamais, un gouvernement rationnel, puissant de vues et d'actions, en un mot large et solide. Ils assumèrent sur leur tête la mission de relever la noble fierté du patriotisme et de forcer les hommes d'état d'Haïti, à la pratique des vertus gouvernementales.

C'est à la presse à seconder les nobles intentions qui animèrent les premiers révolutionnaires, à les développer, à les étendre ou à les resserrer, c'est à la presse à poser hardiment ses objections aux propositions solennelles qui vont s'établir, à seconder les nouvelles mesures, ou à les dénoncer à la communauté ; c'est enfin à la presse particulièrement qu'appartient le droit de soulever les discussions sur le nouveau mode constitutionnel qui va régir le pays; ce mode doit-il être représentatif ou populaire ?

Le gouvernement représentatif qui n'est rien autre chose que le gouvernement de l'élection indirecte, est un enchaînement d'intrigues formées par des tuteurs contre des mineurs ; ce n'est qu'en vertu des bases de ce gouvernement, qu'il a été proclamé que les peuples ne sont rien et que les chefs sont tout ; mélange bizarre d'égalité et de génuflexion, de liberté et de servilisme ; en France c'est le gouvernement du *juste milieu*, c'est la domination de l'intérêt matériel du bourgeois sur l'ouvrier, sur le laboureur ; c'est la puissance de Mr. Guizot sur M. Lamenais ; en Angleterre c'est la domination du gentil homme ou du riche capitaliste sur l'ouvrier de la cité ; c'est le haut orgueil nobilier de lord Palmerston sur sir O'coneel ; en Haïti, c'était Inginac et dans les derniers tems Beaubrun Ardouin entouré d'un sénat proscrivant les chambres, étouffant toutes les pensées généreuses, prescrivant une immobile dépravation ; voilà ce que c'est que le gouvernement représentatif et pour éviter ses dangers, son influence pernicieuse contre la liberté des peuples, son but toujours constant de l'écraser, de l'anhiler et de s'emparer de l'omnipotence, il ne suffit pas que comme en Angleterre et en France, il y ait une puissance pondérative entre la législature et l'exécutif ; qu'en Haïti il y ait un président même réélectif tous les quatre ans entouré d'une chambre des députés et d'un sénat, les mêmes dangers la même influence pernicieuse existera toujours parce que ce sera toujours le mortifère gouvernement représentatif que vous aurez à la tête des affaires publiques, gouvernement qui soutient tantôt que le peuple est trop jeune pour lui donner part au travail politique, tantôt qu'il est trop virile pour lui laisser la libre disposition de ses forces et qu'il convient d'avoir recours à la corruption pour ralentir son ardeur ; tantôt qu'il est trop vieux pour se conduire lui même, gouvernement hypocrite et pervers, tournant toujours dans le cercle vicieux du mal, que le chef soit roi ou président ; que ce roi soit électif ou à hérédité, que ce président soit à vie ou temporaire !

Aussi dans ces derniers temps que de voix généreuses tant en Angleterre qu'en France qui ont élevé leurs accents pour demander la réforme, cette réforme que ces deux peuples magnanimes réclament avec tant d'instances et que leurs égoïstes gouvernemens leur refusent avec tant de cruauté.....

Le peuple haïtien, après avoir donné au monde civilisé, qui en restera étonné, l'exemple d'une sage révolution, peut-il consentir à se courber sous le joug de plomb de ce gouvernement représentatif ? n'aurait-il pas forfait à sa gloire ?

Ah ! comme l'a dit à peu près Rousseau, un peuple abruti par le despotisme, enraciné au vice qui renait à la liberté doit être sagement dirigé mais ce même peuple ne renait jamais deux fois à la liberté ; il faut profiter de l'instant propice pour former son éducation ! Que les patriotes se souviennent continuellement de ces paroles du grand citoyen de Genève, qu'ils y réfléchissent dans leurs foyers, qu'ils y réfléchissent sur les places publiques, que ces pensées ne les abandonnent enfin jamais.

Le gouvernement démocratique ou populaire est l'inverse du gouvernement représentatif ; ici le peuple fait toujours entendre sa voix forte, magnanime et toujours intelligente ; malgré son ignorance apparente, il a le bon sens de ses intérêts ; sous une espèce de dérèglement de mœurs, il porte un culte fervent à la piété filiale ; à l'amour conjugal ; il aime la gloire ; il a les grandes passions, il sait repousser loin de lui les ennemis de son bonheur et couvrir de bénédictions ceux qui travaillent à sa félicité : ces vérités conviennent à tous les peuples et surtout au peuple haïtien et les peuples sont les mêmes partout ; aussi propres à la civilisation, aussi aptes à la moralisation, alors il faut lui donner la plus grande extension d'influence dans ses affaires ; il faut en quelque sorte qu'il fasse par lui-même et que ses agents deviennent ses serviteurs. *A continuer.*

St.-RÉMY fils.

(*) Voir le numéro 51 du Manifeste.

Deux hypothèses ressortent de la belle révolution qui s'accomplit dans notre île et occupe tous les esprits. Tous les vrais patriotes se demandent si l'on conservera la forme militaire contre laquelle le peuple vient de se manifester ou bien s'il y aura complète réformation dans les institutions du pays, par l'organisation d'un système gouvernemental représentatif.

Quant à ce qui est du gouvernement militaire, nous en sentons tous les inconvéniens, sans démêler un seul de ses avantages pour l'état présent du pays. Nous comprenons que les premiers gouvernemens qui surgirent après la fuite des colons dussent être militaires pour maintenir l'édifice de liberté que nous avons élevé avec tant de peine. Alors, nous n'avions pas encore la solution de notre querelle avec l'étranger ; tout n'était pas encore décidé entre nous et nos féroces oppresseurs : nous nous attendions chaque jour à voir débarquer sur nos plages une nouvelle expédition française. Le pays devait donc être constamment debout : les citoyens devaient nécessairement s'accoutumer au cliquetis des armes, à l'odeur de la poudre et se façonner à une certaine discipline indispensable au succès d'une armée. Les règnes de Toussaint Louverture, de Rigaud, de Dessalines étaient un état permanent de guerre. Petion, cet homme aux grandes idées, au génie civilisateur a consacré le principe du gouvernement militaire par la plus grande des nécessités ; le salut de la République. Environné d'ennemis soudoyés par l'or de l'étranger, il lui fallait se tenir sur un pied de guerre respectable, il lui fallait intimider, par une attitude ferme et résolue, les tentatives d'invasion que ses voisins entreprenaient contre la durée de sa République ; il lui fallait en outre réprimer l'insatiable ambition de ses propres généraux. La forme militaire était donc la seule qui convint à son gouvernement ; mais aussi, il travaillait de tout son pouvoir par l'instruction qu'il commençait à répandre dans la masse, à préparer une nouvelle ère pour l'avenir de sa patrie. Malgré toutes les entraves qui embarrassaient sa marche progressive vers la civilisation d'Haïti, malgré cette forme inique de gouvernement, il laissa en mourant son pays libre, prospère et propre à recevoir les plus belles institutions démocratiques.

Son successeur en arrivant au pouvoir trouva le pays dans la voie du progrès, tous les citoyens étaient disposés à accepter en quelque sorte un nouvel ordre de chose et le demandaient. Mais quoique destiné à une si belle immortalité, Boyer naturellement leger et superficiel était incapable de former un plan solide et de suivre son exécution dans toutes ses ramifications. Il n'eut pas le courage de rien entreprendre, de rien réformer ; et il suivit avec un coupable esprit de routine la forme du gouvernement de son prédécesseur. Jusqu'en l'année 1825, il fut l'enfant gâté de la fortune, il ne sut pas habilement profiter de ses faveurs ; l'étroitesse de son esprit l'en empêcha. Il s'engagea depuis dans une série d'actes despotiques qui devaient sans nul doute entraîner sa chûte. Après la réunionn du nord et de l'est, après la pacification de la Grand'anse et le traité de 1825, sa politique devait changer. Le terrain sur lequel il avait à opérer devenant plus vaste, la base

Figure 7.1 *Le Manifeste* (Port-au-Prince), Bibliothèque Nationale de France, Paris.

shared his appreciation of communal self-organization and local institutions as schools of civic spirit and democratic virtue.

Tocqueville's influence went beyond mere ethnography, however. His name and work constituted a broader terrain of ideological dispute between Liberals and loyalists to President Boyer. Writers in *Le Manifeste*, supporting the Liberal position, had a close affinity with Tocqueville's communal institutionalism. In contrast, the Boyerists writing in the competing paper *Le Temps* found bases in Tocqueville's work to support Boyer's heavy-handed authoritarianism. *Le Temps* was a loyalist paper that advertised itself as a proponent of public order. Its editors selectively quoted passages in which Tocqueville worried about the tyranny of democratic majorities and the way they imposed limits on speech and thought in America.[4] Ironically, *Le Temps* used these passages to defend Boyer's own suppression of speech and thought. Such limitations seemed acceptable in their view when exercised by a strong executive authority, but not by the people.

While holding Tocqueville's name sacred, neither side seemed to notice his fascination with French colonialism. He was in fact a vigorous proponent of forceful colonialization as a way of regenerating French society—surely not the kind of regeneration the Liberals had been envisioning. In this regard, Tocqueville was a key theorist of what Verena Erlenbusch-Anderson calls "the science of colonial war," a project that places him squarely in her genealogy of terrorism.[5] Both Liberals and Boyerists read him selectively, however, ignoring the senses in which he might be quite opposed to postcolonial freedom while emphasizing themes in his works more suitable to their separate interests.

In these ideological struggles, Tocqueville stood in not only for the example of America but also for European upheavals of the previous decade. In France, the July Revolution of 1830 had overthrown the Bourbon monarchy and replaced it with the populist Orléans branch of the royal family. Tocqueville had a complicated position in these events. He was connected to the House of Bourbon by family ties but allied with the Orléans camp by his progressive sympathies. Given his celebrity at the time, invoking Tocqueville's name was a convenient way to position oneself within these strands of French revolutionary politics. The Liberals echoed Tocqueville's progressivist hopes that American-style civic education could provide means for a new, regenerated French—or Haitian—society. The Boyerists used him to draw analogies with the French royal house as a guarantor of authority and public order. At times the July Revolution featured more directly in the writings of both sides.[6] Such references were relatively risky, however, particularly for the opposition. It was difficult to refer directly to French revolutionary politics without provoking strong action from Boyer's government. For the most part, then, both Liberals and Boyerists refrained from talking about French politics directly and used "Tocqueville" as a proxy for such arguments.

One can easily imagine why this particular history and principles were invoked in ideological struggle. As Karl Marx noted, the July Revolution was above all a clash between conflicting elite interests.[7] The Bourbon restoration of 1815–1830 had represented the interests of the old landed gentry, while the Orléans monarchy that replaced it represented the interests of ascendant industrial capitalists. Although the July Revolution was dressed up as a movement of democratic reform, Marx says, it was really an internal struggle between two factions of the dominant class.

One could make similar observations about the tensions between Liberals and Boyerists. In 1840s Haiti, landed gentry did not face off against ascendant industrialists. There was little industry, and land continued to be the primary source of wealth. Both sides of the political dispute were equal in this regard: most of the prominent Liberals and Boyerists were influential landowners. Thus the conflict primarily revolved around who would rule and who would benefit from that rule. In Marx's terms, it was a struggle over material interests within the racially and economically dominant class.

These intraclass tensions intensified as the 1840s proceeded. Increasingly dissatisfied with Boyer's autocratic rule, the Liberals formed the Société des Droits de l'Homme et du Citoyen (Society of the Rights of Man and Citizen) in the fall of 1842. Their name explicitly echoes the *Declaration of the Rights of Man and Citizen* that served as a preamble to the French revolutionary constitution of 1789. The Société's first meeting was held on the Praslin plantation on September 1, 1842. At that meeting, the members drafted a manifesto that became known as the *Manifeste de Praslin*.[8]

The *Manifeste de Praslin* provided an ideological roadmap for the reforms that the Société des Droits de l'Homme hoped to undertake. Popular sovereignty was its central value. The *Manifeste* characterizes this as the "great principle of the sovereignty of the people," which it identifies as a basis both for the original Haitian revolution and for a regeneration of the current order. It invites "citizens of diverse parts of the Republic to join us to change the Constitution, undertake the regeneration of Haiti, have a better government, and install in our dear and beautiful homeland the reign of liberty, democracy, morality, national felicity, and public virtue."[9] In other words, the transformation of Haitian society will occur with the participation of Haitian citizens, and it will be transformative because of their participation. This vision of popular sovereignty is framed in terms of constitutionalism, regeneration, and public virtue, giving it a distinctively French Jacobin flavor.

Strands of Jacobin constitutional liberalism—those of Brissot and other Girondins—were particularly prominent in the Liberal movement. The Haitian Constitution of 1816 was alleged to have created many of the nation's current problems, especially its tendency to concentrate power in the executive rather than separate legislative and executive power from one another.[10] Thus constitutional reform was foremost on the revolutionaries' agenda. The new constitution would be democratic and enshrine the sovereignty of the people as its most important feature. A strong notion of constitutional rights was central to this vision. The *Manifeste* characterizes them as "sacred, inalienable, imprescriptible," closely echoing language of the French revolutionary constitution of 1791.[11]

Even small administrative details of the Société reflect a conscious turn toward France. It established a ruling committee called the Committee of Public Safety (Comité de Salut Publique).[12] This name has strong reverberations of the French Revolution, referring back to the fearsome committee that was the power base of the Jacobin Montagnards during the Revolutionary Terror. Charles Rivière Hérard was chosen as the group's leader, bearing the title "Executor of the Sovereign Will of the People," a phrase laden with French revolutionary overtones.

Freedom of the press was another favorite Liberal theme. The newspaper *Le Manifeste* was launched with this encomium to press freedom: "The periodical press is noble, beautiful, forthright, and radiant. It heaps praise on the good; it abhors and dishonors evil. It strews flowers on the virtuous and capable functionary who, measuring the extent of duties and the grandeur of the power the people have entrusted to him, works for their wellbeing and their future. It strikes, flagellates, and tramples upon the perverse minister devoured by ambition and egoism, who dreams only of the shame and the subjection of his country."[13]

Press freedom was clearly a value in itself, but that value had a pointedly political valence. To some extent this is a classic expression of the Enlightenment's devotion to free thought and free expression, codified as a civil liberty.

More pointedly, though, it reflected the particular weight that the Liberals placed on public discourse. Here free expression took the tangible, material form of press freedom. It also reflected the developing ideal of public opinion, an epistemic innovation of the late eighteenth century that gave new, intangible form to earlier ideas of popular sovereignty.[14]

Quite often, Liberal defenses of the free press were most pointed when the press itself was attacked. The *Manifeste de Praslin* makes a number of such charges, and they appear frequently in the periodical press as well.[15] We learn that Boyer often suppressed public criticism by imprisoning, exiling, or killing newspaper editors. The protection of a free and thriving public sphere thus became a principal revolutionary goal.

Despite coming closer to the edge of revolution, the Praslin group remained relatively quiet about its intentions. There was no immediate mention of them or their manifesto in the local media. The *Feuille du commerce*, the newspaper of record in Haiti at this time, carried no notice of the Liberal revolutionaries during the early months of their organizing. Even *Le Manifeste* remained silent about their activities and confined itself to more general news.

In January 1843, however, these intentions were finally realized in open revolt. The Société des Droits de l'Homme issued statements removing Boyer and his adjutants from power and assuming control of the government. They formed revolutionary armies in considerable numbers and went to battle against government forces. Charles Rivière Hérard was designated president of the provisional government. By March 1843 President Boyer was ousted from power and went into exile.

The revolutionary army was reportedly received in the capital with great popular approval and the highest hopes. Their arrival was not without incident: Thomas Madiou reports that "the people" took advantage of the situation to sack the palace and destroy its archives.[16] We might think of this as a self-inflicted silencing by "the people" of its own past, or an effort to silence the government. In either case, it may explain some of the opacity of Haitian history to us today. Nonetheless, the overall mood was reportedly an optimistic one. Foreign consuls of various nations attended the inauguration of the provisional government, indicating a certain degree of international recognition for this upstart reform movement.[17]

Meanwhile, the fall of the Haitian president attracted a great deal of attention in the United States and Europe. The *Courrier des États-Unis*, a French-language newspaper in New York, carried breathless, issue-by-issue coverage of the goings-on in Haiti. After receiving direct news in February, the *Courrier* strained to make out what might be happening there. On April 11, 1843, it reported news from a Captain Leland, newly arrived from Cuba, who heard from an English steamer coming from Jamaica that President Boyer had fled Port-au-Prince to Kingston with three million piastres from the Haitian treasury. Then began a sort of news vigil for Boyer, who was eventually tracked from Jamaica to Pensacola, Florida. Having printed this choice morsel, the *Courrier* was forced to retract it in the next issue after learning that it was just a joke promulgated by the *Mobile Herald*.[18] This was somewhat typical of the nineteenth century Pan-American public sphere: news often followed very circuitous routes, ship's captains were often a favored source of overseas reportage, and newspapers used a great deal of space reporting on the reports of other newspapers.

Meanwhile, the principal Haitian papers were reprinting a flurry of proclamations and orders that had been issued during the months of upheaval. *Le Manifeste* added a burst of commentary about "the revolution that just happened on our island." Both it and the *Feuille de commerce* published the *Manifeste de Praslin* as well as a large number of proclamations and orders from the new provisional government.[19]

Although it was not widely publicized before the revolution, the *Manifeste de Praslin* itself was framed partly as a call to action. At times it blossomed into quite expressive revolutionary prose:

> Dearest fellow citizens, peoples are always criminal to abandon their rights. Citizens, observe Haiti, unhappy, suffering, ragged, almost enslaved, quaking under the weight of injustice and arbitrary will, dulled under this regime of immorality! Hear this people, crying from all quarters that the abuse and pain have reached their limit. . . . Hear the complaints, lamentations, reproaches, the just reproaches of your wives, your mothers, your daughters, your sisters, who accuse you of laxness, pusillanimity, and torpor.[20]

These passages aim to excite the insurrectional sympathies of Haitian citizens. At the beginning of the revolution in January 1843, Hérard issued another proclamation with much the same aim. He writes,

Haitians,

The hypocritical and perverse tyranny that weighs on the country and devours the fruits of the glorious work of our ancestors aims to strike the final blows to patriotism, striking at the heart of the generous opposition that defended your rights with so much constancy and disinterest!

The proclamation ends, "To arms, Haitians! Rise up! The fatherland counts on all of its children! Haitians, you will justify its hope!!"[21]

Again, these proclamations seem to aim at incitement and driving the insurrection forward. However, other, less obvious agendas also seem to be at work. The proclamations exercise a powerful justificatory function. While detailing reasons that might stir one to action, they also provide a rationale for the revolution to anyone else who might be reading. Indeed, this was arguably the primary aim of such proclamations, since the revolution was already moving forward at great speed when they were published.

This justificatory function can be seen in the widespread distribution of revolutionary proclamations. The Liberals deployed their arguments well beyond Haiti's borders, publicizing their cause in the United States as well. A favored venue was the *Courrier des États-Unis*. On March 1, 1843, a group of insurgents from the People's Committees of Les Cayes and Jérémie sent an account of their actions to the *Courrier*. The account took the form of another manifesto, "Official Statement and Manifesto of the Haitian Insurgents."[22] It acquainted the American audience with the recent events surrounding the *Manifeste de Praslin*. The writers characterize the *Manifeste* itself as "a long, passionate, and lucid exposé of the grievances of Haitians against the odious and intolerable reign of the current leader."

A similar agenda can be seen in the retroactive publication of the *Manifeste de Praslin* itself. The *Manifeste* was written in September 1842, but it seems to have been kept secret until the revolution was actually underway. It thus shares a temporality with the French Declaration of the Rights of Man and Citizen, which was issued in the midst of a revolution, rather than, say, the American Declaration, which initiated one. The *Manifeste* functioned more as legitimation for actions already being taken than as a true call to action.

The American Declaration states that, "a decent respect to the opinions of mankind requires that they should declare the causes which impel them to the separation." "To prove this," it says, "let facts be submitted to a candid world." It then lays out a case for revolution in terms of the tyranny of the British king, listing specific charges against him.

The Haitian rebellion against Boyer was justified in strikingly similar terms. It draws on the legacy of that earlier revolution, echoing not just the intentions of the American Declaration but also its rhetorical structure. Hérard substantiated the proclamation removing Boyer from office with a carefully formulated list of grievances.[23] That document is remarkably similar in tone, style, and substance to the charges made against the British king in the American Declaration. It draws on familiar concepts of despotism, usurpation, and tyranny, ones that can be traced through the American Declaration back to Locke's *Second Treatise*.[24] Boyer is accused of undermining the independence of representative bodies, usurping powers not granted him by the constitution, imposing illegitimate taxes, altering laws and failing to promulgate them, arbitrarily appointing and dismissing officials, and plunging public finance and administration into disorder and anarchy. He is charged with using a system of lying, spying, and denunciation to corrupt public opinion and morality, and sow division among the citizenry. He is said to be acting with the most odious tyranny, imposing his will on the country with profound ignorance of people's rights and bad faith in international relations. He has compromised the honor of Haiti and threatened its national independence. In short, the Liberal revolutionaries make pointed charges against him, mimicking the stylistic conventions of the American Revolution and thereby availing themselves of its cultural currency.

Regeneration, a principal theme of the French Revolution, also occupies great pride of place for the Liberal revolutionaries. The *Manifeste de Praslin*, for instance, declares that "The hour of Regeneration has sounded!"[25] The members of the Société des Droits de l'Homme et du Citoyen were asked to swear an oath to promote the health and regeneration of Haiti.[26] It is an idea that is constantly repeated in their proclamations.[27] Consider, for instance, a statement issued by the Municipal Committee of the Commune of Plaisance: "The sublime revolution that opens up the era of regeneration for us has solidified our liberties. We are all descendants of the African race, we are all brothers of the same family, so let us join together and be one to support the principles of our memorable regenerative revolution."[28]

The Liberals even adopted the French revolutionary device of restarting the calendar to mark their new order as an epochal rupture in history. The year 1843 was thus notated "year 40 of Independence and year 1 of the Regeneration" in their manifestos and documents.

In spite of taking Haitian independence as its point of origin, this idea of regeneration rarely looks back to the legacy of the Haitian Revolution. There is no move to reactivate the revolutionary spirit of Louverture or Dessalines, who are blamed for putting Haiti on a path of despotism. Similarly, the Liberals seem ambivalent about the constitutionalism of Alexandre Pétion. He is embraced as a founding president from the early years of independence, but his 1816 constitution is singled out for institutionalizing democracy in a totalitarian form. All of these early moments of postcolonial politics are seen as lost opportunities for freedom and democracy. In the Liberal view, there seems to be little in the Haitian past that is worth reclaiming.[29]

Like its prior use in the French Revolution, the idea of regeneration lacks an originary model here. Really, it is more an idea of *generation*, a fresh start like the one that Hannah Arendt found so intriguing in French revolutionary thought.[30] This emphasis on recreating past virtues while implicitly making a break with the past does some important work. It wraps change in the cloak of an already legitimate past without having to specify exactly which past that is. The Liberals' ideological reference points suggest this would be a French and American past, however, rather than the one developed through forty years of Haitian independence. In an important sense this "regeneration" seems to be a rupture and fresh start for Haiti, a new beginning along French and American lines.

To anchor their fresh start, the Liberal revolutionaries formed a Constituent Assembly (another name with reverberations of the French Revolution) and authored a new constitution.[31] As I have detailed elsewhere, this was a wildly original document with some strikingly unprecedented ideas.[32] It extended citizenship outside of the Westphalian frame of the Haitian nation-state, enfranchising all Caribbean Indians and their descendants and all Africans and their descendants. In principle, the entire African continent and its diaspora were thereby given Haitian citizenship, as was the diaspora of peoples pushed out of the way and partly exterminated by European colonization. Here the Liberal Revolution shows itself to be much more than a timid reflection of European ideals. It reveals vividly original political thinking that goes well beyond anything being imagined on the European continent before or since. The Liberals may have adopted many ideals from revolutions before them, but this did not preempt highly original thought of their own.

The process of drafting the constitution was well publicized in the foreign press, though without seeming fully to realize its radical implications. The *Courrier des États-Unis* covered it extensively. The *Emancipator and Free American*, the newspaper of the Massachusetts Abolition Society, printed an English translation of the constitution and several articles supporting it.[33] The *Weekly Elevator* of Philadelphia, another abolitionist paper, praised the republicanism of the new constitution, saying, "In the origin, rise, progress, and consummation of the Revolution, even the prejudiced disparager and enemy of Haytien welfare, cannot but mark the extraordinary qualification for self-government, and knowledge of political science and legal jurisprudence, and their judicious appliance, to the successful establishment of that most difficult form of government, viz. REPUBLICAN."[34] The Liberal Revolution seemed to capture the imagination of these far-flung public spheres in part because of its unique fusion of liberal-constitutionalist ideals and Haiti's unparalleled example of the abolition of slavery. As we have seen, of course, the Liberals were careful to manage the reception of their movement in the international press. They publicized their ideas widely and received sympathetic recognition in return.

The Liberals' attempts at justification and publicity ultimately aimed at a broader form of self-legitimation. By taking this orientation, they were following genre conventions that had been developing for some time around the idea of revolution itself. The great eighteenth-century revolutions had established the idea that revolutionary actions should be justified in the public domain. As we have seen, this was most famously expressed in the American Declaration of Independence and its solicitude to "let facts be submitted to a candid world." The Haitian Revolution of Dessalines's era featured its own set of forceful justifications, aimed at the evils of French colonialism and slavery. Such practices were now fully developed and available for use, and they had a powerful pull on the Liberal imagination.

Liberal efforts at self-legitimation reflected two imperatives. The first was one shared with the American, French, and Haitian Revolutions: legitimating acts of revolutionary change themselves. Since revolution operates outside the bounds of normal political procedure, it bears an extra burden of legitimation. It is a legitimation that must be improvised, because there is no formal procedure that could supply it.[35]

The second imperative is unique to postcolonial Haiti. It reflects the extent to which the new nation and its citizens had been constituted as global subalterns even after independence. Haiti was viewed with alarm by the existing world powers. As a former slave colony that converted itself into an independent republic—strikingly, ruled by Black and mixed-race people—it constituted a potential example of self-liberation for the other colonies and groups of enslaved people. There was great fear of "contagion" on the part of American and European elites. The result was a politics of quarantine, expressed as lack of diplomatic recognition and an abiding hostility to Haiti's interests.[36]

In this sense, Haiti occupied a difficult position on the global stage: both successful and marginal, unavoidable and delegitimated. This ambiguous status generated a potent form of subaltern silence, one articulated within global public spheres themselves. It was a form of *silencing through delegitimation*. I mean this in Pierre Bourdieu's sense: a person is judged to be a "legitimate" member of a given community when she is seen as a competent speaker and actor according to the implicit standards of that community.[37] Legitimacy here is a broad judgment of social worth and competence, recognition as someone whose actions are worth noting and whose speech is worth listening to. Delegitimation, correspondingly, is anything that undermines that status and damages perceptions of a person's social worth.

Legitimacy and delegitimation operate as forms of symbolic struggle. In subaltern politics they are latter-day developments of *silencing through resignification*, which we have been tracing since the early eighteenth century. In that earlier era, resignification was seen in the slow consolidation of racial thinking, which resignified the identities of the subjects to which it applied. By the 1840s, a century and a half later, it has evolved into a more specific and flexible practice of silencing by denying people value and social competence. In retrospect, we can see the germs of such delegitimation already at the origins of racial thinking: to be racialized was to be delegitimated, to have one's social competence and value decreased. Over 150 years of development, these practices have become much more flexible and autonomous. Delegitimation no longer needs to be attached strictly to race or any other single identity category; it can now travel relatively independently as a potent practice of silencing in many different ways. In addition, it has also become quite flexible in its choice of objects. By the mid-nineteenth century, delegitimation no longer applies only to abstract identity categories like race. It can now be applied to individuals, to abstract social positions, to concrete groups, or collectivities of all sorts.

We can see all of this at work in Haiti in the mid-nineteenth century. As a nation, Haiti and its representatives were visible in the transatlantic public spheres of their time and were participants in them to some extent. However, their presence was always delegitimated. They were not silenced in the thoroughgoing manner in which slaves had been before independence, nor in the way that the agrarian populace was after independence. Rather, their silence was one of devaluation, of being thought to have nothing worth listening to. This is a striking new development in the history of silence and one well worth noting. Its importance would continue to grow in coming decades, and we will have much more to say about it.

The Liberal theme of regeneration takes on new meaning in this light. If "regeneration" implicitly meant refounding the Black Republic on a new basis, the Liberals may well have been trying to create a legitimacy for themselves that had been denied to the first Haitian Republic in 1804-1805. This would be a liberal, constitutional-democratic Haiti, one that was more familiar, more legible, and less threatening to global powers. In this case, Liberal uses of the French revolutionary idea of regeneration may indeed have been calls for a new beginning. This would also explain their preference for French and American rather than Haitian revolutionary precedents. Those had a symbolic value on the international stage not possessed by the original Haitian revolution.

Public spheres across the Americas and Europe took notice of these efforts. This can be seen in the increased attention to Haiti in the French-language print media in 1843-1845 (figure 7.2).[38] Haiti had already captured the world's attention during the mid-1820s, largely due to the infamous indemnification payments negotiated between the Boyer government and France. In exchange for French recognition of the Haitian state, Haiti agreed to crippling "reparation" payments for the loss of French property during the Revolution. These payments were enormously unpopular in Haiti and severely depleted the Haitian treasury for decades. Haiti came back into public attention in the 1840s, this time as the Boyer regime lost its grip and the Liberals seized power.

Here we see that the proliferation of discourse around the Liberal Revolution was not simply a result of its own efforts of publicity. Rather, those efforts incited much broader discussion, analysis, news-chasing, and interpretation—efforts to discern what was really happening in that former colony that still very much held the attention of Europe and the United States. This attention did not necessarily add up to increased legitimation of the Haitian state, however. At

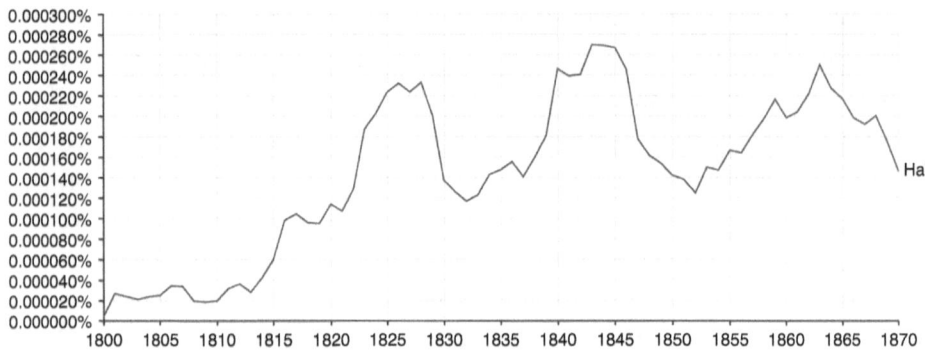

Figure 7.2 The published frequency of "Haïti" in French from 1800 to 1870. Google French dataset of 2012, courtesy of Google Labs.

times it did, as we have seen in the warm reception that the Liberal Revolution received in the foreign press. On other occasions, such attention merely created distraction, problematization, and an undertow of delegitimation.

In sum, the Liberal Revolution of 1843 provides a classic example of the public sphere's revolutionary potential. It was an outward-looking, internationalist, reform-minded, liberal-constitutionalist, progressive political movement. It was strongly oriented toward American and French precedents. Above all, it displayed a consistent preoccupation with self-legitimation. This was a revolution of words, slogans, political clubs, newspapers, and manifestos. It was highly discursive and savvy about publicity. Its members drew on an eclectic mix of ideas to force an authoritarian president from power and "regenerate" the republic. Some of their ideas were adapted from American and French revolutionary thought, some were imported from more recent upheavals in France, and some were unique and unprecedented creations. All of this made signature contributions to an emerging paradigm of modern revolution, developing a highly original constitutional regime while further building on earlier ideological precedents.

REVOLTS OF THE VOICELESS: THE ARMY OF SUFFERERS

In the midst of the well-spoken, highly regarded Liberal Revolution, other currents were also brewing. The Liberal Revolution was a struggle within the dominant class, but it occurred against a broader background of highly racialized class relations. Boyer's rule had been characterized by a sharply delineated racial politics.[39] The abolitionist Victor Schoelcher visited Haiti in 1841 and described social conditions under the Boyer regime. Foremost in his account was the domination of the mixed-race elites, the *gens de couleur*, over blacks. Adopting racial descriptors already circulating in Haiti at this time, he referred to this as "the aristocracy of yellow skin."[40] Those racial tensions had a long history, going back well into the colonial era. Mixed-race men had been pressed into service in the paramilitary *maréchaussée* to hunt down fugitive slaves. Such service was framed as a way of demonstrating one's allegiance to the colony and proving the worth of one's citizenship, so it sometimes elicited a fair amount of zeal among the men pursuing it.[41] As we have seen, mixed-race agitators would later press the case for their own equality within the colonial system. This came at the expense of (mostly black) slaves, because the case for mixed-race equality was held to be perfectly consistent with slavery. All free citizens would be equal as property owners regardless of race. There would be racial equality within classes but not between them: equality among property owners, but no equality between owners and those owned.[42]

In sum, racial tensions between mixed-race and black citizens had a long and complex history in the Haitian Republic. Boyer's racial politics were a continuation of this. They were not swept away by the Liberal Revolution but continued without reflection. The stakes of the Revolution lay between Boyer and other members of his ruling class. It was a narrowly political struggle in which the social questions of the day were not addressed. In this sense, the Haitian struggle of the 1840s was also very much a conflict internal to the bourgeoisie, quite similar to the one Marx described in France.

Against this background, it is not surprising that the Liberal revolutionaries maintained tight control on the revolution itself. In spite of their commitments to popular sovereignty, Hérard explicitly ordered that rural farmers were not to be included in the revolutionary forces, which could consist only of landowners, farm managers, and their sons.[43] In other words, the revolutionary forces were to be composed of the landowning classes and their allies. This contradiction between universalist principles and exclusionary practices was a sign of deeper tensions that would soon surface.

Having been excluded from the Liberal Revolution, the rural farmers now continued the upheaval, raising their own army and seizing control of southern

Haiti. They were poor and had few weapons. An improvised solution to this problem was the use of long, pointed pikes tipped with poison. As a result, the insurgents were sometimes referred to as Piquets—"Pikes." They called themselves l'Armée Souffrante, the Suffering Army or Army of Sufferers, because of their generally destitute condition. This movement was led by Louis-Jean-Jacques Acaau, who also functioned as its spokesperson.

The Army of Sufferers moved through the southern part of the island, defeating government troops and taking various cities in the region.[44] Caught up in the midst of these events, the U.S. consul in southern Haiti sent a series of panicked reports back to Washington. He told of eight thousand revolutionary troops waiting outside of the city where he was stationed and frantically requested that American ships of war be stationed in Haitian ports. He also wrote in some haste of Americans and mixed-race Haitians evacuating from the island. Later his tone turned even darker as he told of having his office ransacked by the revolutionaries, who took his official papers, private letters, funds, and the official seal for authenticating public documents.[45]

As the Army of Sufferers gained success after success, it became a potent revolutionary force and marched on the capital. Dissatisfied with Hérard's rule and his response to this crisis, a group of prominent citizens in Port-au-Prince declared their opposition and named a new president on May 3, 1844.[46] Hérard was forced from office and sent into exile. He was replaced by a black army general, the first in a series of presidents selected to appease the broader movement that the Army of Sufferers represented. Acaau was named military commander of an area in the south, and some of his allies occupied other positions in the government.

There are few documents mapping out the words, principles, or ideals of the Army of Sufferers. They wrote no treatises, did not quote foreign precedents, and were largely rebuffed in their attempts to publicize their cause. Many of the documents we do have are thanks to the Saint-Domingan press.

The editor of *Le Manifeste* had followed other prominent citizens in Port-au-Prince by breaking with Hérard at the beginning of May 1844. He published a bruising editorial saying that Hérard's "brutal and bloody tyranny" had caused the popular uprising, and that he was a traitor to the revolution against Boyer.[47] In the next issue, the newspaper printed a large group of documents from Acaau. They were published with a cover letter from him, dated two days after *Le*

Manifeste's condemnation of Hérard, saying that he was sending the paper a number of documents for publication.[48] Plainly Acaau sensed that the political tide had turned in ways that might allow his movement to speak to a wider audience.

These writings rehearse some familiar points. One early proclamation begins, "I owe my fellow citizens a faithful account of the cause of the counter-revolution that broke out, the events that accompanied it, and the goal to which it aspires."[49] Almost the same wording shows up several weeks later, "I owe my fellow citizens an exact and faithful account of the cause for which I just undertook a counter-revolution that opposed the events preceding it."[50] Here we see an attention to justification, much the same as the Liberal revolutionaries and the revolutionary tradition before them.

The reasons given navigate familiar points as well. The Boyer regime was one that kept them "long bent under the degrading yoke of despotism," and the revolution against it was greeted with hope. Hérard, leader of the Liberal Revolution, claimed to be a "regenerator of the fatherland." Unfortunately, the new government has followed a similar path, engaging in the same kind of arbitrary and illegal acts as the Boyer regime. It is wielding whips, chains, and deceptions against a free and independent people, raising a new specter of slavery in the Republic. Thus the people have risen up en masse against Hérard. Leading their new revolution, Acaau himself has "exterminated and uprooted this heresy that was planted in so many generous, free, and independent souls."[51]

Much in these documents sounds quite familiar. Their objections to tyranny and "the yoke of despotism" echo the Liberal objections to Boyer most directly and follow the Liberals in echoing American and French revolutionary rhetoric before that. This could well be an effective stylistic strategy, turning the revolutionary doctrines of the Liberals back on themselves in the same way that Thomas Jefferson had coopted John Locke's revolutionary doctrines in his declaration of independence from the British.

Indeed, a comparison with Jefferson's writing skill is quite apt. In these proclamations, handbills, and broadsheets, Acaau shows himself a masterful prose stylist who can use language to potent effect. His statements are beautifully written, packed with forceful pronouncements, sharp invectives, and vivid phrases. A broadsheet attacking Hérard provides a beautiful example, so well written that it is worth quoting in the original (figure 7.3). It opens with the following lines:

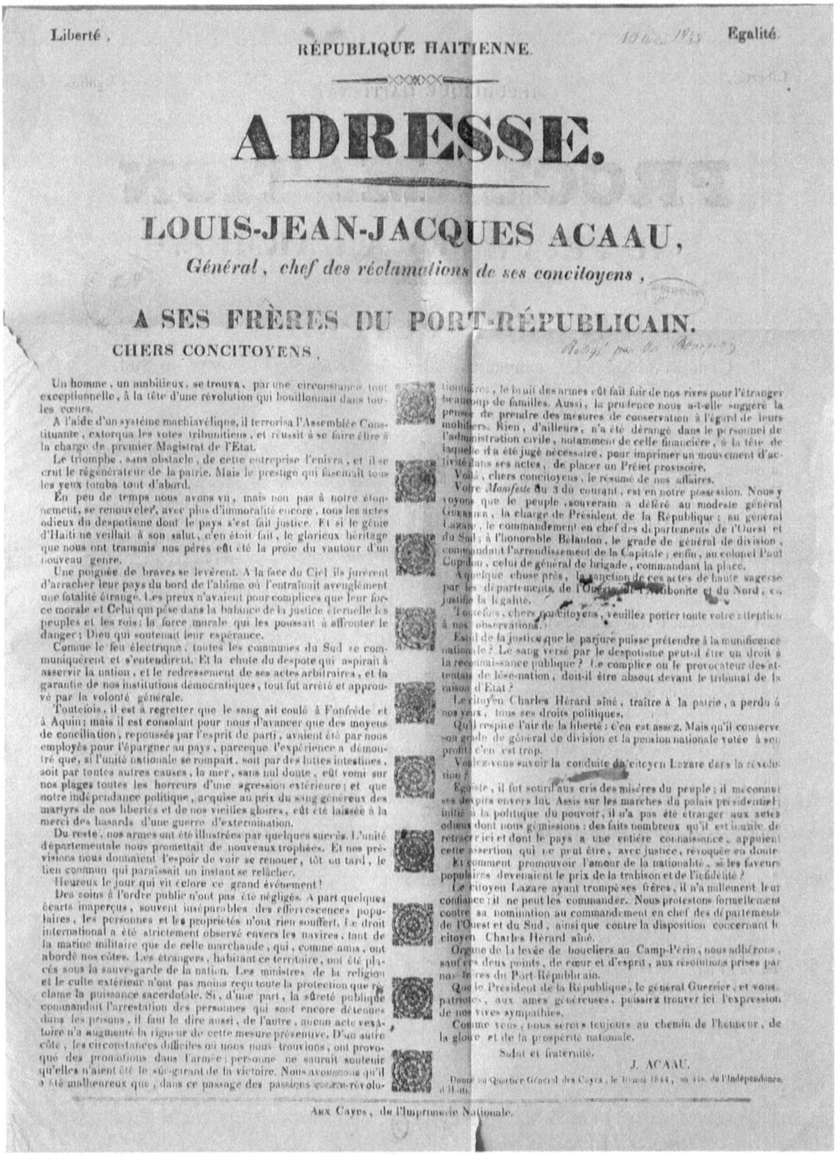
Liberté, RÉPUBLIQUE HAITIENNE. Egalité.

ADRESSE.

LOUIS-JEAN-JACQUES ACAAU,

Général, chef des réclamations de ses concitoyens,

A SES FRÈRES DU PORT-RÉPUBLICAIN.

CHERS CONCITOYENS,

Un homme, un ambitieux, se trouva, par une circonstance tout exceptionnelle, à la tête d'une révolution qui bouillonnait dans tous les cœurs.

A l'aide d'un système machiavélique, il terrorisa l'Assemblée Constituante, extorqua les votes tribunitiens, et réussit à se faire élire à la charge de premier Magistrat de l'État.

Le triomphe, sans obstacle, de cette entreprise l'enivra, et il se crut le régénérateur de la patrie. Mais le prestige qui fascinait tous les yeux tomba tout d'abord.

En peu de temps nous avons vu, mais non pas à notre étonnement, se renouveler, avec plus d'immoralité encore, tous les actes odieux du despotisme dont le pays s'est fait justice. Et si le génie d'Haïti ne veillait à son salut, c'en étoit fait, le glorieux héritage que nous ont transmis nos pères eût été la proie du vautour d'un nouveau genre.

Une poignée de braves se levèrent. A la face du Ciel ils jurèrent d'arracher leur pays du bord de l'abîme où l'entraînait aveuglément une fatalité étrange. Les preux n'avaient pour complices que leur force morale et Celui qui pèse dans la balance de la justice éternelle les peuples et les rois: la force morale qui les poussait à affronter le danger; Dieu qui soutenait leur espérance.

Comme le feu électrique, toutes les communes du Sud se communiquèrent et s'entendirent. Et la chute du despote qui aspirait à asservir la nation, et le redressement de ses actes arbitraires, et la garantie de nos institutions démocratiques, tout fut arrêté et approuvé par la volonté générale.

Toutefois, il est à regretter que le sang ait coulé à Fonfrède et à Aquin; mais il est consolant pour nous d'avancer que des moyens de conciliation, repoussés par l'esprit de parti, avaient été par nous employés pour l'épargner au pays, parceque l'expérience a démontré que, si l'unité nationale se rompait, soit par des luttes intestines, soit par toutes autres causes, la mer, sans nul doute, eût vomi sur nos plages toutes les horreurs d'une agression extérieure; et que notre indépendance politique, acquise au prix du sang généreux des martyrs de nos libertés et de nos vieilles gloires, eût été laissée à la merci des hasards d'une guerre d'extermination.

Du reste, nos armes ont été illustrées par quelques succès. L'unité départementale nous promettait de nouveaux trophées. Et nos prévisions nous donnaient l'espoir de voir se renouer, tôt ou tard, le lien commun qui paraissait un instant se relâcher.

Heureux le jour qui vit éclore ce grand événement!

Des soins à l'ordre public n'ont pas été négligés. A part quelques écarts inaperçus, souvent inséparables des effervescences populaires, les personnes et les propriétés n'ont rien souffert. Le droit international a été strictement observé envers les navires, tant de la marine militaire que de celle marchande, qui, comme amis, ont abordé nos côtes. Les étrangers, habitant ce territoire, ont été placés sous la sauve-garde de la nation. Les ministres de la religion et le culte extérieur n'ont pas moins reçu toute la protection que réclame la puissance sacerdotale. Si, d'une part, la sûreté publique commandait l'arrestation des personnes qui sont encore détenues dans les prisons, il faut le dire aussi, de l'autre, aucun acte vexatoire n'a augmenté la rigueur de cette mesure préventive. D'un autre côté, les circonstances difficiles où nous nous trouvions, ont provoqué des promotions dans l'armée: personne ne saurait soutenir qu'elles n'aient été le sûr-garant de la victoire. Nous avouerons qu'il a été malheureux que, dans ce passage des passions contre-révolutionnaires, le bruit des armes eût fait fuir de nos rives pour l'étranger beaucoup de familles. Aussi, la prudence nous a-t-elle suggéré la pensée de prendre des mesures de conservation à l'égard de leurs mobiliers. Rien, d'ailleurs, n'a été dérangé dans le personnel de l'administration civile, notamment de celle financière, à la tête de laquelle il a été jugé nécessaire, pour imprimer un mouvement d'activité dans ses actes, de placer un Préfet provisoire.

Voilà, chers concitoyens, le résumé de nos affaires.

Votre *Manifeste* du 3 du courant, est en notre possession. Nous y voyons que le peuple souverain a déféré au modeste général Guerrier, la charge de Président de la République; au général Lazare, le commandement en chef des départements de l'Ouest et du Sud; à l'honorable Bélanton, le grade de général de division, commandant l'arrondissement de la Capitale; enfin, au colonel Paul Cupidon, celui de général de brigade, commandant la place.

A quelque chose près, la sanction de ces actes de haute sagesse par les départements de l'Ouest, de l'Artibonite et du Nord, en justifie la légalité.

Toutefois, chers concitoyens, veuillez porter toute votre attention à nos observations.

Est-il de la justice que le parjure puisse prétendre à la munificence nationale? Le sang versé par le despotisme peut-il être un droit à la reconnaissance publique? Le complice ou le provocateur des attentats de lèse-nation, doit-il être absout devant le tribunal de la raison d'Etat?

Le citoyen Charles Hérard aîné, traître à la patrie, a perdu à nos yeux, tous ses droits politiques.

Qu'il respire l'air de la liberté: c'en est assez. Mais qu'il conserve son grade de général de division et la pension nationale votée à son profit, c'en est trop.

Voulez-vous savoir la conduite du citoyen Lazare dans la révolution?

Egoïste, il fut sourd aux cris des misères du peuple; il méconnut ses devoirs envers lui. Assis sur les marches du palais présidentiel; initié à la politique du pouvoir, il n'a pas été étranger aux actes odieux dont nous gémissions: des faits nombreux qu'il est inutile de retracer ici et dont le pays a une entière connaissance, appuient cette assertion qui ne peut être, avec justice, révoquée en doute.

Et comment promouvoir l'amour de la nationalité, si les faveurs populaires devenaient le prix de la trahison et de l'infidélité?

Le citoyen Lazare ayant trompé ses frères, il n'a nullement leur confiance: il ne peut les commander. Nous protestons formellement contre sa nomination au commandement en chef des départements de l'Ouest et du Sud, ainsi que contre la disposition concernant le citoyen Charles Hérard aîné.

Organe de la levée de boucliers au Camp-Périn, nous adhérons, sauf ces deux points, de cœur et d'esprit, aux résolutions prises par nos frères du Port-Républicain.

Que le Président de la République, le général Guerrier, et vous, patriotes, aux âmes généreuses, puissiez trouver ici l'expression de nos vives sympathies.

Comme vous, nous serons toujours au chemin de l'honneur, de la gloire et de la prospérité nationale.

Salut et fraternité.

J. ACAAU.

Donné au Quartier Général des Cayes, le 10 mai 1844, an 41e. de l'Indépendance d'Haïti.

Aux Cayes, de l'Imprimerie Nationale.

Figure 7.3 Louis-Jean-Jacques Acaau, "Adresse à ses freres du Port-Républicain," May 10, 1844, FOL-PU-145. Bibliothèque Nationale de France, Paris.

Un homme, un ambitieux, se trouva, par une circonstance toute exceptionnelle, à la tête d'une révolution qui bouillonnait dans tous les coeurs. À l'aide d'un système machiavélique, il terrorisa l'assemblée Constitutante, extorqua les votes tribunitiens, et réussit à se faire élire à la charge de premier magistrat de l'État. Le triomphe, sans obstacle, de cette entreprise, l'enivra, et il se crut le régénérateur de la patrie. Mais le prestige qui fascinait tous les yeux tomba tout d'abord. En peu de temps nous avons vu, mais non pas à notre étonnement, se renouveler, avec plus d'immoralité encore, tous les actes odieux du despotisme dont le pays s'est fait justice.[52]

A man, an ambitious man, found himself through exceptional circumstances at the head of a revolution that boiled in every heart. Using a Machiavellian system, he terrorized the Constituent Assembly, extorted tribunal votes, and succeeded in getting himself elected as premier magistrate of the State. The triumph without obstacle of this undertaking energized him, and he believed himself to be the regenerator of the homeland. But the prestige that had transfixed our attention suddenly dried up. In a short time we saw, without astonishment, the revival with even more immorality of the most odious acts of despotism that the country had already brought to justice.

This passage has a beautiful cadence; it is poetic, persuasive, and forceful. It paints a vivid picture of flawed character traits and illegitimate acts, leading the reader through an emotional arc that ends in condemnation. This piece also shows an awareness of Liberal ideology, with its barbed comment their self-chartered goal of regeneration.

The broadsheet continues,

Comme le feu électrique, toutes les communes du Sud se communiquèrent et s'entendirent. Et la chute du despote qui aspirait à asservir la nation, et le redressement de ses actes arbitraires, et la garantie de nos institutions démocratiques, tout fut arrêté et approuvé par la volonté générale.[53]

Like an electric current, all the communes of the South communicated with and understood one another. And the fall of the despot who hoped to enslave the nation, the recovery from his arbitrary acts, and the guarantee of our democratic institutions were all agreed and approved by the general will.

Here the poetry continues with a vivid image of electric current lighting up the revolutionary energies of the South. It again condemns Hérard's despotism and finishes on an elevated note with a reference to Rousseau. This is clearly revolutionary rhetoric of the highest order.

When *Le Manifeste* went to press with these proclamations, they had not yet appeared in the *Feuille du commerce*. The *Feuille* occupied the same position in the Haitian press that the *Gazette de Saint-Domingue* and *Affiches américaines* had during the colonial years. It was a commercial paper whose front page was always full of the comings and goings of ships in port, the prices of commodities, and so on. It also functioned as the mainstream paper of record in Haiti at this time. Félix Courtois, its editor, had been harassed and jailed by the Boyer regime for his liberal sympathies.

In an episode of subaltern silence that needs no theoretical elaboration, Courtois admits that he had declined to print statements sent to him by Acaau for many months. He reports, "We haven't thought it necessary to give publicity to pieces coming from the South, which we've read one after the other, especially those sent by General L. J. Jacques Acaau, in his name, addressed to his *Fellow Citizens* of Port-Républicain [i.e., Port-au-Prince]." Now, in a fit of bad conscience—likely spurred on by their appearance in *Le Manifeste*—Courtois printed a torrent of documents from Acaau. He claims, with evident hypocrisy, that they had not been published before because there had been no one to respond to Acaau's appeals, given that all of the governmental bodies were suspended during the crisis. Now the pieces are being printed as "*historical materials*" so that the subscribers of the *Feuille du commerce* can evaluate their merit.[54]

The foreign press also took little notice of these events. The *Courrier des États-Unis* devoted almost no attention to Acaau, especially compared to what it lavished on the Liberal Revolution. The *New York Journal of Commerce* was one notable exception. It referred to Acaau as a "monster... of detestable memory; composed of the lowest and most despicable of the Black race."[55] Overall, though, the Army of Sufferers drew relatively little attention from the outside world. To the extent that it did, it was characterized as yet more upheaval and chaos in a long line of disturbances that interrupted trade and threatened foreign interests.

SUBTERRANEAN PROBLEMATICS

What, then, to make of Acaau and the Army of Sufferers? Their silencing by the Haitian press requires little comment. It rendered the subaltern silent in a straightforward way: what we earlier called *silencing through exclusion*. It is a form of silencing that is made possible only once there is a well-developed public sphere. The subaltern attempts to speak and is simply denied access to the public sphere. That silence might have been a durable one had not *Le Manifeste* decided to print their proclamations. Because they were printed in the end, we see what profound silence Acaau's movement could have fallen into if they had been left to the mercies of other press outlets.

Reading beyond these relatively obvious forms of silence, however, we might well ask what the subaltern was trying to say. Here the issues become more interesting. Acaau's appearance in the archive presents us with a number of puzzles that reveal other forms of silence. Most obviously, there are substantial tensions among the various images we have of Acaau's movement. The Army of Sufferers was described as poor and destitute, and Acaau himself was portrayed as a shabby figure. He was said to wear a straw hat full of holes, a vest with a torn collar, pistols attached to a belt, and sandals.[56] This vivid image of a ramshackle revolutionary seems rather at odds with the beauty and sophistication of his prose. Given the depth and subtlety of Acaau's writing, it is somewhat striking that no refers to him as a great orator, a charismatic leader, or a deep thinker.

There are a number of ways one might reconcile the apparent tensions between these images. On one hand, we could conclude that the physical description of Acaau was misleading and that his writing is the true gauge of his abilities. After all, the account of a ramshackle Acaau with a straw hat did come from Thomas Madiou, a member of the *de couleur* elite with Liberal sympathies. Given the counterrevolutionary force of Acaau's insurgency, we might suppose that Madiou's description had a political valence and Acaau was not as shabby as he was made out to be. Perhaps the image of him was a kind of character assassination through description, or at least an attempt to undercut the force of his writing.

On the other hand, we might view Madiou's description as accurate and conclude that Acaau was not the author of the statements bearing his name. Attributions of authorship are always tricky for political figures, even more so in postcolonial Haiti. We know that literacy was precarious among Haitian leaders and that the words published in one's name may have been crafted by someone else. Acaau was known to be literate, unlike the other principal leaders of the Army of Sufferers. Recent Haitian President Leslie Manigat, who has read some of Acaau's papers, says he "knew how to sign his name and could be assisted in his correspondence and executive tasks" by two *de couleur* secretaries—hardly a stirring endorsement of his literary abilities.[57] It is possible that the statements attributed to Acaau were ghostwritten, as were Jean-Jacques Dessalines's best-known proclamations. Dessalines famously relied on Louis Boisrond-Tonnerre to craft some of "his" most important prose, though he exercised a firm hand in shaping its tone and message. Similarly, the author "Acaau" may not have coincided with the person Acaau.[58]

This interpretation supposes that Acaau's writings were crafted by someone else, likely someone fluent in the new rhetorical conventions of revolutionary prose, someone who knew how to work the levers of publicity by providing justification. In other words, someone similar to the Liberal revolutionaries themselves, probably one of Acaau's *de couleur* aides or a disgruntled Boyerist seeking to score points against the Liberals. In this case, Acaau could well have been semiliterate and destitute, while someone else was doing the writing.

There is of course a much simpler possibility. That is that Acaau was a man of humble origins, an organic intellectual from the countryside, who rose through the military ranks and went on to become a great writer and leader. The point is that we simply do not know. Acaau and the Army of Sufferers have such an ambiguous place in the archive that we do not know exactly what to make of them. That ambiguity is a result of silence. Their movement was effectively obscured in the records of the time, subject to heavy-handed treatment and often excluded from being able to give an account of itself. As a result, their ideas, intentions, agency, and voice remain uncertain to us now, as they seem to have been to nineteenth-century Haitian elites.

AGRARIAN IMAGINARIES

There is a second, more political puzzle surrounding Acaau. His beautiful prose is put to fairly minimal use. Acaau's proclamations make specific demands, typically focusing immediate political issues. He wants an end to martial law, the resignation of President Hérard, dissolution of the Liberal government, upholding of the constitution, and release from prison of specific compatriots. The rest is primarily a recitation of military events and vague statements about the justice of their cause. These proclamations pack a solid rhetorical punch, but they are ideologically sparse. They make few claims and contain no elaborate justifications. Acaau makes a number of specific statements about the events at hand but says little about the broader motivations animating them. What the subaltern may have been trying to say here is largely left to our interpretation. His statements are narrowly specific and indeterminate in a way that adds up to a kind of silence.

However, there are certain connecting threads underlying this silence. They are *sotto voce* to the point of near inaudibility. In the course of their more specific demands, the Army of Sufferers often mention agrarian reform and the maintenance of small landholdings. For instance, an early list includes the requirement that "measures shall be taken to restore peace and public tranquility in town and countryside, and the general in command of the *arrondisement* will give orders to prevent the decline of agriculture."[59] In a proclamation around the same time, Acaau asks, "What should the rural farmer say, whom the revolution promised a decrease in the price of foreign merchandise and an increase in the value of his goods? Only one response is possible: *He was deceived!*" This comment prefaces a demand to safeguard the constitution, so that "agriculture will be honored and respected."[60] Indeed, constitutionality and agriculture often appear together in these documents. The point, never fully articulated, seems to be that the constitution would protect small landholdings and agricultural labor in ways that Boyer and Hérard had violated.

In all of this we see echoes of the agrarian imaginary of "three free days" during the early slave revolts. In the last chapter I conjectured that "three free days" revealed a suppressed imaginary of freedom that was obscured by the creative modernity of the Haitian Revolution. The relatively inchoate and underspecified character of the Army of Sufferers' position seems similar to those earlier revolutionaries who demanded three days free from plantation work, but never explained why. As I argued in chapter 6, this very silence is quite suggestive. It seemed to stake out an alternative vision of life after slavery, one rooted in independence and agricultural self-sufficiency.

There are reasons to see lines of continuity between the agrarian imaginary of the revolutionary period and the understated position of the Army of Sufferers. Some fifty years later, it displays a similar vision of agrarian independence and a similar hostility to the modernity of the postcolonial economy, state, ruling class, and its political doctrines.

To trace these lines, we must examine the threads of "three free days" after the Revolution. The end of slavery brought the colonial plantation system to the verge of collapse. This occurred almost immediately with the emancipation of Saint-Domingan slaves in 1793 and continued after Haitian independence in 1804. When they were able to choose, newly freed slaves left the plantations in favor of the small-scale subsistence farming that they had already practiced under slavery. Without forced labor, plantations were no longer able to attract workers. The result was a generalized economic crisis.

The first attempts to shore up the plantation system came from the Jacobin civil commissioners who ruled Saint-Domingue during the revolution. Although they had abolished slavery, they nonetheless tried to preserve the plantations as engines of wealth. As a result, the commissioners turned to enforcing work requirements on former slaves.[61] When Toussaint Louverture became governor of Saint-Domingue, also before independence, he continued to issue agricultural labor requirements with similar lack of success.[62] These attempts to compel labor were repugnant to former slaves and were always fraught with problems.[63]

The crisis in plantation agriculture only continued after the revolution. Many former combatants built a life for themselves in the countryside through subsistence farming, generalizing and expanding agricultural practices that were common before the revolution. These practices continued in tension with the new nation's rulers, however. The first Haitian head of state, Jean-Jacques Dessalines, instituted mandatory agricultural work requirements. Dessalines's successor Henri Christophe had the same problems and opted for similar solutions.

In this sense, the early decades of the new Haitian state were marked by continual tensions between the plantation system, favored by the government, and subsistence farming, chosen by rural farmers. The tension was a sharp one, etched between the economic modernism of a cash-crop economy operating on a world market through forced labor, and the localism of small-plot farming and individual self-sufficiency.

These tensions over agriculture and independence were still a problem several decades later under the presidency of Jean-Pierre Boyer. Like the Jacobin commissioners, Louverture, Dessalines, and Henri Christophe before him, Boyer tried to legislate agricultural labor as a way of restoring the plantation system. His Code Rural of 1826 was an attempt to establish agriculture on a military model.⁶⁴ It prohibited farmers from moving to cities or towns without a permit (article 4). It banned the sale of agricultural produce in the countryside, eliminating small-scale profits from extra produce. Cash crops such as sugarcane and cotton, on the other hand, could still be sold to local refineries and mills (art. 7). The Code Rural stipulated that agricultural holdings must be carefully tended, under penalty of fine (art. 37). On the other hand, it did have some protections for laborers. Larger farms were required to provide small subsistence plots for the use of their laborers (art. 38 and 39), and the law stipulated certain kinds of profit-sharing, dividing out portions of the proceeds of sales in terms of the "class" of the laborer (art. 57). In sum, however, the Code Rural was widely hated. The law was seen as draconian and punitive, aiming to reinforce the plantation system and biased against small subsistence farming. Boyer's ruthless enforcement of it only enhanced his reputation as a dictator.⁶⁵

Haiti was not alone in its controversies over agriculture. This became a generalized problematic in the Caribbean during the early nineteenth century. As slavery ended in the British colonies, the collapse of the plantation economy became a problem for them as well. This was the source of Thomas Carlyle's biting, racist attack on Caribbean ex-slaves after the emancipation of the British colonies. His remarks focus on the impossibility of finding workers in the colonies after abolition: "Sitting yonder with their beautiful muzzles up to the ears in pumpkins, imbibing sweet pulps and juices; the grinder and incisor teeth ready for every new work, and the pumpkins cheap as grass in those rich climates; while the sugar-crops rot round them uncut, because labour cannot be hired, so cheap are the pumpkins...."⁶⁶

The particular source of Carlyle's ire was the collapse of the cash-crop economy in favor of subsistence agriculture. Former slaves preferred to grow their own food and could do so relatively easily. They were quite happy to leave the plantation system behind, with its concentrated capital, international commodities markets, and brutal labor. Carlyle's vicious rhetoric is an index of the problematic character of the situation. The former slaves were silently stating a preference for agrarian subsistence over a modernized regime of plantation labor. They now had the freedom to act on their preferences, and the only thing that people like Carlyle could do was complain.

With all this in the background, we can make better sense of Acaau's calls for agrarian reform. Here the demands of the Army of Sufferers appear rather similar to revolutionary demands for "three free days." In both cases, a quiet, barely articulated set of claims seems to surface favoring rural independence and subsistence farming. It reveals a recurrent—or in my view, persistent—set of imaginaries focusing on rural independence through small-plot farming.

Revolutionary demands for "three free days" and the quiet claims of the Army of Sufferers reveal similar views, ideas, and efforts at articulation. They suggest the existence of an agrarian imaginary aiming at a rather different notion of freedom. It was not the freedom of nation- and empire-building during the early 1800s or the freedom of liberal revolution during the 1840s. Rather, it associated small landholding, subsistence agriculture, and small scale produce-marketing with freedom. This vision surfaces twice in the genealogy I have drawn: in the 1780s–1790s in chapter 6, and here in the 1840s. It is subaltern speech in a resurgent mode. During the intervening years, this rural, black, agrarian voice largely disappears from view. Based on the lines of continuity I have just drawn, I conclude that it did not disappear during the intervening years but was silenced. This postulates a durable imaginary that appears and disappears from view. In Adom Getachew's felicitous phrase, echoing Paul Gilroy, we might suppose that it forms one of the "lower frequencies" of Haitian political life.[67]

This insight connects with the fertile line of work tracing a countermodern culture in rural Haiti. Armand Thoby noted tensions over agriculture already in 1888 in *La question agraire en Haiti*. It was Jean Price-Mars, however, writing in 1928, who exercised an enormous influence by bringing Haitian rural culture into view. Jean Casimir extended this analysis in an equally influential way. His influential history of the "counter-plantation" traces the formation of an oppositional culture in sociopolitical terms across several centuries of Haitian history. Gérard Bartélemy amplifies those themes, arguing that rural Haitian culture is an achievement rather than a sign of underdevelopment, one that deliberately opposes the modern liberal economic framework's culture of progress. Johnhenry Gonzalez follows a similar path, thematizing marronage as a more general ethos of distance and escape in rural Haitian culture.[68]

Each of these goes some way to reconstructing a rural political imaginary that opposes the plantation and nineteenth century capitalist modernism. These analyses tend to focus on social forms and modes of production, however: village life and rural agriculture versus imperial capitalism as the marker of modernity. While agreeing with the general tenor of their insights, I am following a somewhat different path. The Army of Sufferers rose up above all as a political movement, and it is important to engage their views from that perspective. I aim to trace the contrasting political imaginaries of the two revolutions and the unique ways in which they expressed and realized those visions. Here I join others who have focused on the political valences of Haitian rural politics. Neil Roberts follows a path similar to that of Gonzalez, but in a more narrowly political sense. He develops the idea of marronage into a more idealized reconstruction of postcolonial politics. Adom Getachew and Nick Nesbitt focus more on the concrete specificities of rural life in Haitian history, particularly in the period immediately after the Revolution.[69] These authors provide important reconstructions of subaltern agency and point in the political direction I seek to follow.

None of these accounts operates at a fine enough level of detail to reveal the silences I have been examining, however. To do this, we need a more subtle engagement with the archives, doing interpretive work that can reveal the commitments, tensions, contradictions, and moments of silence in these views. Otherwise one risks developing an overgeneralized construction that substitutes its own vision for the specificities of individual views and archival fragments. One might accidentally smother the voices of the subaltern in good intentions rather than letting them speak. This need for careful interpretation and theoretical self-restraint is essentially the project that Spivak has called a "critique of postcolonial reason."

Here we contrast the political modernity of the Liberal revolution with the relative silence of the Army of Sufferers. One vision is carefully articulated and strategically publicized. The other is plagued with hesitations, inarticulacies, and silence. These are two contrasting versions of the politics of revolution that offer important insights about the way silence can be inscribed *within* revolutionary action. That silence registers in the archive, and it registers in contemporary commentaries that do not elucidate it.

We can see how these risks play out in the treatment of Acaau. When Acaau is mentioned in this context, he is invariably placed in the fraught history of tensions around agriculture and rural life.[70] This placement seems correct in a general sense, but it has a tendency to sweep him and his movement up into broad historical currents and theoretical agendas. The danger here is one of reduction, placing the Army of Sufferers in a grand narrative of urban/rural, elite/peasant, plantation/counter-plantation, *créole/bossale*, *de couleur/noir* oppositions in which rural culture is the oppositional Other of nineteenth-century capitalist modernity.

Such a narrative has many merits, but it fails to grapple with the fine grain of Acaau's actions and utterances. It glosses over the moments of hesitation, the stops and starts, appearances and disappearances, the faint voices and silences, the episodic character of those voices and the ways they appear and disappear from the archives. We miss the mysterious eloquence and ambiguity of Acaau's speech, as well as the way it is channeled into rhetorical forms that seem foreign and ill-fitting. In short, we risk missing the silences themselves, and the broader politics of silencing within these modern/countermodern tensions. This is a kind of *silencing through interpretation*. It arrives a falsely or prematurely determinate conclusion about the meaning of subaltern practices. The damage can be reckoned as a matter of ignoring inherent ambiguities and foreclosing broader possibilities.

Romuald Lepelletier de Saint-Remy, commenting on Acaau's agenda during his uprising, said he was "demanding the prosperity of agriculture by the voice of his cannon."[71] Lepelletier may be onto something. The cannon and armed uprising in general are what dominate our attention in Acaau's insurgency. The voice of the subaltern in this case may well be that of the cannon—the act of revolt itself. Acaau and the Army of Sufferers were clearly saying something. They clearly captured the attention of the Haitian ruling classes and to a lesser extent of global public spheres. What they were saying was quite underspecified, however. The clearest message was that of the cannon itself: "we hereby dissent, we hereby revolt, we hereby express our dissatisfaction," in deeds if not in words.

This takes us back to the internal tensions within Acaau's proclamations: their high degree of rhetorical polish while containing very few demands. One has the feeling that much is left unsaid. There is a sense in which gestures are made without fully articulating the positions they might represent. Floating behind Acaau's demand that "agriculture will be honored and respected" seems to be some broader vision, but it is never presented as such. Yet the very fact of the Army of Sufferers' speech—not only their words, but their presence and action—is itself somewhat unexpected. This movement rose up out of the countryside and achieved a brief moment of infamy before being defeated. This is, I believe, the expression of a subaltern voice that had been largely suppressed since the Revolution. This voice emerges in an episodic fashion. It appears at particular moments, largely moments of disruption, then dissolves back into the background. It surfaces in certain moments as an ambiguous, quiet voice, then returns to silence.

INNOVATIONS IN SILENCING

By focusing on these moments of silence, we can gain some purchase on the circumstances of their production. As the horizon of modernity shifted in the postcolonial period, so did the *dispositifs* of silencing. The episodic appearance of rural black voices provides us with a number of clues about how they were silenced between such episodes. These play out as possible interpretations of Acaau and his time, each manifesting new developments in forms of silencing that we have seen before. It is not clear which of these might have ultimately been responsible for the Army of Sufferers' silence, but each seems to be represented on that scene in specific ways: ghostwriting, conscription by modernity, false equivalence, and delegitimation.

We have seen that there is a kind of political and ideological silence at the heart of Acaau's proclamations. His extraordinary prose soars when landing revolutionary punches, but he rarely has much to say about the demands of the people he claims to represent. If these documents were indeed ghostwritten, particularly by someone with a more elite political background, their seeming silence could be due to the mismatch between the production of prose and the actual agendas being enunciated. An elite ghostwriter might provide well-polished revolutionary rhetoric but would still need to rely on the Army of Sufferers for concrete complaints and demands. The idea here is that ghostwriters could only go so far: they could state one's opposition to the government very strongly, but not conjure up a full political agenda where one was lacking. The agenda would have been lacking, this interpretation suggests, because Acaau and his confederates may not have been up to that task. Their ultimate program remained ambiguous—effectively silenced—even though their rebellion found a voice in other ways. There is a kind of *self-silencing through opacity* here. It may not have been the strategic opacity I have attributed to maroon slaves or insurgents demanding "three free days," but it is opacity nonetheless. This would be a form of self-silencing simply because Acaau and compatriots left their voices—intentionally or not—suspended in ambiguity. Such an interpretation seems to trace lines of continuity between three free days and Acaau's movement several decades later: rural farmers who simply want to be left alone. It would also explain the seeming mismatch between highly polished revolutionary rhetoric and the seeming lack of demands, claims, and ideological principles.

Acaau makes occasional attempts to frame the army's position in the language of rights. "The population of the countryside, woken from the sleep into which it had fallen, murmurs its misery and resolves to work towards the conquest of its rights."[72] He refers at other times to "imprescriptible rights." Acaau never develops these claims in depth, however, by specifying what those rights might be or whence they arise. Rather, his use of this language seems vague and tentative, raising questions about its purpose in his proclamations.

In this regard, Acaau often seems to be drawing on the language of rights for its auratic power: the way it functions as a privileged category, particularly within Liberal ideology. We might view these statements, then, as a way of justifying a counterrevolution to Liberalism on its own terms. This could be an attempt to convert the ideals and claims of the movement into idioms more familiar to the Liberal revolutionaries as a way of making those claims more forceful or comprehensible. Indeed, Félix Courtois, an ally of the Liberal cause, seemed sympathetic to these rights-based claims. Further, we could even see this as a deft tactic for turning the Liberals' own ideologies back against their movement. It would call them to task for failing in some of their key commitments when it came to the treatment of rural farmers.

In either case, this strategy could constitute a form of self-silencing. Here the very effort to express the positions of the Army of Sufferers in the language of rights, never well-wrought or convincing, would be a sign of being on ideologically foreign ground. A kind of self-effacement could arise from translating its concerns into an idiom legible within the new regimes of publicity and new scripts of revolution. Their true commitments could have been lost in translation, converted into an idiom that distorts their character, foreclosing original thought and silencing what otherwise would be said. This would be an unusual form of *silencing through interpretation*. It is a kind of self-interpretation, a self-translation that fixes meanings in a way that is ultimately foreign and distorting. As such, it might have functioned as a kind of epistemic trap. We might see it as what David Scott has called "conscription by modernity:" being transfixed by Euro-American culture and concepts in a way that preempts more radical, autochthonous positions.[73] In this sense, the Army of Sufferers would have been silenced in the very attempt to legitimate their own cause.

Eventually, *Le Manifeste* equated the Liberal revolution against Boyer with Acaau's revolution against Hérard, saying that there were two risings of the people during this time.[74] In their view, the first, against Boyer, was an uprising of the people fatigued by the insistent requirements imposed on them by the head of state. The second, against Hérard, was an uprising of the people reacting to the treason and cruelty of the new head of state. Both of these were victories of the people. This judgment seems sympathetic towards the Army of Sufferers, giving their cause the same dignity and status as the Liberal Revolution itself.

Drawing such an equivalence is also a form of silencing, however. It elides the substantial differences between the two revolutions. By calling both "uprisings of the people," it ignores the sense in which the first "people" was an elite and privileged group, while the second "people" was a largely destitute, racially stigmatized group who was rebelling against the first. These were not two equivalent uprisings of "the" people. Arguably the first uprising, the Liberal Revolution, was not popular in any sense. It did not come from the people, but rather from an elite fraction of the governing class. Similarly, the second revolution was also not a movement of the "entire" people, but rather the most destitute and marginalized of society. The equivalence, then, is a false if flattering one that adds up to a form of silence. It is a different way of silencing through interpretation, this time one imposed from without rather than initiated from within.

Perhaps the most formidable strategy of silencing came in the form of verbal image-making, however. It came, for instance, in Madiou's description of Acaau as wearing a straw hat full of holes, a vest with a torn collar, pistols attached to a belt, and sandals—a shabby revolutionary who was more comic than threatening. The same can be said of the *New York Journal of Commerce*, which characterized Acaau as "the monster," "of detestable memory; composed of the lowest and most despicable of the Black race." Such images served to reduce Acaau and his movement to absurdity, or at least cast a pall of ridicule over them.

Even more biting is the characterization of Maxime Raybaud, a former French consul to Haiti. Raybaud is fairly laudatory about the Liberal Revolution. He describes the *Manifeste de Praslin* as "remarkably written," for instance.[75] His attitude toward Acaau, however, is decidedly more venomous. He lists the various "black generals" who rose up quickly in opposition to the Liberal Revolution: Salomon, Dalzon, Pierrot, and Guerrier. But, says Raybaud, they were merely black (*noir*). Following them came a *nègre*, a "honey-tongued, humanitarian *nègre*" (*nègre humanitaire et beau diseur*): "He was called Acaau, 'General in Chief of the Demands of his Fellow Citizens.' He wore gigantic spurs on his naked heels and, followed by a troop of bandits armed for the most part with pointed stakes instead of guns, swept through the villages depopulated by the terror of his approach, in the interests of 'unfortunate innocence' and 'the *eventuality* of national education.'"[76] Raybaud's description of Acaau is hyperbolic in a very pointed way. It reduces Acaau to a kind of caricature, just as Madiou had. The absurdity of naked heels with gigantic spurs describes someone who is both destitute and pretentious. Acaau terrifies the villagers, yet he is a honey-tongued orator and humanitarian. This sarcastic description already has a sharp edge, but it is then racialized to cut even deeper. Acaau is not just black, he is a *nègre*. It is not clear exactly what Raybaud means by this, only that it intensifies the insult by racializing it. All of this creates a powerful undertow of delegitimation for Acaau. He was not a capable or creative revolutionary leader, but a honey-tongued absurdity.

In contrast to Raybaud's biting commentary, Acaau's treatment by Félix Courtois, editor of the *Feuille du commerce*, seems downright subtle. Yet it had much the same delegitimating effect. Silence had been directly enacted when Courtois refused to print Acaau's words. Even their belated publication was silencing, however. Silence was constituted by Courtois's account of his actions: the powerfully delegitimating force of his assertion that the documents he had received were not worth the readers' attention. Even when Courtois gave the Army of Sufferers a voice, his remarks undercut it as something not worthy of serious consideration. This deft delegitimation constituted a powerful form of silencing, even though Acaau's words were now in print.

These forms of *silencing through delegitimation* continue a developmental trajectory that we first saw at the beginning of the nineteenth century. They strip subaltern speech of its value rather than literally silencing it. Delegitimation operates through more minimal and efficient means than other forms of silence. Here silence need not be achieved in any literal sense. Instead, the subaltern can still speak, but that speech is effectively muted by being rendered worthless, meaningless, absurd, ridiculous, or comical. Acaau, the wild-eyed revolutionary with naked heels and a straw hat, can say whatever he wants, but we may not have any reason to listen or care.

In retrospect, we can see similarities between delegitimation and earlier forms of silencing. From the 1680s onward we observed the formation of racial categories that silenced through resignification. They subtly repositioned the meaning and associations of various people within society, reducing their value and constructing them as natural subjects of violent and exploitative treatment. This resignification was, in many way, an embryonic form of delegitimation.

However, it did not yet function independently as such. These nascent forms of delegitimation served to buttress and justify more absolute prohibitions on speech, those enacted through law, violence, and terror. They did not operate in an autonomous fashion to create silences of their own. By the mid-nineteenth century, however, we find silencing through delegitimation in a mature, autonomous, fully functioning form. Now the subaltern is fully allowed to speak and act, while nonetheless having their words and actions stripped of value.

This form of silencing appears in very particular circumstances: ones in which the subaltern had actually succeeding in speaking and could not easily be silenced. It is no accident that it arises in postcolonial conditions. Subaltern speech could no longer easily be silenced, now that liberal principles prevented overt threats of violence against individuals, and colonies were independent. We have seen this new strategy in a relatively halting, piecemeal form in the attacks on the new Haitian Republic in 1804-1805. It was used to undercut the legitimacy of the newly independent nation and its people. Several decades later, that strategy has achieved a more fully mature form. Ironically, it was used within the Haitian Republic itself to delegitimate the speech and action of internally subordinated people and render them of lesser value.

With these developments, we arrive on new terrain. The nineteenth-century conjunction of liberal democracy and postcoloniality forced innovations in subaltern silence. Those innovations made full use of the modern media of the 1840s to push back against the independence and voice of formerly colonized, formerly enslaved people.

PUBLICITY, LEGITIMATION, AND SILENCE

We can see new layers and forms of silence folded within the Liberal reform project, marking innovations in the development of subaltern silence. The very modernity and progressiveness of this agenda constitutes silences, creates epistemic opacities, and subordinates peoples and points of view.

We can see how this occurs mostly clearly by comparing the Liberal Revolution with the original Haitian Revolution. Both the Haitian Revolution (1791-1804) and its Liberal successor (1843) picked up the thread of an emerging script of revolution, one in which conflicts were fought out partly in the public sphere. A signature feature of this script is a keen concern for self-legitimation, publicizing one's principles to solicit the support of "a candid world." Both political movements were fighting an uphill battle against subordination. Haiti was pervasively delegitimated on the world stage following the revolution. Thus each generation of revolutionaries faced the challenge of gaining acceptance and international support. As we have seen, this happened with only partial success during the original Haitian Revolution. Haiti remained an international pariah and a target of fears about "contagion" for many decades. Things were easier for the Liberal revolutionaries of the 1840s. They were greeted enthusiastically by the international press as democratic constitutionalists. Diplomatic correspondence from the American and British consuls reveals a similar enthusiasm.

This relative success was no doubt due to changing circumstances during the intervening decades, particularly the sense in which the Liberals were viewed as a political corrective to the excesses of Boyer. However, the Liberal adoption of American and French revolutionary idioms was likely a particular advantage in making this case on the world stage.

We have seen that both the original Haitian Revolution and its Liberal successor were quite novel, yet they also adopted many conventions from the Euro-American revolutions that preceded them. These familiar revolutionary languages and scripts created legibility. They made the ideological preoccupations of postcolonial movements more easily acceptable. To some extent this might have been shrewd politics, given the importance of international acceptance to the fledgling Haitian state. The candid world could best accept Haitian independence in terms that were already familiar. In addition, however, the Liberal revolutionaries seemed genuinely committed to the ideals they had chosen. A modern, free, commercially successful Haiti could be built by following ideological lines pioneered in America and France.

In spite of and because of these liberal-democratic commitments, however, each revolutionary movement subordinated other currents of revolutionary thought. Each created what Elisabeth Anker might refer to as an "ugly freedom:" one premised on the unfreedom of others.[77] The Haitian Revolution drove the agrarian vision of "three free days" into silence. We see much the same dynamic at work during the Liberal Revolution. The Army of Sufferers erupted in anger to oppose this self-anointed reform movement, revealing long-simmering problems that had been relegated to silence. The Army largely succeeded in derailing that other revolution, but never did make itself understood. It played the game of publicity only in a halting and ineffective way.

This insurgency does reveal a certain attempt at voice when we view it from the distance of a century and a half, however. It suggests lines of continuity over several decades of postcolonial history. The tantalizing perspective we are presented with is a dappled pattern of silence and voice: subaltern silence perpetuated first by the Haitian Revolution itself, then by a series of postcolonial leaders, then by a rectifying Liberal Revolution that aimed at regeneration, with occasional moments of subaltern speech in between. In this case, we must conclude that even well-intentioned, principled, carefully justified movements of national liberation and democratization can have a dark side. During Haiti's early years they perpetuated forms of subaltern silence that were either the same or remarkably similar to one another. Even with the noblest and best of intentions, new and unexpected forms of subordination can be folded within the project of freedom.

CHAPTER 8

The Force of Farce

Emperor Soulouque and the Art of Racial Caricature

1824–1861

If colonialism takes power in the name of history, it repeatedly exercises its authority through the figures of farce.

—Homi Bhabha

The quip that all great, world-historical events occur twice—first as tragedy, then as farce—was originally a comment on the politics of nineteenth-century France.¹ It seems well echoed in nineteenth-century Haiti, however. The first Haitian empire of Jean-Jacques Dessalines ended in tragedy, only to be recapitulated as farce by Faustin Soulouque in 1849. In many ways the parallel is not merely rhetorical. Dessalines's Haitian empire was formed in deliberate defiance to that of Napoléon I. The second Haitian empire, that of Soulouque, preceded just a bit the coronation of Napoléon's nephew as the farcical emperor of France in 1852. There is, then, a kind of historical doubling: tragedy and farce in France was simultaneous with the same dynamic in postcolonial Haiti.

Farce was not as amusing as one might suppose in Haiti's case, however. It functioned in deadly earnest as a form of subordination that was highly individualized while simultaneously operating at a national and international level. New print technologies were brought together with new genres of pictorial representation to create new forms of silence. Here subaltern silence appears in a fully contemporary form. Subaltern subjects can now be silenced in full view as objects of public representation. The subaltern can speak and be rendered silent at the same time. Caricature and race come together in a particularly potent form of this new *dispositif* of subordination. It operates in abstract, distant, and categorial ways, silencing whole groups of people at once. As a result, it has an unprecedented power and reach.

AGRARIAN INSURGENCY AND THE POLITICS OF CONTAINMENT

As we have seen, 1843 and 1844 were turbulent years in Haitian history. Members of the dominant classes succeeded in overthrowing long-serving President Jean-Pierre Boyer. They represented themselves as a progressive, internationalist, pro-trade, reform-minded corrective. The new government they established was universally applauded in the European and North American press. This liberal, *de couleur* revolution was not universally applauded at home, however. Louis-Jean-Jacques Acaau and the Army of Sufferers rose up shortly afterward and forced the new government out of office, throwing the nation once again into chaos.

Liberal elites tried to appease the army's revolutionary energies and regain some measure of control by putting a series of dark-skinned presidents in office. The presidency changed hands three times in less than three years. In each case, a black president was installed as a puppet of *de couleur* elites, a practice that came to be known as *la politique de doublure*—the politics of understudies. The "understudy" in each case appeared to represent black rural interests while secretly continuing elite dominance. This sham of popular politics employed political optics, appearances, and false representations in new ways. It promised racial representation while stripping subaltern racial and economic groups of political impact. It seemed to respond to black rural concerns while deflecting, dissipating, capturing, and silencing them.

As such, the *politique de doublure* was yet another permutation of subaltern silence. In Spivak's language, it played on representation in both of its English senses: that of a political delegate (expressed by her in German as *vertreten*) and that of a symbol or image (*darstellen*).[2] Here political symbols were misleadingly deployed in a sham of political delegation. The *Darstellung* of a black presidency was substituted for the *Vertretung* of an actual representative of the rural black population. This substitution constituted a new form of subaltern silence. The representation (*Vertretung*) of a political delegate would have given rural black farmers some mediated voice. By turning that representation into a sham (*Darstellung*), voice also became an illusion. The result was the *illusion* of voice substituting for actual voice and a resubordination of the rural population. This amounted to an inversion of *silencing through substitution*. When we have seen it before, subalterns were silenced by attributing their agency to someone else, typically Europeans. Here agency is attributed to the subaltern while it is actually being foiled. This legerdemain creates silence by substituting an appearance of agency for real agency.

After moving rapidly through a series of presidents, the *politique de doublure* finally reached a stable form in 1847. Faustin Soulouque, a black, formerly enslaved military officer, was named the fourth in the series of understudy presidents. He was chosen because he had the right profile to appeal to discontented rural farmers, yet he seemed controllable. His presidency began favorably enough in that regard. He issued proclamations against the insurgent activities of the Army of Sufferers and tried to win them over as participants in government. At the same time, he seemed to shield *de couleur* elites from the former insurgents. For instance, he protected Félix Courtois, the same newspaper editor who had suppressed Acaau's proclamations, from a death sentence for incitement. All of this was much to the relief of the elite classes.

Soulouque was not content to remain an understudy, however. He proved adept at outmaneuvering the people who had put him in office, seizing power that was supposed to remain in the hands of others. He dismissed a number of his puppet masters from their positions in the Senate and took control of the Haitian state. This was accompanied by purges and executions of prominent *de couleur* citizens. By 1849, he had successfully campaigned to have the Haitian Senate name him emperor, styling himself Emperor Faustin I. He established an imperial court filled with titled nobles, most of whom were drawn from the black revolutionary circles of the movements against the Liberals. These events were a final repudiation of the sham politics into which Soulouque had been recruited. He thereby gained a strong position to fulfill the goals of the Army of Sufferers and restore some voice to rural peasants.

CARICATURE

Unfortunately, those interested in silencing this subaltern had the last laugh. For reasons that are unclear, Faustin I—most often referred to as "Emperor Soulouque" in the foreign press—became an object of international ridicule. He had the misfortune of taking the throne during an era in which a rich tradition of caricature was developing in France. Caricature advanced significantly as a print genre during the nineteenth century. It was made possible through a confluence of rapidly advancing lithographic technologies and a culture that enjoyed sharp-edged criticism as a form of entertainment. Publications such as *Le Caricaturiste*, *La Silhouette*, *L'Illustration*, and, most important, *Le Charivari* pioneered a new style of political critique through images. In its most optimistic moment, this was seen as a tool of democratization, a symbolic means for tearing down the powerful or at least deflating their pretensions. An eighteenth-century historian of caricature put these developments on a par with the newspaper as a technology of popular expression: "Caricature, along with the newspaper, is the voice of the citizens."[3] As we will see, however, this visual populism also had a dark side. Pierre Bourdieu has commented on this insightfully. Citing *Le Charivari* as an example, he says that the most potent weapon of conservative denunciation in this era was "the laughter of the people."[4] Being shown to be ridiculous was a formidable tool of conservative populism.

By far the most prolific and well-known caricaturist of the time was Cham, the pen name of Amédée-Charles-Henri de Noé. He was the eighth child of Count Louis-Pantaléon-Judes-Amédée de Noé, a highly respected French nobleman. The name Cham plays on this heritage. In the French translation of the Bible, Cham is Ham, the cursed younger son of Noah. Noé, Amédée's family name, means Noah in French. Amédée de Noé the caricaturist thus positions himself as the cursed younger son of the count, an elaborate conceit fitting his puckish personality.

The Noé family itself had a storied past. It was a famed noble lineage with a large estate in southern France and plantations in Saint-Domingue. Toussaint Louverture was enslaved by Cham's relatives until he was freed in 1776, and he continued to work on one their plantations up to the Revolution.[5] Indeed, the broadsheet listing burned plantations that I discussed in chapter 4 includes a number of Cham's family properties: the Noé plantation in Accul and two Bréda properties in the Plaine du Nord (figure 4.6).

Cham was a wide-ranging satirist with finely tuned sensitivities to the issues of the day. He gleefully taunted politicians across the political spectrum, including members of the Second Republic government and their socialist opposition. His attention was by no means limited to politics, however. He often drew caricatures pointing out the foibles of daily life and sometimes relished a silly subject just for the laugh it might produce.

Cham's drawings of Emperor Soulouque are a mixture of these impulses. He seems to have been first to single out Soulouque for satire, publishing the opening salvo of caricatures in *Le Charivari* on October 14, 1849. It was a panel of six drawings, largely making fun of Soulouque's imperial ambitions and the poverty of the Haitian state. One of these, entitled "Soulouque reviewing his guard," shows the Emperor with a gaudily dressed general making his way along a line of soldiers (figure 8.1). They stand ramrod straight at attention, but they wear loincloths. With a thoughtful look on his face, Soulouque says to the general, "This

Figure 8.1 Cham, *Soulouque passant la revue de sa garde*, Le Charivari, October 14, 1849, 3. Bibliothèque Nationale de France, Paris.

isn't bad for full dress, but for informal wear I'd need to find something simpler." Soulouque is a buffoon who sets his sights low, commanding a ragtag army with no resources.

Cham's venture into Haitian politics was quickly imitated. Within a week of his first six drawings, competitors began rolling out Soulouque caricatures of their own. *La Silhouette*, for instance, quickly amplified the apelike qualities of Cham's Soulouque, turning him into a monkey with a crown, epaulettes, and a frock coat (figure 8.2). This image is captioned "His Majesty Napoléon Soulouque, Emperor of Haiti, King of the Monkeys, Protector of the Confederation of Macaques, etc., etc."

S. M. Napoléon Soulouque, Empereur d'Haïti, Roi des Singes, Protecteur de la Confédération des Macaques, etc., etc.

Figure 8.2 Fabritzius, *S. M. Napoléon Soulouque, empereur d'Haiti, roi des singes...*, *La Silhouette*, October 21, 1849, 1. Bibliothèque Nationale de France, Paris.

A drawing in *Le Caricaturiste* went in a different direction, crowning Soulouque with a laurel wreath and decking him in ermine robes. It was captioned "Fauxteint 1er, empereur d'Haïti, et son auguste famille" (Falsetint I, emperor of Haiti, and his distinguished family).[6] "Fauxteint" plays on the name Faustin while also working in a reference to skin color. Cham's colleague Charles Vernier took yet another direction. He delivered a grandly absurd Soulouque, dressed in full Napoleonic uniform with a star pinned on his chest, dictating a letter to the "Duke of Marmalade" (figure 8.3). (Soulouque really did create a Duke of Marmalade as well as a Duke of Lemonade, but no humor was intended. Marmelade and Limonade were long-established districts of Haiti, and the titles were toponymic.)

This wave of attention quickly established Emperor Soulouque as a butt of jokes in the satirical press. Cham continued to use him as a stock character in *Le Charivari*. I discussed one of those images, *Soulouque après sa mort*, at the beginning of this book (figure 1.1.). It shows a very lively but supposedly embalmed Soulouque peering curiously out of a giant bell jar at a spectator who is trying to examine him. Another of Cham's caricatures shows Soulouque having his portrait painted. He appears somewhat stupefied and perplexed, drawn with the same racial grotesquery that animates Cham's other renderings of him (figure 8.4). His outfit is again a Napoleonic officer's uniform. Examining his boots while an exasperated artist applies paint to them, the caption explains that "Soulouque, having his portrait done, takes advantage of the *flesh tones* used by the artist to put a coat on his boots." Here Cham adds verbal sting to racial imagery, equating Soulouque's skin color with shoe polish. Overtones of stupidity, both visual and implied by the caption, supplement the raciality of the image.

On the rare occasions when he drew Soulouque in a more finely wrought way, Cham accentuated his raciality even more fully. A full page lithograph in 1850, for instance, shows Soulouque trying to raise funds for a New Year's gift for his empress "Ourika" by filing a defamation suit against *Le Charivari* (figure 8.5). This is likely just a joke—the artists at *Le Charivari* loved to portray themselves as hapless jokers constantly under attack by outraged victims. Attempts at humor aside, however, the racialization and bestialization of Soulouque go even further here, accentuating traits found in Cham's smaller plates and rendering them more precisely and deliberately.

The "Empress Ourika" in this drawing became a minor character in other of Cham's Soulouque images as well. In figure 8.6, for instance, we see her in the

Figure 8.3 Charles Vernier, *Une carotte impériale*, *Le Charivari*, November 12, 1849, 3. Bibliothèque Nationale de France, Paris.

Souloque, faisant faire son portrait, profite des *tons de chair* employés par l'artiste pour faire donner une couche à ses bottes.

Figure 8.4 Cham, *Soulouque, faisant faire son portrait...*, Le Charivari, January 10, 1850, 3. Bibliothèque Nationale de France, Paris.

gowns of a nineteenth-century empress, flying into a rage with an impressive, muscular physique somewhat at odds with her elegant, feminine attire. "Empress Ourika," we are told, is "furious at her piano teacher, who dared to claim that a white woman [*blanche*] was worth two black women [*noires*]." Empress Ourika is a rageful and aggressive counterpart to the hapless and confused Soulouque. In this particular case, the empress's rage is humorously misdirected. The caption is an elaborate pun: *blanche* and *noire* are also the names of musical notes, and the piano teacher is merely saying that one is twice as long as the other. The message

Figure 8.5 Cham, *L'empereur Soulouque désirant se procurer des fonds...*, Le Charivari, January 1, 1850, 3. Bibliothèque Nationale de France, Paris.

is clear: Empress Ourika is quick to anger, especially at a perceived racial slight, and does not pause long enough to consider alternative explanations.

RACIAL IMAGINARIES

Ernst Kris and Ernst Gombrich write that caricature uses distortion to "produce a likeness more true than mere imitation could be."[7] The Soulouque caricatures show why this is a dangerous generalization. In certain circumstances, it could indeed be the case that caricature uses distortion to say something true. However, putting too much faith in that idea obscures its truth-*constituting* functions as a form of representation. Really, caricature uses distortion to reposition ideas, fabricate truths, and reproduce already existing beliefs. It can reinforce existing

Figure 8.6 Cham, *L'impératrice Ourika furieuse contre son professor de piano...*, Le Charivari, January 10, 1850, 3. Bibliothèque Nationale de France, Paris.

biases and preconceptions or launch new ones. Caricature can be said to reveal something truer than mere imitation chiefly when we are already prepared to agree with the ideas being represented. Its truths *seem* true, either because we are accustomed to them or because we are prepared to believe them.

In these cases, caricature says something true not about its subject, but about the person constructing the caricature and the context of its reception. It says something true not about the subject but about us. That something is likely to be a finely tuned indication of what it is we already believe and in which new directions we are prepared to extend those beliefs. Caricatures rely on rich background knowledge for interpretation. Without that, it is impossible to get the joke. As such, they are carefully calibrated in their effect and reveal the extent to which both artist and audience have expert knowledge of a shared set of practices.

We can see these dynamics in action with Cham. He was a careful student of the culture of his day, but also an innovator who developed new conventions of visual representation with powerfully racializing effects. Cham pushed the raciality of Soulouque in directions that others had not. Consider, for instance, some of the relatively crude work of his competitors. The etching in *La Silhouette* that we have already examined portrays Soulouque *as* a monkey (figure 8.2). It is a drawing of a monkey labeled "Soulouque," a relatively straightforward form of name-calling. Verneir's Soulouque, in contrast, is completely human (figure 8.3). His posture and manner are distorted for comic effect as one would expect in caricature, but that distortion remains within the bounds typical of the genre. What distinguishes Cham is his fusion of the human, the animal, and the absurd with preexisting racial genre conventions. He rolls all of this into a Soulouque who is racialized, bestialized, rendered absurd, yet presented with a substantial amount of pathos. This combination was biting, stigmatizing, and delegitimating but was also infused with enough warmth and humor to appeal to a white, metropolitan French audience. Because Cham's drawings were "all in good fun," they seemed to avoid provoking any guilty conscience. As a result, Cham's Soulouque circulated widely and became one of the most predominant and durable public images of the Haitian emperor. It appeared frequently in the pages of *Le Charivari* and was instantly recognizable to anyone glancing casually at the newspaper.

With an eye toward genealogy, it is worth teasing out some of the strands of racist culture that Cham so effectively combined and developed. We have already seen that Cham had a rather unusual family background. It provided him with a number of influences that would contribute to his innovations as a racial caricaturist. Cham's father was sent to England as a boy during the French Revolution. He lived there for many years and married the daughter of an English noble family. They moved to India, where the count served in the British colonial military. Cham was born in Paris shortly after their return to France. He was raised by a British nanny who never learned to speak French, so Cham was effectively a native speaker of both French and English. (He supposedly affected an English accent when speaking French.) As a result of family and fluency, he had full access to the British culture of his day, including the British tradition of caricature that

250   *Postcolonial Transformations*

extended back into the eighteenth century. Cham actually went on to be quite influential as an innovator in this tradition, collaborating with the principal British caricature journals *Punch* and *The Illustrated London News*.

Given these connections, it is not surprising that Cham's work shared some features with the already developing, transatlantic visual language of racial caricature. His joke about "flesh tones," for instance, is remarkably similar to one that appeared in the American Edward W. Clay's series "Life in Philadelphia" in 1828–1830 (figure 8.7). In that image, a gaudily over-dressed black woman asks a white clerk for "<u>flesh</u> coloured silk stockings." "Flesh" is underlined to indicate

Figure 8.7 Edward W. Clay, *Have You Any Flesh Coloured Silk Stockings . . . ?* from *Life in Philadelphia* (Philadelphia: W. Simpson, 1829). Library Company of Philadelphia.

the absurdity of her request, the implicit premise being that "flesh tone" should be something like a light peach color. "Silk stockings" indicates another aspect of absurdity, a high-priced luxury good for the rich, which fits the woman's costume and manner but clashes with stereotypes of her race. The resourceful clerk is part of the joke, responding with deference and a French accent that indicates the quality of the establishment. He presents a pair of grey stockings, which completes the joke by responding to the incongruous request for "<u>flesh</u> tone." The humor, such as it is, turns around the impossibility that a black woman would have "flesh colored" flesh, that she would be wealthy, well-dressed, and have the bearing of a patrician white dame. Cham's later attempt to invoke "flesh tone" works in a similar manner. It plays on racial hierarchies in a way that was humorously counterintuitive—or perhaps implicitly unstable and therefore problematic—for its audience. That the humor carries a racialized sting was undoubtedly part of the attraction, a feature that we will consider in a moment.

The silk stockings plate is the only one of Clay's that thematizes "flesh" explicitly, though most of them follow similar lines in satirizing the supposed upper-class pretensions of middle-class Blacks in Philadelphia. The racial animus displayed in Clay's drawings has a very particular place in the white supremacy and racial anxiety of Jacksonian-era United States. Their specific themes of Black class pretension are eerily similar to ones explored in Michael Warner's study of the "African Theatre."[8] Actually called the American Theatre, this was a Black drama company in 1820s New York that specialized in Shakespeare and other serious theatrical productions. It drew attacks from the white press alternating between satire and vitriol, often focusing on the upwardly mobile pretentions of Black citizens. While mocking the troupe itself, the *National Advocate*, New York City's primary paper, spoke of "black dandies and dandizettes," "balls and quadrille parties," and "a tea garden and evening serenades for the amusement of our black gentry."[9] It reported, "They run the rounds of fashion; ape their masters and mistresses in every thing; talk of projected matches; reherse the news of the kitchen, and the follies of the day; and bating the 'tincture of their skins,' are as well qualified to move in the *haut ton*, as many of the white dandies and butterflies, who flutter in the sun shine."[10]

In other words, the "African Theatre" was seen as part of a more alarming trend of Black self-confidence and affluence. Warner interprets a principal source of these attacks as alarm at the growing free Black population of New York, along with the impending 1827 abolition of slavery in the state. From this perspective, satire was a thinly veiled attack on Black upward mobility. Against

252 *Postcolonial Transformations*

this background, Clay's drawings in nearby Philadelphia appear as a similarly phantasmatic projection of white fears and anxieties.

These themes had a very specific location in American racial politics, but they also found an audience in Europe. Several years after its American publication, Gabriel Shire Tregear began reprinting "Life in Philadelphia" in London. Tregear seems to have understood the potential appeal of such racial caricature in Great Britain. Britain was on the verge of abolishing slavery in its colonies. Tregear capitalized on this highly charged environment with an engraving series of his own, "Tregear's Black Jokes." Like "Life in Philadelphia," "Tregear's Black Jokes" took aim at what it portrayed as the pretentious habits of Britain's Black citizens. Tregear's graphic style and execution are clearly much superior to Clay's, however. He uses that sense of visual style to intensify the parody of his subjects. One plate, for instance, puts forward what is intended to be an incongruous scene of a grand ball attended only by Black bourgeoisie (figure 8.8).[11] The characters are drawn with a stylized absurdity. They have exaggerated features with

Figure 8.8 Gabriel Shire Tregear, *The Route*, from *Tregear's Black Jokes* (London, 1834). Michael Graham-Stewart Slavery Collection, © National Maritime Museum, Greenwich, London.

bulbous noses and strange, piled-up hairdos. The women have rather masculine faces, and no one is portrayed in a flattering manner. Yet there is richness and finery in abundance: the assembled company is dressed in the most elegant silk fashions; many are holding crystal glasses. The central couple leer at one another in a knowing, suggestive way as they take to the dance floor.

A signature characteristic of these drawings is a kind of satire by substitution. The "joke" in Tregear's Black Jokes is the presumed incongruity of Black characters adopting the habits and manners of the white upper classes. Clearly that presumption is not enough, however, because Tregear goes to extra lengths to make the characters seem absurd. He seems to imply that such a situation would be completely unthinkable, a sort of surreal nightmare. Thus the leers and other odd expressions, strange hairdos, mannish women, and overwrought scenarios that give Tregear's subjects a pungent unlikability. All of this does not really seem to achieve the effect at which he is aiming, however. It is as if Tregear wants to reduce his subjects to absurdity, but lacks the visual means, the graphic vocabulary, to do so.

Backgrounded by these cultural currents, we see Cham importing English precedents into a French context but modifying them as well. Unlike, say, the aggressively grotesque images produced by Tregear, Cham's have a certain warmth. Soulouque is portrayed as a loveable simpleton, puzzling his way through a situation too complex for his limited understanding. Cham renders this pathos by giving Soulouque a wider range of expression: not the aggressive leering of Tregear's Blacks, but curiosity, confusion, befuddlement, pride, and irritation. As a result, Cham's treatment of Soulouque has a sentimental aspect that is wholly lacking in the British and American caricaturists.

Somewhat paradoxically, Cham also uses apelike features in his figurations of Soulouque. Soulouque's very human expressions are mapped onto these features in a way that combines humanity and animality. This practice was not unusual for Cham. He regularly drew the prominent (white) politician Adolphe Thiers as a fusion of human and owl, and the celebrated (white) socialist Pierre-Joseph Proudhon as having a chimpanzee-like face. The advantage of these human/animal fusions for Cham was to telegraph characteristics normally associated with animals onto the human subject. This required a talented graphic hand, one that could make the specific person recognizable while also blending their appearance with that of the animal avatar. In the case of Thiers, for instance, his likeness is recognizable even as his round face and sharp, pointed nose are turned into the face and beak of an owl. When this effect is well achieved, it creates an instant visual commentary on the subject. Thiers appears small, alert, and somewhat stunned to be awake in the sunlight.

Cham had a gift for rendering human expressions within this human/animal mix. He infused his creations with recognizable emotions, often ones that were both comic and endearing. Thus we can read the expressions of the apelike Soulouque even though his features seem distinctly nonhuman. In his better moments, Cham even overlays multiple emotions in a complicated blend. In Soulouque's case, this is often a combination of confusion and vanity. Soulouque is overly proud of himself, his position, and his dress, yet is also completely perplexed by whatever situation he is in. If such figures were meant to *be* animals we would refer to this as anthropomorphization. Since they are meant to be human, it is instead a form of racially coded bestialization. We are not presented with the features of the real Soulouque, but a more generic, apelike person inhabiting a specific racial imaginary.

The combination of sentimentality, animality, expressivity, and racialization is seen in another of Cham's works, a "portrait" of a family servant. Cham grew up with Tombey, a black servant who had been brought from India. In this undated drawing, Tombey is elegantly dressed in a frock coat and starched collar, yet the clothing has a hard time fitting his oddly shaped frame. His appearance is both comical and grotesquely nonhuman. He has a gigantic protruding mouth and reed-thin arms and legs; his proportions look more frog than human. His eyebrows are arched and hands gesturing frustration in seeming objection to something that is occurring outside the picture frame (figure 8.9).

Cham's nineteenth-century biographer Félix Ribeyre recounts various stories about Tombey, including both his gullibility and his vanity. They seem to be based on recollections of Cham himself; as such, we should take them as no more than verbal caricatures that accompany his drawn delineations. Of course, Cham may have had very real affection for Tombey, but one must always be wary of white affection for servants and enslaved people as well as other forms of nostalgia for colonialism, however genuinely they may have been felt. Whether or not Tombey was gullible and vain is not really the point, nor is Cham's attitude toward him. Rather, the real Tombey is fully transformed into a kind of mythology of Cham's childhood and thus plastic material to be drawn as he sees fit. As Ribeyre notes, "One can see that Cham had, under his very eyes, a perfect model to exercise his youthful energies, and as soon as he could hold a pencil he amused

Figure 8.9 Cham, *Portrait du nègre Tombey*, in Félix Ribeyre, *Cham: Sa vie et son oeuvre* (Paris: Plon, 1884), plate between pp. 20 and 21.

himself by sketching Tombey's portrait."[12] Youthful energies, in this case, seem to have focused on transforming Tombey into a particular kind of racialized concoction. His wildly distorted appearance does not match any reality, nor could it, because it exceeds the bounds of actual human anatomy. It is, rather, a product of Cham's fertile imagination. In this case as in Soulouque's, that is a set of visual conventions that represent race through signature bodily features, distorted beyond any reasonable basis in fact. We might suppose that Tombey provided an early opportunity to develop this vocabulary. Extended more widely in later years, these conventions become a stylized language that represents race and associates various other characteristics with it.

Cham's racial vocabulary was very much his own, but the idea that facial features are a mirror of the soul would have been quite familiar to a nineteenth-century audience. So too would be the idea of comparing human facial features with those of animals, a comparison aimed at revealing similar dispositions. Those ideas were cornerstones of physiognomy. Like phrenology, mesmerism, and eugenics, physiognomy is one of the great discredited sciences of the nineteenth century. It was organized around the idea that a person's external appearance registered the traces of their internal, psychic tendencies. A person's most often repeated inner experiences were supposed to literally shape their outer appearance. Thus people could be quickly understood and sorted into types by their expressions. This insight founded an intensive study of different kinds of expressions and what they revealed about those inner typologies.

Physiognomy had its roots in the seventeenth century, but its popularity increased markedly at the beginning of the nineteenth. Johann Casper Lavater first published his *Physiognomische Fragmente* in the 1770s. The book was a runaway success and was quickly translated into French and English. By 1845 the French translation alone had gone through some fifteen editions. After some tinkering with the title, it now appeared as *La physiognomonie, ou l'Art de connaître les hommes: D'après les traits de leur physionomie, leurs rapports avec les divers animaux, leurs penchants, etc.* (Physiognomy, or the Art of Knowing People from the Traits of their Physiognomy, their Relations with Various Animals, their Tendencies, etc.).[13] Indeed, there are extensive discussions of the visual similarities between animals and people, as well as exhaustive catalogs of the different types of people as revealed by their characteristic expressions.

These ideas were circulating widely in France and England when Cham began drawing Soulouque, and they would have been familiar to many members of his audience. *Le Charivari*, for instance, had a recurring feature called "La physionomie de l'Assemblée," which caricatured facial and bodily features of prominent politicians in the National Assembly to poke fun at their characteristic foibles. In this sense, physiognomy provided caricature with a powerful new set of tools and genre conventions. Rather than being driven solely by absurd situations or captions, the very image of a person could now comment on his or her personality. Cham capitalized on these insights very effectively. His characters had a much expanded expressive range compared with his British predecessors. This in turn allowed him to portray an expanded palette of absurdities in their behavior and personality.

Cham's innovations had additional consequences, however. Physiognomy often distinguished specific types of people by their emotional tendencies ("the choleric type," "the disdainful type") or occupation (the bourgeois, the public scrivener). Cham, however, deployed these insights in *racial* caricature, distinguishing racial types by their allegedly distinctive inner lives. This quickly came to include pride, vanity, and confusion in Cham's drawings. Such ideas were increasingly commonplace in the racist cultures of Europe at this time, but they had not found such effective means of expression. Cham's unique combination of physiognomy, animality, raciality, sentimentality, and expressivity gave such ideas a new force and popularity.

Minstrelsy is another strand of racist popular culture that was starting to appear in Britain at this time. American minstrel shows began traveling across the Atlantic in the 1840s, and eventually homegrown British versions were established there as well.[14] Cham's equation of Soulouque's skin color and shoe polish thus taps into associations that would have been familiar to anyone patronizing the London theater scene. A reference to shoe polish in a racial context suggests the means that white actors used to impersonate blacks on the minstrel stage.[15]

Minstrelsy seems not to have had a wide following in France at this time. However, Parisian audiences would have been familiar with the idea of racial impersonation that Cham is playing on. A landmark of the 1850 cultural season was Alphonse de Lamartine's play *Toussaint Louverture*. Lamartine was a famous poet, writer, politician, aristocrat, and member of the Académie Française. The title role of Louverture was played by a famous white actor, Frédéric Lemaitre, who was tinted a sort of chocolate color for the role (figure 8.10).

This particular play seems not to have aimed at racial parody in the way that the American and British minstrel shows did. It did operate with the same tools

Figure 8.10 Alexandre Lacauchie, *Frédérick Lemaitre dans Toussaint Louverture* (Paris: Martinet, 1850), Toussaint Louverture d'Alphonse de Lamartine: Documents Iconographiques, 4-ICO THE-3490. Bibliothèque Nationale de France, Paris.

of racial mimicry and substitution, however: tinting the skin of a white actor in imitation of a black character. The play drew a crowd of two thousand to its opening performance. It also received a rapturous review in *Le Charivari*, with no trace of irony.[16] The review compares the play favorably to others in the Paris theaters of the time and says that the character of Toussaint Louverture is one of Lamartine's most brilliant creations. The play is praised for its poetry and its sensitive portrayal of the tragic choices faced by Louverture.

Soulouque also received high-profile treatment on Paris stages around this time, though aiming at satire rather than pathos. The Vaudeville farce *La nuit blanche, fantasie noire* by Joseph Méry and Gérard de Nerval (writing under pseudonyms) premiered in 1850 and was quickly shut down by the police.[17] In spite of its brief run, notice was taken in the papers. *L'Argus*, a daily performing-arts journal, reports that the actual Emperor Soulouque had demanded the extradition of the authors to Haiti.[18] It claims that the French government denied the request on the grounds that the authors had provided the most convincing proof that they were not black and were not Haitian citizens. *Le Daguerréotype théatral* mentions the play briefly and acerbically, calling it an ephemeral confection. Sarcastically referring to the second half of the title, "Fantasie Noire," it says that it was a "black fantasy of three white men." They wrote under a pseudonym, the journal says, because of their shame at having soiled the stage of the Odéon with this piece.[19] It is unclear whether the "black fantasy" staged at the Odéon drew on conventions of minstrelsy for comic effect. The editor of *Le Daguerréotype théatral* clearly found it objectionable and shameful but did not explain why.

These stage productions give us some indication of how Cham's joke about shoe polish would have been understood by French audiences. The joke reverses the minstrel formula. Rather than a white actor using shoe polish to impersonate black skin, a black person is using "flesh-toned" paint to polish his boots. The humor lies in the unexpected and risqué character of this reversal, and Soulouque becomes the butt of the joke for having flesh that looks like black paint. His race thus moves front and center as an object of humor, the implication being that it is somehow absurd to have skin the color of one's boots.

Cham's work inherits more than just cheap jokes about blackface from the stage. In a more diffuse sense, it absorbs some of minstrelsy's ethos. The minstrel shows centered around the racialization of foolishness and hapless antics. Their black characters had a kind of exaggerated talkativeness, gullibility, and foolishness, or absurd imitation of upper-class manners and mock dignity. Cham's Soulouque displays many of the same foibles. Minstrel shows were driven by certain stock characters: Tambo, Bones, Zip Coon, Jim Crow, Old Dan Tucker, Mr. Interlocutor.[20] Soulouque certainly comes to fill that function for Cham. Here Cham brings the antics of the minstrel show together with the core insights of physiognomy. Antic behavior accompanies absurd appearance to reveal debased character. The shows peddled both parody and sentimentality: a form of parody based on racial stereotypes and a sentimental portrayal of slavery, plantation life, and race relations. Cham certainly adopts racial stereotypes as a basis for parody as well and does so in a sentimental vein of his own.

In sum, Cham's Soulouque drawings mark a significant evolution in racial caricature. They denigrate Soulouque by bringing together a number of other elements. In addition to Cham's skill as a draftsman and observer of human nature, there are reverberations of physiognomy, now taken in a racial direction, and the racial comicry of the minstrel shows. The result is a highly effective stew of humanity, pathos, and a loose-limbed sense of comic antics. All of this builds on existing elements of racist culture in powerful new ways.

We are used to such visual conventions today, so it is worth trying to see them as they might have appeared in the mid-nineteenth century. Clay's "Life in Philadelphia" had aimed nasty satirical barbs at black Americans. The satire was conveyed primarily through captions and dialogue and the situations its images portrayed. In these images, black people were rendered for comic effect, but the visual language remained largely within the genre conventions of caricature at the time. The facial expressions and features in both Clay's and Tregear's drawings are oddly monotonous and static. They are pretentious, leering, or menacing, regardless of the situation. Obviously, the intent was a negative one, but clumsily so. Those artists seemed unsure how to adapt the portrayal of faces and expressions to racial parody, so they relied on more conventional means to achieve negative effects.

Cham makes a double move beyond his American and English colleagues. He has a much greater talent for rendering a wide variety of expressions, and he simultaneously moves racial imagery out of the range of human appearance to draw on animals as various avatars of human character. He fuses these innovations together in a new vocabulary of racial caricature and sets them into motion with the visual antics of racialized stage drama. Cham uses the resources of pictorial representation in new ways to promote the fuller, more visual development of nineteenth century racial imaginaries. They are all the more damaging because of their enhanced capabilities to convey meaning.

It is not clear that Cham had any particular ax to grind by drawing Soulouque. He seems to have been relatively apolitical, with vaguely royalist leanings that made him oppose republic, empire, and socialism equally. His barbs were aimed all across the political spectrum and at all classes of French society. In contrast to someone like his colleague Honoré Daumier, he had no pretensions to be known as a great artist. Cham appealed to a lower-middle class audience in comparison to Daumier's high culture followers. He preferred quick, topical, and numerous drawings over Daumier's more artistically ambitious production.[21] He would often doodle out a panel of nine drawings on a page, in contrast to the finely drawn, full-page creations of Daumier. Cham's images of Soulouque were almost always in this format. In other words, they were mostly quick laughs, not the more careful puncturing that Cham reserved for other topics. They may simply have been a case of his impish sense of humor combined with a no-holds-barred attitude toward satire.

Whatever Cham's intentions, they in no way minimize the racial and political impact of his Soulouque images. Those images had a powerfully pejorative influence on the rule of a postcolonial leader. More broadly, they pioneered new ways of imagining race, ones that were more vivid and thus more effective in their potential to denigrate, delegitimize, and silence.

In this light, we can see how mistaken it is to say that caricature "produce[s] a likeness more true than mere imitation could be." In the rapidly developing racial caricature of nineteenth-century France, caricature *constituted* truth rather than imitating it. Pictorial representation says by showing, establishing truths by rendering them visible. It provides a kind of tangible verisimilitude, even when it aims at absurdity. When such images are rendered as humor, they are all the more sugar-coated and easier to swallow. As a result, it became an accepted truth that Soulouque was a buffoon, a simpleton, a quasi-person with apelike curiosity who was baffled by the mysteries of the world. It is not the case that racial caricature "produce[s] a likeness more true than mere imitation," but that it produces its own truths, including a complex web of associations between raciality, animality, and absurdity. Those associations appear complex only when we try to tease them apart, however. Unexamined, they have a kind of simple self-evidence. As a result, the caricatured version of Soulouque simply achieved widespread public acceptance and became true.

POSTCOLONIAL *RESSENTIMENT*

It is not surprising that the development of racial images and stereotypes had a profoundly denigrating force. The political context of these developments is worth noting, however, especially the way they intervene in this particular moment in postcolonial politics. An image by Honoré Daumier captures these dynamics well. Following in Cham's footsteps, Daumier contributed a number of memorable images to the Soulouque trope. Among them is a vivid engraving of the emperor waving a hapless and terrified white journalist over his head, preparing to drop him into a boiling cauldron of tar (figure 8.11).

This image intervenes in postcolonial politics in a more pointed way than any of Cham's. Soulouque wears a military officer's uniform, riding boots, and a Napoleonic hat. He is drawn in a manner clearly indebted to Cham: he seems more ape than human. Unlike Cham, however, Daumier gives Soulouque a grotesque combination of animality and aggression. In the background are a number of dimly seen, half-naked figures dancing in the sugarcane. The journalist's pinstripe pants and flapping tails identify him as a member of the upper classes. Shredded papers lay on the ground, and the caption says that he had dared to write an article criticizing acts of the administration. Soulouque's bearlike growl confirms that he is right to be terrified.

The sharp political edge of Daumier's drawing is characteristic of his work, and of many other things appearing in *Le Charivari* at this time. Such drawings of the postcolonial Caribbean pose an additional puzzle, though. It is not clear why this would be such an appealing subject of satire. Barbed caricatures of French politicians seem like a natural enough subject for a satirical French press with a political orientation. But what explains the notoriety and runaway success of Soulouque as a stock character in these same publications?

In 1882 Arthur Bowler hypothesized that Soulouque was a particular target of satire because artists and writers used him as a proxy for the emperor of France.[22] Louis-Napoléon Bonaparte, nephew of the infamous emperor, was crowned Emperor Napoléon III of France in 1852. Caricatures and other criticisms of Soulouque, Bowler claims, were really veiled attacks on the new French emperor. The Haitian historian Dantès Bellegarde repeated this idea in 1938, and since then it has become a commonplace among many who comment on Soulouque's treatment in the French press. Laurent Dubois adds additional detail to the account, noting that the term *soulouquerie* came to be used to deride

Figure 8.11 Honoré Daumier, *L'empereur Soulouque*, *Le Charivari*, June 15, 1850, 3. Bibliothèque Nationale de France, Paris.

Napoléon's court. He tells us that Napoléon was sufficiently stung by this comparison to issue an edict forbidding the word.[23]

If this insight is correct, its implicit comparison between the two emperors would dislocate the conceit I laid out above. Instead of history repeating itself first as tragedy, then as farce, Napoléon III would now become a farcical duplication of the equally farcical Soulouque. We might reframe Karl Marx's quip accordingly: "all great, world-historical events occur twice—first as farce in the Caribbean, then as farce in Europe."

This "politics by proxy" thesis makes an interesting claim. It hypothesizes that the postcolonial world was used to parody the old metropole, tarring metropolitan politics with images of postcolonial degeneracy. One can imagine the sources for such an idea. Marx himself makes such a comparison briefly in his celebrated attack on Napoléon III. He describes Napoléon's court in Haitian terms: "A gang of louts are pushing their way into the court, the ministries, the chief offices in administration and the army, of whom the best to be said is that no one knows where they come from, a noisy, foul, rapacious crowd of bohemians, crawling into gold braid with the same grotesque dignity as Soulouque's stuffed shirts."[24]

Rather than supporting the "politics by proxy" thesis, however, Marx's comments only illustrate its problems. Marx refers to Soulouque elliptically and briefly, without extended explanation. His brief reference is quite telegraphic, but it seems sufficient to make his audience understand how degenerate Napoléon's administration is. That audience was already transatlantic: Marx's account was originally published in the New York magazine *Die Revolution* and is now known as *The Eighteenth Brumaire of Louis Bonaparte*. It was widely read by the German-speaking diaspora of the 1848 revolutions.[25] The brevity and offhand character of Marx's reference to the "grotesque dignity" of Soulouque's court suggests that its meaning is already well established and needs no further explanation. Only a handful of years after the first Soulouque caricatures began to appear, it seems that opinion about him had already settled, not only in France but in Germany and the United States as well.

Most of those who hold the "politics by proxy" thesis site its origins in the parodies of Soulouque's coronation in 1852. However, his reputation had already formed well before that date. Soulouque's debut in the satirical press predates Bonaparte's elevation to emperor by several years. The Soulouque caricatures start showing up in October 1849, well before Bonaparte's coup d'état at the end of 1851 and his coronation as emperor in 1852. At that time, Bonaparte was still the elected president of the Second Republic, and *Le Charivari* was mostly busy lampooning members of the National Assembly and its socialist opposition. There was no Emperor Napoléon III to be satirized by proxy during the formative years of Soulouque caricatures.[26] On the other hand, *President* Bonaparte was actually available as a target of direct caricature and was frequently so targeted in *Le Charivari*. It may well have been the case that he was derided as a white Soulouque once he became emperor, but that was only possible because of a primary, preexisting denigration of Soulouque well before that time.

More important, the grotesque racial stereotypes used to parody Soulouque go far beyond the limits of domestic French politics. Such problems are evident, for instance, in Dantès Bellegarde's remark that the more one blackened Soulouque, the more odious would appear his imitation by Napoléon.[27] This notion of parody by racialization reveals core problems in the "politics by proxy" thesis. The grotesque raciality used to render Soulouque absurd does not find a parallel in Louis Bonaparte. The younger Bonaparte might have illusions of imperial grandeur; he might be accused of *soulouquerie*, but he could not be identified with racial grotesquery as the Haitian emperor was. The satire of Soulouque has a racial sting and animus all its own.

Soulouquerie could find a target in Louis Bonaparte—if indeed it did—only after it had already been established as a trope. Emperor Soulouque was first racialized and rendered absurd on his own, and only then could he be used to parody others. Any later use of him as a standard of absurdity in a "politics by proxy" could only have been a matter of convenience, a clever employment of materials already at hand. It *presupposes* that Soulouque had already been created as an independent object of ridicule rather than explain *why* he received this treatment. In short, the idea that the Soulouque caricatures were *images à clef* is simply not a good explanation for their success. It provides a satisfying reassurance that this was, in the end, all about Europe. In so doing, it ignores the quite targeted racialization of Soulouque, the denigration of postcolonial Haiti, and the subaltern silence that was thereby created. These images were not, in the end, all about Europe, but something much more complex and problematic. To suppose otherwise is to silence Soulouque twice over: first, as racialized and absurd; and second, by making his poor treatment really be all about political battles between white, European elites.

To understand the work being done by the Soulouque caricatures, it is important to place them in the broader cultural currents at the end of Caribbean colonialism. Where there was once tight control over colonial possessions—with considerable anxiety about the effectiveness of that control, as we have seen—there was now considerably less that the European powers could do to force their will on the former colonies. In this context, it might be tempting to say that caricature emerges as a new tool of postcolonial domination to fill that gap. This would be too direct and reductive, however. As Michael Pickering succinctly notes, "In popular culture, trends don't originate in carefully laid plans conceived to fulfil a perceived need, but they do often show where a need is strongly felt."[28] We can say something similar about the biting humor directed against Soulouque. It quickly found an audience, and we can speculate that there were specific reasons for that enthusiasm. A principal one that leaps to mind is the conjunction of biting forms of racial "humor" with the end of colonial slavery in the Americas.

Minstrelsy and racial caricature both became popular in Britain in the 1840s, during the decade after slavery was banned in the British Empire (1833). Similarly, Faustin Soulouque took the throne just as slavery was abolished for the second time in the French colonies (1848). The political climate on both sides of the channel was one of pervasive problematization of slavery, with all of the accompanying political antagonisms that had been building for decades around the topic. We might speculate that this biting racial humor originated within such political currents and eventually became a source of consolation to some for the failure to resist change. Here the sting of racial parody arises out of *ressentiment* and a desire to injure. In this interpretation, the will to inflict injury and pain through satire is a salve for the injured white colonial psyche. It takes solace in satire when domination was no longer possible.

Such dynamics seem borne out by the extended attack on Soulouque published by the former French consul to Haiti, Maxime Raybaud. Writing under a pseudonym in the well-respected *Revue des deux mondes*, he published a series of accounts of Soulouque in 1850–1851. These reports contained rich detail of characters and events that were only receiving vague, impressionistic reporting in the newspapers. Maintaining his anonymity, Raybaud did not explain the sources of his information, but they were clearly those of an eyewitness. He even took advantage of this hidden identity to narrate the crucial role played by Raybaud, who is said to have acted effectively and scrupulously to restrain Soulouque's wild tendencies. Several years later these accounts were republished as a very successful book, *L'Empereur Soulouque et son empire* (Emperor Soulouque and His Empire).[29]

In Raybaud's account, Soulouque is timid, soft-spoken, aggrieved, superstitious, and impressionable. He bears strong hostilities toward the mixed-race elites of the island, which inspire him to murderous aggression against them on many occasions. At the same time, Soulouque struggles to manage the "ultra-African" faction, as Raybaud likes to call it: poor blacks who were mobilized and politicized with Acaau and the Army of Sufferers. Soulouque draws his power base from this faction and solicits their support, particularly those who recognize his authority as a practitioner of Vaudou. At the same time, the Army is a largely leaderless grassroots movement. Their energies are chaotic and difficult to control.

Raybaud reports that these conflicting forces frequently taxed Soulouque beyond his abilities. Soulouque was thus highly insecure about his own power, with a resulting tendency toward excessive and erratic violence. This is manifest in the attacks that he mounted on the nation's *de couleur* elites. Their lives were always precarious under his reign, and many fled the island or were killed as a result. Life in Soulouque's inner circle was reported to be similarly precarious. He allegedly conducted frequent purges and executions of his own ministers and generals. Their tenure could be opulent and privileged until he turned against them. The picture that emerges most strongly from Raybaud is a bloodbath: continual war, murder, and execution in the name of frequently misguided motives.

Raybaud sees these extreme events as a result of Soulouque's insufficiency for rule. Soulouque's superstition is channeled into a strong belief in Vaudou. That devotion manifests itself in various dysfunctional compulsions, including odd fears about sorcery by his political enemies. These irrationalities only heighten his erratic and violent tendencies. Ironically, however, Soulouque is also portrayed as highly sensitive to ridicule. Writing under a pseudonym, Raybaud relates many stories in which the (amazing and judicious) French consul Raybaud plays on Soulouque's insecurities to manipulate him into doing the right thing, when he had been headed off on some disastrous path. Soulouque lacks the ability to navigate the challenges of his office. Fortunately his need for recognition and esteem allows people like Raybaud to steer him onto a better path occasionally and with great effort.

Raybaud also paints a vivid picture of what he characterizes as Soulouque's self-aggrandizing tendencies. Soulouque had apparently gotten ahold of a commemorative album published for the coronation of Napoléon I, some forty years before. He allegedly used this as a template for his own imperial splendor. Raybaud relates stories of crowns, scepters, robes, and thrones made to order in France. He says that dressing was one of Soulouque's greatest preoccupations, and that he sometimes wore three or four outfits per day. Raybaud also details the opulence of Soulouque's coronation and notes the large number of noble titles that he created to populate his imperial court.[30]

In the end, Raybaud's account is a hard-hitting indictment. Soulouque emerges as an irrational fool, overwhelmed by the challenges of rule. His outbursts of anger and suspicion have murderous consequences. This account is well-written, readable, yet also highly racist, dismissive, and self-congratulatory. It presents a palpable rendition of Soulouque as a person. Raybaud arguably had a unique perspective on this, yet there is much in the work to put one on warning against placing too much faith in its vivid details. Raybaud presents a particular image of Soulouque, but it may be one that conceals as much as it reveals. There is a strong element of verbal caricature in Raybaud's account. Admittedly, it is much more fine-grained than Cham's portrayals. It is not ribald nor comic and thus not obviously overstated. That only increases the danger of a false verisimilitude, however. Like Cham's caricatures, this account seems to plunge Soulouque into deep silence by providing such a powerful indictment of his personality and actions.

Raybaud's accounts of Soulouque seem to have been well received. They were widely read and highly influential in creating the popular image of Soulouque in France.[31] The book version was published in a revised second edition a mere four years later, then translated into English the following year.[32] Interestingly, the English translation was published in the American slave-trading city of Richmond, Virginia, a scant two years before the outbreak of the American Civil War. The translator makes clear that he is bringing it to American audiences as a warning of what abolition might look like in the United States. He intends this book as a direct intervention in controversies over the potential abolition of American slavery.

The attacks on Soulouque were not about slavery in any appreciable way, however. They were parodies of a black political figure with considerable power in his own domain. Nonetheless, Soulouque had by now been transformed into a meme in the white, transatlantic public spheres spanning the Americas and Europe. The attacks on him had thus become abstract and typological. That is to say, their bitter edge extended beyond Soulouque to parody Haitians and blacks more generally. Laughter at the expense of blacks seemed to aim at discrediting ideas of black independence and autonomy. Their bitter, satirical edge additionally reveals deeper affective investments. They might provide some comfort, however ill-gotten, for anxieties about the increasingly precarious slave economy in the American South.

Such racial *ressentiment* is often palpable in Raybaud's account. At one point in his narrative, for instance, Raybaud quotes the same "African song" that opened this book. He is clearly sourcing the words directly from Moreau de Saint-Méry, as I did. However, he quotes it without citation, as if it was something he heard himself. His commentary on the song is quite different from Moreau de Saint-Méry's, however:

> Eh! eh! Bomba, hen! hen!
> Canga bafio té
> Canga moune dé lé
> Canga do ki la
> Canga li.

> I don't know whether I have just spoken Senegalese or Yolof, Foule or Bambara, Mindigue or Bouriquis, Arada or Caplaou, Ibo or Moko, Congo or Mousombé. All that I can say is that I just spoke *nègre*. When these uncomprehended words, sung alternately by one or several voices, rose in crescendo from the shadows, the colonists of the former Saint-Domingue had their slaves counted, and the *maréchaussée* was on the march.[33]

For Raybaud, this song is emblematic of the "ultra-African" forces unleashed since Haitian independence. He says that since the elevation of Soulouque, those voices sing at their own pleasure. The primitive impulses of African culture have been given free rein through Soulouque's indulgence and his inability to control them.

Because we examined the "African song" at the beginning of this study, it is worth commenting on the way it reflects transformations since that time. Moreau de Saint-Méry copied the song down in the 1770s. When I discussed it in chapter 1, I noted a kind of casual disregard for subaltern voices, one that banished them to a footnote and thereby constituted forms of subaltern silence. In comparison, Raybaud's treatment in the 1850s is brash, aggressive, and bluntly racist. He still treats the origins and meaning of the song as cryptic but says that does not matter because it is all *nègre*. Back in Saint-Méry's time, the description "*nègre*" oscillated between meaning "enslaved person" and "black." For Raybaud it is a racial slur. The ethnic affiliation of the people singing does not matter, nor does the meaning of their words. It is all *nègre*: illegitimate, dismissible, of no value. We have passed from a form of subaltern silence built on disregard to one built on hostility, dismissal, and delegitimation. The first seems like the slight of a culture that does not care or notice. The second is the intentional insult of a culture that cares too much. These attitudes mark two points in the evolution of subaltern silence that I have been trying to describe in this book.

Similar *ressentiment* seems echoed in the words of the Englishman Thomas Carlyle quoted in chapter 7. They were written in 1849, sixteen years after abolition in the British colonies and just as Soulouque was becoming emperor. His words evoke images as biting as any that Cham or Daumier produced: "Sitting yonder with their beautiful muzzles up to the ears in pumpkins, imbibing sweet pulps and juices; the grinder and incisor teeth ready for every new work, and the pumpkins cheap as grass in those rich climates; while the sugar-crops rot round them uncut, because labour cannot be hired, so cheap are the pumpkins...."[34]

Carlyle's remarks trade in not only animality but also images of the torpor of rural life in the tropics, where pumpkins are as cheap as grass and no one wants to work. These visions are ramified and repeated through his essay; for instance, in references to former slaves as "indolent two-legged cattle...'happy' over their abundant pumpkins." This imagery is just as vivid as that of Cham or Daumier, and quite similar in type. Indeed, the similarity between Carlyle's prose and the caricaturists' images suggests the possibility of genres of satire shared between English and French publics at this time, spanning both prose and image.

Carlyle was not ignorant of the opportunities for satire at Haiti's expense. In the same essay, he intensifies his condemnation of Britain's former slaves with a reference to all of the recent upheavals in Soulouque's empire. He warns that if the former slaves in the British colonies are not put back to work, the consequences may be even worse than they are now: "Alas, let [the former slave] look across to Haiti, and trace a far sterner prophesy! Let him, by his ugliness, idleness, rebellion, banish all White men from the West Indies, and make it all one Haiti,—with little or no sugar growing, black Peter exterminating black Paul, and where a garden of the Hesperides might be, nothing but a tropical dog-kennel and pestiferous jungle."[35] In short, the symbolic residues of the agrarian problematic are still very much at work here. Soulouque is not only a political representative of poor, rural farmers, but he is also tarred and dismissed as one of them, out of place in his high office and fancy Napoleonic clothes. His rule has led to a collapse of the agrarian economy, blacks exterminating one another, and the whole country reduced to a tropical dog kennel.

Carlyle had no particular stake in Haiti other than hostility toward the model of black liberation it represented. He sees it as a *reductio ad absurdum* of abolition run to its natural conclusion. Haiti thus becomes a stalking horse for the abolition of slavery in the British colonies. As for the American planters reading Maxime Raybaud, Soulouque seems to stand in for hostilities and anxieties that were very much located at home as well. Here, then, we arrive at a new "politics by proxy" thesis. Soulouque becomes a metaphor for abolition, postcoloniality, black autonomy, and black sovereignty. By extension, he also serves as a vehicle for white pique and *ressentiment*. Displacement, slander by proxy—all of this is possible because of the polymorphous and typological nature of racial caricature. This version of the thesis is much more compelling than the one that had him standing in for a French emperor.

COUNTERIMAGE AS COUNTERSPEECH?

Racial representations like those of Soulouque have become so familiar that it is sometimes hard to see past them. It is worth noting, then, that not all contemporary commentators shared the opinions of Cham, Daumier, Raybaud, and Carlyle.

Mark Bird, a longtime Protestant missionary in Haiti, saw Soulouque's elevation as an attempt at national unity. From his perspective, it was a response to "the spectacle of a nation rent and torn by intestine commotions and mutual recriminations." Thus, he writes about the prospect of empire in general: "It was thought that, considering the almost chaotic state of things, some great national diversion of thought from the sad scene which had afflicted all might prove salutary." Bird's account of the coronation ceremony follows this line of thought. He comments on its tasteful and impressive character, noting that "notwithstanding all the ridicule which attached to the whole case, it was an imposing spectacle."[36]

Bird's hypothesis about the need for national diversion provides a dramatic recontextualization of Soulouque's seeming excesses. In this view, the empire and the pomp surrounding it are symbols of national power and achievement, a kind of collective self-reassurance that Haiti had fortitude and standing in the world. Thus, Bird says, "a nation, small as it was, was here represented, and it must be supposed that the motive, on the part of the well meaning, was national and individual security, even though it might be under the name of an empire."[37] From this perspective, Soulouque's empire looks like an attempt to resolve divisions, promote internal unity, and improve Haiti's standing in the world. In other words, Soulouque's empire seems above all like an attempt at subaltern speech.

John Bigelow, an American visitor to Haiti, provided a similarly positive interpretation. He gives a very favorable account of his meeting with Soulouque in 1850. The Imperial Palace did not impress Bigelow, but he found Soulouque himself quite commendable, well-mannered, and elegant. He says "his features are pleasing, and there is a peculiar sweetness in his smile." Bigelow further observes that "From the regularity of his features, his profile looks like that of a Roman Emperor."[38]

Interestingly, Bigelow does not attribute the usual vainglorious motives to Soulouque for becoming emperor. He says, "The name of Emperor expresses nothing Napoleon-like at Haiti; it supposes only an authority better respected than that of President, and recalls to the Haitians the popular recollection of Dessalines, who, in reward to the services rendered to his country, had been proclaimed Emperor." In other words, Bigelow interprets Soulouque's elevation as an affair completely internal in the domestic politics of Haiti, and as having a specific meaning within the Haitian cultural context, rather than as an attempt to glorify himself on the world stage. In Bigelow's estimate, the honor of being named emperor was bestowed upon Dessalines by the Haitian people, and he believes the same was true of Soulouque.[39]

Finding Soulouque quite different from his reputation in the European and American press, Bigelow sympathetically notes that Soulouque "is greatly annoyed at the caricatures of him published in the Paris *Charivari*, and the jokes of the press in general. On this point he is susceptible to an incredible extent."[40] It is a mark of how well-known and widely circulated the caricatures were not only that Soulouque was aware of them but also that Bigelow could refer to them in such an off-handed way, confident that this awareness was widely shared by his readers.

There are substantial differences in attitude between the accounts of Bird, Bigelow, and Raybaud, even though all were eyewitnesses to Soulouque's reign. What emerges from both Bigelow and Raybaud, however, is Soulouque's sensitivity to outside opinion. Raybaud tells us that Soulouque read the American and European papers; there was also a rumor that he sued the French government to censor the play satirizing him in Paris.

Karen Salt makes the provocative claim that Soulouque went even further to fight back against the attacks leveled against him in the international press. To commemorate his coronation, Soulouque commissioned an album of twelve engravings made from daguerreotypes, the *Album impériale d'Haïti*. This is the one mentioned by Raybaud, based on an album that Soulouque had studied from the coronation of Napoléon I. The images are sober, dignified, and designed to reflect the solemnity of the occasion (figure 8.12). They are formally posed portraits of the imperial family and images of the coronation itself. The goal is clearly to represent the gravitas and power of the new Emperor. Salt sees the publication of this *Album* as an attempt to rebut Soulouque's treatment in the French press. In her interpretation, he was using images to push back against the images deployed against him.[41]

Salt's idea of viewing the *Album impériale* within the same frame as the Soulouque caricatures is an insightful one. This juxtaposition certainly fits what we have been told of Soulouque's sensitivity to the foreign press, and it places the *Album* squarely within the problematic of subaltern silence. In this view, Soulouque would be deploying imperial grandeur and realist portraiture to displace caricature. A symbolic stratagem of this kind would serve as a novel form of subaltern speech. It could be an effort to reclaim voice by resymbolizing the meanings being established in the French press. The use of a symbolic strategy on Soulouque's part would be particularly perceptive, because it would respond in kind to the symbolic attacks being leveled against him.

Having said this, it is worth noting that the *Album* would have been a rather poor response to the French drawings. Soulouque was caricatured as vainglorious, presumptuous, and unfit for authority. A commemorative photo album, produced as a prestige object to glorify Soulouque's coronation, could have played right into this image, making him appear to be playacting an imperial role for which he was not fit. Indeed, this kind of playacting is exactly the theme of many of the caricatures. This is not to say that Soulouque was not taking aim at the French press by commissioning the *Album*, only that it may have served only to dig him deeper into the hole that was already being dug by his critics.

With such complexities in mind, I am hesitant to draw any determinate conclusion about how the *Album* may have functioned as subaltern speech. We must recognize how hegemonic representations of Soulouque displaced and silenced

Figure 8.12 Theodore Lacombe, *Faustin Ire, empereur d'Haïti*, 1852. Harry T. Peters "America on Stone" Lithography Collection DL.60.3119. National Museum of American History, Smithsonian Institution.

any potential countermove against them. They silenced what Soulouque might have been trying to say, and they stand in the way of our understanding today.

Consider, for instance, the place of Soulouque's empire in the Haitian political scene. Maxime Raybaud gives a clear account of the powerful domestic crosscurrents with which Soulouque had to contend. Soulouque stood at the intersection of two powerful revolutionary movements: the *de couleur* Liberals who had overthrown Boyer and the rural blacks he was put in office to appease. He did not seek political office, but had it thrust upon him. Soulouque owed his power to people who intended to use him as a puppet. He thus had a great need to wipe away the legacy of the *politique de doublure* and claim his legitimacy directly as a self-created leader. At the same time, he had an equivalent need to legitimize his rule with the agrarian movement that had given rise to the Army of Sufferers, the people Raybaud refers to as the "ultra-African party."

In this context, Soulouque may have been attempting to thread the needle of Haitian domestic politics by establishing the empire. It may have been a strategy for legitimating his regime, quieting internal dissent, and naturalizing his status as a ruler by elevating it to the heights of the emperor before him. The great pomp, the proliferation of noble titles, the expensive French costumes, and the *Album impériale* may have been aimed at navigating powerful currents of racial and political division in a highly unstable postcolonial environment. True, Soulouque was pilloried in the international public sphere for his grandiosity and pretention, but it is completely possible that the international public sphere was not his primary audience. In that case, the symbolic display of imperial majesty may well have fulfilled an important domestic function, even if it resulted in ridicule abroad.

The latter interpretation gives us a quite different view of Soulouque. Here he is not a self-aggrandizing buffoon, but a more calculating politician who used a Napoleonic script, with local flavorings of Dessalines and Christophe, as a strategy of postcolonial rule. Unfortunately, all of these possibilities remain only hypothetical. Whatever Soulouque might have been trying to say with the pomp and glory of his reign is now ambiguous to us, and it may well have been so at the time as well. It could have been an attempt to talk back to European racism, refuting racial caricature with the splendor of a black empire. It could have been a project of global vanity undertaken by a dandy unfit for rule. It might have been a shrewd maneuver of domestic politics, invoking the symbolics of imperial power to placate allies and intimidate rivals. Unfortunately, we do not have a basis for choosing between these possibilities. As a result, I do not feel confident attributing any one message to Soulouque's *Album*, even if it was that of subaltern speech. That would ignore the ambiguity of this situation, the extent to which Soulouque was in fact silenced. The *Album*'s message remains caught in limbo by a silence created by other, much more widely distributed images. Whatever Soulouque might have been trying to say, it remains silent to us today.

Despite the ambiguity of the *Album impériale*'s message, we can locate the source of its silence with some precision. Anything Soulouque may have been trying to say through the *Album* was silenced by his treatment in the French press. Caricatures and dismissive reports dominated his public image outside of Haiti, and they continue to do so today. They created ambiguity and doubt, undercutting whatever he might have been trying to say. The pomp and splendor of his coronation were well publicized, and the *Album* circulated as a monument to that event. However, the Soulouque caricatures did an effective job of throwing all of this into doubt. They subverted the seriousness of the message and coopted it through satire. Whatever message Soulouque might have aimed at, it now appeared as vanity and foolishness. Any value that might accrue to him through this ceremony was now drained away in laughter.

Even though the *Album impériale* remains silent, it does give us an important perspective on the Soulouque caricatures. It is a commonplace that caricature distorts a person's features for humorous effect. We see here, however, that the caricatures of Soulouque were on an altogether different level of distortion. Even allowing for a certain amount of cosmetic improvement in Soulouque's appearance, the *Album* suggests that the actual Soulouque bore no resemblance to the caricatures beyond his preference for military uniform.

This shows a departure from our typical assumptions about caricature: that they are based on an accentuation of actually existing traits, habits, and features. In the case of Cham's Soulouque drawings, something rather different seems to be at work. It is a visual language with very particular genre conventions, ones that have a pointedly racial and derogatory character. Soulouque is portrayed not as a person with features that can be accentuated for comic effect, but as someone whose race is the feature most worthy of parody. His politics are subsumed under these racial images, and the developing visual conventions of racial caricature become the means to comment on that politics.

INTERSECTIONAL SILENCING

Earlier I commented that women rarely appear in the archives, and it is worth taking note when they do. Cham's drawings of "Empress Ourika" provide a vivid example of the benefits of such an examination (figures 8.5 and 8.6).[42] Here we see complex forms of silencing across axes of race and gender, which illustrate the broader dynamics that Soulouque encounters as well.

"Empress Ourika" was yet another elaborate confection of Cham's imagination. She appears in his drawings as Soulouque's wife and the Empress of Haiti. In fact, Faustin Soulouque's wife was named Adélina. There was an actual woman named Ourika, however: a young slave girl brought to France by the governor of Senegal in 1786 and given as a gift to his aunt and uncle. This actual Ourika had a complicated relation with the fictional world of her time and the fashionable salons around which it revolved. The celebrated society figure Germaine de Staël adopted her name for a fictional African princess in the 1786 abolitionist novella *Mirza*.[43] In 1799, Ourika's death at age sixteen became a celebrated cause in the intellectual circles of the day and was memorialized in highly emotional terms by Maréchale Princesse de Beauvau, one of Ourika's owners.[44] The most famous treatment, however, came in Claire de Duras's novella *Ourika* in 1824.[45] This bestseller went through several printings in its first year and was immediately translated into English and Spanish. It attracted attention from intellectual notables such as Goethe, Chateaubriand, and Alexander von Humboldt and was so popular that it gave rise to a number of theatrical adaptations, poems, novelistic imitators, and even clothing styles.[46] The novella enjoyed a renaissance in 1849-1850, with several new editions appearing, the same years that Cham began drawing "Empress Ourika."[47] Thus Ourika's name and its connotations would have been easily recognized by his audience.

Duras's *Ourika* tells the story of a slave girl raised by enlightened nobles as their daughter. It is a sentimental and tragic tale. Ourika is a beautiful, thoughtful, and intelligent girl who grows up with no sense of her own racial difference. This naïve harmony comes to an end, however, when she reaches the age of marriage. Now blackness proves to be an impassable barrier that confronts her with great force. Ourika eventually perishes from her sorrows.

This fictional Ourika is a highly sentimentalized figure, and her death is framed as an indictment of racial prejudice. Duras fashions a passionate inner world for her heroine that is narrated in the first person. The vivid psychological depth of her writing creates a powerful sense of verisimilitude, giving readers the illusion of experiencing the thoughts and passions of the actual Ourika. This substitution of the author's voice for the character's inner thoughts is a substantial ventriloquism of the actual person by the fictional portrayal, however. It creates a form of silence in which any thoughts or utterances of the actual

Ourika are replaced by a sentimentalized, fictionalized narrative as imagined by someone else.[48] The ventriloquism is all the more problematic because it occurs across lines of race, nationality, and aristocratic status. Having said that, Duras's narrative was a striking feat of empathy for its time, a probing indictment of the psychological effects of racism.[49] Nonetheless, it ventriloquizes the actual Ourika in favor of a more general abolitionist message. Ourika's thoughts and passions are imagined and fictionalized by the pen of the Duchesse de Duras, a white French noblewoman, and in this situation the actual Ourika is silenced.

When Cham taps these associations, he enacts a similar substitution for the actual Haitian Empress Adélina. Cham's use of the name Ourika repositions Adélina as an innocent slave girl who has been elevated beyond her station. Race is a tragic barrier of which she is blissfully unaware, but it puts invisible limits on what she can attain. In stark contrast, Cham's actual drawings of this character portray her as potent, muscular, and aggressive. She perceives racial slights even when they are not present. The substantial tension between these two representations is a humorous device in Cham's hands. Word and image pull in opposite directions to create a form of racialized parody.

As a result, the silencing of Empress Adélina is quite complex. She is completely displaced by the name, image, and associations that Cham creates, silencing her through substitution. The wide circulation of an ersatz name and image in *Le Charivari* displaces anything that might have been known about the real empress of Haiti. At the same time, the cocktail of associations that Cham brews up for "Empress Ourika"—aggression, muscularity, racialized orphanhood in a white world—is highly delegitimating. She is a large, muscular, belligerent black woman who is easily angered, especially when her racial sensitivities are piqued. This empress is potent but absurd. Thus there is an additional silencing through delegitimation in this case. On the whole, this is an intersectional silencing: both Adélina's race and gender are played for laughs. In the end, the actual Empress Adélina is completely displaced by substitution of a name, an image, and characteristic behaviors. Adélina's voice and presence are gone, leaving an almost absolute silence.

SILENCING THROUGH DELEGITIMATION

We can see many of the same dynamics at work around Soulouque. The central stakes there were struggles over legitimation and delegitimation. The caricaturists, essayists, and journalists making sport of him discredited his ability to rule, racialized him, and undercut the legitimacy of his regime. More broadly, they damaged his legitimacy in the very broadest sense: not simply as a leader but as a person with credible actions and meaningful things to say. They propagated images of Soulouque as incapable and incompetent, undermining his worth in the perception of others. The caricaturists, essayists, and journalists might not have described their project as delegitimation, but it very much had that effect.

In reaction, Soulouque consistently sought to defend his own legitimacy as a person and ruler. Many of his actions can be read in that register. At times this may have been through heavy-handed terror tactics like those portrayed by Maxime Raybaud. At other times, it may have been through the symbolics of empire. He may have tried to resist the undertow of delegitimation by engaging in his own image-making: the *Album impériale*, for instance. This would have been an attempt to recenter his own image in the face of its delegitimation. For Soulouque, this would have been a kind of primary self-signification (or *re-resignification*) in opposition to the considerable work by others to resignify him. All of this constitutes a series of struggles over semantic positioning, attempts to resignify how Soulouque was perceived. In all of these cases, Soulouque would have aimed to improve his standing in public opinion. As he did so, he would have been fighting against a strong undertow of delegitimation.

Overall, it is not clear to what motives may have been at play in the European press. Caricaturists like Cham may simply have been aiming at a cheap laugh, and Soulouque may have seemed like a ripe target. They may not have had any concern with Haiti, postcoloniality, or Soulouque himself. Similarly, we are told that Soulouque read the international press and was sensitive to his reputation beyond Haiti's shores. However, he also had important concerns about legitimacy at home, and this may explain the majority of his efforts in this register. Regardless of the intentions of any of these actors, the result was a potent struggle over legitimation and delegitimation.

These struggles occurred as a politics of representation. They took place in multiple media, both words and images. The developing symbolic vocabulary of the Soulouque caricatures makes a significant contribution to this. It fuses racialization and humor in a particularly vicious way. This racialized vocabulary folds delegitimation into the very image of Soulouque. He is not portrayed as a politician or an emperor but as a pretentious ape who is perplexed by the task of ruling. There is an enormous compression of means and effects in these portrayals. They undercut Soulouque's reputation in a very blunt and far-reaching way.

Words and images have synergistic effects in this politics of representation. Accounts like Maxime Raybaud's substantiate the potent delegitimation enacted by the images. They add detail to what is only elliptically represented in the caricatures, supporting the dismissive character of those images. The images are powerful forms of representation that are easily consumed and circulated. Words add verisimilitude and detail. In short, these two forms of representation reinforce one other to create broader imaginaries.

The ultimate impact of this symbolic politics was to enact complex forms of subaltern silence. It was a latter-day form of silencing through resignification. These practices were focused on resignifying Soulouque in a way that rendered him absurd. As a result, anything he did or said was seen through that prism. These forms of delegitimation devalue the voice of a person or group even while their speech is being heard. The subaltern can speak, but that speech is discounted or rendered worthless. Soulouque was not literally silenced; instead, his actions and words were stripped of their validity and worth. The publicity Soulouque sought only served further to confirm the image of his absurdity. As a result, the profound delegitimation of Soulouque created a situation in which he was effectively silenced, even while speaking.

CATEGORIAL DELEGITIMATION

To unpack the complex politics of silence around Soulouque, it is helpful to observe how their effects propagated well beyond the immediate context. Here silencing operates through new technologies and takes on new forms. It relies on two principal features. First, it operates through more subtle means, no longer forbidding speech but simply devaluing it. Second, it exercises this delegitimation on entire categories of people at once, silencing them by *type*. The combination of these two features produces a new, efficient, and especially effective technology for imposing silence. We can call it *categorial delegitimation*.

Karl Marx's offhand references to *soulouquerie* reveal a great deal about the ways categorial delegitimation functions. Soulouque could not have been rendered absurd through racialization if raciality itself was not already functioning as a genre of devaluation. This included not simply racial hierarchy and racial violence, but more particularly, images of racialized subjects as absurd and grotesque. Such images drew on a whole genre of symbolic expression that coded them as racial, and further associated them with other demeaning ideas. In this sense, Soulouque's degradation relied on preexisting racial vocabularies. When those background understandings were implicitly invoked in caricature, they were creatively reimagined and reproduced. Soulouque's moment as farce relied on racial stereotyping at the same time that it developed new modes of racial representation. It helped to pioneer an elaborate shorthand of words and images that degraded people by type.

Regardless of the intention behind the attacks on Soulouque, their effect was clear enough. Cham, Daumier, and the others succeeded in controlling the narrative about Soulouque and setting the terms under which he was understood in metropolitan France. This included the image of him as a simpleton (Cham's contribution) and somewhat paradoxically, the image of him as a totalitarian ogre (Daumier). It may well be the case that *ressentiment* influenced the reception of these portrayals, producing a highly effective smear campaign with broad political reach. In any case, these ideas circulated widely in accounts and images of Haitian politics. Portrayals of stupidity, degeneracy, pretension, and excess had a broad enough reach to give rise to a popular shorthand, *soulouquerie*, that allowed Karl Marx to make unflattering comparisons to Soulouque without having to explain what he meant.

The broader cultural politics exemplified by "*soulouquerie*" are my ultimate interest here. They went well beyond Soulouque himself to constitute new forms of subaltern silence, ones that could not have been imagined during the earlier days of white colonial publicity. Such forms of delegitimation are complex, ranging from very specific to quite abstract. We can trace out four of them, all material in their manifestations but increasingly general in reach. They play out across the typological categories of the *individual*, the *national*, the *postcolonial*, and the *racial*. The case of Soulouque demonstrates the astonishing variety, flexibility, and power of these modes of subordination.

The most obvious casualty of these attacks was Soulouque himself. As we have seen, Soulouque faced an enormous legitimacy deficit coming into office. His location within the *politique de doublure* was intended to subordinate him to other powers and undercut any independence he might have as Haiti's president. Soulouque managed to subvert that control to a large extent, establishing himself as the independent ruler of Haiti. Where Haiti's *de couleur* elites could not control him, however, French caricature provided a surprising riposte. Those attacks resymbolized Soulouque's independence as totalitarian degeneracy and racialized idiocy. They very efficiently accomplished something that his political competitors could not: undercutting Soulouque's legitimacy as a ruler.

In the best of all worlds, the attention focused on Soulouque might have destabilized the *politique de doublure* and allowed subaltern voices to resurface. It might have created openings for the rural black constituencies that Soulouque represented to make their voices heard, perhaps by rebutting the negative portrayals they were subjected to. This fantasy, however, seriously underestimates the power of images to subordinate and delegitimate. Soulouque remained in office until 1859, but as a kind of international laughing stock. The *politique de doublure* was wiped out by Soulouque's aggressive measures against it, but he was hamstrung in new ways. The result was a different form of disempowerment, one in which Soulouque was not a puppet so much as a weakened and delegitimated ruler. Cartoons, in this case, proved more effective than the *de couleur* elites who had tried to silence Soulouque.

The attacks on Soulouque had strong spillover effects for Haiti as a whole. He was viewed as representing Haitian blacks and rural peasants. In the transatlantic public spheres, this image took the form of the "King of the Monkeys" who commanded a threadbare army while his subjects danced naked in the sugarcane. Black Peter exterminated black Paul; the country was "nothing but a tropical dog-kennel and pestiferous jungle." This treatment rendered Soulouque absurd while also disparaging his government, Haitian politics, and the entire idea of "the black republic." It treated the two as elements of the same absurd picture.

In short, the degradation of Soulouque was not merely individual, but also typological. It painted with a broad brush, caricaturing the tiny Caribbean nation he ruled. Soulouque was rendered absurd as the second-rate emperor of a degenerate state, which reflected back upon, activated, and creatively perpetuated those stereotypes themselves. Haiti was the background against which Soulouque appeared absurd, and it thus also became a place of absurdity. By extension, the agrarian vision that Soulouque represented, the vision of "three free days," Acaau, and the Army of Sufferers, was once again silenced. This time the silencing came from France rather than Haiti itself, and it came in the form of ridicule.

The broader effects of delegitimation go well beyond Haiti to postcoloniality in general. Attacks like that of Thomas Carlyle speak volumes in this regard. Carlyle calls up the image of Haiti under Soulouque to criticize the abolition of slavery and argue for its reinstatement. The idea of British colonies becoming "a tropical dog-kennel and pestiferous jungle" evokes a potent image of collapse and chaos. It is aimed not at Soulouque or his regime directly but at discrediting the whole enterprise of abolition and colonial independence.

For Carlyle this agenda is quite intentional. He expresses great *ressentiment* over the loss of the slave economy, plantation property, and other colonial possessions. We might conclude that his biting attacks on *soulouquerie* may have provided some consolation. They could be read as spite, as attempts to inflict pain in new ways.

Such motivations may or may not have been shared by Raybaud. The intentions of Cham and Daumier are even less clear. However, we know that all of their publications found an avid audience, one that paid to consume representations of postcolonial collapse and ruin. From this perspective, the caricatures would appear as a kind of counterstrike within a broader anti-postcolonial politics. They would be rearguard actions, attempts at revenge, when a restoration of the old order was no longer possible.

This shows us some important things about the broad sweep of genealogy we have been examining. The affective investments of the metropole have changed. Under colonialism they centered on fear, anxiety, and paranoia. In this postcolonial period, those investments are transformed into spite, vicious humor, and *ressentiment*.

Ultimately, the Soulouque caricatures have a significance even broader than postcolonial politics. They were important contributions to the nascent racist popular culture of the time, particularly the developing genre of racial caricature. They developed potent visual conventions to buttress other forms of racialized thought and representation.

It is informative to revisit the "politics by proxy" thesis from this perspective. That hypothesis claims that Soulouque was "blackened" only to "blacken" Napoléon III. It postulates racial imagery as a means to an ostensibly more important political end, located within French domestic politics. Perhaps the most problematic feature of this hypothesis is the extent to which it lets racism off the hook. It ignores the extent to which postcolonial politics had a direct and primary relationship to racial imagery and racist culture. It also ignores the ready market for racial stereotyping and postcolonial *ressentiment*. Regardless of their high-minded motives, publications like *Le Charivari* were, in the end, profit-driven businesses. They were purveyors of a product, and race-based humor seems to have been a product that sold well in metropolitan France and England.

The market for racist culture seemed to be growing steadily in Europe during the mid-nineteenth century. British minstrelsy and racial caricature were early signs of this trend, preceding Cham's drawings by several years. They would be accompanied by the appearance in 1853 of Arthur de Gobineau's highly influential *Essai sur l'inégalité des races humaines* (Essay on the Inequality of Human Races).[50] Gobineau's tract argued for the natural character of white supremacy and the dangers of racial mixing. It purported to establish the superiority of whites across a number of important domains: intellectual capacity, physical strength, and beauty. This was greeted as a landmark in the scientific study of race and was quickly translated into English and German. The racial agenda of the Soulouque caricatures was not as blunt as Gobineau's, but they found a similar market. They were the humorous counterpart to his alleged science. Both were highly successful publishing phenomena and tapped a growing demand for racist cultural products. In this sense, Raybaud, Carlyle, Gobineau, Cham, Daumier, and many others show the formidable amount of energy that was devoted to establishing notions of racial difference and racial inferiority. The Soulouque caricatures contributed to this phenomenon in a primary and direct way, rather than an accidental one.

This reveals the formation of racial imaginaries from a somewhat different angle than is typical. It stands apart from ideas of race as an intellectual tradition or a series of specific institutional innovations. Here we observe the creation of a racial imaginary that is specifically visual. It aims at delegitimation through visual representation and develops a specific visual vocabulary for investing race with various other characteristics. Caricature serves a function in this endeavor that would be difficult to achieve through other genres of visual representation: a kind of slanderous delegitimation through humor that connects individuals, nations, and races with absurdity, animality, and exaggerated personal characteristics.

Delegitimation occurs across a number of registers in this history. It is directed at the person of Soulouque, the nation of Haiti, at postcolonial politics more generally, and it promotes racial thinking and racist culture in the broadest sense. In this sense, the targeted delegitimation of Soulouque as an individual is also abstract and typological. It occurs in a *categorial* sense: whole types of people are subordinated and delegitimated in the national, postcolonial, and racialized imaginaries under construction. Those imaginaries are further attached to other stereotyped caricature images: the indolent tropics with their cattle-like citizens, half-naked savages dancing in the sugarcane, "black Peter exterminating black Paul." The ensemble of this racialized and geographically targeted imagery delegitimizes entire categories of people.

BOTH TRAGEDY AND FARCE

The case of Faustin Soulouque follows twists and turns that are sometimes quite strange yet also strikingly modern. Soulouque was put in office as a political puppet to quell a popular uprising. He was tasked to represent a movement formed out of previously silent subjects. His presidency was engineered as a new way to push them back into silence. Nonetheless, Soulouque succeeded in escaping his controllers and enfranchising the political energies of this silenced subaltern. Unfortunately, what could not be defeated politically was skewered by ridicule. Emperor Soulouque became a transatlantic laughingstock, a victim of emerging global public spheres. As a result, the agrarian revolution that put him in power ended both in tragedy and in farce.

Soulouque stood at an important crossroads in the genealogy of subaltern silence. Ruling a young, postcolonial nation in the 1850s, he was subject to landmark innovations in subaltern subordination. Technologies of print publicity and pictorial representation were brought forward for new purposes in European popular culture. They made it possible to silence people on a massive new scale, both individually and by type, in ways that had not been possible before. Delegitimation was the cultural and political counterpart of those technologies, the thing that gave them traction and political effect on such a broad scale. Those interested in maintaining slavery and racial hierarchy in the United States, Great Britain, and France were early innovators in these techniques.

We typically think of subaltern silence as a matter of being left alone, excluded, pushed to the margins of social existence. Yet here we see something rather different. Here the subaltern subject is brought forward into the spotlight and singled out for attention—a form of excessive visibility similar to the ones we discussed in the maroon slave notices. In this case, the very character of that attention is silencing. This is a new form of subaltern silence in which speech is not literally silenced but stripped of its value. As a result, the subaltern can now be silenced in plain sight, while speaking. This amounts to a new kind of epistemic trap: being visible, audible, and delegitimated at the same time.

Soulouque's fate reveals important things about the problematic of subaltern silence. Regardless of what might disrupt silence and constitute genuine expression on the part of the subaltern, that expression is mediated in many ways. Subaltern speech matters only when it finds an audience, and only when it is valued as important. It depends on conditions of reception, interpretation, and comprehension that are largely set by circumstance and by others. When these conditions are shaped in the wrong ways, silence can be the result, even when the victim seems to be an active, speaking subject.

All of this amounts to a reassertion of subaltern silence in a striking new mode. The full weight of the public sphere is brought into play in novel ways. This constitutes a modernization and radicalization of the project I began tracing in chapter 2. What began as silence brutally imposed through law and violence has slowly changed character. The apparatus of enslavement that maintained silence—irons, chains, guns, Spanish dogs, sexual violation, and gratuitous violence—here gave way to something seemingly more enlightened, more consistent with the self-understanding of a society that had embraced abolition and respected the exchange of ideas in the public sphere. By the time we reach Soulouque, pen and paper are fulfilling those same functions. The printing press turns out to be a more flexible and efficient way to impose silence. It does not need to be deployed on individual bodies to render them silent. It does not need to be present at the site of silencing. It does not operate by rendering people literally mute. Rather, it functions in a new, diffuse modality. The circulation of images can strip people's words and actions of their value. These representations silence in a new way: by delegitimating the speaker, rendering their voice meaningless or of lesser value. The result is silence just as it was under the Code Noir, but of a whole new type. In this new silence, the subaltern speaks without being heard, or without being credible, or without having meaning. The means of imposing such silence are compact and efficient. They can be deployed at great distance, and they masquerade as fun, humor, and critique.

In sum, tragedy and farce describe not only Soulouque's reign but also the mode of subaltern silence that muzzled it. In this novel configuration, farce becomes a potent weapon of delegitimation. It imposes silence on subaltern subjects, deepening the tragedy of their subordination. At this juncture in postcolonial politics, history does not repeat itself first as tragedy, then as farce. Rather, tragedy and farce are merged into a particularly potent combination. These postcolonial developments do not repeat history with faded colorations. Instead, they reflect dynamic innovations that set the stage for forms of subordination in which new, intangible means are weaponized simultaneously to enact both tragedy and farce.

CHAPTER 9

Silent in Plain Sight

We Are All Postcolonial Now

Our investigation proposes to show how . . . the new forms of behavior and the new economically and technologically based creations that we owe to the nineteenth century enter the universe of a phantasmagoria.

—Walter Benjamin

All had an ephemeral existence; all passed before the avid public like a phantasmagoria.

—Panayoty *fils*

The history of subaltern silence reveals a broad tableau of constantly evolving forms. Wrapped into this history is a corresponding array of aporias and problems. Quiet subaltern voices are threaded through the story: the non-voice of maroon slaves, the silence of the tricolor cockade, the stubborn insistence on "three free days," the barely voiced imaginary of agrarian self-sufficiency that appears sporadically after independence. What was the subaltern trying to say? Their message was constantly drowned out by the noise of others. In that light, the conclusions I have drawn about subaltern silence are only one tentative interpretation of this highly fragmentary archive. I have pieced together some provisional suggestions about what that might have been, with all due cautions of overinterpretation and speaking on behalf of those who have been silenced. Navigating a path through the complexities of this story, let me draw together some of its lessons.

THE SHIFTING HORIZON OF MODERNITY

We can now return to that horizon of modernity briefly traversed by Placide Camus, apprentice printer, across the Atlantic and back. Camus experienced the transition between the colonial and the postcolonial in a very direct way. He left France as a junior member of the colonial public sphere and evacuated the Caribbean in haste as that colonial world crumbled in the formation of a new, postcolonial future.

The worlds that preceded and followed Camus were characterized by constantly shifting, permuting forms of subaltern silence. During the colonial era, subalternity was produced in ways both blunt and subtle. Enslaved people were rendered silent through direct and violent means. Prohibitions on speech and action were legally encoded in colonial law. The Code Noir of 1685, for instance, prohibited slaves from assembling or holding office. It specified that their testimony in court could be used only as an aid to remind whites of past events, not as proof that something happened. More broadly, their silence was a corollary to a lack of personhood, implied by a careful, systematic reduction to property. In addition, the specifications of the Code Noir were frequently ignored to enact even more blunt silencing measures: violence, intimidation, and abusive treatment in excess of an already extreme legal code. Enslaved people in Haiti figured as silenced subalterns in the most profound sense.

The development of racial thinking was an important part of this dynamic. In the late seventeenth century we saw the fitful, piecemeal invention of the idea of the *nègre*. It was a complex form of racialization that was intertwined with ideas of devaluation and enslavement in a complex, not fully consolidated way. It was slowly brought into correspondence with and eventually made identical to the category of the enslaved person. Precise forms of racial thinking were by no means necessary to the functioning of the colonial apparatus of violence. As a result, they could develop in a relatively uncoordinated and organic way. Concepts of *esclave* and *nègre* consolidated slowly during this time, sometimes overlapping and sometimes traveling separate paths.

This genealogy started at a point when subaltern silence was rapidly modernizing. In retrospect, we can see the beginnings of more subtle practices of silencing during this time. The loud discourse of the press, legislatures, and other public spheres produced subaltern subjects who were visible but politically and culturally absent. The casual disregard that Moreau de Saint-Méry exhibits towards "the African song" is, in retrospect, an early precursor of what would become silencing through delegitimation a century later. Even the bustling rectitude of the abolitionist public sphere presented problems: its participants tended to talk *about* enslaved people rather than with them. All of this was made possible by European innovations in mass communication, in both a cultural and a technological sense. The public sphere in the age of its technical mediation meant, already in the eighteenth century, print media like books, treatises, pamphlets, and newspapers; physical spaces like salons, parliamentary chambers, and learned societies; and correspondence carried over distance by newly established postal systems.

The first newspaper in Saint-Domingue in 1764 quickly became a tool of subordination. It provided more efficient means for pursuing and repatriating maroon slaves, utilizing the new print public sphere to create excessive visibility for those who had escaped. The silence it articulated was an ambivalent one, however. It gave enslaved people a kind of presence as agents that they otherwise would not have had. To be sure, this presence had a sharp double edge. Maroons were made present as slaves and fugitives, but in the mind of the press-consuming public they thereby acquired an identity as agents repossessing their own freedom and at the same time as threats to the colonial slave economy and the safety of those benefiting from it.

The modern apparatus of publicity served as a tool of subordination, but it also helped to propagate anxieties across the colony and metropole. Fear and paranoia about what *could* happen became a gnawing presence in colonial discourse. Fear of poisoning loomed large at certain points. Paranoia even became self-reflexive as colonial planters imagined what might happen if the apparatus of publicity itself were to be weaponized against them. The ambiguities of the tricolor cockade provoked similar worries, raising the specter of European revolutionary doctrines turned back against the people who had developed them. Fugitivity, poison, publicity, and revolutionary ideas took their turns as objects of fear that provoked concern and incited discourse. These worries all had an epistemic dimension. They were the result of subaltern silence, of the unknowability of the subordinated subjects of colonial exploitation. Silence was instituted as a strategy of subordination, but it also became a source of anxiety because it made subaltern intention and action unknowable.

Here we see the complex, multifaceted character of subaltern silence under colonialism. On one hand, silence was pursued as a primary tool of colonial domination and enslavement. It was encoded into law, backed by a formidable apparatus of legally sanctioned violence as well as violence exceeding the limits of this already brutal code. On the other hand, we also observe subtle cracks in this seemingly airtight system. What most captures one's attention are the ways in which this well-funded, state-backed regime of silencing failed to work, or it encountered difficulties in working. Here we see both silence imposed and silence undermined.

These tensions particularly register in colonialism's material and affective dimensions. Technologies and practices of publicity, the investment and control of enslaved bodies, the spatiality of the plantation and colonial hinterlands, and the unsettling currents of affective problematization all come together in unique ways. Particular regimes of subaltern silence and speech become possible in these conditions.

In keeping with Spivak's cautions, we cannot say that this is a heroic story of subaltern agency. It is not a straightforward example of the "weapons of the weak," of subordinate subjects intentionally subverting the system. Rather, it was a highly ambiguous and complex situation, filled with rumor, supposition, misfired meaning, and occasional openings for limited forms of subaltern action. The subaltern may not have spoken. exactly, but on occasion, consciously or unconsciously, they did exploit the levers of such opportunities to throw the system of subordination off its tracks. This is not really "subaltern agency," but tantalizing hints of a creative exploitation of occasional, unexpected opportunities.

Slavery was gradually stripped away as a legal status in the late eighteenth and early nineteenth centuries, but the public sphere stepped in to generate new forms of subordination. Racialization was still quite present, but it became a broader and more multifarious enterprise. It was propagated through new media and developed into new forms. This in turn allowed it to be put to more precise uses, producing new forms of silence.

In principle, dominant public spheres were accessible to all free people. Thus free *gens de couleur* were able to protest their unfair treatment by colonial whites through various public means: by maintaining a civil profile in organizations like the *maréchausée*, filing lawsuits and *cahiers de doléance* (grievance petitions), and lobbying legislative bodies in France. Within that formal accessibility, however, publicity was effectively partitioned along lines of race and class. *De couleur* citizens faced an undertow of racialization in entering these domains. Their voice was discounted as that of *mulâtres*, a racialized term with subtly demeaning connotations. In retrospect, we can see this kind of racialization as an early form of categorial delegitimation, a way of silencing people by type.

In short, racialization developed in striking new ways during this colonial history. It served to justify the brutal treatment of enslaved people, especially through a slow merging of racial identities with the idea of enslavement itself. Such ideas began to travel more freely with the development of publicity in the late eighteenth century, converging with other techniques of delegitimation and devaluation. By the time slavery was abolished in 1793, all of these could become more generalized phenomena. The new techniques of subordination were well suited for the abstract, intangible character of the public domains in which they now took root.

The Haitian Revolution forced a sudden transition from colonialism to postcoloniality. Placide Camus's hasty departure was emblematic of that transition. He represented a certain version of the colonial public sphere, one with a commitment to open dialogue and the propagation of knowledge as well as great utility for subordination. Saint-Domingan slaves liberated themselves and gave the world remarkably original contributions to political history, seizing the colonial public sphere for their own purposes while Camus and his compatriots took flight.

The horizon of modernity shifted with the achievement of independence. The revolution transformed the status of subaltern subjects in complicated ways. For some it meant entering into the project of European modernity as a new kind of political actor. Both the Haitian Revolution of 1791–1804 and the Liberal Revolution of 1843 followed the emerging script of modern revolution, particularly the modern ethos of public discourse, justification, and the use of print technologies. Here actions were chosen from a set of modern options governing what it means to conduct a revolution. In David Scott's terms, this amounted to kind of self-conscription into modernity.[1] It used the resources of the revolutionary script as an oppositional practice, deploying it against the Europeans and Americans who had pioneered it. Modernity was thereby both embraced and weaponized. As Scott has characterized it, such a choice can be an ambivalent one. It is a freely chosen tactic, but one that bears costs of its own. In this case, embracing modernity also inscribed Haitian revolutionaries in an international order that found new ways to deny them agency and voice.

While modernity was ambivalent for revolutionary elites, it had decidedly negative consequences for others. The revolutionary project of freedom produced new forms of subalternity. While developing a dynamic new political order in dialogue with Euroamerican traditions, this project also silenced new categories of people. They were the formerly enslaved insurgents who made cryptic claims for free time under colonialism, and whose descendants rose up against the mixed-race elites of the Haitian Republic. Their voice emerged briefly during the Haitian Revolution, but it was displaced by other, louder visions. Rural blacks, the underclass of the new national state, were now pushed into new kinds of obscurity, ones that permuted quietly from 1804 to the 1850s. They occasionally attempted to renegotiate the terms of subalternity, surfacing in new political movements, only to be rendered obscure yet again through new means.

SHIFTING PRACTICES OF SILENCING

During this time there was continuous evolution in the techniques of silencing. Old *dispositifs* took on new forms under changing conditions. In the early years of French colonialism, silence was widely imposed through law and violence. The law prohibited speech for certain categories of people, and extralegal violence bluntly silenced them. Even at this time, however, silencing operated through symbolic means in addition to direct, physical ones. Torture, for instance, had subsidiary, symbolic effects in addition to its directly silencing ones. Accounts of torture, passed from person to person, exercised a potent symbolic effect, causing a kind of self-silencing out of fear. In addition, speech extracted through torture also constituted a kind of abstract silencing. When a victim was forced to speak, that coerced speech displaced anything the subaltern may have wanted to say voluntarily. The subaltern said things but did not "speak" in a true sense. This silencing operated in a symbolic register, producing speech that displaced other speech.

Symbolic forms of silencing also occurred through the gradual resignification of particular categories of people. Racialization redescribed enslaved people and thereby helped to silence them. As we have seen, the law was one site in which the gradual consolidation of racial thinking occurred, but it existed within a much broader cultural milieu. In any case, the symbolic dimensions of silencing were supplementary to other, more direct effects of these practices.

This changed with the introduction of formal public spheres in the Caribbean. Now symbolic practices of silencing developed at a rapid rate. We see this almost immediately in the *Gazette de Saint-Domingue* of 1764: maroon slaves were silenced through the excessive visibility made possible by the new medium. At the same time, those very people were reimagined as free agents who have seized their own freedom—what I have referred to as an imaginary unsilencing. They were doubly displaced in this symbolic sense, first as fugitives to be described and recaptured, then as capable and wily adversaries. The transmutation of their identities was silencing in both of these ways, and it occurred through symbolic means.

As the century wore on, symbolic practices of silencing continued to proliferate amid the predominant force of law and violence. Various forms of displacement, interpretation, ventriloquism, substitution, and imaginary unsilencing were all part of this picture. They amounted to a multiplication of new practices of silencing. This very profusion, and the many names I have attached to it, may seem confusing. Indeed, there is an unsatisfying lack of systematicity in this picture. That is because the practices themselves proliferated in such a dynamic way with no single root, cause, or origin. At the same time, the increasingly symbolic character of these new practices did constitute a core of family resemblance. Here silence was produced not by means of prohibition, but by producing and displacing subaltern identities, actions, and voices.

As these practices developed, they also became increasingly autonomous. People could increasingly be silenced in purely symbolic ways that did not ultimately rely on law or violence for their compelling force. Thus we observe a gradual shift of balance, in which the predominant practices of silencing became increasingly abstract and symbolic. This trend took a dramatic turn with the end of colonialism in Saint-Domingue. Colonial law and violence were uprooted, leaving the new forms of silencing in place in a fully autonomous sense.

Above all, we see here a continuous permutation and modernization in the means of producing subaltern silence. Those means were varied, ranging from the agrarian laws of the early 1800s to the noisy publicity of the Liberal Revolution of 1843 to the *politique de doublure* and its inscription into caricature. No single phenomenon underlay these changes, but they were all facilitated by the fact that social existence itself was also becoming more abstract and symbolic.

What it meant to be seen and heard in eighteenth-century society was already changing, and subaltern silence changed with it. Speech, voice, and presence increasingly became mediated through public spheres: to be seen or heard meant to appear in the new media of newspapers, journals, and prints. As a result, people were increasingly silenced by such means as well.

The affective orientation of the former colonizers also changed during this time, accompanied by a shifting relation to subordination and silence. Where white fear, anxiety, and paranoia once problematized subaltern silence and created openings for speech and action, they were now replaced by white spite, *ressentiment*, and parody. These affective investments became the source of new forms of silence.

Delegitimation was the ultimate expression of these phenomena. By the early nineteenth century, powerful means had developed to resignify the value of identities in a very broad sense. This silencing through delegitimation was rooted in earlier practices of resignification, but it acquired a distinctive and autonomous character. Caricature and parody brought that project to a new level. Individuals, nations, races, and the postcolonial world in general could now be silenced even while they spoke. These forms of categorial delegitimation muted entire groups of people by type. Here subaltern silencing entered its fully modern form: abstract, symbolic, and flexible, with substantial powers of resignification and displacement.

SILENT IN PLAIN SIGHT

Faustin Soulouque is a signature example of silencing in the modern age. His case is complex. On one hand he was a political leader with significant powers of violence and oppression. In this sense he seems far from subordinated and far from silent. However, the seeming advantages of his situation were undercut by the steady flow of laughter at his expense. White supremacy and metropolitan domination over the postcolonial world were deployed by new, efficient, and powerful means. The practices of silencing went through their own forms of modernization, becoming more diffuse, abstract, efficient, and ubiquitous. Even a person who commanded an entire country could be subordinated by these techniques. His subordination was not absolute, of course: he still wielded considerable power within his domain. Nonetheless, Soulouque was silenced by this potent set of innovations. His credibility as a leader was enormously damaged by his treatment in the international press, and anything Soulouque might have had to say was drowned out in laughter.

The case of Emperor Soulouque may seem quite singular, the peculiar misfortune of an unusual personality subject to unusual treatment. However, it actually exemplifies broader changes in silencing in the mid-nineteenth century. Soulouque's treatment marks the consolidation of new techniques for producing subaltern silence. The former colonial powers seem not to have lost their zeal for domination as they lost their former colonial possessions. Postcoloniality made old techniques impossible, however, and required new modes of subordination. The techniques of silencing that I have described seem to fit that bill. Subaltern silence now blossomed into an increasingly abstract, virtualized means of postcolonial subordination. Ironically, those techniques worked partly through the intense presence and visibility of the silenced subject.

At this point we arrive at techniques of silencing that should seem familiar because they have become so common. To the extent that they are *not* familiar, that is likely a function of their ubiquity in the contemporary world. This genealogy has critical force to the extent that it brings them back to our attention. In that regard, it is worth focusing on some of the signature features of these developments. They are characterized above all by *abstraction, excessive visibility,* and *pervasiveness*.

Practices of abstraction like those experienced by Soulouque can be quite tangible. For instance, his features were abstracted into a supposedly comic fusion of person and animal, one that used physiognomy to represent confusion, disorientation, and incapacity. Soulouque's actual features were so completely abstracted that they became irrelevant. The portrayals aimed not to represent his actual physical appearance so much as his social meaning.

Such abstraction allowed silencing to occur much less directly than it had in the past. It was now propagated through mass media. This occurred in the highly abstracted form of images, symbols, and the synthesis of new meanings. It reflected the use of representation as a tool of communication. Whereas enslaved people in the colonies had been literally silenced through violence and exclusion, someone like Soulouque could now be silenced by having his words, actions, and identity drained of value. It did not matter what Soulouque said or did, because the weight and meaning of his words were determined by other means. Similarly, Soulouque's struggles to speak had an entirely symbolic importance: they were struggles for legitimacy. This was not the kind of sovereign legitimacy attached to his status as emperor, but rather social and symbolic legitimacy, a struggle to be valued and taken seriously. There was a substantial abstraction away from the specifics of his case. Delegitimation translated fights over Soulouque's voice to an abstract, mediatized domain far from the site of his speech and action.

One of the more striking characteristics of postcolonial silencing is the way it occurs in full view. Emperor Soulouque is again a paradigm case. He was made the center of attention, but in a highly delegitimating way. He was made visible, and *excessively* visible, through ridicule.[2]

In Spivak's work we are used to thinking of the various terms describing the sensorium as roughly interchangeable. People who are silent are also invisible or unintelligible in much the same way: they are not heard; they are not seen; they escape our notice. By the mid-nineteenth century, however, the practices of silencing had become much more complex, and we need an expanded sensorium to describe their new modes of subordination. It involves the simultaneous visibility and silence of subaltern people, where the two descriptors work in complex ways both with and against one another. Intense, excessive visibility allows people like Soulouque to be delegitimated. They are thereby silenced in plain sight in all the multifarious senses of "silence" we have been using. Not only that, but they are silenced *by means of* plain sight, by the excessive visibility to which they are subjected.

In retrospect, we can see more rudimentary uses of excessive visibility emerging during the early years of the colonial public sphere. It is part of a developmental trend that we located all the way back to the maroon notices of the 1760s. Visibility was excessive through the mass distribution of the new newspaper and the careful scrutiny focused on the subjects of those notices. This practice functioned as an extension of slavery law and the punitive apparatus of the state. The excessive visibility of that era individualized fugitives as lawbreaking agents, inscribing them in a punitive apparatus. Publicity sought to make them visible—even excessively visible—as a tool of surveillance and control. It thereby communicated certain subliminal meanings as well, often at cross purposes with one another: both delegitimation on one hand and the unspoken implication that these people were in fact capable agents on the other. They had, after all, chosen to break the law and succeeded at it. In other words, the excessive visibility of the eighteenth century was utilitarian, task-oriented, and individualizing. Its valorizing effects occurred in an odd, unintended way.

The excessive visibility of the 1840s was a wholly different creation. It was not utilitarian and task-oriented but frivolous, resentful, and gratuitous. It was not individualizing, but categorial. It was not partially valorizing, but solely delegitimating. Here whole categories of people were rendered silent in plain sight. Categorial delegitimation employed excessive visibility in entirely new ways, functioning on multiple scales at the same time, from the individual to the national, the racial, and the postcolonial.

In sum, excessive visibility is a technology of silencing that became highly flexible, abstract, and pervasive in its modern form. The arc of its development reveals characteristic changes in the techniques of subordination: an intensification, concentration, and abstraction of subaltern silence.

By the mid-nineteenth century, subordination had entered a new era. The silence experienced by Soulouque was made possible by an alignment of particular registers, categories, and technologies. New developments in print media and print culture made possible new forms of representation. They in turn facilitated a new kind of cultural politics, a delegitimation by category. This politics of categorial delegitimation operated not only at multiple scales but also by attacking different categorial types at each of those levels. Thus race, which had been under formation for several centuries, was painted with the same brush as nation and postcoloniality: all were delegitimated together. The particular elements of this assembly were contingent—a product of historical strands coming together in accidental ways at a particular time. But they served deeper cultural and political purposes connected with the end of colonialism and the aftermath of slavery. All of this formed a rather potent mix of political delegitimation on a grand scale. In sum, these elements created a broad realignment of subaltern silence.

Abstract, excessively visible, pervasive silencing reveals important characteristics of political modernity. It is made possible by modern institutions of publicity. Silences are constantly generated from the apparatus of publicity itself—that which makes things public. In this situation, publicity for some can easily become silence for others. The character of this relationship changes from the mid-eighteenth to the mid-nineteenth century, but the basic fact remains the same. The lesson is that publicity is not universally liberating, and it can easily constitute a means of subordination in ways that are almost undetectable.

This history is important for what it reveals about the developing public spheres of the eighteenth and nineteenth centuries. They were not simply spheres of reasoned discourse, but also technologies of subordination. Thus the view of the public sphere made famous, for instance, by Jürgen Habermas's *Structural Transformation of the Public Sphere* is only part of the story. Another important part is found in the ways that practices of publicity become tools of subordination themselves. In that sense, the genealogy of subaltern silence serves as a counterhistory to Habermas's well known genealogy of the bourgeois public sphere.

This counterhistory becomes even more important in postcoloniality. As colonialism ended, the most brutal forms of subordination became illegal, but subordination was not eliminated. It merely changed form, adopted new technologies, and adapted to changing circumstances. It became much more flexible, efficient, and economical. Such advantages allowed these new techniques to travel widely and become deeply embedded throughout contemporary societies.

IGNORANCE/POWER

The shifting practices of silencing raise the question of how silences are "produced" in the first place. Foucault would normally theorize such phenomena as effects of productive power: power relations constituting the object of genealogy itself. He famously argued that knowledge and power form a complex that he called *savoir/pouvoir*: knowledge/power. The crucial characteristic of this formation is its productive force. It can make up new kinds of people, subjectify individuals into new identities, and create new forms of understanding that have a constituent force on our social world.[3]

The relation between knowledge and power is one of the central themes of Foucault's work. He writes, "The exercise of power perpetually creates knowledge, and inversely, knowledge brings with it effects of power." He continues, "Modern humanism deludes itself in establishing a division between knowledge and power. They are integrated; it is not a matter of dreaming of a moment when knowledge no longer depends on power.... It isn't possible that power is exercised without knowledge, and it isn't possible that knowledge does not give rise to power."[4] Subaltern silence is certainly an effect of power. The question is whether it could be produced in this way. Do knowledges about certain kinds of subjects constitute them *as silent*? Are some subalterns unable to speak because of the effect of knowledge/power? In other words, is Foucault correct to say, "It isn't possible that power is exercised without knowledge?"

The genealogy of subaltern silence suggests that the answer is no, with some important exceptions. Colonial practice was of course heavily populated with *dispositifs* of knowledge and power. Some of those aimed at subaltern silence in a very direct way. In the colonial period, silencing the subaltern was the specific focus of a kind of practical knowledge. It was a knowledge of constraint, intimidation, torture, and violence that aimed at producing docile slaves and pliable colonial subjects. This included legislation, administrative correspondence, pamphlets, how-to guides, and other helpful advice about plantation discipline.[5] Silence was an explicit goal of this literature and the practices it described. In these moments, knowledge/power operated as Foucault described it, producing subordinated subjects.

However, the forms of silence that my genealogy focuses on are primarily *not* those. Such bluntly enacted forms of silence were simple products of power, and they are well understood. Much more interesting are the ineffable, problematic, aporetic silences that sprang up around them. Forms of knowledge aiming at subaltern silence were often destabilized by *other* forms of silence, ones *not* aimed at. They crept onto the scene unbidden and wreaked havoc there. So, for instance, the fearsome figure of the maroon became a destabilizing influence in the colonial order. While attempting to constitute a technology of containment to prevent marronage, colonists created a figure that inhabited their imagination in unexpected ways. This was not a knowledge for producing silent subjects but an unexpected side effect of other knowledges that aimed at other effects. A form of subaltern silence was the outcome, but not the one aimed at. This other silence was a disquieting and destabilizing one.

The same was true of poisoning, where knowledge failed because poison was undetectable. Here the imagination filled in with a productive power of its own, conjuring dangers both real and imaginary, and populating the colony with suspected knowledge and figures who were alleged to hold it. The phantasmatic public sphere and the "Black Jacobins" wearing the tricolor cockade were other examples. They conjured new figures endowed with agency and intent. These were made-up people, produced not by knowledge exactly but by ambiguity, a proliferation of discourse, and the psychic excess of trying to anticipate dangers that may not have existed.

We see a production of new subjectivities in all of these cases. It was not through knowledge, though, but as an accidental effect of knowledge-like mechanisms: attempts to grasp a mysterious and threatening colonial reality with too little comprehension and too little information. The effect was nonetheless productive in Foucault's sense. It produced subjectivities and endowed them with agency and intent. At times those subjectivities were wholly imagined, but their psychic reality was nonetheless a product of power. In these moments, however, there was no knowledge of subaltern silence nor proliferation of discourse around silence that interpellated people into such identities. They were not direct products, but indirect ones—cases in which knowledge was set aside, ignored, or misfired and produced something else. Often the incomprehension, misunderstanding, and disregard of colonists produced such silences. We might better say that these were forms of silence produced by *ignorance* rather than knowledge.

In an insightful reading, Gayatri Spivak points out some of the subtleties in Foucault's notion of knowledge/power. She notes the sense of "can-do"-ness in "*pouvoir*," linked as it is with French terms for being able to do something. There are similar resonances in *savoir*, as we see in expressions like *savoir-faire* and *savoir-vivre*. Read in this way, *savoir/pouvoir* becomes an idea of being able to do something because it makes sense to you. It has a pragmatic, hands-on, "homely" feel.[6]

We might see ignorance operating in a similarly rich way. It is the sense in which one is *not* aware of doing, or knows *not* what one does, and yet in this lack of awareness, does things. It highlights the extent to which *not* knowing often enabled doing in the history we have just examined. Subordination seems to be linked to ignorance in deep ways, at least in this particular history. Here I am reminded of Charles Mills's crystalline formulation:

> One could say, then, as a general rule, that *white misunderstanding, misrepresentation, evasion, and self-deception on matters related to race* are among the most pervasive mental phenomena of the past few hundred years, a cognitive and moral economy psychically required for conquest, colonization, and enslavement. And these phenomena are in no way *accidental*, but *prescribed* by the terms of the Racial Contract, which requires a certain schedule of structured blindnesses and opacities in order to establish and maintain the white polity.[7]

These insights take on a whole new meaning when backgrounded by the genealogy I have just traced. We do not find a productive power developing out of concentrated knowledge about a particular topic—knowledge/power. Instead we find an absence of attention, misplaced attention, or, as Mills so wonderfully puts it, "misunderstanding, misrepresentation, evasion, and self-deception." In the scene I have examined this is not the case only for race, as Mills says, but much more broadly for subaltern subordination. There is an official production of subaltern silence under colonialism, but it morphs into new and less tangible forms as colonialism comes to an end. This continuity of practice, even in a variety of new and different forms, can be explained by the underlying dynamic. It is misunderstanding, misrepresentation, evasion, and self-deception, not simply in the understanding of race, but more broadly in the entire worldview of those who subordinate and create silences. It is testament to the powerful combination of affect and epistemology that we see in colonialism. The imagination can be populated by things largely of its own creation, presumably with roots in reasonable anxieties, given the situation. At the same time, the production of white domination and subaltern silence, in all of its forms, is to some extent fostered by equally potent psychic forces of self-repression, avoidance, and self-deception: believing what is comfortable, convenient, and profitable to believe, without consciously taking note of the self-deception.

In short, the most complex and contemporary forms of subaltern silence result not from knowledge/power, but from what we might call *ignorance/power*. Foucault was correct to point out the many ways in which knowledge and power are intertwined. However, we see here that other arrangements are possible as well. This reversal of his formula shows that considerable power can be exercised through ignorance. Misunderstanding, misrepresentation, evasion, and self-deception can have a constitutive effect. Ignorance can also serve as a condition of possibility for subaltern silence.

With regard to such forms of ignorance, we might talk about a productive power that is frequently accidental in its effects. It is power that aims at other targets and produces collateral damage and unintended results. It is not the kind of productive power that produced "the insane," "the sexual pervert," or "the delinquent." Rather, in the colonial and postcolonial histories I have examined, subjects were sometimes allowed to slip into obscurity through ignorance, and other times given agency in unintended ways.

At times, this ignorance can take the form of substitution. That is to say, silence can be produced through *some other* productive power, a power manufacturing an identity that stands in for, substitutes for, the one silenced. The figure of Soulouque stood in for the real Soulouque, whoever he may really have been. The figure of the maroon stood in for the many people who took fate into their own hands and achieved some measure of silence by actively creating it for themselves. The figure of the poisoner provided a tangible form to fears that were quite intangible, also furnishing a warped justification for working out that surplus anxiety on the captive bodies of other people. The archives of colonialism and postcoloniality are full of such stories. In all of these cases, new kinds of people were summoned into being through ignorance masquerading as knowledge. Those people were constituted as silent.

In many ways, this phenomenon is similar to what George Shulman and Sibylle Fischer describe as disavowal.[8] For each of them, disavowal names various phenomena of refusal or avoidance connected with race and white privilege. Sometimes it can take the form of an intentional refusal to acknowledge white agency in creating racial subordination. Here white agency is disavowed in the sense of refusing to admit what one knows. At other times, however, disavowal can be rooted in complex psychological dynamics of self-deception and avoidance. In these cases, the knowledge of white agency in the maintenance of racial subordination remains invisible to whites themselves. It is disavowed in a complex affective and epistemological sense: an inability to see or understand that which is painful, reprehensible, disturbing, or self-inculpatory. The latter form is the one that would interest us here. It traces much the same phenomenon that Charles Mills notes: white misunderstanding, misrepresentation, evasion, and self-deception on matters related to race.

Shulman's and Fischer's insights help to anchor my own point about subaltern silence. The production of silences can occur in many ways, sometimes intentional and sometimes generated out of complex affective, psychological, and epistemological dynamics. All of this requires great attention to unpack. Therefore, we cannot read subaltern silence out of a theory of power in any simple sense. Subaltern silence does not primarily arise from straightforward practices of subjectification like those described by Foucault, in which types of people are conjured into existence by being postulated as objects of knowledge. It can be produced by such means, to be sure. However, it can also arise from complex, unacknowledged psychological dynamics like those we observe repeatedly in this genealogy. Or it can even arise as collateral damage from other practices: lack of attention can cause unknowable, scarcely observable kinds of people to be buried in silence. In short, this genealogy reveals very different dynamics at work than those theorized by Foucault. Knowledge/power has some role here, but by far the dominant tendency is a contrasting phenomenon, in which complexly layered forms of ignorance produce subaltern silence. We might say, with Foucault, that this is a productive theory of power—but in a new and different sense.

A GENEALOGY OF WHAT IS NOT

For connoisseurs of genealogy, it is worth commenting on several features of the arc I have traced in this book. As I noted in the beginning, a study of subaltern silence entangles itself in profound paradoxes by aiming to research the lives, thoughts, and actions of silenced subalterns. If subaltern silence is a problem of invisibility, of the denial of presence and meaningfulness, then that silence is defined by lack and absence. It is a negativity, a nonobject, something that is problematic precisely because it does not exist. It does not have the same kind of positivity as, say, the human sciences, carceral institutions, sexuality, or even subaltern speech. Rather, the object is defined by negativity, and its history is a genealogy of what is not. This line of investigation has required a number of innovations and traversed some unusual ground.

Writing a history of something that is inaccessible and potentially nonexistent has required a great deal of methodological soul-searching. By definition, the kinds of silences and invisibilities that characterize subalternity force us to proceed with great interpretive care and epistemic subtlety. This must be a delicate excavation, one thoroughly chastened by Spivak's cautions. The objects of this genealogy are by no means clearly given. They are sometimes accessible in indirect ways, however. Thus, I have worked around the edges of some of these silences, observing their effects among those who still had voice, presence, and legitimacy.

In the early, colonial years these effects frequently took an affective form. Silence was a deliberate product of slaveholding policies, but it also had an unnerving effect on its architects. A silent subaltern was also an unknowable, untraceable, and unpredictable one. As a result, we have seen silences register in the fear, anxiety, and paranoia that they provoked among colonial elites. The inferences we can draw on this basis are always quite complex, and often they yield incomplete or indeterminate results. Yet they do give us some picture of the ways people were silenced during this time, as well as the undercurrents of self-critique and resistance that undermined that silence.

The postcolonial era requires similar working around the edges. The upstart movements of "three free days" and the Army of Sufferers seemed to be struggling to express something, but we do not know exactly what. I have used genealogy to stitch together a picture of how they were silenced, observing their interactions with other movements of those who could speak. The case of Emperor Souloque presents its own interpretive complexities. Souloque seems to speak quite loudly, so it requires some attention to note the ways in which he was silenced. Once we identify this silence, however, it becomes clear that we really did *not* know what Souloque was saying while he was speaking so loudly. His speech was silenced in new ways, stripped of meaningfulness and distorted in its reception. This again is a form of silence, one whose edges are registered in the foreign press, in foreign commentaries, and in the reception of his own attempts to speak. These penumbrae of Souloque's silence are highly revealing even if we cannot pierce the veil of that silence itself.

The strategies I have just described do not resolve problems of subaltern silence nor provide conclusive interpretations of them. They are improvisations and approximations, cobbled together to pursue a project that would otherwise remain elusive. What they do reveal is an irreducible ambiguity in these situations. As Spivak has taught us, ambiguity is an inherent characteristic of subaltern silence. The goal must be to locate and describe such ambiguities rather than to master or dissolve them. As a genealogy, this project tries to work with ambiguity and find ways to avoid distorting our interpretation of it.

The genealogy nonetheless gives us a number of concrete insights. It reveals a rather uncoordinated set of techniques that have produced and reconfigured subalternity. Silencing has occurred in a variety of modes: violent suppression, racialization, naïve disregard, puppet government, and the force of ridicule, among others. This is not a linear trajectory so much as a durable tendency that permutes in constantly novel forms. It is a kaleidoscopic story of changes that nonetheless reveal common strands within their very discontinuity.

For instance, the growing transatlantic public sphere is a constant presence and influence on both the Haitian and Liberal revolutions, but in constantly changing ways. It often serves as a venue of self-legitimation for revolutionaries trying to use the tools of modernity to their advantage. However, it also becomes a venue of subordination for rural blacks, including Acaau and his movement. Much the same fate befalls Emperor Soulouque. He attempts to legitimize his rule in the public domain but is sucked into a vortex of delegitimation instead. The new print technologies of the mid-nineteenth century take on an increasing role as conditions of possibility for subordination during his reign. The developing genre of caricature and new lithographic technologies come together in a striking new apparatus of subordination, one made possible by the conjunction of new forms of publicity and political constellations that had not existed in the past.

Such heterogeneity reflects the opportunism involved in subordination. It can be economical to draw on techniques that are already in circulation, but one is not limited to them. Because subordination is typically resisted, there is a tense play of action and reaction that keeps its manifestations on the move. We see that particularly during the colonial phase of this genealogy, when silence plays out across practices of enslavement, marronage, and the fear of poisoners, abolitionists, and Black Jacobins. At the same time, we observe lines of similarity across these differences. The affective character of their traces is one connecting thread. The steady accumulation of racial meanings is another.

Such histories substantiate my reasons for focusing on subaltern silence rather than subaltern "speech." A fine-grained examination of subalternity requires us to trace the ensemble of conditions and practices that produce its characteristic forms and qualities. This includes not just discourse, but institutions, practices, cultures of publicity, and technical developments in the print media of the day. It is a heterogeneous ensemble of practices, arrayed across many different modes of sociability.

Because no one set of practices produces silence, the genealogy of subaltern silence has a rather different character than some of the others we are used to. Silences are produced in a variety of ways, and their manifestations can be quite different from one another. This is what Foucault referred to as "discontinuities, ruptures, gaps, entirely new forms of positivity, and ... sudden redistributions."[9] The very heterogeneity of the practices we have examined implies the absence of any straightforward, linear path of development. Silence is eclectic, episodic, and disunified in its manifestations, so the genealogy must mirror that discontinuity.

In many ways this discontinuity fits the character of Gayatri Spivak's work. Her early concerns about silence focused on the danger of complete oblivion: a subaltern who was invisible or incomprehensible to us because she could not speak. What I have called its pointillism may simply be a reflection of the underlying heterogeneity and discontinuity of silence itself.

Based on my argument in chapter 6, one may be tempted to read "three free days" that way. The agrarian vision that surfaced in a tentative form in the 1790s seems to have been completely pushed aside by later revolutionary projects. It is from this perspective a dead end, a pit of silence that constituted a terminus for a certain sets of perspectives, claims, and beliefs.

Here, however, we see that discontinuity is not the final word. This investigation also suggests long, subterranean lines of continuity within the evolving scene of subordination. "Three free days" had later reverberations among the Army of Sufferers. Each was sidelined by other ideals of freedom and autonomy: the doctrines of the Haitian Revolution in one case and Liberal attempts to "regenerate" Haitian society along French lines in the other. This suggests a more comprehensive project of silence was being enacted during the early nineteenth century, one enacted through similar but not strictly connected means in each case. In my interpretation, the lines of continuity between these two movements suggests the existence of silenced subalterns during the entire time span of this history: a rural population denied voice and presence throughout most of this time.

The interpretive strands connecting three free days with the Army of Sufferers reveal important lessons about the use of genealogy to study subaltern silence. It allows us to make inferences about silences that we could not otherwise observe, revealing longer lines of continuity within a seemingly discontinuous scene. Of course, Spivak's cautions always apply, so we cannot say with certainty that this is the same movement or the same silence. All of my earlier cautions about ambiguity and heterogeneity continue to apply. However, the particular combination of continuities and differences in this case is suggestive.

Genealogy is a valuable tool for surveying this shifting and complex scene. We gain insights into that which has been silenced by patiently observing what is adjacent to it, contiguous with it, or by tracing temporal disruptions and reappearances of subaltern agency. We can track moments of rupture when received orders and meanings are disturbed by the appearance of those heretofore silent or invisible. Here the subaltern becomes politically, culturally, and socially visible in fleeting ways. These forms of working around the edges help us to assemble a critical picture of silence as a historical phenomenon.

This investigation shows that silence is a quite variable phenomenon. Subaltern subjects are not simply silent. Rather, they are silenced in quite varied and heterogeneous senses. Their silencing takes many different forms, occurs in many different registers, and has a complex history. Sometimes silences are produced as a form of diminished presence, sometimes as complete absence. Sometimes the subaltern speaks without being understood, as is the case with "three free days." Sometimes subalterns speak, are heard, and are nonetheless stripped of the legitimacy of having anything important to say, as happened to Haitian Blacks under Soulouque. The challenge is to characterize the complex forms of silence appearing in each situation, being aware of the radical differences between them.

The enslaved people wearing the tricolor cockade were engaging in an intentional act, for instance. They were "speaking" in some important sense; we simply do not know what the content of that message might have been. This is a silence of lost or incomplete meaning. In contrast, the delegitimation experienced by Acaau and the Army of Sufferers and brought to an apogee with Soulouque shows intentional silencing of the subaltern through very different means. Here a subtle devaluation saps subaltern speech and action of its value. It thus operated through mechanisms very different from the others we have examined: subtle symbolic means that rendered whole categories of people absurd and unworthy of attention.

Silence can also be produced in seemingly paradoxical ways, such as when a victory against subaltern silence in turn produces new silences. We observed these dynamics playing out in both the Haitian Revolution and the Liberal Revolution. In these movements, the achievement of freedom and agency for some produced silence for others. In these most modern of revolutions, even the proliferation of discourse produced symmetrical forms of subaltern silence. Discursive ferment around new revolutionary doctrines, with all of the novelty of those creative endeavors, crowded out the ideas, speech, and presence of others. Similarly, the performative enactment of liberty, the actual revolution itself, launched a series of actions and institutional reforms that sidelined others. At the same time, these very forms of silencing produced their own undercurrent of resistance. In the interpretation I have given, the silenced voices of rural blacks resurfaced in anger forty years after the Revolution, revealing the durable dissatisfaction of being silenced by broader currents in world history.

Foucault's work, particularly in the 1980s, often focused on histories of subjectivity: the different qualities and constructions of being a subject. Such an analysis is much more problematic in the study of subaltern silence. Spivak shows how dangerous it can be to interpret subaltern subjectivities. Such interpretations often rearticulate silence in new ways, a phenomenon she refers to as ventriloquism. Similarly, she is also quite cautious about attributions of blocked or frustrated subaltern agency. This would imply that the subaltern subject has an already formed set of intentions and capabilities, and our task is merely to remove blockages from their path. Again, this presupposes a fully formed subject in ways that risk essentialism and overinterpretation.

All this said, subaltern silence does describe a particular way of being a subject. Subaltern subjects are created as silent and as occupying liminal spaces. They are made to be present yet absent, visible yet invisible, observed yet silent. Thus a history of subaltern silence is a history of non-, partial, missed, ambiguous, unknown, or unknowable subjectifications—ambivalent and ultracomplex subjectifications.

Consider, for instance, the way subjectification plays out in Soulouque's turbulent career. Soulouque the person seemed quite different from his representation in the media. Caricatures of him were thoroughly detached from reality, tethered to him by name only. There was, in other words, a doubling of identities: the Soulouque of the caricatures was very different from Soulouque the head of state. The gap between them created a space of silence: the representation of Soulouque passed as the real Soulouque, displacing anything the other may have wanted to say. This is subjectification of a very complex sort. It is not the meticulous training of bodies nor the practices of self-cultivation that Foucault describes. Rather, it is a political legerdemain in which the material Soulouque is pushed aside, displaced, and thereby silenced by representations of him. This is the creation of a subaltern subject, one fabricated through substitution and silencing. Really, subjectification becomes a kind of simulacrum in this case; the "actual" subject is someone else, and he is significantly impacted—resubjectified—by the free-floating double that circulates in the media.

In short, the idea of subjectification has some interesting things to say about subaltern silence, but largely because it becomes such a fraught category. Subaltern silence significantly problematizes the entire idea of the "hermeneutics of the subject" as a genealogical enterprise, at least in the highly problematic cases we are examining.[10] These considerations move us away from a focus on subject formation as central to the enterprise. We are not concerned with who is subaltern and what they might say, but rather the conditions under which such agency is precluded or silenced. This is not a history of subjectivities or subjectifications, but of the epistemic conditions of possibility for speaking and acting, and equally importantly, of the conditions of *impossibility* for doing so.

One of the more surprising aspects of this genealogy is the way it occasionally inverts the significance of subaltern silence. We have good reasons to think that maroons and those demanding "three free days" during the Haitian Revolution were actively *seeking* silence. Each in its way reflects a desire to be left alone. In that case, the subaltern had no reason to explain or justify, but only to withdraw. It had nothing to signify. The message may have been "we have nothing to say to you." This gives us a rather different view of subaltern silence. Here it is an achievement rather than a form of epistemic violence. This suggests that subaltern silence might sometimes function as an important improvisation within otherwise unfavorable circumstances, a way of navigating subordination in a colonial context.

Foucault's genealogies tend to be histories of texts. They trace evolutions in thought: how our notions of subjectivity, discipline, madness, the medical gaze, and the human sciences have changed over time. Of course, it is true that the texts he most revels in are ones *about* material practices. These are ones describing the means of spatialization in training, the care of the self, how to design the ideal prison, and so on. They are nonetheless texts reflecting *on* such practices, and thus remain one step removed from practice itself.

The genealogy of subaltern silence taps a somewhat different archive. It is one that is more directly *material* and *performative*. We have been looking at material practices in the very direct sense of following the traces of actual revolutions, suspected insurgencies, and infiltrations. There is a strong performative element here in the many practices that produce meaning, contain it, or propagate it. Among these are the success of people who have performatively seized their own freedom or succeeded in establishing their own regime of silence, people who engage in material practices that seem to have symbolic importance, and even texts that directly enact subordination and silence.

Here we see that such materialities and performativities do not always have a clear meaning, or perhaps, that we cannot necessarily access their meaning in a clear and determinate way. This in itself can be a form of silence. There is, in this sense, a dense set of connections between subaltern silence, materiality, and performativity. I believe this is very much the same phenomenon that Banu Bargu and Stacey Liou have observed, for instance, in silent protest movements.[11] These are contemporary examples of silent, symbolic, bodily protest that are both performative and semantically underdetermined. They examine practices that seem to telegraph some meaning *within* or *through* silence, but what that meaning is, exactly, remains ambiguous.

To say that the archive of subaltern silence is frequently material and performative is not to make those silences positive phenomena, of course. They remain nonobjects defined by absence. Positivity, materiality, and performativity instead lie in the practices surrounding them, the ones we have access to. The genealogy of subaltern silence relies on an interpretation of this material to make indirect inferences about that which is missing. In this sense and the many others described here, it is a rather unusual sort of genealogy.

WILD COUNTERNARRATIVES

The genealogy of subaltern silence follows a path rather different from those traveled by either Spivak or Foucault. We might adopt Spivak's observation in this regard: "This picture is outside of Foucault's beautifully organized system, so beloved by the disciplines, but also 'inside,' for this is the wild counternarrative ... that keeps the story of efficiency and leniency going in the metropolis."[12] The picture I have presented is indeed outside of Foucault's beautifully organized system, though it describes a counternarrative that is vital to understanding the developments he studied. It is also, I should add, rather different from Spivak's artfully disordered one.

This genealogy has tacked back and forth between the metropolitan world that Foucault documented and the colonial world that he ignored. The tacking in itself shows how inseparable one is from the other. The kind of intellectual activity that Foucault celebrated in Europe had colonial correlates. The Cercle des Philadelphes constituted itself as a scientific society in the colonies, similar in form and content to the circles traveled by Condillac, Diderot, Quesnay, and the other Enlightenment figures that fascinated Foucault. The Enlightenment intellectuals of the Classical Age were busy arguing over the justice of colonialism and propagating their ideas in transcontinental public spheres, while that very colonial economy funded their intellectual and political pursuits. The new periodical press had a vital importance to the development of European culture in its Classical Age—which strangely, Foucault never took note of—and it also had a pivotal force of constituting reality in the colonies.[13] Despite these tight entwinements, Foucault always wrote histories of European practices without acknowledging their colonial involvements.

This book treats metropole and colony as an intimately interconnected pair. I have tried to highlight the important relations of thought and practice between the two. This includes much that is not the normal concern of genealogy: influence at a distance between groups across physical space, mediated by extended public spheres, feedback relations between elite and subaltern in both directions, stark cultural fissures that lead to misunderstandings, and constituent misinterpretations. It surveys transatlantic relationships and decouplings on multiple scales. It exposes regional, hemispheric, and transcontinental dimensions of subaltern silence. It follows the transmutation of institutions, ideas, technologies, and practices as they are transmitted from metropole to periphery and vice versa.

Such an approach captures the spatial and material character of subordination, its institutional and social mediation, and its changing character over time. It throws into relief the complex texture of action and reaction that creates forms of subordination. This includes the subtle epistemological means through which they are articulated: the connections of thought, discourse, and exchange between Europe and its colonies. In short, it provides a detailed look at the complex nexus of discursive and material practices that create subaltern silence.

This genealogy of a nonobject takes us quite far beyond Foucault in other ways as well. It explores the conditions under which silences occur. It points toward a horizon beyond which things disappear, warning us that the practices creating such a horizon are particularly dangerous. As such, this genealogy attacks the apparatus of power. It does not "desubjugate" by telling the truth of some silent subaltern. Rather, it traces out the conditions under which power can enact silence, exposing and destabilizing those conditions.

This picture also proceeds in terms quite different from the artful disorder of Gayatri Spivak's approach. She has done us the great service of highlighting the aporetic character of subalternity. She shows how many traps lie in the path of public visibility and how difficult—or impossible—it can be to navigate such paths. Spivak herself is clear about the desirability of subaltern speech, but she is also wary of declaring victory or claiming to discover any magic formulas of success.

I have embraced the central insights of Spivak's project while also expressing reservations about the way it has been carried out. She tends to limit her attention to the particular aporias faced by particular individuals or situations. This has the advantage of specificity, but it has the corresponding disadvantage of being limited to exemplary instances. Rather than engage in a pointillist examination of individual cases, I have tried to trace broad lines of change in the creation of subaltern silence. I have tried to do this by using Foucault's fertile intuitions about how to write a history of the present while trying to work around some of the problems inherent in such a project.

In essence, Spivak accuses Foucault of a latent romanticism combined with epistemic overreach in trying to liberate subaltern voices. I have tried to walk a middle line between them here, following out the traces of subaltern silence without hypostatizing any subject or attributing agency to it. When we turn to Foucault's more methodological insights, we see the great value of genealogy for furthering this kind of project. Its historical sweep provides us with a much richer analysis of subaltern silence. If carefully crafted, it need not totalize nor essentialize subaltern speech. Nor is it necessarily associated with romantic tendencies to liberate subaltern agency. Instead, it can reveal the fine texture of subaltern silence over an extended span of time, highlighting interconnected appearances and disappearances, continuities and discontinuities, and the changing character of silence and subordination. There is no developmental logic in this story, but it does reveal important patterns. At the same time, it also makes visible some of the striking innovations in such histories: the creative cosmopolitanism of the Liberal constitution of 1843, for instance, as well as the equally unanticipated response of the Army of Sufferers. Here we see point and counterpoint, action and reaction, the production of a silenced population and its performative seizure of agency. The haphazard and contingent connections between these moments can only be illuminated by observing their complex historical dynamics. In this sense, Spivak may be correct to curb some of Foucault's cryptoromanticism, but his genealogical insights, properly reconfigured, reveal a great deal that we might otherwise miss.

WE ARE ALL POSTCOLONIAL NOW

The history of subaltern silence is very much a history of our present moment. It is still with us today in many ways, as damning images circulate and condition our perceptions of particular people and their words and actions. In this sense, Emperor Soulouque turns out not to be an aberration but an early victim of something that would become ubiquitous in our era. His seemingly unique treatment migrated into new registers and categories over subsequent decades. Today's world is populated by Soulouques of all kinds: people whose identity is devalued by the circulation of images and imaginaries, especially those mediated by modern tools of communication. As diasporas and displacements have spread people around the globe, geographical and spatial forms of subordination have been replaced by other mechanisms not dependent upon location or spatial control. Diffuse, despatialized mechanisms of categorial delegitimation work quite well in this regard. They have surgical accuracy, regardless of the location of their target. The technology of the disparaging image—in the very broadest sense of "image"—proves a valuable tool for the control of subordinate peoples. This is particularly the case when such identities are understood in typological terms, be it by region, subculture, nation, or race. The signature feature of this treatment is a differential silencing, one that can occur even while a person is acting or speaking. The phenomenon Soulouque acutely experienced was the pervasive delegitimation of what he had to say, the silencing of those words even while audible, the devaluation of his self-representations even while visible. This silencing in plain sight was a slowly developing innovation of the colonial and postcolonial world, and it has diffused throughout modern societies in its mature form.

Foucault liked to talk about a surveillance society that had become broadly generalized into a carceral continuum.[14] We could talk similarly about a society of diffuse and pervasive delegitimation. This would amount to the transformation of caricature into more generalized logics of subordination.

I have been arguing, in agreement with many others, that we cannot separate metropolitan and colonial histories. This is particularly true at the present moment. We often have the idea that the metropole is still metropole, while the former colonies are "postcolonial." However, this idea is mistaken. We see here that the postcolonial lies at the heart of contemporary experience. It turns out that we are all postcolonial now. That means, in part, that practices of colonial subordination and their postcolonial descendants traveled freely when liberated from colonial existence. Those techniques found use in a wide variety of contexts, including in the former metropole. Subaltern silence continues to mark out distinctions between "core" and "periphery" in the global economy, tracing the lines of old colonial distinctions in new ways.[15] However, it also does much more than that, both on a local and global scale.

This history teaches us that we cannot treat subalternity in any simple and straightforward way. It is a plastic, changing status that is not always evident to us. Silence can take many different forms across many different registers. Similarly, silenced and invisible peoples sometimes manifest themselves in surprising ways. The challenge is to trace out the conditions of that silence and to be alert for manifestations we are currently missing.

All of this poses the challenge that we, now, are ignorant of silences in our midst. They are by definition that which is beyond notice, an ever-present possibility that remains out of reach in important ways. The critical insights I have assembled here may allow us to push back the horizon of such silences and find new ways to discern them. We must be aware, however, that they remain always... elusive.

Notes

1. THE SOUNDS OF SILENCE

1. Médéric-Louis-Elie Moreau de Saint-Méry, *Description topographique, physique, civile, politique et historique de la partie française de l'isle Saint-Domingue* (1797), 3 vols. (Saint Denis: Société Française d'Histoire d'Outre-Mer, 2004), 1:67.
2. All translations are mine unless otherwise noted.
3. Julius von Schlosser, *Art and Curiosity Cabinets of the Late Renaissance*, trans. Jonathan Blower (Los Angeles: Getty Research Institute, 2021).
4. Ralph Ellison, *Invisible Man*, 2nd ed. (New York: Vintage Books, 1995), 3.
5. Jürgen Habermas, *The Structural Transformation of the Public Sphere: An Inquiry Into a Category of Bourgeois Society*, trans. Thomas Burger with Frederick Lawrence (Cambridge, MA: MIT Press, 1989).
6. Dumas Malone, ed., *Dictionary of American Biography* (New York: Scribner, 1934), 7:156–57.
7. Collection Moreau de Saint-Méry, sous-série F3, Archives Nationales d'Outre-Mer, Aix-en-Provence, France.
8. Julius S. Scott, *The Common Wind: Afro-American Currents in the Age of the Haitian Revolution* (London: Verso, 2018); James Scott, *Weapons of the Weak: Everyday Forms of Peasant Resistance* (New Haven, CT: Yale University Press, 1985).
9. Michel-Rolph Trouillot, *Silencing the Past: Power and the Production of History* (Boston: Beacon Press, 1995).
10. Gayatri Chakravorty Spivak, *A Critique of Postcolonial Reason: Toward a History of the Vanishing Present* (Cambridge, MA: Harvard University Press, 1999), 266–67.
11. Spivak, *Critique of Postcolonial Reason*, 269, emphasis in the original.
12. Spivak, *Critique of Postcolonial Reason*, 271–74.
13. Spivak, *Critique of Postcolonial Reason*, 257.
14. Spivak, *Critique of Postcolonial Reason*, 266–67.
15. Spivak, *Critique of Postcolonial Reason*, 274–79, quote at 279.
16. Michel Foucault, *"Society Must Be Defended": Lectures at the Collège de France 1975–1976* (New York: Picador, 2003).
17. Carl Schmitt, *The Concept of the Political*, expanded ed., trans. George Schwab (Chicago: University of Chicago Press, 2007). Ladelle McWorter's discussion of this material is

particularly insightful; see *Racism and Sexual Oppression in Anglo-America: A Genealogy* (Bloomington: Indiana University Press, 2009).

18. Foucault, *"Society Must Be Defended,"* 34, 45–46.
19. Ann Laura Stoler, *Race and the Education of Desire: Foucault's* History of Sexuality *and the Colonial Order of Things* (Durham, NC: Duke University Press, 1995); see also Pheng Cheah, "Biopower and the New International Division of Reproductive Labor," in *Can the Subaltern Speak? Reflections on the History of an Idea*, ed. Rosalind Morris (New York: Columbia University Press, 2010), 179–212.
20. Michel Foucault, *The History of Sexuality, Volume 1: An Introduction* (New York: Vintage Books, 1980), 26, 54, 64, 117–19, 122–27, 136–37, 147–50.
21. Arlette Farge, *The Allure of the Archives* (New Haven, CT: Yale University Press, 2013), 94.

2. SILENCE AS AN ACHIEVEMENT

1. Orlando Patterson, *Slavery and Social Death: A Comparative Study*, 2nd ed. (Cambridge, MA: Harvard University Press, 2018).
2. Laurent Dubois, "Translator's Introduction," in Achille Mbembe, *Critique of Black Reason* (Durham, NC: Duke University Press, 2017), xiv.
3. Franz Fanon, *Peau noir, masques blancs* (Paris: Seuil, 1952), 90. My translation. The published translation of this passage remains entangled in the same problems Dubois describes: "*Maman*, look, a Negro; I'm scared!" *Black Skin, White Masks*, trans. Richard Philcox (New York: Grove, 2008), 91.
4. E.g., Aimé Césaire, *Cahier d'un retour au pays natal* (Paris: Presence Africaine, 1983); Léopold Sédar Senghor, "Negritude: A Humanism of the Twentieth Century," in *The Africa Reader: Independent Africa*, ed. Wilfred Cartey and Martin Kilson (New York: Vintage, 1970), 179–92; see also Gary Wilder's wonderful history, *Freedom Time: Negritude, Decolonization, and the Future of the World* (Durham, NC: Duke University Press, 2015).
5. Achille Mbembe, *Critique de la raison nègre* (Paris: Découverte, 2013), 67.
6. Gayatri Chakravorty Spivak, "Can the Subaltern Speak?" (1988), in *Can the Subaltern Speak? Reflections on the History of an Idea*, ed. Rosalind Morris (New York: Columbia University Press, 2010), 237–91, at 238.
7. Louis XIV de France, *Edit du roy, touchant la police des isles de l'Amerique françoise, du mois de mars 1685*. Reprinted in René-Josué Valin, *Nouveau commentaire sur l'ordonnance de la marine, du mois d'août 1681*, 2 vols. (La Rochelle: Mesnier, 1760), 1:405–9.
8. Michel Foucault, *Security, Territory, Population: Lectures at the Collège de France 1977–1978*, trans. Graham Burchell (New York: Palgrave, 2007), 45, 110, 278, 312–54.
9. Louis XV de France, *Édit du roi, touchant l'état et la discipline des esclaves nègres de la Louisiane, donné à Versailles au mois de mars 1724* (Paris: Imprimerie royale, 1724).
10. Louis XIV de France, *Le code noir ou edit du roy, servant de reglement pour le gouvernement et l'administration de justice et la police des isles françoises de l'Amerique, et pour la discipline et le commerce des negres et esclaves dans ledit Pays, donné à Versailles au mois de mars 1685* (Paris: Claude Girard, 1735).
11. "Memoire sur les deux questions suivantes . . . ," May 10, 1742, Archives Nationales d'Outre-Mer, Aix-en-Provence (hereafter ANOM), and "Memoire questions proposées, 1. Si les negres doivent etre reputés meubles . . . ," May 10, 1742, both F3/90/57.

12. E.g., "Extrait d'un rapport fait au conseil-supérieure de la Guadeloupe..." 1758, ANOM F3/90/75; "Propositions de M. Nadau et Marin, pour la reforme...du Code Noir...." 1758, ANOM F3/90/85.
13. Charles Mills, *The Racial Contract* (Ithaca, NY: Cornell University Press, 1997), 73-74.
14. Michel Foucault, *Discipline and Punish: The Birth of the Prison*, trans. Alan Sheridan (New York: Vintage Books, 1995), 32-69.
15. Gabriel Debien, "Le marronage aux Antilles françaises au XVIIIe siècle," *Caribbean Studies* 6, no. 3 (1966): 3.
16. Anon., "De l'introduction des negres à St. Domingue, de leurs révoltes, de leur traitement...," n.d., ANOM F3/94/1.
17. The dimensions of this idea are richly explored in Neil Roberts, *Freedom as Marronage* (Chicago: University of Chicago Press, 2015).
18. Séguy de Villevaleix to the Comte de Polastron, September 31, 1790, reprinted in Gabriel Debien, *Études antillaises XVIIIe siècle* (Paris: Colin, 1956), 170.
19. Willy Apollon, *Le vaudou: Un espace pour les "voix"* (Paris: Galilée, 1976), 59-67.
20. David Geggus, *Haitian Revolutionary Studies* (Bloomington: Indiana University Press, 2002), 81-92.
21. Jean Casimir, *La culture opprimée* (Delmas, Haiti: Lakay, 2001), 110-20; Carolyn Fick, *The Making of Haiti: The Saint Domingue Revolution from Below* (Knoxville: University of Tennessee Press, 1990), 50-52.
22. Bryan Edwards, *Observations on the Disposition, Character, Manners, and Habits of Life, of the Maroon Negroes of the Island of Jamaica: And a Detail of the Origin, Progress, and Termination of the Late War Between Those People and the White Inhabitants*, in *The Proceedings of the Governor and Assembly of Jamaica, in Regard to the Maroon Negroes* (London: Stockdale, 1796); Alvin O. Thompson, *Flight to Freedom: African Runaways and Maroons in the Americas* (Kingston, Jamaica: University of the West Indies Press, 2006).
23. Saidiya Hartman, *Scenes of Subjection: Terror, Slavery, and Self-Making in Nineteenth-Century America* (Oxford: Oxford University Press, 1997), 51.
24. Julius S. Scott, *The Common Wind: Afro-American Currents in the Age of the Haitian Revolution* (London: Verso, 2018), 7-15.
25. Édouard Glissant, *Poetics of Relation*, trans. Betsy Wing (Ann Arbor: University of Michigan Press, 1997), 111-20, 189-94.
26. Brandeis's phrase is "the right to be let alone." *Olmstead v. United States* 277 US 438 (1928), quotation at 478.
27. E.g., ANOM F3/91/101, 141; F3/94/18, 19, 29, 43, 51, 56, 60, 71, 76, 78, 87, 88, 110, 112, 116, 118, 136, 138, 139, 140, 142, 145, 170.
28. Grégoire Chamayou, *Les chasses à l'homme: Histoire et philosophie du pouvoir cynégétique* (Paris: La Fabrique, 2010), 65-113; Patrick Chamoiseau, *L'esclave vieil homme et le molosse* (Paris: Gallimard, 1997); Sara E. Johnson, *The Fear of French Negroes: Transcolonial Collaboration in the Revolutionary Americas* (Berkeley: University of California Press, 2012), 21-48; Stewart R. King, "The Maréchaussée of Saint-Domingue: Balancing the Ancien Régime and Modernity," *Journal of Colonialism and Colonial History* 5, no. 2 (2004), https://muse.jhu.edu/article/173267; Marcus Rainsford, *An Historical Account of the Black Empire of Hayti: Comprehending a View of the Principal Transactions in the Revolution of Saint Domingo; with its Antient and Modern State* (London: Albion Press, 1805), 420-29; Yvan

Debbasch, "Le marronnage: Essai sur la désertion de l'esclave antillais, seconde partie, La société coloniale contre le marronnage," *L'année sociologique* 13 (1962): 117-95.
29. Louis XIV de France, *Edit du roy 1685*, in Valin, *Nouveau commentaire sur l'ordonnance de la marine*, 1:405-9, esp. §38; Joseph Elzéar Morénas, *Précis historique de la traite des noirs et de l'esclavage colonial: Contenant; l'Origine de la traite, ses progrès, son état actuel, et un exposé des horreurs produites par le despotisme des colons* (Paris: Firmin Didot, 1828).
30. "Extrait de la Lettre du Ministre à M. Bégon, 27 mai 1705," ANOM F3/90/19.
31. "A la Martinique 8 Oct 1741..." ANOM F3/90/41.
32. "Propositions de M. Nadau et Marin, pour la reforme...du Code Noir...." ANOM F3/90/85.
33. Foucault, *Discipline and Punish*, 32-69.
34. Louis de Jaucourt, "Supplice," in Denis Diderot et al., *Encyclopédie, ou dictionnaire raisonné des sciences, des arts et des métiers, par une société de gens de lettres*, 28 vols. (Geneva, 1754-72), 15:674.
35. Jean Fouchard, *The Haitian Maroons: Liberty or Death*, trans. A. F. Watts (New York: Blyden, 1981), 63-68.
36. Saidiya Hartman, *Scenes of Subjection: Terror, Slavery, and Self-Making in Nineteenth-Century America* (Oxford: Oxford University Press, 1997), 17-23.
37. "Interrogatoire d'un negre de l'habitation de la dame de l'isle Adam, du 25 janvier 1775," ANOM F3/90/160. The interrogator accurately states section 38 of the Code Noir.
38. Benedict Anderson, *Imagined Communities: Reflections on the Origin and Spread of Nationalism*, rev. ed. (London: Verso, 1991), 32-36.
39. *Gazette de Saint-Domingue* (Cap Français), February 8, 1764, 16.
40. *Virginia Gazette* (Williamsburg, VA), October 15, 1736, 4.
41. *Gazette de Saint-Domingue*, February 15, 1764, 26-27; February 22, 1764, 34.
42. I am grateful to Jason Frank for suggesting this formulation.
43. *Affiches américaines*, October 15, 1783; November 19, 1783; December 3, 1783; February 4, 1784. See Fouchard, *The Haitian Maroons*, 9-10.
44. Alexandre-Stanislas, Baron de Wimpffen, *Voyage à Saint-Domingue, pendant les années 1788, 1789 et 1790* (Paris: Cocheris, 1797), 2:86-89; Hartman, *Scenes of Subjection*, 79-86.
45. "Extrait de la lettre du Ministre...," June 24, 1727, ANOM F3/91/94. See also ANOM F3/91/93, 95, 96, 99, 123, 125; Joan Dayan, *Haiti, History, and the Gods* (Berkeley: University of California Press, 1995), 189-99, 225-26, 237-40.
46. Oskar Negt and Alexander Kluge, *Public Sphere and Experience: Analysis of the Bourgeois and Proletarian Public Sphere* (London: Verso, 2016), 79.
47. Médéric-Louis-Elie Moreau de Saint-Méry, *Description topographique, physique, civile, politique et historique de la partie française de l'isle Saint-Domingue* (1797), 3 vols. (Saint Denis: Société Française d'Histoire d'Outre-Mer, 2004), 1:351-54. See M.-A. Ménier and G. Debien, "Journaux de Saint-Domingue," *Revue d'histoire des colonies* 36 (1949): 424-27; Adolphe Cabon, *Un siècle et demi de journalisme en Haïti* (Worcester, MA: American Antiquarian Society, 1940), 6.
48. The full title of the *Journal Économique* reveals much about its editor's intentions: *Journal économique, ou Mémoires, notes et avis sur les arts, l'agriculture, et tout ce qui peut avoir rapport à la santé ainsi qu'à l'augmentation des biens de famille*, Paris, 1751-1772. See Steven Kaplan,

Bread, Politics, and Political Economy in the Reign of Louis XV (The Hague: Martinus Nijhoff, 1976), 706.
49. *Gazette du commerce* (Paris), prospectus, January 1, 1763, 2.
50. *Gazette du commerce* (Paris), January 31, 1763, 65-72.
51. Jeremy Popkin, *Revolutionary News: The Press in France, 1789–1799* (Durham, NC: Duke University Press, 1990).
52. Data from the French Atlantic History Group, McGill University, http://www.marronnage.info/en/.
53. Phillip Curtin, *The Atlantic Slave Trade: A Census* (Madison: University of Wisconsin Press, 1969), 79.
54. *Follicules caraïbes* (Guadeloupe), no. 8, February 1785, ANOM F3/94/166.
55. E.g., *Gazette de la Guadeloupe*, May 29, 1788, 90.
56. Johnson, *Fear of French Negroes*, 12–13.
57. *Affiches américaines*, March 17, 1787, 138.
58. Michel-René Hilliard d'Auberteuil, *Considérations sur l'état présent de la colonie française de Saint-Domingue: Ouvrage politique et législatif* (Paris: Grangé, 1776).
59. See "Moreau de Saint-Méry, Médéric-Louis-Elie," in *Dictionary of American Biography*, ed. Dumas Malone, (New York: Scribner, 1934), 7:156-57.
60. Moreau de Saint-Méry, *Description*.
61. Moreau de Saint-Méry, *Description*, 1131–36, quote at 1135.
62. Moreau de Saint-Méry, *Description*, 1133. Emphases in the original.
63. See Dena Goodman, *The Republic of Letters: A Cultural History of the French Enlightenment* (Ithaca, NY: Cornell University Press, 1994).
64. ANOM F3/81/128.
65. *Follicules caraïbes* (Guadeloupe), February 1785, 61–62, ANOM F3/94/166; see Michel Foucault, *The Order of Things: An Archaeology of the Human Sciences* (New York: Vintage Books, 1994), esp. 56-58.
66. ANOM F3/81/130. Cf. ANOM F3/81/131, 132, 134, 138, 140, 141, 143, 145, 146.
67. Karl Marx and Frederick Engels, *The German Ideology, Part One with Selections from Parts 2 and 3 and Supplementary Texts*, ed. C. J. Arthur (New York: International Publishers, 2016), 64-68.
68. Antoine de Labarre de Beaumarchais, "Lettre cinquième," in *Amusements littéraires* (La Haye: van Duren, [1729] 1741), 3:60-65.
69. See Jean-Baptiste Michel et al., "Quantitative Analysis of Culture Using Millions of Digitized Books," *Science* 331, no. 6014 (January 14, 2011): 176–182. This tendency also holds of the term "*marron*," but that is hard to examine at an aggregate level because of confusion over multiple meanings. As a noun "*marron*" can mean either "fugitive" or "chestnut," as an adjective either "escaped" or "chestnut colored." To look for changing tendencies, therefore, one must examine each occurrence of the word. "Marronage" does not have this polyvalence, a suggestive fact in itself.
70. There is a steady increase of attention to "*marronage*" from 1790 to 1802. While the overall increase is striking, it is important to note that its absolute magnitude is not. The peak of attention to "*marronage*" in 1802 is constituted by forty-six uses of the term in sixteen different publications. Compare that to 17,254 uses of "*amour*" in 1,211

different publications during the same year. In other words, the French-speaking public was not transfixed by *marronage* to anything like the extent it was by *amour*.
71. Michel Foucault, *The History of Sexuality, Volume 1: An Introduction* (New York: Vintage Books, 1980), 17.
72. Foucault, *History of Sexuality, Volume 1*, 23.
73. Michel Foucault, *Lectures on the Will to Know: Lectures at the Collège de France 1970–1971*, trans. Graham Burchell (New York: Palgrave Macmillan, 2013); *On the Government of the Living: Lectures at the Collège de France 1979–1980*, trans. Graham Burchell (New York: Palgrave Macmillan, 2014); *Wrong-Doing, Truth-Telling: The Function of Avowal in Justice* (Chicago: University of Chicago Press, 2014).
74. Le Comte de la Lauzerne, Gouverneur de Saint-Domingue, au Ministre des Colonies, September 8, 1786, ANOM C9A/85. Quoted in Apollon, *Le vaudou*, 62-63.
75. David Geggus, "Marronage, Voodoo, and the Saint Domingue Slave Revolt of 1791," *Proceedings of the Meeting of the French Colonial Historical Society* 15 (1992): 22-35.
76. See Foucault, *Discipline and Punish*, 3-6.
77. "Propositions de M. Nadau et Marin, pour la reforme…du Code Noir.…" 1758, ANOM F3/90/85.
78. See Kevin Olson, *Imagined Sovereignties: The Power of the People and Other Myths of the Modern Age* (Cambridge: Cambridge University Press, 2016), 94-96.
79. See Michel Foucault, *The Use of Pleasure: The History of Sexuality, Volume Two* (New York: Vintage, 1986), 10-24; Michel Foucault, "Polemics, Politics, and Problematizations: An Interview with Michel Foucault," in Foucault, *Ethics: Subjectivity and Truth, Essential Works of Foucault, 1954–1984*, ed. Paul Rabinow (New York: New Press, 1997), 111-19; Colin Koopman, *Genealogy as Critique: Foucault and the Problems of Modernity* (Bloomington: Indiana University Press, 2013), 87-153; Isabelle Stengers, "Putting Problematization to the Test of Our Present," *Theory, Culture, and Society* 38, no. 2 (2021): 71-92; Olson, *Imagined Sovereignties*, 168-70.
80. Moreau de Saint-Méry, *Description*, 1131-34.
81. Particularly eloquent in this regard are Chamayou, *Les chasses à l'homme*, chaps. 5 and 6; and Chamoiseau, *L'esclave vieil homme et le molosse*.
82. See Albert Hirschman, *Exit, Voice, and Loyalty* (Cambridge, MA: Harvard University Press, 1970).
83. Judith Butler, *Gender Trouble: Feminism and the Subversion of Identity* (New York: Routledge, 1999), esp. 163-80; *Bodies That Matter: On the Discursive Limits of "Sex"* (New York: Routledge, 1999).
84. James Scott, *Weapons of the Weak: Everyday Forms of Peasant Resistance* (New Haven, CT: Yale University Press, 1985).

3. UNSETTLING SILENCES

1. Médéric-Louis-Elie Moreau de Saint-Méry, *Loix et constitutions des colonies françoises de l'Amérique sous le vent*, 6 vols. (Paris: Privately printed, 1784), 1:371-75.
2. *Edit du roy, touchant la police des isles de l'Amerique françoise. Du mois de mars 1685*, later republished as *Le code noir ou edit du roy, servant de reglement pour le gouvernement et l'administration de justice et la police des isles françoises de l'Amerique, et pour la discipline et le*

commerce des negres et esclaves dans ledit pays, donné à Versailles au mois de mars 1685 (Paris: Claude Girard, 1735).

3. "Du 7 jan 1712," signé M. de Vaucresson, Archives Nationales d'Outre-Mer, Aix-en-Provence, France (hereafter ANOM), F3/88/204; "Du 22 may 1712," signé M. de Vaucresson, ANOM F3/88/205.
4. [Jacques-Charles Bochard de] Champigny de la Croix, "A la Martinique 8 Oct 1741...," ANOM F3/90/41.
5. "Lettre des Administrateurs au Ministre sur 1. les empoisonneurs, 2. la fustigation des empoisonneurs avec du médicinier, 3. le témoinage des esclaves," Léogane, March 18, 1746, ANOM F3/88/206. Quotation at 3.
6. Anon., *Relation d'une conspiration tramée par les negres, dans l'isle de S. Domingue; défense que fait le Jésuite confesseur, aux negres qu'on suplicie, de révéler leurs fauteurs et complices* (Paris?: n.p., 1758).
7. Anon., *Relation d'une conspiration*, 5.
8. Michel Foucault, *Discipline and Punish: The Birth of the Prison*, trans. Alan Sheridan (New York: Vintage Books, 1979), 3-6.
9. Moreau de Saint-Méry, *Loix et constitutions des colonies françoises*, 4:217-18.
10. Anon., *Relation d'une conspiration*, 3-4.
11. Anon., *Relation d'une conspiration*, 1-2.
12. Anon., *Relation d'une conspiration*, 5.
13. ANOM F3/88/212, 215, 219, 221, 223, 224, 227, 231, 235, 236, 238-57.
14. [Charles] Fournier de la Chapelle, "Mémoire pour servir à l'information des procès contre les nègres devins, sorciers, et empoisonneurs," 1758, ANOM F3/88/236. See also Pierre Pluchon, *Vaudou, sorciers, empoisonneurs: De Saint-Domingue à Haiti* (Port-au-Prince: Karthala, 1987), 248-49.
15. Kevin Olson, *Imagined Sovereignties: The Power of the People and Other Myths of the Modern Age* (Cambridge: Cambridge University Press, 2016), 56-58.
16. Thomas Hobbes, *Leviathan*, ed. Richard Tuck (Cambridge: Cambridge University Press, 1996), chap. 6, 41.
17. American Psychiatric Association, "Anxiety Disorders," in *Diagnostic and Statistical Manual of Mental Disorders*, 5th ed. (Arlington, VA: American Psychiatric Association, 2013). Emphasis in the original.
18. Sara Ahmed, *The Cultural Politics of Emotion*, 2nd ed. (Edinburgh: Edinburgh University Press, 2014), 64-68.
19. Ahmed, *The Cultural Politics of Emotion*, 69. Emphasis in the original.
20. Ann Laura Stoler, *Along the Archival Grain: Epistemic Anxieties and Colonial Common Sense* (Princeton, NJ: Princeton University Press, 2009), 95-102, 152-55.
21. Stoler, *Along the Archival Grain*, 106; referring to Jacqueline Rose, *States of Fantasy* (Oxford: Oxford University Press, 1996), 5.
22. Gayatri Chakravorty Spivak, *A Critique of Postcolonial Reason: Toward a History of the Vanishing Present* (Cambridge, MA: Harvard University Press, 1999), 271-74.
23. Spivak, *Critique of Postcolonial Reason*, 267, quoting an early translation of Foucault by Kate Soper in *Power/Knowledge: Selected Interviews and Other Writings, 1972–1977*, ed. Colin Gordon (New York: Pantheon, 1980), 82.
24. Spivak, *Critique of Postcolonial Reason*, 255.

3. Unsettling Silences

25. Spivak's critique is chiefly leveled against the published conversation between Foucault and Gilles Deleuze, "Intellectuals and Power," in Michel Foucault, *Language, Counter-Memory, and Practice: Selected Essays and Interviews*, ed. Donald Bouchard (Ithaca, NY: Cornell University Press, 1977), 205-17.
26. C. L. R. James, *The Black Jacobins: Toussaint L'Ouverture and the San Domingo Revolution*, 2nd ed. rev. (New York: Vintage Books, 1989), 20-22; Carolyn Fick, *The Making of Haiti: The Saint Domingue Revolution from Below* (Knoxville: University of Tennessee Press, 1990), 59-75.
27. Fick, *Making of Haiti*, 66-68.
28. David Scott, *Conscripts of Modernity: The Tragedy of Colonial Enlightenment* (Durham, NC: Duke University Press, 2004), 105-7, 132-35, 167-69.
29. M. de C., "Makandal, histoire véritable," *Mercure de France*, September 15, 1787, 102-14; Anon., *La caverne des brigands, ou recueil des assassinats, des vols, des brigandages, des scélérats qui ont expié leurs crimes* ... (Paris: Locard et Davi, 1814), 10-23; and subsequent editions of 1829 and 1845.
30. Michel-René Hilliard d'Auberteuil, *Considérations sur l'état présent de la colonie française de Saint-Domingue* (Paris: Grangé, 1776), 137-39.
31. Pierre de Vaissière, *Saint-Domingue: La société et la vie créoles sous l'ancien régime (1629–1789)* (Paris: Perrin, 1909), 240-41.
32. Médéric-Louis-Elie Moreau de Saint-Méry, *Description topographique, physique, civile, politique et historique de la partie française de l'isle Saint-Domingue* (1797), 3 vols. (Saint Denis: Société Française d'Histoire d'Outre-Mer, 2004), 1:56; 2:629-31.
33. Olson, *Imagined Sovereignties*, 94-96.

4. PHANTASMATIC PUBLIC SPHERES

1. Abbé Guillaume-Thomas-François Raynal, *Histoire philosophique et politique des établissemens et du commerce des européens dans les deux Indes*, 10 vols. (Geneva: Pellet, 1780).
2. Raynal, *Histoire*, 6:221; see also C. L. R. James, *The Black Jacobins: Toussaint L'Ouverture and the San Domingo Revolution*, 2nd ed. rev. (New York: Vintage Books, 1989), 24-25, 171, 250.
3. Anatole Feugère, *Un precurseur de la révolution: L'Abbé Raynal (1713–1796)* (Geneva: Slatkine, [1922] 1970), 175-200.
4. Marguerite Glotz and Madeleine Maire, *Salons du XVIIIème siècle* (Paris: Nouvelles Editions Latines, 1949), 326-29.
5. Michèle Duchet, *Diderot et l'histoire des deux Indes, ou l'écriture fragmentaire* (Paris: Nizet, 1978).
6. David Brion Davis, *The Problem of Slavery in the Age of Revolution, 1770–1823* (Ithaca, NY: Cornell University Press, 1975), 92.
7. Gabriel-François Coyer, *Discours sur la satyre contre les philosophes*, in *Collection complète des oeuvres de M. L'Abbé Coyer* (Neuchatel: Société Typographique, 1780), 226-27; Frère [?] de la Coste, *Voyage philosophique d'Angleterre, fait en 1783 et 1784* (Paris: Poinçot, 1787), Lettre V, 1:103.
8. Jacques-Pierre Brissot, *Discours sur la nécessité d'etablir à Paris une societe pour concourir* . . . *à l'abolition de la traite et de l'esclavage des negres*, February 19, 1788, in La Société des Amis

des Noirs, *La révolution française et l'abolition de l'esclavage*, 12 vols. (Paris: Editions d'Histoire Sociale, 1968), 6:1-32; Jeremy Popkin, *Revolutionary News: The Press in France 1789-1799* (Durham, NC: Duke University Press, 1990), 28-29.

9. Archives Nationales de France, series D, subseries XXV (hereafter AN D/XXV).
10. "Adresse présentée à l'Assemblée Nationale, par les propriétaires de biens aux colonies françaises, résidants à Bourdeaux," November 28, 1789, AN D/XXV/78/770/63, 4, 7.
11. "Adresse Présentée à l'Assemblée Nationale," 4.
12. "Adresse Présentée à l'Assemblée Nationale," 5.
13. "Ville du Havre-de-Grace, adresse à l'Assemblée Nationale," December 26, 1789, AN D/XXV/78/770/62, 3.
14. Richard Hofstadter, "The Paranoid Style in American Politics," *Harper's Magazine* (November 1964), 77-86, at 80.
15. Hofstadter, "The Paranoid Style," 81.
16. "Lettre du Ministre à M. le Duc de Choiseul, du 24 nov 1767," Archives Nationales d'Outre-Mer, Aix-en-Provence, France, Series F3, 81/40.
17. E. Stanley Abbot, "What Is Paranoia?," *American Journal of Psychiatry* 71, no. 1 (July 1914): 29-40.
18. Heather Munsche and Harry Whitaker, "Eighteenth Century Classification of Mental Illness: Linnaeus, de Sauvages, Vogel, and Cullen," *Cognitive and Behavioral Neurology* 25, no. 4 (December 2012): 227-28, 233.
19. Timothy Tackett, *The Coming of the Terror in the French Revolution* (Cambridge, MA: Harvard University Press, 2015), esp. 135-41; David Brion Davis, ed., *The Fear of Conspiracy: Images of Un-American Subversion from the Revolution to the Present* (Ithaca, NY: Cornell University Press, 1971), 23-65.
20. Eve Kosofsky Sedgwick, *Touching Feeling: Affect, Pedagogy, Performativity* (Durham, NC: Duke University Press, 2003), 130-31.
21. Sedgwick, *Touching Feeling*, 138-39.
22. See Kevin Olson, *Imagined Sovereignties: The Power of the People and Other Myths of the Modern Age* (Cambridge: Cambridge University Press, 2016), 94-96.
23. *Moniteur général de la partie française de Saint-Domingue*, November 15, 1791, 1-2.
24. Anon., *My Odyssey: Experiences of a Young Refugee from Two Revolutions, by a Creole of Saint Domingue*, trans. and ed. Althéa de Puech Parham (Baton Rouge: Louisiana State University Press, 1959), 32-34, quote at 34.
25. Olson, *Imagined Sovereignties*, 127-28.
26. Laurent Dubois, *Avengers of the New World: The Story of the Haitian Revolution* (Cambridge, MA: Harvard University Press, 2004), 102-3; Carolyn Fick, *The Making of Haiti: The Saint Domingue Revolution from Below* (Knoxville: University of Tennessee Press, 1990), 110-11; Illan rua Wall, *Human Rights and Constituent Power: Without Model or Warranty* (London: Routledge, 2012), 17-18. James Martel, in contrast, expresses a much more subtle skepticism about the passage in *The One and Only Law: Walter Benjamin and the Second Commandment* (Ann Arbor: University of Michigan Press, 2014), 152-53.
27. Félix Carteau, *Soirées bermudiennes, ou entretiens sur les evénemens qui ont opéré la ruine le la partie française de l'île St.-Domingue* (Bordeaux: Pellier-Lawalle, 1802), 74-75, 85, 105-6.
28. Carteau, *Soirées bermudiennes*, 120.

326   4. Phantasmatic Public Spheres

29. Carteau, *Soirées bermudiennes*, 121. Emphasis in the original.
30. Carteau, *Soirées bermudiennes*, 74-76, 93. Quotations at 76.
31. Carteau, *Soirées bermudiennes*, 75-77.
32. Carteau, *Soirées bermudiennes*, 82-83.
33. Hugh Honour, *From the American Revolution to World War I: Slaves and Liberators* (Cambridge, MA: Harvard University Press, 2012), 43-44.
34. Cheryl Finley, *Committed to Memory: The Art of the Slave Ship Icon* (Princeton, NJ: Princeton University Press, 2018), 31-52.
35. Finley, *Committed to Memory*, 19-23.
36. Gustavus Vasa, The African [Olaudah Equiano], "To the Committee for the Abolition of the Slave Trade at Plymouth," *The Public Advertiser* (London), February 14, 1789, 2.
37. Olaudah Equiano, *The Interesting Narrative of the Life of Olaudah Equiano, or Gustavus Vassa, The African, Written by Himself* (New York: W. Durrell, 1791).
38. Charles Boilly after Pierre Rouvier, *Soyez libres et citoyens*, frontispiece to Benjamin Frossard, *La cause des esclaves noirs*, vol. 1, 1789.
39. Susan H. Libby, "The Color of Frenchness: Racial Identity and Visuality in French Anti-Slavery Imagery, 1788-94," in Adrienne L. Childs and Susan H. Libby, *Blacks and Blackness in European Art of the Long Nineteenth Century* (Surrey, UK: Ashgate, 2014), 19-45.
40. Olson, *Imagined Sovereignties*, 119-24.
41. Nancy Luxon, "Gender, Agency, and the Circulations of Power," in Nancy Luxon, ed., *Archives of Infamy: Foucault on State Power in the Lives of Ordinary Citizens* (Minneapolis: University of Minnesota Press, 2019), 308-18.
42. Chris Bongie, "A Flexible Quill: Abbé de Lahaye's Role in Late Colonial Saint-Domingue, 1787-1791–The Legend and the Life," *Atlantic Studies* 15, no. 4 (2018): 476-503.
43. "Procès-verbal d'interrogatoire, subi par le Curé du Dondon...," February 1, 1793, AN D/XXV/14/128/18, 7.
44. "À l'Assemblé Nationale, mémoire et accusation contre les Amis des Noirs," n.d., signed Du Budehouychamp [?], AN D/XXV/110/867/20.
45. Hofstadter, "The Paranoid Style," 78.
46. Hofstadter, "The Paranoid Style," 81.
47. Hofstadter, "The Paranoid Style," 82.
48. Here I am further developing ideas that I have explored elsewhere. Olson, *Imagined Sovereignties*, 136-37, 142.
49. Renko Geffarth, "The Masonic Necromancer: Shifting Identities in the Lives of Johann Georg Schrepfer," in *Polemical Encounters: Esoteric Discourse and Its Others* (Leiden: Brill, 2007), 181-97.
50. E. G. [Étienne-Gaspard] Robertson, *Mémoires récréatifs, scientifiques et anecdotiques du physicien-aéronaute E. G. Robertson: Connu par ses expériences de fantasmagorie, et par ses ascensions aérostatiques dans les principales villes de l'Europe* (Paris: Privately printed, 1831).
51. Laurent Mannoni, *The Great Art of Light and Shadow: Archaeology of the Cinema*, trans. Richard Crangle (Exeter: University of Exeter Press, 2000), 136-75.
52. Edmé-Gilles Guyot, *Nouvelles récréations physiques et mathématiques* (Paris: Gueffier, 1770), 3:185-90.
53. Mannoni, *The Great Art of Light and Shadow*, 143-44, 148-49; quote at 148.
54. Fulgence Marion, *L'optique*, 3rd ed. (Paris: Hachette, 1874), 208-52.

55. Jean-Philippe-Gui Le Gentil, Comte de Paroy, *Mémoires du Comte de Paroy: Souvenirs d'un défenseur de la famille royale pendant la révolution (1789-1797)* (Paris: Plon, 1895), 281-83.

5. DISRUPTIVE OBJECT

1. Dominique Doncre, *Le Juge Pierre-Louis-Joseph Lecocq et sa famille*, 1791, Musée de la Révolution Française (Vizille, France), MRF 1984-263.
2. Abbé Guillaume-Thomas-François Raynal, *Histoire philosophique et politique des établissemens et du commerce des européens dans les deux Indes*, 10 vols. (Geneva: Pellet, 1780), 6:221.
3. See, for instance, Société des Amis des Noirs, *Adresse à l'Assemblée Nationale, pour l'abolition de la traite de noirs*, February 5, 1790 (Paris: Potier de Lille, 1790).
4. Claude Nicolet, *L'idée républicaine en France: Essai d'histoire critique* (Paris: Gallimard, 1982), 47-114; Biancamaria Fontana, ed., *The Invention of the Modern Republic* (Cambridge: Cambridge University Press, 1994), 63-138; Pierre Bouretz, *La république et l'universel* (Paris: Gallimard, 2000), 35-82.
5. Augustin Cochin, *La révolution et la libre-pensée* (Paris: Copernic, 1979), 39-51; Jeremy Popkin, *Revolutionary News: The Press in France 1789–1799* (Durham, NC: Duke University Press, 1990).
6. Médéric-Louis-Elie Moreau de Saint-Méry, *Considérations présentées aux vrais amis due repos et du bonheur de la France, à l'occasion des nouveaux movemens de quelques soi-disant Amis-des-Noirs*, March 1, 1791 (Paris: Imprimerie Nationale, 1791), 6.
7. Société des Amis des Noirs, *Adresse de la Société des Amis des Noirs, à l'Assemblée Nationale . . . ,"* (Paris: Imprimerie de Patriote François, March 1791), iii.
8. Anon, *My Odyssey: Experiences of a Young Refugee from Two Revolutions, by a Creole of Saint Domingue*, trans. and ed. Althéa de Puech Parham (Baton Rouge: Louisiana State University Press, 1959), 34. See p. 112.
9. Joseph-Paul-Augustin Cambefort, *Mémoire justificatif de Joseph-Paul-Augustin Cambefort. . . .* (Chartres: Frères Chaignieau, 1793), 38-39.
10. Cambefort, *Mémoire justificatif*, 46-47.
11. Félix Carteau, *Soirées bermudiennes, ou entretiens sur les événemens qui ont opéré la ruine de la partie française de l'île St.-Domingue* (Bordeaux: Pellier-Lawalle, 1802), 85; see p. 113.
12. John Garrigus, *Before Haiti: Race and Citizenship in French Saint-Domingue* (New York: Palgrave, 2006), 205, 217.
13. For a more detailed account of the trial. see Mercer Cook, "Julien Raimond," *Journal of Negro History* 26, no. 2 (1941): 158-63.
14. Comité de la Marine et des Colonies, "Assertions Extraits de la Correspondance de Raimond," Archives Nationales de France, series D, subseries XXV, carton 56, dossier 549, document 7 (hereafter, e.g., AN D/XXV/56/549/7).
15. "Colonies: 12 Pièces . . . ," AN D/XXV/56/549/7.
16. Quoted in Pierre de Vassière, *Saint-Domingue: La société et la vie créoles sous l'ancien régime, 1629–1789* (Paris: Perrin, 1908), 368.
17. Anon., "Mémoire historique des dernières révolutions des provinces de l'Ouest et du Sud, de la partie française de St. Domingue . . . ," n.d., AN D/XXV/56/549/7, AN D/XXV/110/872, 3.
18. AN D/XXV/56/549/7, AN D/XXV/59/583-586, AN D/XXV/110/867.

19. Laurent Dubois, *Avengers of the New World: The Story of the Haitian Revolution* (Cambridge, MA: Harvard University Press, 2004), 78–79.
20. Michel-Rolph Trouillot, *Silencing the Past: Power and the Production of History* (Boston: Beacon Press, 1995).
21. Trouillot, *Silencing the Past*, 49.
22. Maurice Agulhon, *Marianne Into Battle: Republican Imagery and Symbolism in France, 1789–1880* (Cambridge: Cambridge University Press, 1981).
23. Ronald Paulson, *Representations of Revolution: 1789–1820* (New Haven, CT: Yale University Press, 1983), 23.
24. Paulson, *Representations of Revolution*, 26.
25. Ferdinand Pouy, *Histoire des cocardes blanches, noires, vertes, et tricolores*, 2nd ed. (Paris: Baur et Détaille, 1872), 50.
26. Pouy, *Histoire des cocardes*, 17–23, quote at 26.
27. Pouy, *Histoire des cocardes*, 33.
28. Lynn Hunt, *Politics, Culture, and Class in the French Revolution* (Berkeley: University of California Press, 1984), 58–59.
29. Pouy, *Histoire des cocardes*, 35–37.
30. Paulson, *Representations of Revolution*, 18–20; Pouy, *Histoire des cocardes*, 33–37; Mona Ozouf, "La Révolution française et l'idée de l'homme nouveau," in *The Political Culture of the French Revolution*, ed. Colin Lucas (Oxford: Pergamon Press, 1987), 213–32; Bouretz, *La république et l'universel*, 41, 45–48.
31. Nicole Pellegrin, *Les vêtements de la liberté: Abécédaire des pratiques vestimentaires en France de 1780 à 1800* (Aix-en-Provence: Alinea, 1989), 118.
32. Richard Wrigley, *The Politics of Appearances: Representations of Dress in Revolutionary France* (Oxford: Berg, 2002), 102–3.
33. Hunt, *Politics, Culture, and Class*, 59; Pouy, *Histoire des cocardes*, 45; Wrigley, *Politics of Appearances*, 103.
34. Pouy, *Histoire des cocardes*, 49–50.
35. *Collection générale des décrets rendus par la Convention Nationale . . . , mois de septembre 1793, jusqu'au 21 inclusivement* (Paris: Baudouin, [1793]), 210–11. See Joan Landes, *Women and the Public Sphere in the Age of the French Revolution* (Ithaca, NY: Cornell University Press, 1988), 110, 142, 165; D. Levy, H. Applewhite, and M. Johnson, eds., *Women in Revolutionary Paris, 1789–1795* (Urbana: University of Illinois Press, 1979), 146–47, 197–204.
36. Lynn Hunt, "Freedom of Dress in Revolutionary France," in *From the Royal to the Republican Body: Incorporating the Political in Seventeenth- and Eighteenth-Century France*, ed. Sara Melzer and Kathryn Norberg (Berkeley: University of California Press, 1998), 224–28.
37. *Moniteur général de la partie française de Saint-Domingue* [Cap Français], Prospectus, no date [c. November 1791], 1.
38. Kevin Olson, *Imagined Sovereignties: The Power of the People and Other Myths of the Modern Age* (Cambridge: Cambridge University Press, 2016), 115–19. See, for instance, the satirical poem "Ode à la Philantropie," discussed in chapter 4. *Moniteur général*, November 15, 1791, 1–2.
39. Joan Dayan, *Haiti, History, and the Gods* (Berkeley: University of California Press, 1995), 4–5.
40. Clinton Hutton, *The Logic and Historical Significance of the Haitian Revolution and the Cosmological Roots of Haitian Freedom* (Kingston, Jamaica: Arawak, 2005), 59–72.

41. Dayan, *Haiti*, 29-39; Maureen Warner-Lewis, *Central Africa in the Caribbean: Transcending Time, Transforming Cultures* (Kingston, Jamaica: University of the West Indies Press, 2003), 138-75; Wyatt MacGaffey, *Kongo Political Culture: The Conceptual Challenge of the Particular* (Bloomington: Indiana University Press, 2000), 78-96.
42. Hutton, *Logic and Historical Significance*, 82-84.
43. John Thornton, "'I Am the Subject of the King of Congo': African Political Ideology and the Haitian Revolution," *Journal of World History* 4, no. 2 (1993): 193-214. The original quotation is from François-Joseph-Pamphile de Lacroix, *Mémoires pour servir à l'histoire de la révolution de Saint-Domingue*, 2 vols. (Paris: Pillet Aîné, 1819), 1:253.
44. See Carolyn Fick, *The Making of Haiti: The Saint Domingue Revolution from Below* (Knoxville: University of Tennessee Press, 1990), 243-50; Sibylle Fischer, *Modernity Disavowed: Haiti and the Cultures of Slavery in the Age of Revolution* (Durham, NC: Duke University Press, 2004), 13-24; Hutton, *Logic and Historical Significance*, 36, 46-52; Olson, *Imagined Sovereignties*, chap. 7.
45. Pierre Bourdieu, *Language and Symbolic Power* (Cambridge, MA: Harvard University Press, 1991); Kevin Olson, "Legitimate Speech and Hegemonic Idiom: The Limits of Deliberative Democracy in the Diversity of Its Voices," *Political Studies* 59, no. 3 (2011): 527-46.
46. Jane Bennett, *Vibrant Matter: A Political Ecology of Things* (Durham, NC: Duke University Press, 2010), 1-19.
47. Charles Mills, *The Racial Contract* (Ithaca, NY: Cornell University Press, 1997).

INTERLUDE

1. "De Placide Camus, garçon imprimeur," Archives Nationales de France, series D, subseries XXV, carton 83, dossier 807, documents 20-23 (hereafter, e.g., AN D/XXV/83/807/20-23).
2. "Répertoire des Proclamations des Commissaires Civils de la République," AN D/XXV/28/285/12.
3. Comité de Salut Public, "Memoire pour Placide Camus né à Chartres..." 10 Frimaire [*An* 3, i.e., December 5, 1794], AN D/XXV/83/807/20.
4. Michel-Rolph Trouillot, *Silencing the Past: Power and the Production of History* (Boston: Beacon Press, 1995), 70-107.
5. Ann Laura Stoler, *Duress: Imperial Durabilities of Our Times* (Durham, NC: Duke University Press, 2016), 13.
6. Juliet Hooker, *Theorizing Race in the Americas: Douglass, Sarmiento, Du Bois, and Vasconcelos* (New York: Oxford University Press, 2017), 57-66; Kevin Olson, *Imagined Sovereignty: The Power of the People and Other Myths of the Modern Age* (Cambridge: Cambridge University Press, 2016), 155-61.
7. Michel Foucault, *The Archaeology of Knowledge*, trans. A. M. Sheridan Smith (New York: Pantheon Books, 1972), 169.
8. Michel Foucault, "Réponse à une question" (1968), in *Dits et écrits I: 1954–1975* (Paris: Gallimard, 2001), 701-8, quotation at 705.
9. Foucault, "Truth and Power," in *Power/Knowledge: Selected Interviews and Other Writings, 1972–1977*, ed. Colin Gordon (New York: Pantheon Books, 1980), 111. The actual dictionary phrase is *"Auteur d'une philosophie de l'historie fondée sur la discontinuité."* "Foucault, Michel," *Petit Larousse illustré* (Paris: Librairie Larousse, 1973), 1343.

10. Foucault, "Réponse à une question," 711.
11. Foucault, "Truth and Power," 112; "Réponse à une question," 714.
12. Olson, *Imagined Sovereignties*, chap. 7.
13. *Constitution impériale d'Haïti*, 1805, reprinted in Louis-Joseph Janvier, *Les constitutions d'Haïti (1801–1885)* (Paris: Flammarion, 1886), 30–41.

6. TIMES OF EXCEPTION

1. Carolyn Fick, *The Making of Haiti: The Saint Domingue Revolution from Below* (Knoxville: University of Tennessee Press, 1990), 91, 116, 137, 138, 141, 143, 145, 268, 305n135, 310n14, 311n29.
2. "Declarations of the Slave Antoine and Sieur Fabvre, Extract of the Minutes from the Register of the Provincial Assembly of the South," Archives Nationales de France, series D, subseries XXV, carton 63, dossier 638 (hereafter D/XXV/63/638), trans. Caroline Fick, in Fick, *The Making of Haiti*, 268.
3. Jean-Philippe Garran de Coulon, *Rapport sur les troubles de Saint-Domingue, fait au nom de la Commission des Colonies . . .*, 4 vols. (Paris: Impimerie Nationale, 1797-1799), 2:570.
4. "Copie de le Lettre écrite par M. Henry Capitaine du Navire la Charlotte Désirée de Nantes, à M.M. Charles le Mesle, Oursel, et Compagnie," Du Cap Français le 27 sept 1791, D/XXV/78/772.
5. "Copie de le Lettre écrite par M. Henry," 4. Emphasis in the original.
6. David Patrick Geggus, *Haitian Revolutionary Studies* (Bloomington: University of Indiana Press, 2002), 81–92.
7. Pamphile de Lacroix, *Mémoires pour servir à l'histoire de la révolution de Saint-Domingue*, 2 vols. (Paris: Pillet Aîné, 1819), 1:147.
8. Eugene Genovese, *From Rebellion to Revolution: Afro-American Slave Revolts in the Making of the Modern World* (Baton Rouge: Louisiana State University Press, 1979), 82–125.
9. Michel-Rolph Trouillot, *Silencing the Past: Power and the Production of History* (Boston: Beacon Press, 1995), 70–107.
10. Guillaume-Thomas-François Raynal, *Histoire philosophique et politique des établissemens et du commerce des européens dans les deux Indes*, 10 vols. (1770) (Geneva: J. L. Pellet, 1780), 6:168.
11. Marcus Rainsford, *An Historical Account of the Black Empire of Hayti: Comprehending a View of the Principal Transactions in the Revolution of Saint Domingo; with its Antient and Modern State* (London: Albion Press, 1805), 89.
12. William Beckford, *A Descriptive Account of the Island of Jamaica: With Remarks upon the Cultivation of the Sugar-cane, throughout the Different Seasons of the Year, and Chiefly Considered in a Picturesque Point of View; also Observations and Reflections upon What would Probably Be the Consequences of an Abolition of the Slave-trade, and of the Emancipation of the Slaves*, 2 vols. (London: Printed for T. and J. Egerton, 1790), 2:129–30; see also 1:233–37, 1:254–57.
13. Beckford, *Descriptive Account of the Island of Jamaica*, 2:137.
14. Beckford, *Descriptive Account of the Island of Jamaica*, 2:136.
15. Beckford, *Descriptive Account of the Island of Jamaica*, 2:152.
16. Beckford, *Descriptive Account of the Island of Jamaica*, 1:256.
17. Beckford, *Descriptive Account of the Island of Jamaica*, 2:153.

18. Raynal, *Histoire des deux Indes*, 6:214-19.
19. Michèle Duchet, *Diderot et l'histoire des deux Indes, ou l'écriture fragmentaire* (Paris: Nizet, 1978).
20. John Stuart Mill, occasional articles on "The Condition of Ireland," published in the *Morning Chronicle*, October–November 1846; see also Mill, "Poulett Scrope on the Poor Laws," *Morning Chronicle*, October 31, 1846, 4. Reprinted in John Stuart Mill, *Collected Works* (Toronto: University of Toronto Press, 1963), 24:879-82, 913-16, 923-26, 930-32, 942-45, 991-93, 1004-8.
21. Michel Foucault, *The Punitive Society: Lectures at the Collège de France 1972–1973*, trans. Graham Burchell (New York: Palgrave, 2015), 70-72, 82-84; Jacques Le Goff, "Labor Time in the 'Crisis' of the Fourteenth Century," in *Time, Work, and Culture in the Middle Ages*, trans. Arthur Goldhammer (Chicago: University of Chicago Press, 1980), 43-52.
22. David Scott, *Conscripts of Modernity: The Tragedy of Colonial Enlightenment* (Durham, NC: Duke University Press, 2004).
23. Thomas Madiou, *Histoire d'Haïti*, 8 vols. (1847) (Port-au-Prince: Henri Deschamps, 1989), 3:144-45.
24. Jean-Jacques Dessalines, *Act d'indépendence*, January 1, 1804 (Port-au-Prince: Imprimerie du Gouvernement, 1804), British National Archives, Kew, CO 137/111/1. Reprinted in *Lois et actes sous le règne de Jean Jacques Dessalines* (Port-au-Prince: Presses Nationales d'Haïti, 2006), 8-11.
25. Jean-Jacques Dessalines, *Proclamation du général en chef au peuple d'Haiti*, January 1, 1804 (Port-au-Prince: Imprimerie du Gouvernement, 1804). Also reprinted in Dessalines, *Lois et actes*, 8-11.
26. Dessalines, *Lois et actes*, 9.
27. Trouillot, *Silencing the Past*, 88-89.
28. Hannah Arendt, *On Revolution*, rev. ed. (New York: Penguin, 1965), 132-206.
29. Mona Ozouf, *L'homme régénéré: Essais sur la Révolution française* (Paris: Gallimard, 1989).
30. Jennifer Harris, "The Red Cap of Liberty: A Study of Dress Worn by French Revolutionary Partisans 1789-94," *Eighteenth-Century Studies* 14, no. 2 (1981), 283-312; Mona Ozouf, *Festivals and the French Revolution* (Cambridge, MA: Harvard University Press, 1988); Alexis de Tocqueville, *The Old Regime and the French Revolution*, trans. Stuart Gilbert (New York: Doubleday, 1955).
31. Dessalines, *Lois et actes*, 8.
32. Dessalines, *Lois et actes*, 9-10.
33. Christian Dupont and Peter Onuf, eds., *Declaring Independence: The Origin and Influence of America's Founding Document* (Charlottesville: University of Virginia Library, 2008), 31-33, 58-61.
34. Deborah Jenson, *Beyond the Slave Narrative: Sex, Politics, and Manuscripts in the Haitian Revolution* (Liverpool: Liverpool University Press, 2011), 122-60.
35. Rosalind Krauss, *The Originality of the Avant-Garde and Other Modernist Myths* (Cambridge, MA: MIT Press, 1985), 151-70.
36. Dessalines, *Lois et actes*, 8, 9.
37. Laurent Dubois, *Avengers of the New World* (Cambridge, MA: Harvard University Press, 2004), 3; Lynn Hunt, *Inventing Human Rights: A History* (New York: Norton, 2007), 160-67; James R. Martel, *The Misinterpellated Subject* (Durham, NC: Duke University Press, 2017), 62-70.

332   6. Times of Exception

38. Adom Getachew, "Universalism After the Post-Colonial Turn: Interpreting the Haitian Revolution," *Political Theory* 44, no. 6 (2016): 821–45; Nick Nesbitt, *Universal Emancipation: The Haitian Revolution and the Radical Enlightenment* (Charlottesville: University of Virginia Press, 2008); Massimiliano Tomba, *Insurgent Universality: An Alternative Legacy of Modernity* (Oxford: Oxford University Press, 2019).
39. Sibylle Fischer, *Modernity Disavowed: Haiti and the Cultures of Slavery in the Age of Revolution* (Durham, NC: Duke University Press, 2004; Scott, *Conscripts of Modernity*.
40. Joan Dayan, *Haiti, History, and the Gods* (Berkeley: University of California Press, 1995), 5.
41. Annette K. Joseph-Gabriel, "Creolizing Freedom: French-Creole Translations of Liberty and Equality in the Haitian Revolution," *Slavery and Abolition* 36, no. 1 (2015): 111–23.
42. Michel-Rolph Trouillot, *Haiti, State Against Nation: The Origins and Legacy of Duvalierism* (New York: Monthly Review Press, 1990), 87.
43. *Constitution impériale d'Haïti*, 1805, reprinted in Louis-Joseph Janvier, *Les constitutions d'Haïti (1801–1885)* (Paris: Flammarion, 1886), 30–41.

7. REVOLUTION WITHIN A REVOLUTION

1. *Le Manifeste* (Port-au-Prince), April 18, 1841, 2; March 13, 1842, 2.
2. *Le Manifeste*, April 23, 1843, 1–2.
3. Alexis de Tocqueville, *De la démocratie en Amérique*, 2 vols. (Paris: C. Gosselin, 1835 and 1840).
4. *Le Temps: Feuille politique, agricole et commerciale* (Port-au-Prince), March 3, 1842, p. 1–3.
5. Verena Erlenbusch-Anderson, *Genealogies of Terrorism: Revolution, State Violence, Empire* (New York: Columbia University Press, 2018), 94–106.
6. [T. Bouchereau], "Souvenir historique," *Le Manifeste*, March 6, 1842, 1–3; *Le Temps*, March 3, 1842, 2.
7. Karl Marx, *The Eighteenth Brumaire of Louis Bonaparte*, in *Later Political Writings*, ed. Terrell Carver (Cambridge: Cambridge University Press, 1996), 56–57.
8. Charles Hérard et al., "Manifeste, ou appel des citoyen des Cayes à leurs concitoyens" (a.k.a "Le manifeste de Praslin"), reprinted in Emmanuel Édouard, *Recueil général des lois et actes du gouvernement d'Haïti et documents historiques*, vol. 7, 1840–1843 (Paris: Pedone-Lauriel, 1888), 118–29. Also reprinted in Beaubrun Ardouin, *Études sur l'histoire d'Haïti* (Paris: Dézobry et Magdeleine, 1860), vol. 11., chap. vi, 243–47.
9. Hérard et al., "Manifeste," 125–26.
10. [T. Bouchereau], "Pourquoi Haïti n'est-elle pas plus avancée en civilisation?," *Le Manifeste*, September 12, 1841, 1–3.
11. Hérard et al., "Manifeste," 124; *La constitution française de 1791*, in *Les constitutions de la France depuis 1789* (Paris: Proux, 1848), Title III, article 1, p. 11; see Kevin Olson, *Imagined Sovereignties: The Power of the People and Other Myths of the Modern Age* (Cambridge: Cambridge University Press, 2016), 81–86.
12. M. B. (Mark Baker) Bird, *The Black Man or Haytian Independence* (New York: Privately printed, 1869), 225.
13. *Le Manifeste*, April 4, 1841, 1.

7. *Revolution Within a Revolution* 333

14. Myrthil Bruno, untitled, *Le Manifeste*, September 19, 1841, 1. See Olson, *Imagined Sovereignties*, 67-68, 74-86; Mona Ozouf, "L'opinion publique," in *The Political Culture of the Old Regime*, ed. Keith Baker (Oxford: Pergamon Press, 1987), 419-34.
15. Hérard et al., "Manifeste," 124; *Le Manifeste*, January 30, 1842, supplement; March 13, 1842, 3-4.
16. Thomas Madiou, *Histoire d'Haïti*, 8 vols. (1846) (Port-au-Prince: Henri Deschamps, 1989), 7:472.
17. Bird, *The Black Man*, 232-34.
18. *Courrier des Etats-Unis* (New York), March 2, 1843, 2; April 11, 1843, 72; April 29, 1843, 111; May 1, 1843, 116.
19. *Le Manifeste*, April 2, 1843, 2-3; *Feuille du commerce*, April 2, 1843, 2-4.
20. Hérard et al., "Manifeste," 125.
21. Charles Hérard, "Proclamation du 27 janvier 1843," in Édouard, *Recueil général des lois et actes*, 7:155-56.
22. Le Comité Populaire des Cayes et Le Comité Populaire de Jérémie, "Relation et manifeste officiels des insurgés haïtiens," *Courrier des Etats-Unis*, March 25, 1843, 1.
23. Charles Hérard, "Acte de déchéance," *Le Manifeste*, March 26, 1843, 3-4.
24. John Locke, *Second Treatise of Government*, in *Two Treatise of Government*, ed. Peter Laslett (Cambridge: Cambridge University Press, 1988), 397-405.
25. Hérard et al., "Manifeste," 126.
26. "Résolution de la Société 'Des Droits de l'Homme et du Citoyen' établie aux Cayes, du 21 novembre 1842," in Édouard, *Recueil général des lois et actes*, 7:139-40, art. 4; and Madiou, *Histoire d'Haïti*, 7:419-20, art. 4.
27. *Le Manifeste*, August 13, 1843; see Mona Ozouf, *L'homme régénéré: Essais sur la Révolution française* (Paris: Gallimard, 1989), 116-57.
28. Ch. Grégoire, Cazimir Audié, and S. Colas, "Discours prononcé par le Comité Municipal de la Commune de Plaisance," *Le Manifeste*, February 15, 1844, 4.
29. [T. Bouchereau], "Pourquoi Haïti n'est-elle pas plus avancée en civilisation?," *Le Manifeste*, June 20, 1841, 2-3; *Le Manifeste*, July 11, 1841, 2.
30. Hannah Arendt, *On Revolution* (New York: Penguin Books, 2006).
31. République Haïtienne, *Constitution de 1843*, reprinted in Janvier, *Les constitutions d'Haïti (1801–1885)*, 154-86..
32. Olson, *Imagined Sovereignties*, 157-61.
33. *Emancipator and Free American* (Boston), February 15, 1844, 167, 168.
34. *Weekly Elevator* (Philadelphia), February [sic—January?] 31, 1844, reprinted in *Emancipator and Free American*, February 15, 1844, 168.
35. Jason Frank, *Constituent Moments: Enacting the People in Postrevolutionary America* (Durham, NC: Duke University Press, 2010), 1-39; Jacques Derrida, "Declarations of Independence," *New Political Science* 15 (1986): 7-15.
36. Gordon S. Brown, *Toussaint's Clause: The Founding Fathers and the Haitian Revolution* (Jackson: University Press of Mississippi, 2005).
37. Pierre Bourdieu, *Language and Symbolic Power* (Cambridge, MA: Harvard University Press, 1991), 43-65.
38. There is no similar increase in the Anglophone media.

334   7. Revolution Within a Revolution

39. James MacQueen, *The Colonial Controversy, Containing a Refutation of the Calumnies of the Anticolonists . . .* (Glasgow: Khull, Blackie, 1825), 80–81.
40. Victor Schoelcher, *Colonies étrangeres et Haiti*, 2 vols. (Paris: Pagnerre, 1843), 2:219–45.
41. Stewart R. King, *Blue Coat or Powdered Wig: Free People of Color in Pre-Revolutionary Saint Domingue* (Athens: University of Georgia Press, 2001), 56–60, 75–76.
42. Olson, *Imagined Sovereignties*, 119–24.
43. Letter from Charles Hérard to Honoré Féry, January 15, 1843, quoted in F. E. Dubois, *Précis historique de la Révolution haïtien de 1843* (Paris: Bourdier, 1866), 60–61; and Thomas Madiou, *Histoire d'Haïti*, 8 vols. (1846) (Port-au-Prince: Henri Deschamps, 1989), 7:435–36.
44. M. Lamour, "Historique de la contre-révolution de Camp-Périn (Mars 1844)," *Le Manifeste*, June 30, 1844, 1–2.
45. William B. Gooch to Honorable Abel P. Upshur, Secretary of State, Aux Cayes, April 27?, 1844; William B. Gooch to John Calhoun, Secretary of State, Aux Cayes, April 29, 1844; May 24, 1844. Despatches from U.S. Consuls in Aux Cayes, Haiti, T 330, roll 2, Jan 7, 1839–April 26, 1850. Records of the Department of State, U.S. National Archives and Records Administration.
46. "Manifeste des citoyens de Port-Républicain, à leurs frères des départements de la république," May 3, 1844, *Le Manifeste*, May 12, 1844, 3–4.
47. "Manifeste des citoyens de Port-Républicain," 1.
48. *Le Manifeste*, May 26, 1844.
49. Louis-Jean-Jacques Acaau, "Proclamation au peuple et à l'armée," April 15, 1844, Bibliothèque Nationale de France, Paris (hereafter BnF), 8-PU-127; reprinted in *Le Manifeste*, May 26, 1844, 1.
50. Louis-Jean-Jacques Acaau, "Au peuple et à l'armée," May 5, 1844, BnF FOL-PU-139.
51. Acaau, "Au peuple et à l'armée," May 5, 1844.
52. Louis-Jean-Jacques Acaau, "Adresse à ses frères du Port-Républicain," May 10, 1844, BnF FOL-PU-145.
53. Acaau, "Adresse à ses frères du Port-Républicain."
54. *Feuille du commerce: Petites affiches et annonces du Port-Républicain* (Port-Républicain, Haiti), June 2, 1844, 2. Emphasis in the original.
55. Reprinted in *The Southern Patriot* (Charleston), April 20, 1846, 2.
56. Madiou, *Histoire d'Haïti*, 8:133.
57. Leslie Manigat, *La Révolution haïtienne de 1843: Essai d'analyse, histoire d'une conjoncture de crise* (Port-au-Prince: CHUDAC, 2007), 98; see Madiou, *Histoire d'Haïti*, 8:135.
58. See Michel Foucault, "What Is an Author?," in *Language, Counter-Memory, and Practice: Selected Essays and Interviews*, ed. Donald Bouchard (Ithaca, NY: Cornell University Press, 1977), 113–38.
59. Les Commissaires des Cayes, "Republique haitienne," April 4, 1844. Despatches from U.S. Consuls in Aux Cayes, Haiti, T 330, roll 2, Jan 7, 1839–April 26, 1850, Records of the Department of State, U.S. National Archives and Records Administration.
60. Acaau, "Proclamation au peuple et à l'armée," April 15, 1844.
61. Archives Nationales de France, D/XXV/28/285, 286, 287, 288.
62. Toussaint Louverture, *Constitution de 1801*, reprinted in Louis-Joseph Janvier, *Les constitutions d'Haïti (1801–1885)*, 7–23 (Paris: Flammarion, 1886), arts. 14–17, 75, 76; "Réglement relative à la culture, le 20 vendémiaire, l'An IX de la République française," October 12,

1800), Archives Nationales d'Outre-Mer, Aix-en-Provence, France, CC 9B 18; "Letter to Laveaux" (February 20, 1796); "Proclamation on Labour" (1800), "Proclamation" (November 25, 1801), in Toussaint Louverture, *The Haitian Revolution*, ed. Nick Nesbitt (London: Verso, 2008), 21-25, 38-39, 65-72.

63. E.g. "Extrait des pièces originales déposées au greffe de la municipalité de Toussaint Louverture," in *Arrêtés des différentes communes de la colonie de St.-Domingue adressées à l'agent particulier du Directoire* (Cap-Français: P. Roux, 1799), 6.

64. M. Linstant Pradine, ed., *Recueil général des lois et actes du gouvernement d'Haïti* (Paris: Durand, 1865), v. 4 (1824-1826), May 6, 1826, 413-48. See Michel-Rolph Trouillot, *Haiti, State Against Nation: The Origins and Legacy of Duvalierism* (New York: Monthly Review Press, 1990), 60, 74.

65. James Franklin, *The Present State of Hayti (Saint Domingo): With Remarks on Its Agriculture, Commerce, Laws, Religion, Finances, and Population, Etc. Etc.* (London: John Murray, 1828), 317-67.

66. Thomas Carlyle (signed as "D"), "Occasional Discourse on the Negro Question," *Fraser's Magazine*, December 1849, 670-79; quote at 671.

67. Adom Getachew, "Universalism After the Post-Colonial Turn: Interpreting the Haitian Revolution," *Political Theory* 44, no. 6 (2016): 821-45, at 838.

68. Armand Thoby, *La question agraire en Haiti* (Port-au-Prince? n.p., 1888); Jean Price-Mars, *Ainsi parla l'oncle* (1928) (Ottawa: Lemeac, 1973); Jean Casimir, *La culture opprimée* (Port-au-Prince: Imprimerie Media-Texte, 2001); Gérard Bartélemy, *L'univers rural haïtien: Le pays en dehors* (Paris: Harmattan, 1990); Johnhenry Gonzalez, *Maroon Nation: A History of Revolutionary Haiti* (New Haven, CT: Yale University Press, 2019).

69. Neil Roberts, *Freedom as Marronage* (Chicago: University of Chicago Press, 2015); Getachew, "Universalism After the Post-Colonial Turn;" Nick Nesbitt, *Universal Emancipation: The Haitian Revolution and the Radical Enlightenment* (Charlottesville: University of Virginia Press, 2008).

70. E.g. Casimir, *La culture opprimée*, 120; Manigat, *La Révolution haïtienne de 1843*, 98-115.

71. Romuald Lepelletier de Saint-Remy, *Saint-Domingue: Étude et solution nouvelle de la question haïtienne*, 2 vols. (Paris: Bertrand, 1846), 1:280.

72. Acaau, "Proclamation au peuple et à l'armée," April 15, 1844, 1.

73. David Scott, *Conscripts of Modernity: The Tragedy of Colonial Enlightenment* (Durham, NC: Duke University Press, 2004); Olson, *Imagined Sovereignties*, chapter 7.

74. *Le Manifeste*, November 24, 1844, 1.

75. Gustave d'Alaux (Maxime Raybaud), *L'Empereur Soulouque et son empire* (Paris: Michel Lévy Frères, 1856), 54.

76. D'Alaux, *L'Empereur Soulouque et son empire*, 56.

77. Elisabeth R. Anker, *Ugly Freedoms* (Durham, NC: Duke University Press, 2022), 37-76.

8. THE FORCE OF FARCE

1. Karl Marx, *The Eighteenth Brumaire of Louis Bonaparte*, in *Later Political Writings*, ed. Terrell Carver (Cambridge: Cambridge University Press, 1996), 31.

2. Gayatri Chakravorty Spivak, *A Critique of Postcolonial Reason: Toward a History of the Vanishing Present* (Cambridge, MA: Harvard University Press, 1999), 257-64.

3. Champfleury, *Histoire de la caricature moderne*, 3rd ed. (Paris: Librairie de la Société des Gens de Lettres, 1885), vi.
4. Pierre Bourdieu, *Manet: Une révolution symbolique—Cours au Collège de France (1998–2000)* (Paris: Raisons d'Agir/Seuil, 2013), 25.
5. The relative in question is often thought to be Cham's grandfather, Louis Pantaléon de Noé, but more likely he was Pantaléon II de Breda, a great-great-uncle. Félix Ribeyre, *Cham: Sa vie et son oeuvre* (Paris: Plon, 1884), 11–12; Philippe R. Girard and Jean-Louis Donnadieu, "Toussaint before Louverture: New Archival Findings on the Early Life of Toussaint Louverture," *William and Mary Quarterly* 70, no. 1 (January 2013): 41–78, at 61.
6. *Le Caricaturiste*, October 21, 1849.
7. Ernst Kris and Ernst Gombrich, "The Principles of Caricature," *British Journal of Medical Psychology* 17, nos. 3-4 (1938): 319–42, at 321.
8. Michael Warner, *Publics and Counterpublics* (New York: Zone Books, 2002), 225–68.
9. *National Advocate* (New York), August 3, 1821; September 21, 1821; September 25, 1821. Reprinted in Warner, *Publics and Counterpublics*, 242, 247, 248.
10. *National Advocate*, August 3, 1821. Sic throughout. Reprinted in Warner, *Publics and Counterpublics*, 242.
11. Gabriel Shire Tregear, "The Route," from *Tregear's Black Jokes* (London, 1834).
12. Ribeyre, *Cham*, 21.
13. Johann Casper Lavater, *La physiognomonie* [sic.], *ou L'art de connaître les hommes: D'après les traits de leur physionomie, leurs rapports avec les divers animaux, leurs penchants, etc.*, trans. H. Bacharach (Paris: Havard: 1845).
14. E.g., *The Illustrated London News*, January 24, 1846, 61.
15. I am grateful to Patchen Markell for suggesting these connections.
16. *Le Charivari* (Paris), April 8, 1850, 2.
17. Léon-François Hoffmann, with Carl Hermann Middelanis, *Faustin Soulouque d'Haïti dans l'histoire et la littérature* (Paris: Harmattan, 2007), 177–78.
18. *L'Argus* (Paris), February 19, 1850, 1.
19. *Le Daguerréotype théâtral: Journal artisitique et littéraire* (Paris), October 23, 1850, 1.
20. Michael Pickering, *Blackface Minstrelsy in Britain* (Aldershot UK: Ashgate, 2008), 15–17; Dale Cockrell, *Demons of Disorder: Early Blackface Minstrels and Their World* (Cambridge: Cambridge University Press, 1997), 54–56, 62–162.
21. David Kunzle, *Cham: The Best Comic Strips and Graphic Novelettes, 1839–1862* (Jackson: University Press of Mississippi, 2019), 3–5.
22. Arthur Bowler, "Article de M. Bowler," in Jules Auguste et al., *Les détracteurs de la race noire et de la république d'Haïti* (Paris: Marpon et Flammarion, 1882), 142.
23. Dantès Bellegarde, *La nation haïtienne*, 3 vols. (Paris: Gigord, 1938), 1:118–19; Elizabeth Childs, *Daumier and Exoticism: Satirizing the French and the Exotic* (New York: Peter Lang, 2004), 111–20; Joan Dayan, *Haiti, History, and the Gods* (Berkeley: University of California Press, 1995), 12–13; Laurent Dubois, *Haiti: The Aftershocks of History* (New York: Henry Holt, 2012), 146; Hoffmann, *Faustin Soulouque d'Haïti*, 75–103.
24. Marx, *The Eighteenth Brumaire of Louis Bonaparte*, 126. Translation lightly altered.
25. Terrell Carver, in Marx, *Later Political Writings*, xii; David McLellan, *Karl Marx: A Biography* (New York: Palgrave, 2006), 225; Robert Tucker, ed., *The Marx-Engels Reader*, 2nd ed. (New York: Norton, 1978), 594.

26. Here Hoffmann is a bit more subtle: he locates the beginnings of politics by proxy back to 1849 and the *fear* that Bonaparte might have imperial ambitions. Hoffmann, *Faustin Soulouque d'Haïti*, 81.
27. Bellegarde, *La nation haïtienne*, 1:119.
28. Pickering, *Blackface Minstrelsy in Britain*, xii.
29. Gustave d'Alaux (Maxime Raybaud), *L'Empereur Soulouque et son empire* (Paris: Michel Lévy Frères, 1856). See also *Revue des deux mondes* 8 (1850): 773-807, 1140-65; 9 (1851): 321-55, 521-45; 10 (1851): 193-224, 459-501.
30. D'Alaux, *L'Empereur Soulouque et son empire*, 204-15, 224-33.
31. Hoffmann, *Faustin Soulouque d'Haïti*, 88-92.
32. Gustave d'Alaux (Maxime Raybaud), *L'Empereur Soulouque et son empire*, 2nd ed. edition (Paris: Michel Lévy Frères, 1860); *Soulouque and His Empire*, trans. John H. Parkhill (Richmond, VA: J. W. Randolph, 1861).
33. D'Alaux, *L'Empereur Soulouque*, 63-64.
34. Thomas Carlyle (signed as "D"), "Occasional Discourse on the Negro Question," *Fraser's Magazine*, December 1849, 670-79, quote at 671.
35. Carlyle, "Occasional Discourse," 675.
36. M. B. Bird, *The Black Man; or, Haytian Independence: Deduced from Historical Notes, and Dedicated to the Government and People of Hayti* (New York: Privately printed, 1869), 291, 296.
37. Bird, *The Black Man*, 304.
38. John Bigelow, "A Visit to the Emperor of Haiti," appendix to *Jamaica in 1850: or, The Effect of Sixteen Years of Freedom on a Slave Colony* (New York: Putnam, 1851), 191.
39. Bigelow, "A Visit," 194-95.
40. Bigelow, "A Visit," 192.
41. Karen N. Salt, "Migrating Images of the Black Body Politic and the Sovereign State: Haiti in the 1850s," in *Migrating the Black Body: The African Diaspora and Visual Culture*, ed. Leigh Raiford and Heike Raphael-Hernandez (Seattle: University of Washington Press, 2017), 52-70.
42. I am grateful to Verena Erlenbusch-Anderson for encouraging me to discuss Ourika in this regard.
43. Anne-Louise-Germaine Necker, Baronne de Staël-Holstein, *Mirza, ou Lettre d'un voyageur* (1786), in *Oeuvres complètes de Mme. la Baronne de Staël* (Strasbourg: Treuttel et Würtz, 1820), 2:221-44.
44. Marie-Charlotte de Beauvau, *Souvenirs de la Maréchale Princesse de Beauvau* (Paris: Techener, 1872), 147-50.
45. Claire Lechat de Kersaint, Duchesse de Duras, *Ourika* (Berlin: Duncker et Humblot, 1824).
46. Thérèse de Raedt, "Ourika en noir et blanc: Une femme africaine en France," PhD diss., University of California, Davis, 2000, 156-216. See also Christopher Miller, *The French Atlantic Triangle: Literature and Culture of the Slave Trade* (Durham, NC: Duke University Press, 2007), 147, 158-73; and Salt, "Migrating Images," 57-58.
47. Raedt, "Ourika en noir et blanc," 245-46.
48. Earl G. Ingersoll, "The Appropriation of Black Experience in the 'Ourika' of Claire de Duras," *CEA Critic* 60, no. 3 (1998): 1-13.

49. David O'Connell argues that her insights about the psychological impact of racism foreshadow those of Franz Fanon. "Ourika: Black Face, White Mask," *French Review* 47, no. 6 (Spring 1974): 47–56, at 52.
50. Arthur de Gobineau, *Essai sur l'inégalité des races humaines* (Paris: Firmin Didot Frères, 1853).

9. SILENT IN PLAIN SIGHT

1. David Scott, *Conscripts of Modernity: The Tragedy of Colonial Enlightenment* (Durham, NC: Duke University Press, 2004).
2. Again, I thank Jason Frank for suggesting this formulation.
3. Michel Foucault, "Pouvoir et savoir" (1977), in *Dits et écrits II: 1976–1988* (Paris: Gallimard, 2001), 399-414.
4. Michel Foucault, "Entretien sur la prison: Le livre et sa méthode" (1975), *Dits et écrits I: 1954–75* (Paris: Gallimard, 2001), 1620.
5. E.g., "Lettre des administrateurs au ministre sur 1. les empoisonneurs, 2. la fustigation des empoisonneurs avec du médicinier, 3. le témoinage des esclaves," Léogane, March 18, 1746, Archives Nationales d'Outre-Mer, Aix-en-Provence, France, F3/88/206.
6. Gayatri Chakravorty Spivak, "More on Power/Knowledge" (1992), in *The Spivak Reader: Selected Works of Gayatri Chakravorty Spivak*, ed. Donna Landry and Gerald MacLean (New York: Routledge, 1996), 150-51.
7. Charles Mills, *The Racial Contract* (Ithaca, NY: Cornell University Press, 1997), 19. Emphasis in the original.
8. George Shulman, *American Prophesy: Race and Redemption in American Political Culture* (Minneapolis: University of Minnesota Press, 2008), 131-73; "Acknowledgment and Disavowal as an Idiom for Theorizing Politics," *Theory & Event* 14, no. 1 (2011); Sibylle Fischer, *Modernity Disavowed: Haiti and the Cultures of Slavery in the Age of Revolution* (Durham, NC: Duke University Press, 2004), 37-8, 114-20, 273-74; see also Michael Rogin, "Make My Day: Spectacle as Amnesia in Imperial Politics," *Representations* 29 (1990): 99-123.
9. Michel Foucault, *The Archaeology of Knowledge*, trans. A. M. Sheridan Smith (New York: Pantheon Books, 1972), 169.
10. See Michel Foucault, *The Hermeneutics of the Subject: Lectures at the Collège de France 1981–1982* (New York: Palgrave, 2005).
11. Banu Bargu, "The Silent Exception: Hunger Striking and Lip-Sewing," *Law, Culture, and the Humanities* (2017), https://journals.sagepub.com/doi/10.1177/1743872117709684; *Starve and Immolate* (New York: Columbia University Press, 2014); Stacey Liou, "Unspoken Insurgencies," *Political Theory* 45, no. 3 (2017): 342-61.
12. Gayatri Chakravorty Spivak, *Other Asias* (Oxford: Blackwell, 2008), 139.
13. Jürgen Habermas and Benedict Anderson provide insightful genealogies of the press where Foucault did not. Habermas traces its Enlightenment self-understanding and Anderson, its reality-constituting functions in the colonies. Habermas, *The Structural Transformation of the Public Sphere: An Inquiry Into a Category of Bourgeois Society*, trans. Thomas Burger with Frederick Lawrence (Cambridge, MA: MIT Press, 1989); Benedict Anderson, *Imagined Communities: Reflections on the Origin and Spread of Nationalism*, rev.

ed. (London: Verso, 1991), 24-46, 61-65, 194. See also Dena Goodman, *The Republic of Letters: A Cultural History of the French Enlightenment* (Ithaca, NY: Cornell University Press, 1994), 136-232.
14. Michel Foucault, *Discipline and Punish: The Birth of the Prison*, trans. Alan Sheridan (New York: Vintage Books, 1979), 293-308.
15. See Immanuel Wallerstein's contributions to Étienne Balibar and Immanuel Wallerstein, *Race, Nation, Class: Ambiguous Identities* (London: Verso, 1991).

Bibliography

Abbot, E. Stanley. "What Is Paranoia?" *American Journal of Psychiatry* 71, no. 1 (July 1914): 29–40.
Acaau, Louis-Jean-Jacques. "Adresse à ses frères du Port-Républicain." May 10, 1844. Bibliothèque Nationale de France, Paris, FOL-PU-145.
———. "Au peuple et à l'armée." May 5, 1844. Bibliothèque Nationale de France, Paris, FOL-PU-139.
———. "Proclamation au peuple et à l'armée." April 15, 1844. Bibliothèque Nationale de France, Paris, 8-PU-127.
Agulhon, Maurice. *Marianne Into Battle: Republican Imagery and Symbolism in France, 1789–1880.* Cambridge: Cambridge University Press, 1981.
Ahmed, Sara. *The Cultural Politics of Emotion.* 2nd ed. Edinburgh: Edinburgh University Press, 2014.
Alaux, Gustave de (Maxime Raybaud). *L'empereur Soulouque et son empire.* Paris: Michel Lévy Frères, 1856.
———. *L'empereur Soulouque et son empire.* 2nd ed. Paris: Michel Lévy Frères, 1860.
———. *Soulouque and His Empire.* Trans. John H. Parkhill. Richmond, VA: J. W. Randolph, 1861.
American Psychiatric Association. *Diagnostic and Statistical Manual of Mental Disorders.* 5th ed. Arlington, VA: American Psychiatric Association, 2013.
Anderson, Benedict. *Imagined Communities: Reflections on the Origin and Spread of Nationalism.* Rev. ed. London: Verso, 1991.
Anker, Elisabeth R. *Ugly Freedoms.* Durham, NC: Duke University Press, 2022.
Anon. *La caverne des brigands, ou recueil des assassinats, des vols, des brigandages, des scélérats qui ont expié leurs crimes. . . .* Paris: Locard et Davi, 1814, 1829, 1845.
Anon. *My Odyssey: Experiences of a Young Refugee from Two Revolutions, by a Creole of Saint Domingue.* Trans. and ed. Althéa de Puech Parham. Baton Rouge: Louisiana State University Press, 1959.
Anon. *Relation d'une conspiration tramée par les negres, dans l'isle de S. Domingue; défense que fait le jésuite confesseur, aux negres qu'on suplicie, de révéler leurs fauteurs et complices.* Paris[?]: n.p., 1758.
Apollon, Willy. *Le vaudou: Un espace pour les "voix."* Paris: Galilée, 1976.
Ardouin, Beaubrun. *Études sur l'histoire d'Haïti.* Paris: Dézobry et Magdeleine, 1860.
Auberteuil, Michel-René Hilliard de. *Considérations sur l'état présent de la colonie française de Saint-Domingue: Ouvrage politique et législatif.* Paris: Grangé, 1776.
Balibar, Étienne, and Immanuel Wallerstein. *Race, Nation, Class: Ambiguous Identities.* London: Verso, 1991.

Bargu, Banu. "The Silent Exception: Hunger Striking and Lip-Sewing." *Law, Culture, and the Humanities* (2017). https://journals.sagepub.com/doi/10.1177/1743872117709684.

——. *Starve and Immolate*. New York: Columbia University Press, 2014.

Bartélemy, Gérard. *L'univers rural haïtien: Le pays en dehors*. Paris: Harmattan, 1990.

Beaumarchais, Antoine de Labarre de. "Lettre cinquième." In *Amusements littéraires*, 3:60–65. La Haye: Van Duren, 1741.

Beauvau, Marie-Charlotte de. *Souvenirs de la Maréchale Princesse de Beauvau*. Paris: Techener, 1872.

Beckford, William. *A Descriptive Account of the Island of Jamaica: With Remarks upon the Cultivation of the Sugar-cane, throughout the Different Seasons of the Year, and Chiefly Considered in a Picturesque Point of View; also Observations and Reflections upon What would Probably Be the Consequences of an Abolition of the Slave-trade, and of the Emancipation of the Slaves*. 2 vols. London: Printed for T. and J. Egerton, 1790.

Bellegarde, Dantès. *La nation haïtienne*. 3 vols. Paris: Gigord, 1938.

Benjamin, Walter. *The Arcades Project*. Trans. H. Eiland and K. McLaughlin. Cambridge, MA: Harvard University Press, 1999.

Bennett, Jane. *Vibrant Matter: A Political Ecology of Things*. Durham, NC: Duke University Press, 2010.

Bhabha, Homi. "Of Mimicry and Man: The Ambivalence of Colonial Discourse." *October* 28 (1984): 125–33.

Bigelow, John. "A Visit to the Emperor of Haiti." Appendix to *Jamaica in 1850: or, The Effect of Sixteen Years of Freedom on a Slave Colony*. New York: Putnam, 1851.

Bird, M. B. *The Black Man; or, Haytian Independence: Deduced from Historical Notes, and Dedicated to the Government and People of Hayti*. New York: Privately printed, 1869.

Boilly, Charles. *Soyez libres et citoyens*. Frontispiece to Benjamin Frossard, *La cause des esclaves nègres et des habitans de la Guinée*. Lyon: Aimé de La Roche, 1789. Library Company of Philadelphia.

Bongie, Chris. "A Flexible Quill: Abbé de Lahaye's Role in Late Colonial Saint-Domingue, 1787–1791—The Legend and the Life." *Atlantic Studies* 15, no. 4 (2018): 476–503.

Bourdieu, Pierre. *Language and Symbolic Power*. Cambridge, MA: Harvard University Press, 1991.

——. *Manet: Une révolution symbolique—Cours au Collège de France (1998–2000), suivis d'un manuscrit inachevé de Pierre et Marie-Claire Bourdieu*. Paris: Raisons d'Agir/Seuil, 2013.

Bouretz, Pierre. *La république et l'universel*. Paris: Gallimard, 2000.

Bowler, Arthur. "Article de M. Bowler." In Jules Auguste et al., *Les détracteurs de la race noire et de la république d'Haïti*. Paris: Marpon et Flammarion, 1882.

Brandeis, Louis. *Olmstead v. United States* 277 US 438 (1928).

Brissot, Jacques-Pierre. *Discours sur la nécessité d'établir à Paris une société pour concourir . . . à l'abolition de la traite et de l'esclavage des negres*, February 19, 1788, in *La Société des Amis des Noirs, La Révolution française et l'abolition de l'esclavage*. 12 vols. Paris: Editions d'Histoire Sociale, 1968.

Brown, Gordon S. *Toussaint's Clause: The Founding Fathers and the Haitian Revolution*. Jackson: University Press of Mississippi, 2005.

Butler, Judith. *Bodies That Matter: On the Discursive Limits of "Sex."* New York: Routledge, 1999.

——. *Gender Trouble: Feminism and the Subversion of Identity*. New York: Routledge, 1999.

C., M. de. "Makandal, histoire véritable." *Mercure de France*, September 15, 1787, 102–14.

Cabon, Adolphe. *Un siècle et demi de journalisme en Haïti*. Worcester, MA: American Antiquarian Society, 1940.

Cambefort, Joseph-Paul-Augustin. *Mémoire justificatif de Joseph-Paul-Augustin Cambefort....* Chartres: Frères Chaignieau, 1793.
Carlyle, Thomas (signed as "D"). "Occasional Discourse on the Negro Question." *Fraser's Magazine*, December 1849, 670-79.
Carteau, Félix. *Soirées bermudiennes, ou entretiens sur les événemens qui ont opéré la ruine le la partie française de l'île St.-Domingue.* Bordeaux: Pellier-Lawalle, 1802.
Carver, Terrell. "Editor's Introduction." In Karl Marx, *Later Political Writings*, ed. Terrell Carver, ix-xx. Cambridge: Cambridge University Press, 1996.
Casimir, Jean. *La culture opprimée.* Delmas, Haiti: Lakay, 2001.
Césaire, Aimé. *Cahier d'un retour au pays natal.* Paris: Presence Africaine, 1983.
Chamayou, Grégoire. *Les chasses à l'homme: Histoire et philosophie du pouvoir cynégétique.* Paris: La Fabrique, 2010.
Chamoiseau, Patrick. *L'esclave vieil homme et le molosse.* Paris: Gallimard, 1997.
Champfleury. *Histoire de la caricature moderne.* Rev. 3rd ed. Paris: Librairie de la Société des Gens de Lettres, 1885.
Cheah, Pheng. "Biopower and the New International Division of Reproductive Labor." In *Can the Subaltern Speak? Reflections on the History of an Idea*, ed. Rosalind Morris, 179-212. New York: Columbia University Press, 2010.
Childs, Elizabeth. *Daumier and Exoticism: Satirizing the French and the Exotic.* New York: Peter Lang, 2004.
Cochin, Augustin. *La révolution et la libre-pensée.* Paris: Copernic, 1979.
Cockrell, Dale. *Demons of Disorder: Early Blackface Minstrels and Their World.* Cambridge: Cambridge University Press, 1997.
Collection générale des décrets rendus par la convention nationale . . . , Mois de septembre 1793, jusqu'au 21 inclusivement. Paris: Baudouin, [1793].
"Constitution de 1791." In *Les constitutions de la France depuis 1789.* Paris: Proux, 1848.
"Constitution de 1843." In Louis-Joseph Janvier, *Les constitutions d'Haïti (1801–1885).* Paris: Flammarion, 1886.
"Constitution impériale d'Haïti," 1805. In Janvier, *Les constitutions d'Haïti.*
Cook, Mercer. "Julien Raimond." *Journal of Negro History* 26, no. 2 (1941): 158-63.
Coste, Frère [?] de la. *Voyage philosophique d'Angleterre, fait en 1783 et 1784.* Paris: Poinçot, 1787.
Coyer, Gabriel-François. *Discours sur la satyre contre les philosophes.* In *Collection complète des oeuvres de M. L'Abbé Coyer.* Neuchatel: Société Typographique, 1780.
Curtin, Phillip. *The Atlantic Slave Trade: A Census.* Madison: University of Wisconsin Press, 1969.
Davis, David Brion, ed. *The Fear of Conspiracy: Images of Un-American Subversion from the Revolution to the Present.* Ithaca, NY: Cornell University Press, 1971.
———. *The Problem of Slavery in the Age of Revolution, 1770–1823.* Ithaca, NY: Cornell University Press, 1975.
Dayan, Joan. *Haiti, History, and the Gods.* Berkeley: University of California Press, 1995.
Debbasch, Yvan. "Le marronnage: Essai sur la désertion de l'esclave antillais, seconde partie, La société coloniale contre le marronnage." *L'année sociologique* 13 (1962): 117-95.
Debien, Gabriel. *Études antillaises XVIIIe siècle.* Paris: Colin, 1956.
———. "Le marronage aux Antilles françaises au XVIIIe siècle." *Caribbean Studies* 6, no. 3 (1966): 3-43.
Derrida, Jacques. "Declarations of Independence." *New Political Science* 15 (1986): 7-15.

Dessalines, Jean-Jacques. "Acte d'indépendence." January 1, 1804. Port-au-Prince: Imprimerie du Gouvernement, 1804. Reprinted in Dessalines, *Lois et actes sous le règne de Jean Jacques Dessalines*, 8–11. Port-au-Prince: Presses Nationales d'Haïti.

———. *Proclamation du général en chef au peuple d'Haïti*. January 1, 1804. Port-au-Prince: Imprimerie du Gouvernement, 1804. Reprinted in Dessalines, *Lois et actes*, 8–11.

Dubois, F. E. *Précis historique de la Révolution haïtien de 1843*. Paris: Bourdier, 1866.

Dubois, Laurent. *Avengers of the New World: The Story of the Haitian Revolution*. Cambridge, MA: Harvard University Press, 2004.

———. *Haiti: The Aftershocks of History*. New York: Henry Holt, 2012.

———. "Translator's Introduction." In Achille Mbembe, *Critique of Black Reason*. Durham, NC: Duke University Press, 2017.

Duchet, Michèle. *Diderot et l'histoire des deux Indes, ou l'écriture fragmentaire*. Paris: Nizet, 1978.

Dupont, Christian, and Peter Onuf, eds. *Declaring Independence: The Origin and Influence of America's Founding Document*. Charlottesville: University of Virginia Library, 2008.

Duras, Claire Lechat de Kersaint, Duchesse de. *Ourika*. Berlin: Duncker & Humblot, 1824.

Edwards, Bryan. *Observations on the Disposition, Character, Manners, and Habits of Life, of the Maroon Negroes of the Island of Jamaica: And a Detail of the Origin, Progress, and Termination of the Late War Between Those People and the White Inhabitants*. In *The Proceedings of the Governor and Assembly of Jamaica, in Regard to the Maroon Negroes*. London: Stockdale, 1796.

Ellison, Ralph. *Invisible Man*. 2nd ed. New York: Vintage Books, 1995.

Equiano, Olaudah. *The Interesting Narrative of the Life of Olaudah Equiano, or Gustavus Vassa, The African, Written by Himself*. New York: W. Durrell, 1791.

———. [As Gustavus Vasa, The African.] "To the Committee for the Abolition of the Slave Trade at Plymouth." *The Public Advertiser* (London), Saturday, February 14, 1789.

Erlenbusch-Anderson, Verena. *Genealogies of Terrorism: Revolution, State Violence, Empire*. New York: Columbia University Press, 2018.

"Extrait des pièces originales déposées au greffe de la municipalité de Toussaint Louverture." In *Arrêtés des différentes communes de la colonie de St.-Domingue adressées à l'agent particulier du directoire*. Cap-Français: P. Roux, 1799.

Fanon, Franz. *Black Skin, White Masks*. Trans. Richard Philcox. New York: Grove, 2008.

———. *Peau noir, masques blancs*. Paris: Seuil, 1952.

Farge, Arlette. *The Allure of the Archives*. New Haven, CT: Yale University Press, 2013.

Feugère, Anatole. *Un precurseur de la révolution: L'Abbé Raynal (1713–1796)*. Geneva: Slatkine, [1922] 1970.

Fick, Carolyn. *The Making of Haiti: The Saint Domingue Revolution from Below*. Knoxville: University of Tennessee Press, 1990.

Finley, Cheryl. *Committed to Memory: The Art of the Slave Ship Icon*. Princeton, NJ: Princeton University Press, 2018.

Fischer, Sibylle. *Modernity Disavowed: Haiti and the Cultures of Slavery in the Age of Revolution*. Durham, NC: Duke University Press, 2004.

Fontana, Biancamaria, ed. *The Invention of the Modern Republic*. Cambridge: Cambridge University Press, 1994.

Foucault, Michel. *The Archaeology of Knowledge*. Trans. Alan Sheridan Smith. New York: Pantheon Books, 1972.

———. *Discipline and Punish: The Birth of the Prison.* Trans. Alan Sheridan. New York: Vintage Books, 1995.

———. "Entretien sur la prison: Le livre et sa méthode" (1975). In *Dits et écrits I: 1954–75*, 1608–21. Paris: Gallimard, 2001.

———. *The Hermeneutics of the Subject, Lectures at the Collège de France 1981–1982.* New York: Palgrave, 2005.

———. *The History of Sexuality, Volume 1: An Introduction.* New York: Vintage Books, 1980.

———. *Lectures on the Will to Know: Lectures at the Collège de France 1970–1971.* Trans. Graham Burchell. New York: Palgrave Macmillan, 2013.

———. *On the Government of the Living: Lectures at the Collège de France 1979–1980*, Trans. Graham Burchell. New York: Palgrave Macmillan, 2014.

———. *The Order of Things: An Archaeology of the Human Sciences.* New York: Vintage Books, 1994.

———. "Polemics, Politics, and Problematizations: An Interview with Michel Foucault." In Foucault, *Ethics: Subjectivity and Truth, Essential Works of Foucault, 1954–1984*, ed. Paul Rabinow, 111-19. New York: New Press, 1997.

———. "Pouvoir et savoir" (1977). In *Dits et écrits II: 1976–1988*, 399–414. Paris: Gallimard, 2001.

———. *Power/Knowledge: Selected Interviews and Other Writings, 1972–1977.* Ed. Colin Gordon. New York: Pantheon Books, 1980.

———. *The Punitive Society: Lectures at the Collège de France 1972–1973.* Trans. Graham Burchell. New York: Palgrave Macmillan, 2015.

———. "Réponse à une Question" (1968). In *Dits et écrits I: 1954–1975*, 701-23.

———. *Security, Territory, Population: Lectures at the Collège de France 1977–1978.* Trans. Graham Burchell. New York: Palgrave, 2007.

———. *"Society Must Be Defended": Lectures at the Collège de France 1975–1976.* New York: Picador, 2003.

———. *The Use of Pleasure: The History of Sexuality, Volume Two.* New York: Vintage Books, 1986.

———. "What Is an Author?" In *Language, Counter-Memory, and Practice: Selected Essays and Interviews*, ed. Donald Bouchard, 113-38. Ithaca, NY: Cornell University Press, 1977.

———. *Wrong-Doing, Truth-Telling: The Function of Avowal in Justice.* Chicago: University of Chicago Press, 2014.

Foucault, Michel, and Gilles Deleuze. "Intellectuals and Power." In Foucault, *Language, Counter-Memory, and Practice*, 205-17.

Fouchard, Jean. *The Haitian Maroons: Liberty or Death.* Trans. A. F. Watts. New York: Blyden, 1981.

Fournier de la Chapelle, [Charles]. "Mémoire pour servir à l'information des procès contre les nègres devins, sorciers, et empoisonneurs." 1758. Archives Nationales d'Outre-Mer, Aix-en-Provence, France, F3/88/236.

Frank, Jason. *Constituent Moments: Enacting the People in Postrevolutionary America.* Durham, NC: Duke University Press, 2010.

Franklin, James. *The Present State of Hayti (Saint Domingo): With Remarks on Its Agriculture, Commerce, Laws, Religion, Finances, and Population, Etc. Etc.* London: John Murray, 1828.

Garran de Coulon, Jean-Philippe. *Rapport sur les troubles de Saint-Domingue, fait au nom de la Commission des Colonies . . .* 4 vols. Paris: Imprimerie Nationale, 1797-1799.

Garrigus, John. *Before Haiti: Race and Citizenship in French Saint-Domingue.* New York: Palgrave, 2006.

Geffarth, Renko. "The Masonic Necromancer: Shifting Identities in the Lives of Johann Georg Schrepfer." In *Polemical Encounters: Esoteric Discourse and Its Others*, 181-97. Leiden: Brill, 2007.

Geggus, David. *Haitian Revolutionary Studies*. Bloomington: University of Indiana Press, 2002.

——. "Marronage, Voodoo, and the Saint Domingue Slave Revolt of 1791." *Proceedings of the Meeting of the French Colonial Historical Society* 15 (1992): 22-35.

Genovese, Eugene. *From Rebellion to Revolution: Afro-American Slave Revolts in the Making of the Modern World*. Baton Rouge: Louisiana State University Press, 1979.

Gentil, Jean-Philippe-Gui Le, Comte de Paroy. *Mémoires du Comte de Paroy: Souvenirs d'un défenseur de la famille royale pendant la révolution (1789–1797)*. Paris: Plon, 1895.

Getachew, Adom. "Universalism After the Post-Colonial Turn: Interpreting the Haitian Revolution." *Political Theory* 44, no. 6 (2016): 821-45.

Girard, Philippe R., and Jean-Louis Donnadieu. "Toussaint Before Louverture: New Archival Findings on the Early Life of Toussaint Louverture." *William and Mary Quarterly* 70, no. 1 (January 2013): 41-78.

Glissant, Édouard. *Poetics of Relation*. Trans. Betsy Wing. Ann Arbor: University of Michigan Press, 1997.

Glotz, Marguerite, and Madeleine Maire. *Salons du XVIIIème siècle*. Paris: Nouvelles Editions Latines, 1949.

Gobineau, Arthur de. *Essai sur l'inégalité des races humaines*. Paris: Firmin Didot Frères, 1853.

Gonzalez, Johnhenry. *Maroon Nation: A History of Revolutionary Haiti*. New Haven, CT: Yale University Press, 2019.

Goodman, Dena. *The Republic of Letters: A Cultural History of the French Enlightenment*. Ithaca, NY: Cornell University Press, 1994.

Guyot, Edmé-Gilles. *Nouvelles récréations physiques et mathématiques*. Paris: Gueffier, 1770.

Habermas, Jürgen. *The Structural Transformation of the Public Sphere: An Inquiry into a Category of Bourgeois Society*. Trans. Thomas Burger with Frederick Lawrence. Cambridge, MA: MIT Press, 1989.

Harris, Jennifer. "The Red Cap of Liberty: A Study of Dress Worn by French Revolutionary Partisans 1789-94." *Eighteenth-Century Studies* 14, no. 2 (1981): 283-312.

Hartman, Saidiya. *Scenes of Subjection: Terror, Slavery, and Self-Making in Nineteenth-Century America*. Oxford: Oxford University Press, 1997.

Hérard, Charles. "Acte de déchéance." *Le manifeste*, March 26, 1843, 3-4.

——. "Proclamation du 27 Janvier 1843." In Emmanuel Édouard, *Recueil général des lois et actes du gouvernement d'Haïti et documents historiques*, vol. VII, 1840–1843, 155-56. Paris: Pedone-Lauriel, 1888.

Hérard, Charles, et al. "Manifeste, ou appel des citoyen des cayes à leurs concitoyens." Reprinted in Édouard, *Recueil général des lois et actes*, 118-29.

Hirschman, Albert. *Exit, Voice, and Loyalty*. Cambridge, MA: Harvard University Press, 1970.

Hobbes, Thomas. *Leviathan*. Ed. Richard Tuck. Cambridge: Cambridge University Press, 1996.

Hoffmann, Léon-François, with Carl Hermann Middelanis. *Faustin Soulouque d'Haïti dans l'histoire et la littérature*. Paris: Harmattan, 2007.

Hofstadter, Richard. "The Paranoid Style in American Politics." *Harper's Magazine*, November 1964, 77-86.

Honour, Hugh. *From the American Revolution to World War I: Slaves and Liberators*. Cambridge, MA: Harvard University Press, 2012.

Hooker, Juliet. *Theorizing Race in the Americas: Douglass, Sarmiento, Du Bois, and Vasconcelos.* New York: Oxford University Press, 2017.

Hunt, Lynn. "Freedom of Dress in Revolutionary France." In *From the Royal to the Republican Body: Incorporating the Political in Seventeenth- and Eighteenth-Century France,* ed. Sara Melzer and Kathryn Norberg, 224-49. Berkeley: University of California Press, 1998.

———. *Inventing Human Rights: A History.* New York: Norton, 2007.

———. *Politics, Culture, and Class in the French Revolution.* Berkeley: University of California Press, 1984.

Hutton, Clinton. *The Logic and Historical Significance of the Haitian Revolution and the Cosmological Roots of Haitian Freedom.* Kingston, Jamaica: Arawak, 2005.

Ingersoll, Earl G. "The Appropriation of Black Experience in the 'Ourika' of Claire de Duras." *CEA Critic* 60, no. 3 (1998): 1-13.

James, C. L. R. *The Black Jacobins: Toussaint L'Ouverture and the San Domingo Revolution.* 2nd rev. ed. New York: Vintage Books, 1989.

Jaucourt, Louis de. "Supplice." In *Encyclopédie, ou dictionnaire raisonné des sciences, des arts et des métiers,* ed. Denis Diderot et al., 15:674. Geneva, 1772.

Jenson, Deborah. *Beyond the Slave Narrative: Sex, Politics, and Manuscripts in the Haitian Revolution.* Liverpool: Liverpool University Press, 2011.

Johnson, Sara E. *The Fear of French Negroes: Transcolonial Collaboration in the Revolutionary Americas.* Berkeley: University of California Press, 2012.

Joseph-Gabriel, Annette K. "Creolizing Freedom: French-Creole Translations of Liberty and Equality in the Haitian Revolution." *Slavery and Abolition* 36, no. 1 (2015): 111-23.

Kaplan, Steven. *Bread, Politics, and Political Economy in the Reign of Louis XV.* The Hague: Martinus Nijhoff, 1976.

King, Stewart R. *Blue Coat or Powdered Wig: Free People of Color in Pre-Revolutionary Saint Domingue.* Athens: University of Georgia Press, 2001.

———. "The Maréchaussée of Saint-Domingue: Balancing the Ancien Régime and Modernity." *Journal of Colonialism and Colonial History* 5, no. 2 (2004), https://muse.jhu.edu/article/173267.

Koopman, Colin. *Genealogy as Critique: Foucault and the Problems of Modernity.* Bloomington: Indiana University Press, 2013.

Kramer, Sina. *Excluded Within: The (Un)Intelligibility of Radical Political Actors.* New York: Oxford University Press, 2017.

Krauss, Rosalind. *The Originality of the Avant-Garde and Other Modernist Myths.* Cambridge, MA: MIT Press, 1985.

Kris, Ernst, and Ernst Gombrich. "The Principles of Caricature." *British Journal of Medical Psychology* 17, nos. 3-4 (1938): 319-42.

Kunzle, David. *Cham: The Best Comic Strips and Graphic Novelettes, 1839–1862.* Jackson: University Press of Mississippi, 2019.

Lacroix, François-Joseph-Pamphile de. *Mémoires pour servir à l'histoire de la révolution de Saint-Domingue.* 2 vols. Paris: Pillet Aîné, 1819.

Landes, Joan. *Women and the Public Sphere in the Age of the French Revolution.* Ithaca, NY: Cornell University Press, 1988.

Lavater, Johann Casper. *La physiognomonie* [sic], *ou l'art de connaître les hommes: D'après les traits de leur physionomie, leurs rapports avec les divers animaux, leurs penchants, etc.* Trans. H. Bacharach. Paris: Havard, 1845.

Lepelletier de Saint-Remy, Romuald. *Saint-Domingue: Étude et solution nouvelle de la question haïtienne*. 2 vols. Paris: Bertrand, 1846.

Levy, D., H. Applewhite, and M. Johnson, eds. *Women in Revolutionary Paris, 1789–1795*. Urbana: University of Illinois Press, 1979.

Libby, Susan H. "The Color of Frenchness: Racial Identity and Visuality in French Anti-Slavery Imagery, 1788-94." In *Blacks and Blackness in European Art of the Long Nineteenth Century*, ed. Adrienne L. Childs and Susan H. Libby, 19-45. Surrey, UK: Ashgate, 2014.

Liou, Stacey. "Unspoken Insurgencies." *Political Theory* 45, no. 3 (2017): 342-61.

Locke, John. *Two Treatise of Government*. Ed. Peter Laslett. Cambridge: Cambridge University Press, 1988.

Louis XIV de France. *Édit du roy, touchant la police des isles de l'Amerique françoise, du mois de mars 1685*. Reprinted in René-Josué Valin, *Nouveau commentaire sur l'ordonnance de la marine, du mois d'août 1681*, 1:405-9. 2 vols. La Rochelle: Mesnier, 1760.

——. *Le code noir ou édit du roy, servant de reglement pour le gouvernement et l'administration de justice et la police des isles françoises de l'Amerique, et pour la discipline et le commerce des negres et esclaves dans ledit pays, donné à Versailles au mois de mars 1685*. Paris: Claude Girard, 1735.

Louis XV de France. *Édit du roi, touchant l'état et la discipline des esclaves nègres de la Louisane, donné à Versailles au mois de mars 1724*. Paris: Imprimerie royale, 1724.

Louverture, Toussaint. *Constitution de 1801*. Reprinted in Louis-Joseph Janvier, *Les constitutions d'Haïti (1801–1885)*, 7-23. Paris: Flammarion, 1886.

——. *The Haitian Revolution*. Ed. Nick Nesbitt. London: Verso, 2008.

Luxon, Nancy. "Gender, Agency, and the Circulations of Power." In *Archives of Infamy: Foucault on State Power in the Lives of Ordinary Citizens*, ed. Nancy Luxon, 295-340. Minneapolis: University of Minnesota Press, 2019.

MacGaffey, Wyatt. *Kongo Political Culture: The Conceptual Challenge of the Particular*. Bloomington: Indiana University Press, 2000.

MacQueen, James. *The Colonial Controversy, Containing a Refutation of the Calumnies of the Anti-colonists* . . . Glasgow: Khull, Blackie, 1825.

Madiou, Thomas. *Histoire d'Haïti*. 8 vols. Port-au-Prince: Henri Deschamps, [1847] 1989.

Malone, Dumas, ed. *Dictionary of American Biography*. New York: Scribner, 1934.

Manigat, Leslie. *La Révolution haïtienne de 1843: Essai d'analyse, histoire d'une conjoncture de crise*. Port-au-Prince: CHUDAC, 2007.

Mannoni, Laurent. *The Great Art of Light and Shadow: Archaeology of the Cinema*. Trans. Richard Crangle. Exeter: University of Exeter Press, 2000.

Marion, Fulgence. *L'optique*. 3rd ed. Paris: Hachette, 1874.

Martel, James R. *The Misinterpellated Subject*. Durham, NC: Duke University Press, 2017.

——. *The One and Only Law: Walter Benjamin and the Second Commandment*. Ann Arbor: University of Michigan Press, 2014.

Marx, Karl. *The Eighteenth Brumaire of Louis Bonaparte*. In *Later Political Writings*, ed. Terrell Carver, 31-127. Cambridge: Cambridge University Press, 1996.

——. "Preface to *A Critique of Political Economy*." In *Selected Writings*, ed. David McLellan, 388-91. Oxford: Oxford University Press, 1977.

Marx, Karl, and Frederick Engels. *The German Ideology, Part One with Selections from Parts 2 and 3 and Supplementary Texts*. Rev. ed. Ed. C. J. Arthur. New York: International Publishers, 2016.

Mbembe, Achille. *Critique de la raison nègre*. Paris: Découverte, 2013.
———. *Critique of Black Reason*. Trans. Laurent Dubois. Durham, NC: Duke University Press, 2017.
McLellan, David. *Karl Marx: A Biography*. New York: Palgrave, 2006.
McWorter, Ladelle. *Racism and Sexual Oppression in Anglo-America: A Genealogy*. Bloomington: Indiana University Press, 2009.
Ménier, M.-A., and G. Debien. "Journaux de Saint-Domingue." *Revue d'histoire des colonies* 36 (1949): 424-75.
Michel, Jean-Baptiste, et al. "Quantitative Analysis of Culture Using Millions of Digitized Books." *Science* 331, no. 6014 (January 14, 2011): 176-82.
Mill, John Stuart. "The Condition of Ireland." Occasional articles published in the *Morning Chronicle*, October-November 1846. Reprinted in *Collected Works* 24:879-82, 913-16, 930-32, 942-45, 991-93, 1004-8. Toronto: University of Toronto Press, 1963.
———. "Poulett Scrope on the Poor Laws." *Morning Chronicle*, October 31, 1846. Reprinted in *Collected Works*, 24:923-26.
Miller, Christopher. *The French Atlantic Triangle: Literature and Culture of the Slave Trade*. Durham, NC: Duke University Press, 2007.
Mills, Charles. *The Racial Contract*. Ithaca, NY: Cornell University Press, 1997.
Moreau de Saint-Méry, Médéric-Louis-Elie. *Considérations présentées aux vrais amis du repos et du bonheur de la France, à l'occasion des nouveaux movemens de quelques soi-disant amis-des-noirs*, March 1, 1791. Paris: Imprimerie Nationale, 1791.
———. *Description topographique, physique, civile, politique et historique de la partie française de l'isle Saint-Domingue* (1797). 3 vols. Saint Denis: Société Française d'Histoire d'Outre-Mer, 2004.
———. *Loix et constitutions des colonies françoises de l'Amérique sous le vent*. 6 vols. Paris: Privately printed, 1784.
"Moreau de Saint-Méry, Médéric-Louis-Elie." In *Dictionary of American Biography*, ed. Dumas Malone. New York: Scribner, 1934.
Morénas, Joseph Elzéar. *Précis historique de la traite des noirs et de l'esclavage colonial: Contenant; l'Origine de la traite, ses progrès, son état actuel, et un exposé des horreurs produites par le despotisme des colons*. Paris: Firmin Didot, 1828.
Munsche, Heather, and Harry Whitaker. "Eighteenth Century Classification of Mental Illness: Linnaeus, de Sauvages, Vogel, and Cullen." *Cognitive and Behavioral Neurology* 25, no. 4 (December 2012): 224-39.
Negt, Oskar, and Alexander Kluge. *Public Sphere and Experience: Analysis of the Bourgeois and Proletarian Public Sphere*. London: Verso, 2016.
Nesbitt, Nick. *Universal Emancipation: The Haitian Revolution and the Radical Enlightenment*. Charlottesville: University of Virginia Press, 2008.
Nicolet, Claude. *L'idée républicaine en France: Essai d'histoire critique*. Paris: Gallimard, 1982.
O'Connell, David. "Ourika: Black Face, White Mask." *French Review* 47, no. 6 (Spring 1974): 47-56.
Olson, Kevin. *Imagined Sovereignties: The Power of the People and Other Myths of the Modern Age*. Cambridge: Cambridge University Press, 2016.
———. "Legitimate Speech and Hegemonic Idiom: The Limits of Deliberative Democracy in the Diversity of Its Voices." *Political Studies* 59, no. 3 (2011): 527-46.
Ozouf, Mona. *Festivals and the French Revolution*. Cambridge, MA: Harvard University Press, 1988.

———. *L'homme régénéré: Essais sur la Révolution française*. Paris: Gallimard, 1989.

———. "L'opinion publique." In *The French Revolution and the Creation of Modern Political Culture*, vol. 1, *The Political Culture of the Old Regime*, ed. Keith Baker, 419–34. Oxford: Pergamon Press, 1987.

———. "La Révolution française et l'idée de l'homme nouveau." In *The Political Culture of the French Revolution*, ed. Colin Lucas, 213–32. Oxford: Pergamon Press, 1987.

Patterson, Orlando. *Slavery and Social Death: A Comparative Study*. 2nd ed. Cambridge, MA: Harvard University Press, 2018.

Paulson, Ronald. *Representations of Revolution: 1789–1820*. New Haven, CT: Yale University Press, 1983.

Pellegrin, Nicole. *Les vêtements de la liberté: Abécédaire des pratiques vestimentaires en France de 1780 à 1800*. Aix-en-Provence: Alinea, 1989.

Petit Larousse illustré. Paris: Librairie Larousse, 1973.

Pickering, Michael. *Blackface Minstrelsy in Britain*. Aldershot, UK: Ashgate, 2008.

Pluchon, Pierre. *Vaudou, sorciers, empoisonneurs: De Saint-Domingue à Haïti*. Port-au-Prince: Karthala, 1987.

Popkin, Jeremy. *Revolutionary News: The Press in France, 1789–1799*. Durham, NC: Duke University Press, 1990.

Pouy, Ferdinand. *Histoire des cocardes blanches, noires, vertes, and tricolores*. 2nd ed. Paris: Baur et Détaille, 1872.

Pradine, Linstant, ed. *Recueil général des lois et actes du gouvernement d'Haïti*. 8 vols. Paris: Durand, 1865.

Price-Mars, Jean. *Ainsi parla l'oncle*. New ed. Ottawa: Lemeac, [1928] 1973.

Rainsford, Marcus. *An Historical Account of the Black Empire of Hayti: Comprehending a View of the Principal Transactions in the Revolution of Saint Domingo; with its Antient and Modern State*. London: Albion Press, 1805.

Raynal, Guillaume-Thomas-François. *Histoire philosophique et politique des établissemens et du commerce des européens dans les deux Indes*. 10 vols. Geneva: Pellet, [1770] 1780.

Raedt, Thérèse de. "Ourika en noir et blanc: Une femme africaine en France." PhD dissertation, University of California, Davis, 2000.

Ribeyre, Félix. *Cham: Sa vie et son oeuvre*. Paris: Plon, 1884.

Roberts, Neil. *Freedom as Marronage*. Chicago: University of Chicago Press, 2015.

Robertson, E. G. [Étienne-Gaspard]. *Mémoires récréatifs, scientifiques et anecdotiques du physicien-aéronaute E. G. Robertson: Connu par ses expériences de fantasmagorie, et par ses ascensions aérostatiques dans les principales villes de l'Europe*. Paris: Privately printed, 1831.

Rogin, Michael. "Make My Day: Spectacle as Amnesia in Imperial Politics." *Representations* 29 (1990): 99–123.

Rose, Jacqueline. *States of Fantasy*. Oxford: Oxford University Press, 1996.

Salt, Karen N. "Migrating Images of the Black Body Politic and the Sovereign State: Haiti in the 1850s." In *Migrating the Black Body: The African Diaspora and Visual Culture*, ed. Leigh Raiford and Heike Raphael-Hernandez, 52–70. Seattle: University of Washington Press, 2017.

Schlosser, Julius von. *Art and Curiosity Cabinets of the Late Renaissance*. Trans. Jonathan Blower. Los Angeles: Getty Research Institute, 2021.

Schmitt, Carl. *The Concept of the Political*. Expanded ed. Trans. George Schwab. University of Chicago Press, 2007.

Schoelcher, Victor. *Colonies étrangères et Haïti*. 2 vols. Paris: Pagnerre, 1843.
Scott, David. *Conscripts of Modernity: The Tragedy of Colonial Enlightenment*. Durham, NC: Duke University Press, 2004.
Scott, James. *Weapons of the Weak: Everyday Forms of Peasant Resistance*. New Haven, CT: Yale University Press, 1985.
Scott, Julius S. *The Common Wind: Afro-American Currents in the Age of the Haitian Revolution*. London: Verso, 2018.
Sedgwick, Eve Kosofsky. *Touching Feeling: Affect, Pedagogy, Performativity*. Durham, NC: Duke University Press, 2003.
Shulman, George. "Acknowledgment and Disavowal as an Idiom for Theorizing Politics." *Theory & Event* 14, no. 1 (2011). https://muse.jhu.edu/article/423098.
———. *American Prophesy: Race and Redemption in American Political Culture*. Minneapolis: University of Minnesota Press, 2008.
Société des Amis des Noirs. *Adresse a l'Assemblée Nationale*. Paris: Potier de Lille, 1790.
———. *Adresse à l'Assemblée Nationale, pour l'abolition de la traite de noirs*, February 5, 1790. Paris: Potier de Lille, 1790.
———. *Adresse de la Société des Amis des Noirs, à l'Assemblée Nationale . . .* Paris: Imprimerie de Patriote François, March 1791.
Société des Droits de l'Homme et du Citoyen. "Résolution de la société 'Des Droits de l'Homme et du Citoyen' établie aux Cayes, du 21 novembre 1842." In Édouard, *Recueil général des lois et actes*, 7:139-40.
Spivak, Gayatri Chakravorty. "Can the Subaltern Speak?" (1988). In *Can the Subaltern Speak? Reflections on the History of an Idea*, ed. Rosalind Morris, 237-91. New York: Columbia University Press, 2010.
———. *A Critique of Postcolonial Reason: Toward a History of the Vanishing Present*. Cambridge, MA: Harvard University Press, 1999.
———. "More on Power/Knowledge" (1992). In *The Spivak Reader: Selected Works of Gayatri Chakravorty Spivak*, ed. Donna Landry and Gerald MacLean, 141-74. New York: Routledge, 1996.
———. *Other Asias*. Oxford: Blackwell, 2008.
Staël-Holstein, Anne-Louise-Germaine Necker, Baronne de. *Mirza, ou Lettre d'un voyageur* (1786). In *Oeuvres complètes de Mme. la Baronne de Staël*, 2:221-44. Strasbourg: Treuttel et Würtz, 1820.
Stengers, Isabelle. "Putting Problematization to the Test of Our Present." *Theory, Culture, and Society* 38, no. 2 (2021): 71-92.
Stoler, Ann Laura. *Along the Archival Grain: Epistemic Anxieties and Colonial Common Sense*. Princeton, NJ: Princeton University Press, 2009.
———. *Duress: Imperial Durabilities of Our Times*. Durham, NC: Duke University Press, 2016.
———. *Race and the Education of Desire: Foucault's History of Sexuality and the Colonial Order of Things*. Durham, NC: Duke University Press, 1995.
Tackett, Timothy. *The Coming of the Terror in the French Revolution*. Cambridge, MA: Harvard University Press, 2015.
Thoby, Armand. *La question agraire en Haïti*. Port-au-Prince? n.p., 1888.
Thompson, Alvin O. *Flight to Freedom: African Runaways and Maroons in the Americas*. Kingston, Jamaica: University of the West Indies Press, 2006.
Thornton, John. "'I Am the Subject of the King of Congo': African Political Ideology and the Haitian Revolution." *Journal of World History* 4, no. 2 (1993): 193-214.

Tocqueville, Alexis de. *De la démocratie en Amérique*. 2 vols. Paris: C. Gosselin, 1835, 1840.
——. *The Old Regime and the French Revolution*. Trans. Stuart Gilbert. New York: Doubleday, 1955.
Tomba, Massimiliano. *Insurgent Universality: An Alternative Legacy of Modernity*. Oxford: Oxford University Press, 2019.
Tregear, Gabriel Shire. *Tregear's Black Jokes*. London, 1834.
Trouillot, Michel-Rolph. *Haiti, State Against Nation: The Origins and Legacy of Duvalierism*. New York: Monthly Review Press, 1990.
——. *Silencing the Past: Power and the Production of History*. Boston: Beacon Press, 1995.
Vaissière, Pierre de. *Saint-Domingue: La société et la vie créoles sous l'ancien régime (1629–1789)*. Paris: Perrin, 1909.
Wall, Illan rua. *Human Rights and Constituent Power: Without Model or Warranty*. London: Routledge, 2012.
Warner, Michael. *Publics and Counterpublics*. New York: Zone Books, 2002.
Warner-Lewis, Maureen. *Central Africa in the Caribbean: Transcending Time, Transforming Cultures*. Kingston, Jamaica: University of the West Indies Press, 2003.
Wilder, Gary. *Freedom Time: Negritude, Decolonization, and the Future of the World*. Durham, NC: Duke University Press, 2015.
Williams, William Carlos. *Paterson*. New York: New Directions, 1963.
Wimpffen, Alexandre-Stanislas, Baron de. *Voyage à Saint-Domingue, pendant les années 1788, 1789 et 1790*. Paris: Cocheris, 1797.
Wrigley, Richard. *The Politics of Appearances: Representations of Dress in Revolutionary France*. Oxford: Berg, 2002.

Index

abolition; in French colonies, 164; opposition to, 102-5, 266; in the public sphere, 78, 101, 104, 115-16; as subaltern silence, 131-32; visual culture of, 116-122
Acaau, Louis-Jean-Jacques, 218-25, 227, 229-34, 266-67
affect, 69, 79-80, 87-88; postcolonial transformations of, 283; and subaltern silence, 100, 295; surplus, 98. *See also* anxiety; fear; paranoia; *ressentiment*
"African song," 4-5, 7-8, 15-16, 20, 58, 269
agrarian imaginary, 181-85, 197-98, 224-28, 285; compared with similar movements, 186; as countermodern culture, 228; delegitimation of, 282; as subaltern speech, 228; as a vision of freedom, 228
Ahmed, Sara, 86-87, 107
Anderson, Benedict, 47
Anker, Elisabeth, 236
anxiety: in colonialism, 87; about abolition, 104-8, 111-130, 145; about race, 251-52; definitions of, 86; about delegitimation, 85; as insightment to discourse, 98; about insurrection, 105; about marronage, 69-72, 75, 77; relation to fear, 86-87; relation to publicity, 107. *See also under* poisoning
archive: problems of interpretation, 27-28, 77-78, 92-95, 166, 198-99, 224, 229-230; revolutionary destruction of, 208

Army of Sufferers, 218-25, 227-29, 236-37, 240, 266-67; silencing of, 222-25, 229-34

Bargu, Banu, 311
Boisrond-Tonnerre, Louis, 189-92, 194, 224
Bourdieu, Pierre, 154, 214, 241
Boyer, Jean-Pierre: agricultural policies of, 225-27; despotism of, 219, 222, 227, 236; flight of, 208-9; racial politics of, 217; references to Tocqueville, 205-6; reparations payments to France, 215; revolution against, 202-3, 211, 215, 218
Brandeis, Louis, 40
Brissot, Jacques-Pierre, 78, 102, 104, 207

Cambefort, Joseph-Paul-Augustin, 113, 141-43
Camus, Placide, 163-66
Carlyle, Thomas, 227, 270-71
caricature. *See* racial caricature
Carteau, Félix, 113-23, 134
Cercle des Philadelphes, 15, 60-61, 67, 122, 311
Césaire, Aimé, 33
Cham (Amédée de Noé): family history, 241, 249-50. *See also under* racial caricature
cockade. *See* tricolor cockade
Code Noir: ignored in colonial practice, 54-55, 175; racial language of, 34-36, 80-81; reforms to, 42, 81; silencing effects, 103, 286, 289; symbolic dimensions of, 41-45, 62, 69-70

colonialism, 3, 15; British, 23; and oppression, 7-10, 12, 13; and the public sphere, 16; race and, 33, 35-36; subaltern silence and, 25, 29-32, 70-71, 79-80. *See also under* Foucault, Michel
Committee on the Colonies, 103-4

Damiens, execution of, 69, 83
Daumier, Honoré, 261-63, 270-71, 281, 283-84
Delahaye, Guillaume, 115, 122-23, 125
delegitimation: categorial, 280-85; contemporary forms, 314-15; defined, 214; dimensions of, 281-85; of Haiti, 215-16, 236; postcolonial transformations of, 234-35, 278-87, 295; resistance to, 215, 236, 279
Dessalines, Jean-Jacques: as emperor, 272; and Haitian independence, 189-91, 193, 212, 224, 226; as tragedy, 238
Diderot, Denis, 78, 102, 140, 185-86
discourse: about marronage, 42, 61-63; enlightened, 15-16; gendered character of, 53, 59; and modernity, 3; and the public sphere, 12, 47; and practice, 70; racial, 35, 37; and silence, 12-13; and subaltern speech, 8, 16, 30. *See also* incitement to discourse
Dubois, Laurent, 33, 195, 262-63

Ellison, Ralph, 11
Emperor Soulouque. *See* Soulouque, Faustin
Empress Ourika. *See* Ourika
Equiano, Olaudah, 118
Erlenbusch-Anderson, Verena, 205, 337n42
esclave: as legal identity, 34-38, 81
exception: epistemic, 186-87; from modernity, 197; spaces of, 40-41, 186-87; time of, 186-89
excessive visibility, 51, 297-98
exit and voice, 73

"Faithful Anne," 59-60
Fanon, Frantz, 33
Farge, Arlette, 27

Fatine, 52-54
fear, 69; definitions of, 86; relation to anxiety, 86-87; of slave insurrection, 145; about the tricolor cockade, 157-58; . *See also* anxiety
Fick, Carolyn, 90-91, 175, 198
Fischer, Sibylle, 195-96, 303
Foucault, Michel: and colonialism, 20-22, 24; criticisms by Spivak, 18-21, 88-89, 313; *Discipline and Punish*, 21, 36, 83; ideas of revised, 68, 311-15; *The History of Sexuality, Volume 1*, 22, 66; knowledge/power, 299-300; *The Order of Things*, 21, 60; and history of the police, 34; on race, 21-22; "Society Must Be Defended," 21; on subjectification, 309-310
Frank, Jason, 320n42, 338n2
Frederick II (King of Prussia), 16-17
freedom; as absence, 74; as agrarian self-sufficiency, 181-89, 198, 228; as national independence, 196-98, 228; silencing effects of, 236-37. *See also under* marronage; "three free days"
French revolutionary ideals: and abolition, 136, 140-41, 143; problematized, 156-57; racial character of, 157; understanding of in the Caribbean colonies, 136-37, 144
fugitivity. *See* marronage

Geggus, David, 69
genealogy: advantages of, 174, 313; Foucault's conception of, 19, 66; methodological considerations, 304-13; as preserving ambiguity, 99; rupture and continuity in, 167-68; of silence, 17, 20, 24-29, 304-11
Getachew, Adom, 195, 228-29
Glissant, Édouard, 30, 40-41
Gobineau, Arthur de, 284

Habermas, Jürgen, 14-15, 299
Haitian independence: performative character of, 191; as national independence, 197-98; proclamations of, 189-91; temporality of, 191

Haitian Revolution: aftermath of, 167; beginnings of, 111-12, 163; consequences of, 168-69, 173-74; fear of "contagion," 214; historiography of, 90-91; importance of justification in, 189-91; importance of publicity in, 192-93; importance of rupture in, 191-92; inconceivability of, 166; modernity of, 194-96; originality of, 191-94; as rearticulation of subaltern silence, 167, 199
Hartman, Saidiya, 39, 43, 173
Henri I (King of Haiti), 16-17, 39, 226
heterotopia, 40
Hobbes, Thomas, 86
Hofstadter, Richard, 100, 107, 126

ignorance, 299-304
incitement to discourse, 63-79, 98, 215-16
incitement to practice, 70, 77
individualization, 50-54, 62

James, C. L. R., 90-91, 157
Jaucourt, Louis de, 43
Jefferson, Thomas, 190, 219

Liberal Revolution of 1843: as movement against Boyer, 203, 208, 211; ideals of, 206-8, 210-12, 221; influence of American Revolution, 211-13; influence of French Revolution, 211-12; influence of Tocqueville, 203-5; justification of, 210-13; modernity of, 229; originality of, 212, 216; silencing effects of, 235-37
Liou, Stacey, 311
Louverture, Toussaint, 90, 124, 212, 226, 241, 257-58
Luxon, Nancy, 119

Madiou, Thomas, 190, 208, 223, 233
magic lantern, 123, 127, 130, 134
Makandal, François: anxiety about, 88, 91; accusations against, 82-83; ambiguities of interpretation, 84-85, 90-97, 99; background of, 39, 82-83; execution of, 83-85, 97; mythology of, 93-94; as revolutionary leader, 90-91
maréchaussée, 41, 188, 217, 269
marronage: anxiety about, 69-76, 79, 87-88; constituent effects on the public sphere, 68-69; defined, 30-31, 38-39; discourse about, 63-78; and freedom, 38-39, 64, 77; measures against, 41-42, 50-51, 57-58, 81; maroon communities, 57-59, 62, 69, 71, 72; networks of communication and, 39-40; and silence, 40-41, 59, 61-63
Martel, James, 195, 325n26
Marx, Karl: *The Eighteenth Brumaire of Louis Bonaparte*, 206, 238, 263-64; on Emperor Soulouque, 264, 280-81; on ideology, 62; on revolution, 163, 206, 217. See also *soulouquerie*
Mbembe, Achille, 33, 79
Mill, John Stuart, 185
Mills, Charles, 35, 158, 301-3
minstrelsy. *See under* racial caricature
modernity, 163-69, 289-93: colonialism and, 21; of Haitian independence, 189-94; the public sphere and, 12; silence and, 24, 29, 289-90; subordination and, 3-4
Moreau de Saint-Méry, Louis-Élie-Médéric: and Guillaume Delahaye, 122; and the "African song," 15-16, 269; on marronage, 58-60, 71; papers of, 15; on poisoning, 94-95, 97; and the public sphere, 58; on revolutionary rhetoric, 140-41

Napoléon Bonaparte, 192, 238, 267, 272
nègre: in contemporary racial discourse, 33; difficulties of translation, 33; early uses, 34-36; *empoisonneur*, 82; *esclave*, 82, 84; *libre*, 35, 84, 94, 114; *marron*, 38, 48, 49, 51, 58-59, 67; postcolonial transformations, 233-34, 269-70; silence and, 36-38, 40; transformations in meaning, 81-82, 102, 114, 269-70
newspapers: caricature journals, 240-41; in colonial Saint-Domingue, 45-58, 62, 64-68; coverage of French revolutionary ideals, 152; coverage of "philanthropy,"

newspapers (*continued*)
111-12; democratic effects, 241; European, 55, 64, 279; in postcolonial Haiti, 203-209, 218-19, 222-23; in the United States, 208-210, 213, 222, 264

Ourika, 244-47, 276-77

paranoia, 77; about abolitionism, 123, 135; compared with fear and anxiety, 108, 126; characteristics of, 109-11; and mass media, 107-8; "paranoid tendencies," 107-8; about poisoning, 98; about the public sphere, 127; public character of, 98, 126; about the tricolor cockade, 145, 157-58
Patterson, Orlando, 32
performativity, 73-76, 77, 160, 191, 199, 310-11
phantasmagoria, 127-30, 134
philanthropy, 102-3, 111-15, 123, 134
physiognomy. See *under* racial caricature
Piquets. See Army of Sufferers
poisoning: ambiguities of, 88-95, 106; anxiety about, 85-88, 96-98, 105-6; compared with abolition, 105-7; legislation against, 80-81; reports of, 80-84
"politics by proxy" thesis, 262-65, 271, 283-84
politique de doublure, 239-40, 275, 282
postcoloniality: transformations of silence in, 173
problematization: anxiety as, 70-77, 96-99, 100, 133; of colonialism, 291; of French revolutionary ideals, 156-57; of the Liberal Revolution, 215-16; by marronage, 57-58, 65-67; performativity as, 30, 75; by poisoning, 98; in racial discourse, 35, 37-38, 51; of slavery, 266, 291; in Spivak's work, 22-24; by tricolor cockade, 157-60
public sphere: abolitionist, 113-26, 131; affective character of, 95, 165; Anglophone, 48; anxiety about, 125-30; circulation of images within, 116-22; colonial, 15-16, 44-47, 54-56, 61, 66, 68, 76, 77, 158-59; counterhistory of, 14-15, 78; democratic, 54-56, 169; epistemic dimensions of, 54, 61, 62, 67, 106, 127; European, 47, 55, 61; fear of, 106-7; Habermas's genealogy of, 14-15, 299; innovations in, 12, 16, 18; pan-American, 209; paranoia about, 125-30; phantasmatic, 126-27, 131-35; revolutionary potential of, 216; as site of subordination, 169, 285-87, 295, 298-99; technologies of, 12, 18, 50, 165; transatlantic, 8, 104, 106, 115-17, 164-65, 305-6; as vector of insurrection, 115-16. See also marronage: constituent effects; publicity; subordination: and the public sphere
publicity, 42-45, 50; ambivalence of, 62; in the Haitian Revolution, 189-94; individualizing, 50-54; normalizing, 58, 61-63; performativity and, 74-76; transformations in, 165, 168-69. See also individualization; public sphere

racial caricature: American, 250-52, 260; British, 249-50, 252-53, 260; Cham's innovations in, 241-43, 253-57, 259-61; and minstrelsy, 257-58; in nineteenth century France, 240-41; and physiognomy, 256-57; role in postcolonial politics, 265-66; truth-constituting capacities, 247-49, 261. See also *under* Soulouque, Faustin
racial thinking: postcolonial, 169, 217, 233-34; transformations of, 81-82, 94, 113-14, 214, 284-85
racist culture, 257, 266-71, 283-85
Raimond, Julien, 119, 143-44
Raybaud, Maxime (Gustave d'Alaux), 233-34, 266-67, 273-75
Raynal, Guillaume: on abolition, 78, 101-2, 114, 140; on subsistence farming, 181-82, 185-86

republic of letters, 60
ressentiment, 266-71, 281, 283-84
rights: in the Code Noir, 175; constitutional, 207; *Declaration of the Rights of Man and Citizen*, 191, 206, 210; of free press, 152; language of, 232; of mixed-race people, 143; in modernity, 3; as revolutionary doctrine, 209-10; Rights of Man, 105, 112, 133, 136, 140-41, 195; violations of, 211
Roberts, Neil, 229, 319n17
rumor, 74, 106, 122, 145

Scott, David, 92-93, 188, 195-96, 232, 292
Scott, James, 16, 77
Scott, Julius, 16, 39
Sedgwick, Eve Kosofsky, 109-10, 127
Senghor, Léopold, 33
Shulman, George, 303
silence: as an achievement, 40-41, 181-82, 187, 310; anxiety and, 71; archival, 122, 147-48, 187; archival traces of, 30; challenges of interpretation, 16-17, 27-29, 77-78, 98-99; and coerced speech, 85; colonial, 41, 58; created by progressive movements, 237; critical force of, 158; defined, 11-12; epistemic dimensions, 32, 58, 103, 133; as evidence of conspiracy, 130; failure of, 132; forms of, 5, 7, 9-14, 25, 78, 314-15; genealogy of, 10-11, 13-18, 20, 24-29; and ignorance, 299-304; as illusion of voice, 239-40; intersection of gendered and racial, 59-60, 276-78; marronage as resistance to, 31, 38, 39-40, 50-51; as a nonobject, 24-26, 304-11; publicity and, 76, 169, 285-87, 295, 298-99; problems of in Foucault's work, 19-20; problems of in Spivak's work, 23; production of, 21, 32; racialization and, 33, 36-38; subaltern, 13-21, 23-29, 30-31, 33, 36-38, 39-41; as subordination, 3-4, 8, 19-20, 56, 71-72; terminology for, 11-12, 297; transformations of, 168, 231, 235-37, 269-70, 279-80, 285-87, 289-93, 314-15;

ventriloquism as, 19, 85, 89, 93, 132, 277-78. *See also* silencing; Soulouque, Faustin: silencing of
silencing: contemporary forms, 296-315; self-silencing through opacity, 41, 51, 187, 231; through coerced speech, 85; through delegitimation, 214, 234-35, 278-87; through displacement, 37, 71, 134; through excessive visibility, 51, 297-98; through exclusion, 148, 223; through imaginary unsilencing, 71, 90, 133; through law, 32, 37, 51, 103; through interpretation, 92-93, 155-56, 230, 232-33; through resignification, 37, 214, 234, 280; through substitution, 133-34, 149, 154, 196, 239-40; through ventriloquism, 90-92, 132, 154, 156, 277-78; through violence, 32, 37, 51; transformations in, 231, 279-80, 293-96, 314-15. *See also* silence
Société des Amis des Noirs: attacks on, 102-5, 114-16, 123-25, 140-41; and the French Revolution, 140; and mixed-race equality, 119, 143
Soulouque, Faustin (Emperor of Haiti): attempts at self-legitimation, 273-75; caricatures of, 5-8, 20, 240-47, 260-63; conflicting accounts of, 266-273; delegitimation of, 281; as farce, 238, 263-64, 285-87; portrayed on Vaudeville, 259; as puppet president, 240; silencing of, 265, 275-76, 295-98
souloquerie, 262-63, 265, 280-81, 283
spaces of exception. *See under* exception
Spivak, Gayatri: "Can the subaltern speak?," 9-11, 17-18, 19, 37, 60, 74, 78, 159; criticisms of Foucault, 18-21, 88-89, 313; exemplification and, 23; ideas of revised, 135, 312-13; ideology and, 33; on knowledge/power, 301; methodological insights of, 17, 22-24, 72, 89-90, 154, 229; problematization and, 22-23; problems of, 10, 23-24
Stoler, Ann Laura, 22, 87

subaltern: agency of, 16–17, 90, 92, 97, 99, 166, 240; interpretation of, 22; speech of, 17, 23–24, 29, 31, 37, 54, 75, 174, 228. *See also under* silence; subordination
Subaltern Studies group, 19
subordination: affective bases, 132; colonial, 3, 30, 51; contemporary forms, 8, 12–13, 18, 23, 295–315; increasing abstraction of, 25–26; invisible forms, 25; modern forms, 3–4, 8–9, 12–14, 16, 29, 174; problems of interpretation, 26–28; and the public sphere, 8, 12–13, 16, 21, 25–26, 61–62, 76; racial, 38; resistance to, 14, 17–18, 38–41, 74, 166, 187; subaltern, 3, 12–14, 21; techniques of 3, 26, 51–52, 61–62; terminology for, 11–12. *See also under* silence
subsistence farming, 181–85, 226–28

"three free days": ambiguity of, 180–81, 185, 188–89; and the Army of Sufferers, 225–26, 228, 231; compared with other agrarian movements, 186; as failure of the imagination, 178–80; as insurgent demand, 175–78; silencing of, 180–81, 196–97; as vision of freedom, 184–89, 196, 228

time of exception. *See under* exception
Tocqueville, Alexis de: on colonialism, 205; on French Revolution, 192; influence on Liberal Revolution of 1843, 203–6
Tomba, Massimiliano, 195
tricolor cockade: ambiguity of, 156; appearance in colonial Saint-Domingue, 141–46; described, 137–38; epistemological aspects, 146, 149, 152, 156, 158; origins, 150; problems of interpretation, 145–57; material character of, 137–39, 148, 158; significance in colonial Saint-Domingue, 152–54; significance in revolutionary France, 139, 149–152; silence of, 148, 154–55, 158
Trouillot, Michel-Rolph: on archival silence, 147–48, 154; on Haitian proclamation of independence, 191; on inconceivability of Haitian Revolution, 166, 179, 189; on interpretation of silence, 16–17

Vaudou, 4–5, 39, 267

"weapons of the weak," 16, 77, 91, 99, 135, 291. *See also* Scott, James
white supremacy, 76, 251, 295

GPSR Authorized Representative: Easy Access System Europe, Mustamäe tee
50, 10621 Tallinn, Estonia, gpsr.requests@easproject.com

www.ingramcontent.com/pod-product-compliance
Lightning Source LLC
Chambersburg PA
CBHW031231290426
44109CB00012B/242